For each type of visa, Allison Lounes writes for, where to apply, various fees, length of vi: naturalization, health insurance responsib savings requirements, work, taxation, maint residency, family members' situation, docun summary. *Foolproof French Visas* answered most, if not all, the questions I had about the French visas and which one would be best for our particular situation and needs. But very importantly it also answered some relevant questions that I had not even thought of.

- Ali Kazemi

I purchased the latest edition of Foolproof Visas and I can highly recommend it as one of the most informative guides to the confusing world of French visas. I'm a big fan of Alison's blog and her monthly overviews on Zoom where she answers all kinds of questions about which visa might be right for you as well as all of the info you'll need to prepare to apply. This easy-to-use and informative guide is well worth the money spent if/when you're planning on a relocation--or, as Allison says: Your Franceformation!

- Kal

Making a move to a foreign country can feel daunting. With Allison Lounes' Foolproof French Visas, she shares a wealth of knowledge about how to navigate this process in France with grace. Allison's experience and guidance helping people make this move takes much of the anxiety out of the process and inspires decision-making that excites rather than terrifies!

- Erin Martin

Allison has laid out a blueprint for individuals who want to move to France whether it is short or long term. The book is well organized and very easy to read. It clarifies the various visa options, as it can be quite confusing with the amount of unreliable resources on the internet. I was hoping there was a more detailed plan for those who are interested in living in France while working remotely but it has certainly given me a good starting point in my research. She is quite knowledgeable in the visa process and has created a wonderful community on Facebook that helps one another with questions related to moving/living in France. She also offers additional services on her Franceformation website that will ensure your dreams of moving to France becomes reality. I really appreciative the positive vibes I got when reading this book. It made me feel like I can really do this. I am very excited to see the updates in the 2022 edition!

- Kevin

Loved this book. It has all the information I needed and I feel well prepared for our move to France.

Foolproof French Visas: Complete 2024-2025 Edition

- DMF, Amazon review

Allison's enthusiastic, straight-talking style makes for a extremely readable and useful book. Her recommendations and non-nonsense advice, based on nearly ten years helping people relocate to France, helps you navigate the minefield of visas and residency criteria that you need to know before you move.

- J Beale

I was lucky enough to receive a copy of Foolproof French Visas 2020 during an online presentation by Allison. I was blown away by the amount of information she has collected! At last, we have a visa guide that lays out each visa in an a very linear, very detailed fashion--something we can't get on the official visa site. Also included are what to do when you land, how to renew, info about naturalization, and some helpful case studies. The one thing that it is missing is some graphics or visual elements to help summarize and break up the text, but this does not reduce the value of the information. Thanks Allison!

- M. Keel

Everything you need to know as you prepare for your move to France. It's dense with info and a good resource!

- Yoga Girl, Amazon review

I love this! It is so detailed and it answered every one of my thousand questions about the visa process and how to renew my visa. Allison did an amazing job of writing this book and making it very easy to process and understand. I definitely would advise buying this book if you are having visa issues or questions.

~Brittney Schwartzendruber

This book was excellent and beyond informative for this novice who sees her future in France, and extremely enlightening for the forms needed; including divorce papers! Who knew! I am thrilled I will be able to read and STUDY your complete book and I can only hope you are still accepting clients when I am ready to jump. It is not a matter of if, but when.

- Terri Ayala

The section on which type of visa to apply for was very useful and informative. As someone who is in the early stages of planning a move to France, I felt overwhelmed by details like which visa to apply for, since there seems to be so many to choose from! Allison's guide broke the different visas down and explained each one in clear and simple terms. After reading this section of the book, I now know exactly which visa I need, and have concrete actions to take now to start the process of applying for the proper authorizations to make our big move. I can't wait to start! Thank you!

- Brooke Plourde Dupuy

As a long time visitor to Paris, it had been my dream to move to France once I retired. With so many bits and pieces of information from multiple sources available, the biggest problem is where do you begin, what to expect, and most importantly how do you avoid making mistakes along the way? *Foolproof French Visas* answers these and many more questions, providing the sort of hand-holding I've been looking for. Thank you Allison Lounes!

- Eleanor Matthews

I am impressed by the amount of information. It is thorough and written with clarity. The checklists you provide are very useful. Your book will be very helpful for those applying for French visas.

- Faith Dugan

Such an interesting and VERY informative read! It will be useful for so many people and save everyone from the headaches that can come with this process!

- Anita Oudega

Filled with so much info, very helpful. I'm still reading sections and taking notes!

- Dar C., Amazon Review

Foolproof French Visas:

Complete 2024-2025 Edition

Revised & Updated

Copyright © 2019-2025 by Allison Grant Lounes

All rights reserved. No part of this publication may be reproduced, distributed, or transmitted in any form or by any means, including photocopying, recording, or other electronic or mechanical methods, without the prior written permission of the publisher, except in the case of brief quotations embodied in critical reviews and certain other noncommercial uses permitted by copyright law. For permission requests, write to the publisher at the address below.

Allison Grant Lounes, Présidente
Your Franceformation SASU, au capital de €1.000
5 avenue du 8 mai 1945 - 95200 Sarcelles - France
SIRET: 897738027 00019 - RCS Pontoise
VAT number: FR72897738027
www.yourfranceformation.com
welcometo@yourfranceformation.com

ISBN (paperback): 9798326438379

Cover Image: Notre Dame de Paris at spring, France, by @sborisov, stock photo on DepositPhotos
Cover design by: Lesia of germancreative,
https://www.fiverr.com/germancreative

Ordering Information: Quantity sales. Special discounts are available on quantity purchases by corporations, associations, and others. For details, contact the author at the address above.

DISCLAIMER

This is very important. Although this book is called "Foolproof French Visas," the process of applying for a French visa is not actually 100% foolproof. Some 3 million visa applications are submitted at French consulates around the world each year, and only a fraction of those are successful. Allison and her company have an excellent track record in successfully getting visas for clients; however, there are several factors to be taken into consideration, including nationality and country of the application, the applicant's overall quality, and the mood of that particular consular official on that day. The consulate can reject your application for any reason, or for no reason at all. In some cases, the consulate can issue a different visa type from the one you requested, or refuse your visa application entirely, without providing any reason.

The book's title should NOT be considered a guarantee that you will get your visa, even if you follow all of the instructions in this book. Allison Lounes, Your Franceformation SASU, and our employees are not legally liable for any costs or damages related to unsuccessful visa applications or to any penalties or costs you might incur from following the advice herein.

To Grant, who would not exist if I hadn't move to France or if I hadn't done TAPIF.

To Auntie Joanne, who taught me my first words of French and made me want to come to Paris.

*. *. *. *. *

To Mom & Dad, who made studying abroad possible.

FOOLPROOF FRENCH VISAS: 5

COMPLETE 2024-2025 EDITION 5

FOOLPROOF FRENCH VISAS 2024-2025 EDITION (5TH VERSION) INFORMATION 13
REGISTER TO RECEIVE A FREE UPDATE 16
TAKE THE FREE VISA QUIZ 17
ATTEND FREE Q&AS WITH ALLISON GRANT LOUNES TO ANSWER YOUR QUESTIONS ABOUT MOVING TO FRANCE 18

PART 1: INTRODUCTION TO FRENCH VISAS 21

1.1 THE EVER-EVOLVING REGULATIONS ON FRENCH VISAS 25
1.2 THE TREND TOWARDS DIGITALIZATION OF PUBLIC SERVICE AND THE MYTH OF "SIMPLIFICATION" 29
1.3 PRIVATIZATION OF THE VISA APPLICATION PROCESS 36
1.4 SCHENGEN TRAVEL RULES 40
1.5 THE ENTRY EXIT SYSTEM (EES) AND EUROPEAN TRAVEL INFORMATION & AUTHORIZATION SYSTEM (ETIAS) 47
1.6 ADMISSION EXCEPTIONNELLE AU SÉJOUR 49
1.7 WORKING REMOTELY LEGITIMATELY & ETHICALLY IN FRANCE 51
1.8 CERTIFICATES OF COVERAGE FOR SOCIAL SECURITY CHARGES 60
1.9 IMPLEMENTATION OF NEW JANUARY 2024 IMMIGRATION REFORM LAW ... 63
1.10 COMPARING & EVALUATING LONG-STAY VISA TYPES 67
1.11 HELPFUL VOCABULARY 75
  Visa, Carte de Séjour, Titre de Séjour Vocabulary 75
  Préfecture Vocabulary 78

PART 2: FRENCH LONG-STAY VISA TYPES 85

2.1 NON-WORK VISAS 86
  2.1-1 Long-Stay Visitor Visa 87
  2.1-2 Long Séjour Temporaire 100
2.2 STUDENT VISA TYPES 106
  2.2-1 Student Visa 108
  2.2-2 Internship Visa 129
  2.2-3 Recherche d'Emploi / Création d'Entreprise Visa 135
  2.3-4 Au Pair 143
2.3 TEMPORARY YOUTH WORK PROGRAMS 151
  2.3-1 Working Holiday / Young Traveller* "Vacances Travail / Jeune Travailleur" Visa 152
  2.3-2 Franco-American Chamber of Commerce Temporary Work Visa 158
  2.3-3 TAPIF Teaching Assistant Program in France Visa 164

  2.3-4 Lecteur d'Anglais / Maître de Langue Visa............................171
  2.4 Long-Term Work Visa Types...179
   2.4-1 Salarié/Travailleur Temporaire Visa 187
   2.4-2 Intra Corporate Transfer (ICT Salarié Détaché) Visa 195
   2.4-3 Passeport Talent Salarié en Mission Visa 203
   2.4-4 Passeport Talent Chercheur-Scientifique........................ 208
   2.4-5 Passeport Talent Recrutement dans une Entreprise Innovante 215
   2.4-6 Passeport Talent - Salarié Qualifié Visa........................... 221
   2.4-7 Passeport Talent Salarié Hautement Qualifié / Carte Bleue Européenne Visa.. 227

2.5 INDEPENDENT WORK VISA TYPES 233
   2.5-1 Profession Libérale ou Indépendante - Liberal or Independent Visa.. 238
   2.5-2 Entrepreneur (artisan, industriel, commerçant).............. 252
   2.5-3 Passeport Talent - Profession Artistique Visa or Renommée Nationale ou Internationale Visa 262
   2.5-4 Passeport Talent Entrepreneur or Passeport Talent Investor 273
  2.6 Family Member Visas...287
   2.6-1 Vie Privée et Familiale: Spouse of a French Citizen 290
   2.6-2 Vie Privée et Familiale: PACSed with a French Citizen..... 301
   2.6-3 Vie Privée et Familiale: Parent of a Minor French Child.... 307
   2.6-4 Vie Privée et Familiale Visa: Spouse of an EU citizen (not French).. 314
   2.6-5 Passeport Talent Famille Accompagnante Visa: Spouse of a Passeport Talent Visa Holder... 320
   2.6-6 Vie Privée et Familiale Visa: Regroupement Familial for Spouse of a CDS Holder 324
  2.7 Getting EU Citizenship through Ancestry...............................328

PART 3: APPLYING FOR A FRENCH VISA 333
  3.1 Accompanying Family Members 334
  3.2 Tips for Using the France-Visas Website 340
  3.3 Where to Apply for Your Visa 342
  3.4 Making a Visa Appointment..344
  3.5 Timeline for Applying 346
  3.6 The Visa Application Submission Process...............................348
  3.7 Common Reasons for Visa Rejections 352
  3.8 Rejections, New Applications & Appeals 357

PART 4: ARRIVING IN FRANCE AFTER RECEIVING YOUR VISA 359

4.1 ARRIVING IN FRANCE WITH YOUR VISA 361
4.2 SIGNING THE CONTRAT D'INTÉGRATION RÉPUBLICAINE (CIR) 367
4.3 SIGNING THE CONTRAT D'ENGAGEMENT RÉPUBLICAINE (CER) 370
4.4 RENEWING YOUR VISA 372
4.5 CHANGING YOUR VISA STATUS IN FRANCE 382
4.6 REQUESTING A 10-YEAR RESIDENT CARD 386
4.7 APPLYING FOR FRENCH NATURALIZATION 390

GETTING HELP WITH YOUR FRANCEFORMATION 393

FRANCEFORMATION RELOCATION SERVICES PACKAGES 399
   Business Creation, Self-Employment, and Artistic Packages ... 399
   Retirement & Sabbatical Packages 400
   French & EU Family Packages 401
   How to Get Started with Us 401
OUR CLIENTS' PRAISE FOR YOUR FRANCEFORMATION 403
FRANCEFORMATION COURSES & DIGITAL PRODUCTS 412
   Fast Track to France 412
   The Complete French Business Incubator 413
   The French Admin Tracker 415
   The Franceformation Relocation Admin Success Survey 416
   Also by Allison Lounes 417
ALLISON GRANT LOUNES, CREATOR OF YOUR FRANCEFORMATION 418
KIMBERLY MOUSSERON, INTERNATIONAL MOBILITY CONSULTANT WITH YOUR FRANCEFORMATION 427
ALLISON'S ACKNOWLEDGEMENTS 429

APPENDIX: LIST OF DOCUMENTS YOU MAY NEED 431

IDENTIFICATION DOCUMENTS 431
BASIC ADMINISTRATIVE DOCUMENTS 432
HOUSING 435
HEALTHCARE DOCUMENTS 436
BUSINESS & ENTREPRENEUR 437
SALARIED WORK VISAS 439

GLOSSARY OF COMMON TERMS, ACRONYMS & INITIALISMS 442

APPENDIX: CESEDA VISA CODES 456

APPENDIX: USEFUL LINKS 457

APPENDIX: PRÉFECTURE AND OFII OFFICES BY DEPARTMENT ... 460

Foolproof French Visas 2024-2025 Edition
(5th Version) Information

Because you need to have the most up-to-date information for your visa application, it is important to know when the most recent changes to French legislation regarding visas went into effect, and when the information contained in this book was most recently updated.

This *Complete 2024-2025 Edition* is completely up-to-date as of its publication date of **October 1, 2024** and contains information on procedures and legislation currently in effect. The most recent changes to legislation reflected in this book are the January 2024 immigration reforms.

The fifth edition or "Complete 2024-2025 Edition" was published on October 1, 2024.

The fourth edition or "Complete 2023 Edition" was published on March 27, 2023.

The third edition was published on January 3, 2022.

The second edition was published on August 1, 2020.

The first edition of *Foolproof French Visas* was published on October 1, 2019.

Revisions, changes, updates, and additions for the Complete 2024-2025 Edition:

- French SMIC is €1767 gross per month and €1400 net per month as July 2024
- Replaced "VFS" (Visa application contractor in the US, Canada, and other countries) or "TLS" (visa application contractor in the UK and other countries) with "VFS Global / TLS Contact" throughout when referencing the appointment process.
- Added details on rules for selecting a visa application center.
- Clarified EES and ETIAS implementation plan
- Added renewal deadline info to online renewals
- Elaborated on evaluation of income and financial requirements for the profession libérale visa.

- Updated the section on the evolution of visa regulations by describing processes that have gone online and new layers of approvals added to certain visa types.
- Added clarifications to minor children's visas and required documents.
- Updated student fees, CampusFrance fees and deadlines, and details on the financial guarantee for students.
- Student visas: Clarified requirements for VAE and two-year degree programs; Rewrote explanation of Diplôme Universitaire and master's programs, along with the application process.
- Internship visa: updated internship gratification, added related terms to glossary.
- FACC-NY Program: Updated requirements, separated lists of required documents into "FACC Application," "Host Company Documents," and "Visa Application Documents." Clarified procedure and requirements.
- TAPIF: Updated program requirements, revised because participants can now do TAPIF 3 times instead of 2 previously, and net salary has increased by €30.
- Maître de langue and lecteur de langue positions: clarified the number of hours for each type of contract and updated salary information for 2024, and separated out the position types more for clarity.
- Clarified additional "highly qualified" and management position requirements for the ICT Salaried Worker visa, and distinguised from the "ICT Trainee" visa available to non-executives and non-managers.
- Chercheur-Scientifique: Clarified updated income and salary requirements for 2024-2026.
- Updated salary requirements and requirement to complete the Contrat d'Engagement for all carte de séjour applicants.
- Clarified that bank
- Slight edits to sections 3.2 and 3.4 on filling out the visa forms and making appointments, as both VFS & TLS changed their appointment booking procedures. Added additional information about fees for extra services, including temporary

visa centers, prime time appointments, and "visa at your doorstep."
- Added "Assembling Your Documents" section to 3.6 "The Visa Application Submission Process"
- Added a section 4.3 on the "Contrat d'Engagement à Respecter les Principes de la République" and renumbered sections.
- Edited chart of renewals done online to reflect updates.
- Revised instructions for making appointments and getting récépissés.
- Added a brief section on citizenship through descent and "double droit du sol."
- Elaborated section on bank statements and bank account requirements for visas and renewals.
- Updated list of documents that will be accepted as a "justificatif de domicile."
- Added new vocabulary and updated administration names, including "France Services," "France Titres," "France Travail," RSA, Mon Master, Parcoursup, and more.
- Updated CVEC fee.
- Removed COVID travel rule and health/vaccine pass links from the "Useful Links" section.
- Verified all préfecture and OFII contact information and indicated that all préfecture websites have now been updated to the new look, except for Paris.

We feel like you probably don't care about the evolution of the previous editions of Foolproof French Visas, so we've removed the section tracking previous updates. However, we have a copy in our records and are happy to satisfy your curiosity if you'd like.

Register to Receive a Free Update

Because we want you to have the most up-to-date information possible while applying for your visa, we are committed to providing one electronic update for anyone who purchases *Foolproof French Visas,* as long as we continue to update and support it.

If you purchased this book on Amazon, you can receive a free electronic version, along with a copy of our Franceformation Readiness Assessment to see how ready you are to move to France, and what you need to do to prepare. Then, when we release the new edition of the book, you will automatically be able to access an updated copy through your customer space online.

Here's what you have to do to receive this bonus:

1. Write a review of this book on Amazon or share it in the Americans in France Facebook group and tag me, the author, so I see it. (The admin, Allison Lounes).
2. Send a screenshot of your review and a copy of your receipt to support@yourfranceformation.com with the subject line "Foolproof French Visas Ebook".
3. We'll grant you free access to the ebook / pdf version of this edition of Foolproof French Visas through our online platform Kajabi, so you can log in and download it now.
4. When we update this book and publish a new edition, you'll receive an email update and be able to log into Kajabi to access the most recent version.

You will also receive a companion worksheet to this book, via email, which will help you to outline your visa options and make decisions about how to best move forward with your Franceformation.

Take the Free Visa Quiz

Trying to figure out the best French visa for you based on all of the different types available can be tricky, which is why we've developed our own special visa assessment, the French Visa Quiz!

Answer a few multiple choice questions about your family situation, your education level, your employment plans, and your level of income, to determine the best visa type for your situation.

Take the visa quiz here: https://www.yourfranceformation.com/visa-quiz/	

Attend Free Q&As with Allison Grant Lounes to Answer Your Questions about Moving to France

One Monday night per month, Allison Grant Lounes hosts a free Q&A live on zoom, where you can come have your questions about French visas, French admin, and moving to France answered. If you're new to the process and just starting to figure out the kinds of things you need to know before you're ready to move, it can be a great opportunity to learn about some of the topics that others have, and to meet Allison if you're considering working with Your Franceformation on your relocation.

Free Q&A sessions are typically held on the first Monday of the month, unless there is a holiday in France or the US. There is no Q&A in August. They are held at 7 PM France time.

Attendees can submit questions in advance, and can also submit questions live through the chat box on Zoom during the call. Registering for any Q&A will ensure you receive reminders with the zoom link for all Q&As, and you will also receive our newsletter, where the replay is sent out a few days after the event.

The next Q&A sessions will be:

• September 9, 2024	• February 3, 2025
• October 7, 2024	• March 3, 2025
• November 4, 2024	• April 7, 2025
• December 2, 2024	• May 5, 2025
• January 6, 2025	• June 2, 2025

[QR code]	Register for the monthly Q&As: (You'll receive the zoom link right before the session) www.yourfranceformation.com/qas/
[QR code]	Submit your questions before the session so Allison answers them in priority order: https://forms.gle/Vw46iXEAvj6wSZE2A
[QR code]	You can watch previous Q&As on our Youtube Channel: https://www.youtube.com/@yourfranceformation

Allison Grant Lounes & Kim Mousseron

Part 1: Introduction to French Visas

The simplest definition of a visa is that it is a travel authorization document designed to keep people - immigrants - out of a country, by allowing them to enter with a specific reason, only with pre-approval and for a limited time.

By definition, a country that issues visas (virtually all countries) intends to keep certain people from entering, or from staying longer than a certain amount of time, by scrutinizing their intentions for travel, identifying their potential risk to a country's security, and analyzing the likelihood that they will overstay the visa length (by immigrating illegally) and assessing whether their verified-by-degree professional skills are economically interesting. Visas determine how long you can stay in a country, and what type of work you are allowed to do.

An immigration visa is like a bank loan: the less you need it, the more likely you are to be able to get it. Our mission at Your Franceformation, and the reason for writing this book, is to help you to get the visa you want, so you can create the life you want to have.

As experts in relocating people to France, our goal at Your Franceformation is to help you identify and implement the best way for you to successfully and sustainably move to France, while retaining the option of one day applying for permanent residency or even French nationality if you choose to do so. In order for you to make your move to France successful, you need to begin the process with a thorough understanding of all of the visa types available to you, and to select the most appropriate visa type for your situation that will enable you to achieve your short and long-term goals. Our aim has always been to make information about French immigration easily available and understandable, so you can assess the implications of each visa type you may choose and make an informed decision based on your personal and professional aspirations.

You should fully understand all visa requirements and make sure you will be able to meet them before you begin preparing your visa application, and especially before you engage any professional services to assist with your relocation journey. A professional's advice and guidance during this process can be invaluable, and we will discuss throughout the book how our services in particular can facilitate your own Franceformation, but you should not expect any surprises about the visa requirements after engaging professional services, from Your Franceformation or from another immigration consultant or attorney.

If you want to move to France, you may not know where to begin in evaluating all of the different ways to move to France, establishing which visas you could potentially apply for, or which types of international mobility programs you may be eligible for. You may also be unaware of the types of visas that can ultimately lead to a permanent stay in France, and which ones are more temporary.

This book will provide an overview of each type of visa so you can determine the visa type most compatible with your move and understand how to apply for it. For each visa type, we'll not only cover the requirements for obtaining each visa, but also what you are and are not allowed to do on each visa type. The goal is to not only help you to choose the visa that is most appropriate for your stay in France, but also to help you create a long-term plan for staying in France if you would like, and for helping you to understand the vocabulary and administrative procedures related to your stay.

Each visa section will also help you to determine what challenges you may face in preparing your visa application and relocation, what type of support you may benefit from during the visa application process, and whether or not our team at Your Franceformation may be a good fit for working with you to make your own Franceformation a reality. You may seriously consider two or three potential paths to moving to France, and be unable to decide. In this case, you may benefit from exploring the career and financial implications of your move in more detail, through our *Fast Track to France* program or a full consultation with Allison to fully develop each of the options available to you and to select the best one.

By the end of this book you should:

✓ Understand the different vocabulary related to the visa application and renewal process.

✓ Learn about the different ways to move to France temporarily or permanently, and understand the pros and cons of each visa type.

✓ Understand the role of different French administrations in awarding your visa and establishing your residency in France.

✓ Know which visa type is most appropriate for you and what documents you will need to submit to apply for it to maximize your chances for success.

✓ Know the timeline of when you should begin acquiring documents and submit your application, and when you expect to arrive in France.

✓ Be aware of the implications of your visa type for taxes, health insurance, residency, and more.

✓ Understand how to maintain and renew your selected visa type.

✓ Understand if you will ever have to change your visa status and whether or not you will become eligible for residency or naturalization.

Who (what nationalities) is this book for?

The guidance in this book can be used for successful visa applications in almost all countries. With that in mind, it's important to know that there are several countries that have special bilateral agreements with France, which means that those countries may have 1) special visa requirements or 2) quotas on the number of visas granted. These special agreements primarily concern former French colonies, especially countries in North or West Africa. Before choosing a visa type, you should verify that your home country does not have special requirements or agreements that limit your visa options.

For people from countries without special bilateral agreements with France, the rules about visas and how to apply are pretty much always the same; however, the choice about whether to award a visa or not to an individual, and how many visas to award to nationals of each country, and when, is always a political choice. It is one that individual consulates or consular officials may not have a lot of control over. For this reason, applicants from countries like the United States, Australia, or Canada may have a very easy time getting a visa approved for France. The French Foreign Ministry opts to give more visas to nationals from those countries because many French citizens also want to go to those countries to live and work. Citizens from countries that have a more lopsided exchange with France may have a more difficult time getting visas, as lower numbers of visas are granted to people from some nations as a matter of diplomatic policy. Many highly qualified Indian citizens, for example, seek visas and residency permits to work in STEM fields, and a fraction of those who are qualified actually obtain their visas successfully.

This book will therefore be most useful to people from countries that do NOT have a special agreement with France. Nationals or permanent residents of the United States, Canada, Australia, New Zealand, and the United Kingdom will benefit particularly from the contents of this book and its explanations. Nationals from other countries in North America, Asia, or non-French-speaking African countries may also benefit from its guidance.

Note that because US persons are obligated to file US tax declarations even while living outside of the US, I have included relevant tax information for US citizens and green card holders who will be required to declare their worldwide income to the IRS. The US tax information can obviously be disregarded by readers who have no ties to the US.

1.1 The Ever-Evolving Regulations on French Visas

Allison Grant Lounes has been in the business of helping people with French visas since she started writing a book-turned-website-turned-business, originally entitled Paris Unraveled in 2010. She began offering services to those moving to France or who needed admin assistance in Paris in 2012. Now, through her company Your Franceformation, the team helps dozens of people each year to successfully navigate the visa application process and move to France to create their dream lives.

Since Allison began working with clients on their visa applications, the different visa types, their regulations and requirements, and the procedures for applying and renewing have continued to change roughly every year and a half. Sometimes, they have changed without much warning. Visa types have been eliminated (Compétences et Talents) and reconfigured (Passeport Talent). In one instance in 2016, she submitted a Compétences et Talents visa application for a client two days before new regulations came into effect, and sure enough, they came back requesting new documents for the updated requirements.

More recently, in 2022, the Ministry of the Interior suddenly implemented a new procedure for Passeport Talent Entrepreneur applicants to request a certificate "attesting to the real and serious nature of the business project" from the Ministry of the Economy, and applied the new requirement retroactively, to applications that had been received over a month prior to this new requirement. The abrupt and retroactive change required us to research a new procedure which had only just been made publicly available, elaborate on the business plan to answer additional questions asked on the form, and wait an additional 4 weeks for a reply, pushing the visa applicants' travel dates later into the spring. Fortunately, we had the information for the Ministry of the Economy requirements available and could quickly and easily submit the relevant paperwork.

We also advise you to consult with multiple sources and to not rely purely on the France Visas website for the visa requirements - which you're already doing by reading this book, so good job! While the site indicates the minimum acceptable requirements for having your visa application approved, it doesn't really tell you how your application will be evaluated, which is subjective based on the type of project you're presenting. Nor does it provide guidance on how to identify or complete other relevant, necessary procedures in order to get the documents you need.

In this book, we will present the different visa types along with the most up-to-date requirements and procedures for getting an application approved, as of its date of publication. Of course, meeting the minimum requirements for obtaining a visa does not necessarily mean that the visa will be granted. You also have to ensure, as an applicant, that you are not providing any contradictory or confusing information that undermines the main parts of your visa application. In a previous conversation with a potential client who had already had a visa application rejected, we realized he had submitted an incoherent set of documents - company creation documents for setting up a French entity (one visa type), along with contracts and financials for being an autoentrepreneur (a completely different visa) when he was actually going to be an employee on a disguised work contract. No wonder the consulate was confused!

We would STRONGLY caution you against taking advice from random people on the internet who have experience only with their own visa, or who applied longer than 1 year ago. You should also consider whether the people offering advice submitted their application at the same consulate or VFS/TLS office as you will, or at the same préfecture. While the standards and general guidelines are the same, the *application* of those guidelines by thousands of people across hundreds of offices in France and around the world can be vastly different. Even factors like nationality, quotas, and the time of year you apply can have an impact on your file and its processing time, outside of the overall quality of your application.

While some visa types have not changed, the types of information consular officials consider while reviewing visa applications changes slightly from year to year, and can sometimes depend on the consulate and the country where it's being reviewed. There are also subjective differences based on who reviews certain business applications and what they are looking for. Many procedures have also moved online in the past several years.

Remember that the awarding of visas - or not - is a political tool. Government officials reviewing your application have evolving instructions on how generously or strictly to review the applications. We have noticed a significant decrease, for example, in consulates reaching out for additional documents, and a corresponding increase in outright rejections of visa applications, requiring applicants to reapply rather than submit additional information by email.

Similarly, document requirements are enforced unevenly across different consulates and jurisdictions. While the consulates in the US and Canada have been emphasizing letters of support from potential clients to accompany profession libérale visa applications, the consulate in the UK has sometimes insisted on a "platform review" of a business plan by a third party agency - something the US has never asked for. Insurance policies accepted for the visa in the US are specifically excluded for applicants in the UK. Review of visas and for residence permit renewals may suddenly become stricter and more difficult, without any overt changes in legislation or requirements. Overall, given the newly appointed right-wing government and Minister of the Interior as this book goes to press at the end of September 2024, that's the direction we think things will be going.

Taking advice from non-professionals who are not invested in the outcome of something as important as your visa application and who do not remain informed of updates to legislation and visa application and renewal procedures can potentially jeopardize the success of your application. Proceed with caution if you are getting free advice on social media rather than professional advice from someone who deals regularly with multiple préfectures, consulates, and visa types.

Before we begin presenting the visa types, we're going to discuss a few of the recent developments and trends in the visa application process, and introduce you to some of the vocabulary and information you'll need before you're ready to learn about the visa types you may apply for.

SMIC and Evolution of Visa Financial Requirements

Most work visa types have minimum income or financial resource requirements for both application and renewal, and these income requirements are linked to French minimum wage, called SMIC, which rhymes with 'speak' and stands for salaire minimum de croissance. SMIC is indexed to inflation and updated every quarter. For this reason, you should always confirm the SMIC amount for the current quarter when submitting your visa application or CDS renewal.

At the time of publication of the Complete 2024-2025 Edition, SMIC is €1.767 gross income per month, or €1.400 net income per month. This corresponds to annual gross income of €21.204, and annual net income of €16.800.

In this edition, we have done our best to update the SMIC amount everywhere it is located in the text, but we may have missed a few and left the outdated number. In most cases, we have removed references to the specific amount within each section to make it easier to update future editions.

1.2 The Trend Towards Digitalization of Public Service and the Myth of "Simplification"

The trend towards digitizing French public services began prior to the Covid-19 pandemic, but the move online was accelerated by work-from-home orders and by public services closing between March and June 2020. Prior to the pandemic, various French departments had already started making the move online, begun providing more information, and created online portals for making carte de séjour renewal appointments.

While the information provided through the various préfecture websites is far more helpful now than it was even five years ago, these modernization efforts have not been without problems. Up until recently, immigrants in certain departments hoping to renew their visas had to line up outside the préfecture at night and sit on cardboard boxes in the cold, in hopes of obtaining a ticket the next morning to get inside for information or to make an appointment. Allison and Kim both experienced renewal appointments under this system. Under the old system, though, you quite literally knew where you stood, and you knew where to go, and you could speak to an actual human who would help you and tell you what to do, even if it meant lining up again somewhere else the next day.

The virtual line to make appointments and have an application processed is dispersed, invisible, and offers no opportunity for photographic evidence of large crowds overwhelming understaffed préfectures to journalists reporting on immigration issues in France. It's a system designed to let people fall through the cracks. Now, it is impossible to even get into the line to enter the préfecture without an appointment, and it can be difficult to get help if your préfecture hasn't anticipated a response to the scenario you need help with or if you have difficulty accessing appointments online.

We frequently encounter problems with members of our Americans in France group being unable to log in to make an appointment, requesting an appointment for none to be available, or entering their residence permit details only to not be found in the system. Journalists have reported bots programmed to snatch up appointments the second they are released, and to resell them on dubious websites. Préfectures with high numbers of immigrants, like Seine-Saint-Denis or Essonne, have been accused of releasing too few appointments and deliberately understaffing to reduce immigration. Associations have organized to call préfectures to account for failing to process applications and renewals in a timely manner.

The Défenseur des Droits, the French administration tasked with defending citizens' rights and access to public services, has published reports on certain préfectures, including Paris, for making public service too difficult to access. It advocates for non-digital alternatives available to all public service users. Paris has responded in part by making a "France Services" kiosk available with computers across from the main préfecture, to provide digital access to various public service websites. In order to schedule a session to use the kiosk, you must scan the QR code displayed on the kiosk's window, using a smartphone. The Paris préfecture's phone answering system has been suffering from consistent "technical issue with call transfers that they are currently working on resolving" since the beginning of 2023, and most préfectures have completely stopped taking calls and walk-ins, and won't answer questions on individual cases.

The "numérisation" (digitalization) of this process has worsened the quality of the service provided by the consulates, companies like VFS/TLS, and the préfectures, and causes ongoing confusion to visa applicants and immigrants renewing their residency permits. Each extra layer of the process removes accountability, and makes it more difficult to get help with an issue that arises.

A recent and relevant example of this is our work with two separate clients, both of whom were accompanying spouses to their partners on Passeport Talent - Entrepreneur visas. Both of these Passeport Talent visa types are issued for 90 days, but the catch is that the primary Passeport Talent holder has to request their carte de séjour through the ANEF website first. In both of these cases - one in Nancy, the other in Nice - we submitted the requests promptly. The first, in Nice, was submitted the day after this couple arrived, since they already owned their home. The other, in Nancy, was submitted within a couple of weeks, but still before the 90 days ended, because they had to find permanent housing first.

Neither application was processed within the 90 day deadline despite our repeated messages and inquiries, which meant both spouses had expired visas before we could submit their online carte de séjour requests. Of course, the visa number didn't work on the website, because the visa was expired. In Nancy, the préfecture still allows walk-ins, so after two attempts to go into the préfecture, our Grand-Est-based client was able to speak with someone who could take her husband's paperwork and issue a récépissé, and then enter the information into the backend. In Nice, we had to make an appointment for the spouse to submit his carte de séjour application in late October, more than 5 months after he arrived with his visa, and we requested his husband's carte de séjour.

Here's the story from the 2023 edition of Foolproof French Visas, about two clients at the end of 2022 who were both attempting to switch from "visitor" status to "profession libérale" status. We are happy to report we now have a resolution! Previously, in Paris, this was done by calling the préfecture to request a change of status appointment, and then attending the appointment with all of the relevant documents. The préfecture would then issue a récépissé allowing the client to register an autoentrepreneur activity, and, upon receipt of the business registration documents from INSEE and URSSAF, send them by email to the préfecture, which would close the file and issue the carte de séjour. Allison did this exact procedure with a client in June 2022. She had to call maybe half a dozen times before finally getting through to an operator who gave her client an appointment about 2 weeks later.

However, sometime in early fall 2022, the procedure changed, without notice, and without a replacement procedure being made available. As these two unrelated clients in Paris had titres de séjour which expired in November and December 2022 respectively, Allison and Kim began attempting to make appointments for them in early October, once their complete applications had been prepared. They made hundreds of phone calls to the préfecture, but only got through to a real person a couple of times, and the response was an abrupt 'the procedure is online' before hanging up and leaving no time to explain or ask for clarification. Reader, the procedure was not online.

They followed every official link they could think of. They wrote messages through the ANEF website (where visitor renewals were processed). They wrote emails to the préfecture. Allison accompanied multiple other Franceformation clients to various préfecture appointments to get inside the building and attempt to get information from someone working there, to no avail. Allison stood outside a préfecture to get assistance, and made an appointment at the (unhelpful) kiosk, which resulted in sending an email through the préfecture's contact page, to no response. After struggling for weeks and attempting all possible solutions, Allison also reached out to an immigration attorney colleague to determine if there were any other possible avenues for changing the status, before attempting to send registered legal letters and encouraging the clients to sue the préfecture in the administrative tribunal as a last resort.

Finally, in early January, as Allison accompanied one of the clients to a random (and ultimately irrelevant) préfecture office for a fruitless visit in the *fin fond du 15ème* (as far in Paris as you can get from where Allison lives, while still being in Paris), Kim reviewed everything we had done so far, and discovered that the website for the change of status procedure had *been updated the previous day* with the new procedure. (We knew the site had only just been updated because it indicated "Mis à jour le 11 janvier 2023…) The saga of this particular administrative undertaking highlights the importance of continuing to attempt all possible solutions and trying to solve problems from many different angles, as the right answer can appear miraculously, out of nowhere, and from something you've already tried. (It also highlights why we don't charge by the hour at Your Franceformation, precisely because of situations like this where it would unduly penalize the client for something that's not their fault and completely outside of anyone's control.) Unfortunately, the new procedure failed to take into account a few key elements of the change of status process, so the saga is still ongoing.

We ended the story here in the last edition, and promised an update, so here it is: The Paris Préfecture had developed their own online submission form on the website demarches-simplifiees.fr, which many prefectures use for a variety of requests. We were able to submit the business plans and other change of status documents through the form. Allison also wrote a letter detailing all of the attempts we had made to make an appointment and change the status, to justify the late submission.

We received responses about a month later, requesting that we register the microentrepreneur activity and submit the required documents, including the INSEE registration, to verify that the businesses were registered. Then, our clients received convocations inviting them in for change of status appointments at the préfecture office on rue Delta that handles profession libérale applications and renewals. They went to the in-person appointments with their documents, which we prepared into a complete file, and they walked out with récépissés extending their stay in France and enabling them to work. A happy ending to a stressful procedure, for two different clients.

The question of digitalization, combined with the préfecture's ongoing reduction of staffing and hiring of contract workers rather than professionals in permanent (CDI) contracts who have passed the concours of the fonction publique, is making things more difficult for everyone. It also means procedures are not uniform throughout France. When we do four or five applications for the same carte de séjour type within the same month, and each file comes back asking for a different document, even within the same préfecture, and none of the requests are similar, it shows that there is something off about the préfecture's procedures and the uniformity of training.

As more and more administrative procedures move online, it is going to become more important than ever to understand the procedure and the requirements before attempting to complete it. Without the human interaction, without the ability to drop into the préfecture to ask a question at the front desk, without the ability to make an appointment by phone or in person if the website glitches, a lot of people could fall through the cracks. Senior and retiree associations are fighting the requirement to do everything and get all information online, and lobbying to keep in-person and analog options.

While these examples don't seem to have much to do with immigration procedures moving online, they were timely examples of how digitalized procedures, implemented quickly and without an alternative or regard for consequences, can be disastrous. If everything moves online, suddenly there's no opportunity to check with the agent reviewing your file in front of you that the document you're providing is sufficient and what she's looking for. There's no opportunity to ask a question that may lead to providing more information and improving the quality of the file. If an online submission gets rejected, it's impossible to know why unless they tell you.

- Was it a digital scan of the document that found an error?
- Was the document out of date or different from what was requested?
- Was an element of your application misread or misunderstood?
- Was it a case of discrimination?
- What happens if an application gets lost or a document gets deleted in the system?
- Do you have an opportunity to clarify and amend the application, and in what timeframe?
- How are applications in the system prioritized? Are certain types of applications processed more quickly than others?

For certain procedures, like visitor visa renewals and passeport talent carte de séjour applications through ANEF, the agents have been getting better about explaining specifically what they need and asking for follow-up documentation. However, we have also noticed that certain applications have fallen through the cracks, and have remained unprocessed, despite multiple follow-up messages through the website's messaging system and through the préfecture. This is despite the files being complete and on-time, and regardless of whether other similar files submitted later have been processed first.

These potential problems are insidious in that the préfectures are not explicitly creating virtual systems to mis-process carte de séjour renewals. But make no mistake: the onus is going to fall on you more than ever to ensure your application is complete and thorough prior to submission, with little benevolent support from public officials. And if there are rejections or delays due to the digital system, or flaws in the system that prevent you from properly submitting a complete file, you are also going to bear the consequences.

Finally, since the publication of the 2023 edition of this book, we have noticed a significant uptick in verifications of paperwork and residency documents, not only for our clients, but for all visa applications and carte de séjour renewals in France. Whether it is certain right-leaning or anti-immigration sentiment empowering individual agents to be more stringent, or a new set of policies gradually being implemented across France, we have seen far more requests for evidence of integration than before. Préfectures are far more likely to ask for translations of bank statements that aren't statements from French banks holding funds in Euros, for example, which can be a significant expense to someone using a non-French investment account with pages-long statements, who never set up a French account. We've seen more requests for French tax declarations, and for additional paperwork for those who have not yet integrated the French healthcare system. All around, the trend seems to be on ensuring people living in France are actually living here, and not just on a long vacation.

All of this to say that reading this book, and applying for the visa, is only the beginning of your new life in France. It's after you arrive that the real work of settling in, and putting down roots, begins. Many people come to France after doing the whole visa process right, but never really settle, and overlook essential paperwork, which is why we help you to focus not just on the visa, but on creating the life you intend to live in France. That starts here, with ensuring you are setting yourself up for success.

1.3 Privatization of the Visa Application Process

A consulate is a localized branch representing the French embassy that issues visas based on whether or not you meet the criteria for a certain visa type. Since 2018, French consulates in the US and Canada, as well as several other countries, have outsourced processing of visas to private companies. VFS Global and TLS Contact are third-party companies which accept visa applications on behalf of the French embassy and consulates and forward them to the consulate for processing. After accepting the applications at their processing centers throughout the world, they forward the applications to the primary French consulate in that country, and theoretically send a series of emails that enable you to track your application from submission through processing and shipping back to you. These are the two companies most commonly awarded contracts for consular services, and they both process visas applications for multiple governments worldwide.

VFS Global, like TLS Contact, is not a French government entity, and the transition from visa processing by the consulates to visa processing by VFS/TLS has been rocky. In many cases, VFS/TLS agents cannot answer questions about visa requests or applications and cannot indicate which documents are necessary. Because they merely pass along documents for processing elsewhere, they are not reliable sources of information for what you need to provide and cannot tell you at the time of your appointment whether the documents you are providing are sufficient for obtaining your visa. Both companies also manage visa application services for many other countries around the world.

When dealing with VFS/TLS, it is advisable to submit ALL documentation you have and that is indicated in the checklists in this book. It is better for you to submit additional, unnecessary documents that support your visa application, rather than to have your application refused because the agent didn't ask for certain documents. YOU are responsible for knowing what is required and for making sure the application they accept is complete and thorough.

The France Visas website now provides a complete list of documents for your visa type if you select the appropriate visa type through their visa wizard, but first, you need to be absolutely sure you're selecting the correct visa and know how to do so within the visa form itself. While the Visa Wizard has significantly improved since the first version of the book, it is still not perfect. It assumes you know what visa type you are applying for, and why, and provides information based on your assumptions. If you are not crystal clear on the type of visa that best suits your project, or if your project could legitimately be shoehorned into a couple of different visa categories, you may be led astray by the Visa Wizard.

If you'd like assistance determining the appropriate visa type for you based on your plans, qualifications, and employment or business goals, you can take our free visa quiz based on *Foolproof French Visas* here: https://www.yourfranceformation.com/visa-quiz/

On more than one occasion, we have received an inaccurate supporting document list from the France-Visas website and had to write attestations or explanations for clients who were "missing" documents not on the list because the documents didn't apply to their situation. When VFS/TLS threatened to mark the file as incomplete, we provided a written note about why the list was incorrect and why these "necessary" documents weren't included, which was accepted, but the situation certainly adds stress to any visa application.

A client making small-talk with the agent during a visa application appointment learned that it takes more than 4 months to be adequately trained on the French visa system, and we have had multiple clients report significant challenges in getting VFS/TLS to understand their documentation.

While VFS/TLS seems to have an adequate understanding of visitor and student visas, the types they process most frequently, it is concerning that they are advertising services for visa assistance, in a clear conflict of interest, when they seem unable to consistently process all visa types correctly.

- One client reported that the VFS agent had told her that her 11-year-old son's visa application as a minor accompanying a passeport talent holder would not be approved because didn't have a work contract.
- Multiple clients reported that the VFS agent reviewing their file did not know what a "profession libérale" visa was and tried to request documents for a French company, or didn't understand the company creation documents listed for Passeport Talent Entrepreneur applicants.
- Some VFS/TLS agents would not take documents we provided like the cover letters, despite those documents being created to ensure the correct visa type is awarded.
- VFS/TLS agents are regularly unable to distinguish between the documents that should go along with the visa application, such as proof of an adequate catastrophic health insurance policy versus a fee quote from an insurance company.
- On multiple occasions, VFS has tried to convince our clients that the insurance policy they purchased may not be sufficient for the visa application, in an attempt to get them to purchase a policy sold by VFS.

In the US, UK, and Canada, it used to be fairly common for the consulate to email applicants within 2-3 business days of receiving the application if they needed any additional information to approve the request. While this is still sometimes true for Talent Passport applications, which have many documents, we've noticed an increase in outright rejections for applications deemed incomplete, even for profession libérale. Instead of requesting additional information, they are flagging the entire application as "unreliable," and rejecting the application, rather than asking for clarification. This change has corresponded with a new Consul General at the help of the French consulate, and unfortunately, this simply means having to revise the application and to reapply.

Moral of the story? Over-prepare, know exactly what you need to provide for the type of visa you want, and make sure they take everything you want them to take. And avoid providing any documentation that could confuse the consulate about what visa type you are requesting.

In our work with Your Franceformation clients, we always provide a complete visa application delivery packet with required documents numbered, and with a cover letter explaining exactly what to provide and in what order, so they are abundantly clear on what to expect at their appointment. We encourage clients to have a final application review appointment with Allison to review their file prior to submission, to answer any questions about the application and appointment process and to ensure everything is printed and in order. Clients go into their appointments confident they have all of their documents in the correct order, the appointment goes smoothly, and if the VFS/TLS agent is unclear on any part of the application, our clients know what to do.

1.4 Schengen Travel Rules

France is part of the European Union (EU), the European Economic Area (EEA, or EEE, 'Espace Economique Européen en français) and the Schengen space. In this section, we will explore the travel rules for being in Schengen as a tourist, and when you will need a long-stay visa.

As of 2024, the Schengen space includes 25 EU countries plus 4 additional countries: Austria, Belgium, Bulgaria, Croatia, Czechia, Denmark, Estonia, Finland, France, Germany, Greece, Hungary, Iceland, Italy, Latvia, Liechtenstein, Lithuania, Luxembourg, Malta, Netherlands, Norway, Poland, Portugal, Romania, Slovakia, Slovenia, Spain, Sweden, and Switzerland.

Note that Cyprus and Ireland are in the EU, but not part of Schengen.

Iceland, Liechtenstein, Norway, and Switzerland are in the Schengen space, but not part of the EU. Bulgaria and Romania became full-fledged members of Schengen in March 2024.

The European Economic Area, which allows free trade between member states, includes all EU countries, plus Iceland, Liechtenstein, Norway, and Switzerland.

The UK is no longer part of the EU or the European Economic Area, so no longer participates in free trade with the EU, and it was never part of Schengen.

What is the Schengen Area?
Schengen is a collection of 29 countries that have eliminated border controls between them in order to allow free movement and strengthen cross-border law enforcement. You will typically only present your passport and visa upon entry into the first Schengen country you travel to. If you leave Schengen to go to a non-Schengen country like Ireland, you will have to re-present your passport and visa to travel to those countries and again when you return to Schengen. Your days spent in Schengen are tracked and your passport is scanned at each point of

entry to and exit from Schengen. Passports are no longer systematically being stamped at the border, so you should keep your boarding passes or train tickets proving your date of entry into the Schengen space.

When traveling between these countries, you should always have your passport and titre de séjour, but your documents will not necessarily be checked at the borders. Random checks are always possible, however, especially in the event of a security incident, so you should always have your papers. It is important to know that having a visa for one of these countries does not give you the ability to stay in the others without restriction.

Tourists from 62 countries who do not require a visa to travel within Schengen (Americans, Canadians, other nationalities who can travel on just a passport) can spend up to 90 days total out of 180 days in any or all Schengen countries without applying for a visa. This period is rolling. Handy online calculators can use your travel dates to ensure you don't overstay your welcome. You can find them by googling 'Schengen trip calculator.'

Any day during which you spend partially in a Schengen country counts as a day spent in Schengen. For example, if you leave Paris on Monday to go to London, and return on Friday, your trip was 5 days, but you only spent 3 days (Tuesday, Wednesday, Thursday) completely outside of the Schengen area. In practice, overstaying by a couple of days isn't going to cause too many problems, especially for tourists traveling from visa-waiver countries. While theoretically passport control can look through your stamps (which are no longer being issued), add up your days and fine you (or even ban you!), they aren't likely to do that without a good reason or a pattern of abusing the Schengen system. Note that the ETIAS system will eventually facilitate the work of counting your days for border control officials.

Understanding the 90/180 Rule

The 90/180 rule applies to traveling as a tourist within the Schengen space, and stipulates that you cannot spend more than 90 days out of any 180 day period. The 180 day period is consecutive looking backwards from the date that you are doing the calculation, while the

90 days would include any and all days spent in whole or in part within Schengen.

In practice, the 90/180 rule looks like this: if you are traveling regularly back and forth to the EU, you need to look backwards from the last day of your trip. If your trip ends April 1, 2025, you would need to count ALL days you spend partially in the EU between October 3, 2024 and April 1, 2025. The number cannot exceed 90 days at any point.

You can do an internet search for a "Schengen Calculator" and enter your departure and arrival dates to ensure you don't overstay your travel authorization. Certain sites will allow you to create an account and save your travel dates so you are more easily able to calculate your Schengen dates.

Applying for a Long-Stay Visa after Schengen Travel

Applying for a visa of any kind (short stay or long stay) removes the limitations of the Schengen visa-free travel rules. For example, if you are enrolled in an academic program that starts in September, but want to spend the summer in France or in Europe, you can spend May 20-August 15 in Europe, apply for a long-stay visa in your home consulate on August 17, and return to France as soon as you receive your passport back in the mail. There is no waiting period between returning to your home country after tourism and applying for a visa and returning. Having spent time as a tourist in France or in Europe is not typically a reason for rejecting a visa application.

The main caveat is that if you have a pattern of overstaying your Schengen tourism travel dates, you can jeopardize your chances for a long-stay visa.

Arriving in Schengen

Your French visa is issued with a start and end date, and you influence these dates by indicating the date of your intended arrival in France on your long-stay visa application form. Typically, you provide the visa start date, a reservation for accommodations beginning on the date of your arrival, and an insurance policy (if necessary for your visa type) which takes effect on your arrival date.

If you have a long-stay visa, you can theoretically arrive in France (or in Europe) before it officially starts, provided that you are able to travel to Europe visa-free. In that case, you will be considered a tourist upon arrival, and your visa rights (to work, for example) will start on the start date of your visa. We cannot validate your visa online through the ANEF system until after your visa's start date.

If you have a French visa, but arrive through another EU country, your travel documents for proof of entry into Schengen will be from that EU country. Normally, there is no border control between the EU states, and so you will not have direct proof of entry into France. In that case, OFII assumes that you arrived in France within 5 days of your arrival into Schengen. As border control in most places is phasing out passport stamping to prepare for ETIAS, you will need to have other evidence of when you arrived if you ever need it.

Overstaying a Long-Stay Visa

If you do not plan on renewing your visa upon its expiration (or are not able to renew it), your visa automatically converts to tourist status upon expiration. Again, this is assuming that you are allowed to travel in Schengen on just your passport, without an official tourist visa. You are therefore allowed to stay up to 90 days beyond the end date of your visa in Schengen countries, but your status will be that of a tourist. And if you are a tourist, you will need to have the valid ETIAS authorization once your long-stay visa expires, if it is not being renewed.

You will not be allowed to work or receive any benefits, including unemployment or housing assistance, after the expiry date of your visa or titre de séjour. There is a short grace period after your visa's expiration date during which you can make a renewal appointment for your visa and renew, and you will pay a tax of 180€ for making your appointment after your visa's expiration date.

This section does not apply if you hold a "Temporaire" visa type. If you want to be 100% safe and free from questions at border control, you can leave Schengen upon your visa's expiration and return immediately for

90 days, with an ETIAS, to continue as a tourist.

The So-Called 1949 Bilateral Agreement Supposedly Still in Effect

Some travel blogger out on the interwebs has an article up with a link to a 1949 "Bilateral Agreement" between France and the United States, which he claims is still in effect and enables American citizens to go to the préfecture and ask for an additional 90 days to remain in France as tourists. Unfortunately, this misinterpretation has made the rounds a few times, but there is no process in place through which Americans can get an extension on a tourist stay beyond 90 days, without leaving France and returning to their home country to apply for a visa.

The agreement's text actually established visa-free entry (i.e. just on a passport, without requesting a visa in advance) for French people entering the US and Americans entering France, for periods up to 90 days. It also specifies that for stays longer than 3 months, the applicant must apply for a visa prior to departure, although the visa will be free.

Beyond that, the text appears to come from an old book - but there are no references to which book that might be. Even if it WERE the case that the text indicated visa extensions to Americans, you'd have a hell of a time making an appointment at the préfecture - which usually requires a visa or carte de séjour number and a significant wait time - and meeting with someone who 1) knows what you're talking about, 2) knows that the text is still in effect from 1949 without having to do lots of legal research, and 3) has the power and the good will to grant your request.

If someone actually has luck with this, please do email us about it, but we would not advise anyone to attempt this type of visa extension.

Traveling in Schengen as a French Resident

While you are a French resident with a valid visa or titre de séjour, you can travel in other Schengen countries, but you remain limited to 90 days out of 180 days in every Schengen country except for France. In practice, there are no border controls between the EU states, and you may therefore "get away with" overstaying the 90 days in other countries. However, in order to maintain your visa status in France and ensure you are able to renew, you should keep a permanent residence and proof of address in France for the duration of your visa. Moving around too much even within France or spending too much time outside of France during the year can invalidate the terms of your visa.

Working in Schengen as a French Resident
Any work rights conferred by your French long-stay visa are limited to France. If you are working for a French company, they may send you on brief work trips to other EU countries, and if you are a French autoentrepreneur, company, or profession libérale, you may bill clients in other EU countries. However, all of your income is reported and your taxes are still paid in France.

While having a 10-year resident card, a "carte bleue européenne," or a vie privée et familiale card may facilitate the process for working in another EU country, you would still need to apply for a work permit from the country where you want to work. Having a residence permit for France valid less than ten years enables you to request a visa for another country from that country's consulate in France. Having a 10 year resident permit or a "Carte Bleue Européenne" allows you to apply for an appropriate residency permit directly in another EU country, without first applying for a visa. However, it does not automatically grant you rights to a similar visa or work permit in another EU country.

Finally, be aware that getting a visa to live and/or work in another country may invalidate your French residence and therefore interrupt your continuous stay in France. If you are planning on applying for a 10 year residence card or naturalization, you should research how getting a visa for another Schengen country would impact your ability to maintain your French visa. French permanent residents with a 10 year carte de séjour can live and work outside of France for up to 3 years without giving up their rights to French residency. If you plan to move between EU countries, you may want to explore opportunities for naturalization in one before moving to another, because you would have freedom of movement as an EU citizen.

Working in France with Another Schengen Country's Visa
In 2019, Allison had a consultation with a potential client who had

gotten rejected for a French visa, and had instead traveled to Germany with just his passport, where he was able to apply for a freelancer visa for Germany upon arrival. He then relocated to France, where he thought he would also be able to apply for a French visa within France and without traveling back to Germany or to his home country. He was quite indignant when she told him that working and living in France indefinitely on his German visa was not allowed and that he would have to apply for a visa in a place where he was a citizen or resident.

If you live and work in another EU country on a visa, you are limited to 90 days out of 180 in France as a tourist. You may come to France on business trips through your company, or bill clients in France for services if you are a registered freelancer or business in another EU country, but you cannot use another country's visa to come live and work in France. In that case, you would have to apply for a French visa at the French consulate in the country where you live, and meet the conditions of the appropriate visa type.

1.5 The Entry Exit System (EES) and European Travel Information & Authorization System (ETIAS)

Within the next year or so, the Schengen area will finalize the creation and implementation of EES, the Entry-Exist System, and ETIAS, the European Travel Information and Authorisation System.

The EES is scheduled to start on November 10, 2024, after the end of the Toussaint holidays and UK half-term holidays.

ETIAS is scheduled to begin in mid-2025, but a precise date has not yet been set.

EES is an improvement on the current entry system of stamps, and it means that when your passport is scanned at border control entering or exiting the European Union, the date of your entry or exit will be logged in a central database, and the EU will be able to more easily track people who overstay their 90/180 days. In the long run, this will likely lead to an increase in overstay fines and visa rejections. People who have been flying under the radar and playing fast and loose with the Schengen travel rules will no longer be able to do so. Attempting to enter the EU if you have already completed your 90/180 days may result in refused entry.

In contrast to the EES, which will track time spent in the EU by non-EU citizens, ETIAS is an information check on travelers arriving to the European Union without a visa (short-stay or long-stay). The ETIAS will collect identity information from all travelers prior to their trip and provide a travel authorization before departure. It will be required for all travelers from visa-waiver countries and be valid for a period of 3 years, for a fee of €7. In this way, it is similar to the ESTA, required by the US, or similar pre-travel clearance certificates created by the UK and Canada.

Implementation of these systems was supposed to occur in 2020, and has been pushed back multiple times for various reasons, including the pandemic and the 2024 Paris Olympics. At the time of publication of the 2024 edition of this book, implementation of the EES system is now to begin on November 10, 2024, but many officials in the UK are concerned about long lines at the Eurostar, ferry, and port transit areas, because there is doubt that there is enough physical space to accommodate long lines and the scanning machines, as people typically clear EU border control and customs prior to boarding the train or boat.

ETIAS will be a simple form submission online, and will result in an immediate travel authorization in 95% of cases. When the form is submitted, an electronic cross-check of your identity information will be completed with the Schengen Information System, the Visa Information System, Europol, the Entry/Exit System, Interpol databases, and databases on lost or stolen identity documents. It will be applied to arrivals by air first, before being expanded to all arrivals into the EU space.

Note that the ETIAS system will store your personal data and may make it easier for border control of Schengen states to track if travelers have overstayed their visa-free travel limits or their visas. If you have a long-stay visa for a Schengen country or hold a carte de séjour, you will not be required to obtain an ETIAS check prior to departure.

For more information about ETIAS and its deployment date, you can follow the European Commission website: https://ec.europa.eu/home-affairs/policies/schengen-borders-and-visa/smart-borders/european-travel-information-authorisation-system_en

1.6 Admission Exceptionnelle au Séjour

It is not possible to arrive in France without a visa and apply for a visa or carte de séjour directly. Anyone who wants to relocate to France needs to apply for a long-stay visa in a country where they have citizenship or permanent residence prior to departing their country of residence for France. It is also not possible to leave France for a nearby country to apply for a visa in a different consulate if you are not a citizen or resident of that country. Taking the train to London to apply is not an option.

The two main exceptions to this rule are spouses of EU citizens, who may not apply for a long-stay visa prior to arriving but must request a carte de séjour directly from the préfecture within 90 days, and people who get married to a French citizen in France and who request a CDS directly without leaving the country. Even in the latter case, it is faster, easier, and ultimately less expensive to return home to get the visa, and we typically recommend doing so if at all possible.

Each year, many people erroneously believe that they can arrive in France without a visa, and apply directly for a carte de séjour through the préfecture, and some have "done their research" and uncovered the procedure of "admission exceptionnelle au séjour." However, this procedure is only available in two main situations:
1. For refugees who were unable to apply in the home country, in accordance with international conventions
2. For people who unexpectedly need serious medical treatment which is not available in their home country.

Admission exceptionnelle au séjour is a long and tricky process, precisely because its scope is very limited and it is not designed for circumventing the normal visa application process. We're not going to cover it in this book, except to say that even during the pandemic when borders were closed and flights canceled, it was not possible to apply for a visa or carte de séjour in France directly, including for people who had unwittingly obtained a "temporary" nonrenewable visa in their home country and then wanted to renew due to the pandemic. It was only possible to get an extension on a tourist authorization, and only until travel restrictions eased enough to enable people to travel home.

Although Allison assisted many people in getting their tourist stays legally extended during the pandemic and attempted with certain clients to request cartes de séjour directly in France due to the exceptional situation, those CDS requests were not granted under any circumstances.

Please do not make the mistake of believing that admission exceptionnelle au séjour can apply to your situation and that you will be able to cajole or coax your way into obtaining a visa or carte de séjour in France. It will be an expensive and fruitless endeavor.

1.7 Working Remotely Legitimately & Ethically in France

With the rise of "digital nomads" over the past ten years, the creation of fully-remote jobs requiring only a computer and an internet connection, and the pandemic accelerating the ability to work from home even indefinitely, many people have taken advantage and have been empowered to work from anywhere, including from other countries. While it may seem exciting to be able to live anywhere, explore a new city and learn a new language by day, then work on your home company's timezone by night, there isn't a sole effective and legal way to do so. The fact is that remote work is relatively new and not well-defined or regulated by existing laws makes it more difficult to ensure you're doing everything correctly.

What makes understanding international remote work situations even more complicated is the fact that consulates, tax offices, accountants, and attorneys often give conflicting information to people seeking to do the right thing. And hundreds, if not thousands, of people have been getting away with undeclared remote work for years, often mistaking the fact that they haven't yet been caught or sanctioned for doing so for official approval of their setup. Many of these same people encourage others to circumvent the rules like they did and dismiss legitimate concerns about the consequences of working under the radar. So let's dispel a few myths about the realities of remote work, and particularly, international remote work.

In the current globalized economy, a company is considered to have a business location in any place where it has an employee. Even within the US, having a single employee in a different state can complicate things significantly for a company, as Ask A Manager author Alison Green explained in a 2016 article.[1] Having an employee in a different state from the company's main headquarters opens the company up to following new labor laws and tax laws, and having an employee in a

---

[1] https://www.askamanager.org/2016/04/why-its-complicated-for-your-employer-to-let-you-work-from-another-state.html

different country is even more complicated. It doesn't really matter whether the company specifically sent you there, or whether they simply allowed you to work remotely and you went to the new place without their knowledge.

It's also not just non-EU employers that have difficulty abiding by these regulations. One of the challenges that some EU countries had to renegotiate during Covid work-from-home orders was the set of regulations surrounding "frontaliers", or people who live in one EU country but work in another. It is common for people living near France's eastern border to work in Switzerland, Luxembourg, or Belgium, where salaries are higher. In this scenario, frontalier workers pay into the social tax system of the country where their employer is located, but pay income tax to the country where they live. So, someone living in Lorraine region of France who works in Luxembourg would pay into the healthcare system in Luxembourg through their employer, rather than into the French system at the rates French employers pay, but still be covered throughout the EU. Over the past few years, there has been debate about how much these employees could work from home (in France) while maintaining their advantageous frontalier status, and various agreements have been reached giving workers access to 25-40[2]% remote work, depending on the country.

EU regulations are quite clear about what the "employee's place of work" means and what requirements are in place to ensure proper taxes get paid: Frontaliers Grand Est, a resource for cross-border workers living near Belgium & Luxembourg, states, *"Le règlement (CE) n°883/2004 et son règlement d'application reposent sur un principe : le travailleur est assuré dans un seul État, à savoir l'État dans lequel il exerce son activité professionnelle, même si l'employeur a son siège ou son domicile dans un autre État membre.*[3]*"*

(Worker are insured in the country where they exercise their professional activity, even if the employer's headquarters are situated in another country.) The article goes on to say that if a cross-border

---

[2] https://www.lesechos.fr/economie-france/budget-fiscalite/fiscalite-accord-entre-la-france-et-la-suisse-sur-le-teletravail-des-frontaliers-1891670

[3] https://frontaliers-grandest.eu/accueil/salaries/france-luxembourg/teletravail/possibilites-et-limites/

worker living in France and working in Luxembourg exceeds 25% work from home in France, the employee's social tax coverage may change, and any other government assistance (like housing and child benefits) could be impacted.

For a company, having an employee in France means abiding by French employment laws, having a French employment contract, paying some amount of French tax, and potentially keeping accounting records of French business activity with a French accountant, a certified expert-comptable. France-based employees would also need to be covered by a European insurance policy, receive benefits like vacation time in line with what a French employee would get, and abide by French overtime hours. They would also have to ensure that their employee is legally allowed to work in France and potentially apply for a work authorization. Not doing any or all of these things can land your employer in hot water with a number of different French administrations, and for this reason alone, most companies are not willing to officially enable remote work from another country like France.

GDPR - the European General Data Protection Regulation law - would apply to any company keeping and collecting client and customer data in the European Union, with significant financial penalties for businesses that don't comply, even accidentally. Having international remote employees access protected business data could jeopardize GDPR compliance.

On the employee - or even contractor - side of the regulations, you would be expected to be properly insured, to have the legal authorization to exercise your activity in France (so anything medical in nature or regulated professional activities like law and accounting are immediately excluded), and to have the proper visa. There are also regulatory issues to consider, like HIPAA in the US for healthcare workers, or financial regulations that prohibit financial data from leaving the country.

You may believe, or be told by the online peanut gallery, that you can circumvent France's rules on work visas by getting a visitor visa, maintaining your job in their home country, and having your salary paid directly into a foreign bank account. Some may even claim that since the job and the company are located outside of France, that technically they are not "working in France," which their visa status prohibits. Your local French consulate may even support this idea, as there is no "digital nomad" visa type for France specifically for this kind of setup. But while other countries, like Croatia, offer a specific digital nomad visa scheme, those visas are strictly regulated and often offer no path to long-term residency or citizenship. And they can create the complications we've discussed above.

Working remotely in an unapproved way is a very bad idea that will become very expensive for you to fix (if it's even possible to fix) once various authorities catch on to what you (and / or your company) are doing. There are significant penalties for you as the undeclared and untaxed employee, and for the business owner running a business with undeclared employees in France.

The simple truth is this: Working + being in France = working in France. An accountant based in France calls it the "rule of butts": wherever your butt is sitting the majority of the time during the year is where you're a tax resident.

If you have a visa to live in France, you become a French tax resident. (The visa presupposes you will be in France for more than 183 days, as you cannot renew the visa without actually living in France for most of the time.) If you are a French tax resident, you are bound to pay French social charges and income taxes on your earned income (salary, business income) in France FIRST, before paying taxes to any other country. This means that regardless of who is paying you and for what work, you need to be set up to pay French social charges and income taxes on that income. Of course, getting set up to pay social charges and taxes requires a work visa and a contract, whether that's a work contract (salarié en mission) or a freelancer contract (autoentrepreneur).

Initially, you may get away with it, as it would indeed be difficult for France to know what deposits are being made to your foreign bank account. However, as a French resident, you are also bound to declare your worldwide income on your French taxes, even if you are not subjecting the income to tax in France. At your visa renewal appointment, the préfecture can and will ask to see your French tax returns and your bank statements. They may also request your US tax returns and bank statements. If you want to transfer large amounts of money for any reason, like buying a house or a car, the bank will also want to know where the money is coming from and will ask you to prove that the income has been properly subjected to tax. We have been aware of people within the expat community who were asked by their bank or notaire to provide an "attestation de l'origine des fonds" and had trouble finalizing a purchase or procuring a mortgage in France because their foreign-sourced income had never been reported on their French tax declarations, despite years of living in France.

Furthermore, if the préfecture or your local tax office gets suspicious that you have income outside of France that is not being taxed properly, they will collaborate and request many documents from you and send you large, scary bills and penalties that you are going to be hard-pressed to prove you don't have to pay. Of all of the French administrations, URSSAF - the Union de Recouvrement des cotisation de Sécurité Sociale et des Allocations Familiales - is the scariest one to cross.

We cannot stress enough that if you plan on staying in France for more than a year or two, you should make every effort to ensure that you are working and/or running your business *legally* with regards to French laws and tax laws, to avoid all potential problems. If there is even a *slight* chance you might want to stay in France, we would advise you to do everything the right way from the beginning rather than get the visitor visa and try to fix it later. You can always leave and abandon the "right" visa if things don't work out, but it will be a long and painful process to try to "fix" your visa situation and make it right if you decide you want to stay long-term - or if you get caught doing things the "wrong" way by the tax office. Allison often discusses these options with our clients in our *Franceformation* consultations.

The challenge is this: if you are living in France, working remotely in an undeclared way, and then want to legitimize your situation by declaring your work, you will have to change your visa status to reflect a remote work option compatible with the visa type you select. (We'll discuss the options in a minute.) Part of that process will be proving the viability of your project as a self-employed person or meeting the salary and sponsorship requirements as an employee. For the first scenario, in which you are a remote contractor and registering as self-employed, you would have to convince the préfecture of your project's viability without referencing the fact that you were, in fact, working for the previous X amount of time, therefore omitting crucial information from your application. Similarly, a current employer wanting to sponsor you to work in France would have trouble preparing a legitimate visa application without admitting you had previously been working remotely in an undeclared capacity. Both of these situations would require some major professional damage control to minimize the consequences of unofficial remote work. And none of the time you spent working in France remotely would benefit your later requests for the ten year residence card or French naturalization.

But, despite the challenges, let's discuss a few ways you can legally and legitimately work remotely in France.

Scenario 1: You don't need a visa to live and work in France.
You have an EU Passport, are the spouse of a French citizen, or are the spouse of an EU citizen exercising their treaty rights to live in France. You therefore have the right to exercise any type of professional activity and do not need to request a visa to do so.

For the record, "exercising your treaty rights" to free movement as an EU citizen to live in another EU country means, in this case, that you can either fully support yourself without working, or that you are a tax resident of France and properly declaring and taxing your income in France. If you are running a foreign business - even an EU based business - from France and not declaring and taxing the income, you are not exercising your EU treaty rights.

Here are your options:
1) You can work as a full-time salaried employee for the European branch of the company you work for. They do not have to sponsor you.

You are paid through their EU payroll.

2A) Your US-based company registers a French office (subsidiary / filiale or branch office / succursale) in order to have employees in France. They create a French work contract for you and pay French social charges.

2B) Your company registers with the Centre National des Firmes Étrangères (CNFE) so they can have employees in France without having a stable company structure.

3) You register with a "portage salarial" which employs you and is responsible for your work contract, social charges, and benefits. The portage salarial invoices your company, takes a 50% cut to pay for these expenses, and provides payslips for your monthly salary. Your employer is the portage salarial company, and the foreign company can be your only client, or you can have multiple clients.

4) You can register your own French company (SAS or SARL), invoice the non-French company as a contractor, and pay your own charges, expenses, and salary. You can have one client or many clients.

5) You can register as an autoentrepreneur and invoice your company as a contractor. You are required to have more than one client per calendar year and are responsible for your own social charges (see the section on "Profession Libérale" for a more complete description of Autoentrepreneur).

Scenario 2: You need a visa to live and work in France.

You do not have a visa or passport which enables you to exercise your professional activity in France, which means your ability to work in France depends on your visa.

Without a visa or EU passport, your options for remote work are more limited:

1) You have already been employed by a foreign company for more than 3-6 months. Your company can send you to France with a specific

mission under an International Company Transfer or a Passeport Talent - Salarié en Mission visa, depending on whether you meet the requirements for one of those visa types.

2) You begin working as a contractor (rather than as an employee) for the company, turn your job description into a business plan, identify other potential clients, including potential clients in the market for your work in France, and apply for a "Profession Libérale" or "Entrepreneur (commerçant, artisan, industriel)" or "Passeport Talent - Entrepreneur" visa to create your own company and work from France. You provide your own insurance and pay your own social charges and taxes through the company, and invoice the home company directly.

3) You register with a "portage salarial" with a salary high enough to sponsor your own Passeport Talent - Salarié Hautement Qualifié visa.

Working remotely is possible, but it typically requires advanced planning and an examination of all of the different factors and potential consequences with an experienced professional.

What about working remotely as a tourist?
Whenever we pontificate about the complications of working remotely, we always get questions about people traveling to France for tourism who happen to do a bit of work on their trip, and we'd like to clarify that point. Generally speaking, if you're traveling in France as a tourist on the visa waiver program and staying under 90 days, you are unlikely to experience any tax or visa issues related to your work. Even salaried workers or performers on temporary assignment in France for less than 3 months are not required to apply for a work-type visa.

The main exception is that if you are a journalist, you may need a short-stay visa, because working journalists traveling to France do not benefit from the visa-waiver program, like foreign journalists traveling to the US for work purposes also need visas.

If you are legitimately in France for tourism, or even a short business trip, there are no issues with checking your work email, responding to clients or messages, attending a conference, or even seeing a France or

Europe-based client for a business meeting. You can even meet up with potential clients, and we often advise our Your Franceformation clients who plan to start French businesses to meet with potential collaborators and to make connections on their trips to France with the goal of requesting letters of support and collaboration for their later visa applications.

Again, you'll have to check regulations for your company to ensure you aren't accessing sensitive data or violating company policies by working from Europe, and you'll want to ensure that your insurance policy would cover work-related incidents, like a stolen laptop with sensitive data, or an accident during a work-related event while abroad.

It becomes slightly trickier if you are self-employed and plan on continuing to work with your full client roster while abroad. The line not to cross as a tourist would be soliciting clients, getting paid, especially in cash or in Euros, and working for French companies while traveling.

1.8 Certificates of Coverage for Social Security Charges

Despite the tax treaty being abundantly clear on which country gets to assess social charges and income taxes on your earned income while you meet the criteria for being a tax resident in France, there are still some consulates and even immigration attorneys who neglect to consider this issue of income sourcing. Ultimately, determining an income's "source" and where it is taxed is based on three important criteria: the type of income (salary, self-employment, interest/dividends, rental, capital gains...), the tax residence of the beneficiary of the income, and the treatment it gets in the tax treaty between France and the country where the income is paid out. For the purposes of social charges, or what's considered "Social Security tax" or "self-employment tax" in the US, we are talking primarily about earned income, that is to say, income which comes from employment, self-employment, or a business that you're working in.

Because of the way the tax treaty covers this income, the only legitimate way to work in France without being liable for paying social charges to URSSAF is to get a document called a Certificate of Coverage from your home country. In the US, this document is issued by the Social Security Administration. In other EU countries, this document is known as an S1. Certificates of coverage are official government documents stating that your healthcare expenses are fully covered by your home country's healthcare system and that you are paying into that system instead of the French system. They were created as a result of the Social Security Totalization Agreement between the US and France (or other countries and France) to eliminate double taxation of social charges on the same earnings.

Employees who are sent to France on an International Company Transfer visa type are required to have this document if they are being sent from a country which has a Social Security Totalization agreement with France. For these employees, the company will keep them on payroll in their home country rather than enrolling them in CPAM and paying French social charges on their salary. This can be a much cheaper option for the company, and various tax rules enable a company to do this for seconded employees for up to 5 years before putting the employees on local French contracts. Note that employees who are sent on ICT visas from countries without a bilateral Social Security agreement will pay all social taxes in France. (Talk to a French expert-comptable used to working with immigrants or expats in France to better understand 'impatriation' and 'expatriation' regimes, which are tax breaks for foreign workers posted to other countries as part of their work contracts and who travel frequently for business.)

In order to obtain a Certificate of Coverage, your employer must request one from the Social Security Administration of your home country and demonstrate that you are temporarily being sent to work overseas. As part of the request, the SSA (or its foreign equivalent) will review the rules for exempting foreign income from social security charges in France, and issue, or not, a certificate. The certificate, along with proof that the applicant has complete comprehensive healthcare coverage for all treatment, including routine procedures, is provided during the visa application and submitted to URSSAF to demonstrate your exemption from social charges. If you are able to procure this document for your salary or business income before relocating temporarily to France, you have a potential defense against significant and unexpected social charge bills.

If you do not procure a Certificate of Coverage, you will be liable for French social charges on all earned income during your time as a French tax resident. And if it's URSSAF that determines you should have been paying social charges in France the whole time, you may be in for an audit, a big accounting bill, and an even larger tax bill, complete with penalties.

Since you are unlikely to be able to procure a Certificate of Coverage for your work unless you meet some specific requirements, you should plan to request the appropriate visa that enables you to register your activity and properly pay social charges in France to URSSAF for the duration of your time in France.

You can read more about the Social Security Totalization Agreement between France and the United States here:

https://www.ssa.gov/international/Agreement_Pamphlets/documents/France.pdf

1.9 Implementation of New January 2024 Immigration Reform Law

A new law on immigration, entitled the "Loi pour contrôler l'immigration, améliorer l'intégration" - to manage immigration and improve integration - was passed in January 2024 after much debate, and many of the applicable decrees and instructional texts about how to apply the law were published in July 2024. After it was passed with many concerning provisions that came from the right wing, President Macron requested a review by the Constitutional Council to validate the law's contents in its entirety, with the result being that many of the initial articles were censured.

We refrained from commenting on the new law and its potential impact until the constitutional review of the text was complete, as there were many extreme measures that we felt would not be finalized and implemented. Certain measures, like requiring the spouses of French citizens to have financial resources and private insurance to obtain a visa or carte de séjour, would have put an undue (and thus illegal) financial burden on French families.

Other provisions, like enabling British second-home owners to have a multiyear card for short stays, would have singled out one non-EU nationality for special privileges. Despite much enthusiasm in the English-speaking press and a representative from the Dordogne who championed the measure, it was unlikely to pass muster from the start, because why would British second homeowners have a special carte de séjour that wouldn't be available to American, Qatari, or Russian second homeowners?

Ultimately, while a sweeping reform was passed, very little was introduced that impacts the lives of ordinary foreigners in France, and anything expressing "national preference" for certain jobs or benefits, or restricting the hiring of foreigners, was eliminated.

The main points of the law are covered on the Vie Publique website:

https://www.vie-publique.fr/loi/287993-loi-immigration-integration-asile-du-26-janvier-2024

Some key points:

Knowledge of French language: The law has increased the language conditions for awarding a multiyear carte de séjour to a minimum knowledge of the French language. Previously, anyone who is engaged with a Contrat d'Intégration Républicaine had to take an initial language exam at the OFII visit, and either test out at the A1 level or take a mandatory language class. The new law will now require people to pass the A1 French class before receiving a *carte pluriannuelle* (a card valid less than 5 years). Salaried employees in France may also be able to take French language classes on their work time. Going forward and beginning by 2026, a B1 level of French will be required to receive a 10-year residence card, and a B2 level of French will be required for naturalization.

Requirement to spend at least 6 months/year in France: For the renewal of multiyear cartes de séjour, a minimum amount of time spent in France may be imposed. Currently, actual number of days spent physically in France is only one criteria of determining residence and tax residence.

Reinforcement of paperwork checks on autoentrepreneurs: With the rise of platforms like Uber and Deliveroo, it has become common for undocumented migrant workers to register for these platforms and sign up as autoentrepreneur, despite lacking a carte de séjour authorizing them to do so. The law reinforces checks on autoentrepreneurs and requires INPI to verify the validity of the carte de séjour before finalizing their business registration. It also applies increased fines and additional penalties to platforms engaging undocumented workers. While we were initially concerned that this measure would prevent someone (like the spouse of a French citizen with a vie privée visa, for example) from becoming a microentrepreneur if they did not have a specific "profession libérale" carte de séjour, this is not the case. Anyone with a "profession libérale" status or a card that enables them to work in non-salaried work can continue to register as microentrepreneur.

Creation of a visa and titre de séjour "métiers en tension": Many industries in France, including service and hospitality, are suffering from recruitment difficulties. While a provision in the "salarié" visa criteria already allows the local DREETS to identify fields where there is a need for foreign workers and make it easier for employees to apply for a titre de séjour directly after working in these jobs for 12 of the last 24 months if they have lived in France for at least 3 years and can demonstrate their integration. This procedure is experimental until 2026 and is left largely to the discretion of the different préfectures.

Creation of a "délit" for hiring undocumented workers: In contrast with facilitating employees requesting a titre de séjour after working under the table, the law has also made sanctions harsher for companies and individuals who employ undocumented workers.

Creation of a visa and carte de séjour "Passeport Talent - Professions Médicales et de la Pharmacie": This new carte de séjour may facilitate the hiring of foreign doctors and medical workers such as midwives, pharmacists, and dentists, who received their degrees and education outside the European Union. It would also decentralize and hopefully accelerate the process of awarding these professionals authorization to practice medicine in France. Currently, it is extremely difficult for medical professionals who studied outside the EU to have their credentials recognized in France. For foreign students who study medicine within the French system, it can also be difficult to get sponsored for certain visa types after earning their degrees, because salaries in the public sector, including hospitals and clinics, are relatively low compared to the current Passeport Talent requirements. This measure may ease the shortage of medical doctors in certain regions of France. The particulars of this new carte de séjour are unknown at the time of publication, but we will certainly feature this visa type in the next edition of Foolproof French Visas or elaborate when information becomes available.

Creation of the *Contrat d'Engagement à Respecter les Principes de la République*: We cover this document more in-depth in Section 4.3, but this document essentially entails agreeing to abide by certain French Republican principals, mainly equality between the sexes and secularism.

Other Provisions: The law also ended protections for certain groups of people which prevented them from being deported (receiving an OQTF - Obligation de Quitter le Territoire Français), including those who arrived in France as minors. It allows judges to sentence those subjected to deportation orders but who would be deported to a war-torn country to be confined to house arrest for a maximum of 3 years. There are a few other measures specifically about managing delinquent minors, who are treated differently by the law based on the age at which they arrived in France. Finally, it simplifies the process for contesting certain immigration-related administrative decisions in French courts.

1.10 Comparing & Evaluating Long-Stay Visa Types

The purpose of this book is to provide an overview of each type of visa for living in France, and to guide you on the conditions of eligibility for that visa type, how to get it, and what you can do with it. The goal of providing this information is to enable you to compare the visa types you may be eligible for and to choose the visa type most appropriate for your situation. We will study each visa in-depth to showcase its advantages and disadvantages, and the different ways in which it can lead (or not) to long-term residency and naturalization.

The explanation for each visa type will provide clarification on each of the following topics, so you can easily compare the different requirements and the pros and cons of each type:

Health Insurance for Visas & Upon Arrival

Since 2016, every person residing regularly in France for more than 3 months has had the right to have access to their own health insurance in the French system through a program called PUMA, Protection Universelle MAladie. In this system, individuals are covered through their jobs or self-employment, and anyone who is not otherwise affiliated with French sécurité sociale can submit PUMA applications to their local CPAM, Caisse Primaire d'Assurance Maladie. The process for registering for PUMA through the individual caisse will be explained for each visa type, as the procedure can vary slightly.

PUMA premiums are income-based and calculated based on your French tax declaration, where you are required to report your worldwide income annually as a tax resident of France. It is not possible to opt out of this system, even if you maintain private healthcare. However, if you are registered to the French healthcare system through work or self-employment, you will pay into the system through social taxes levied on your French-source earned income, rather than a percentage of your total worldwide income from non-pension sources.

Because you cannot opt out of PUMA, and because proof of ongoing health coverage is required for most visa renewals, we recommend registering for the French healthcare system as soon as you become eligible, and dropping the private health coverage once you are able.

Certain visa types and certain individuals require a 12-month Schengen visa insurance policy for catastrophic coverage and repatriation for the visa to be granted, which we will indicate for each visa type.

Income & Savings Requirement

Most visas have a minimum requirement for financial resources, which can vary based on the visa type and the number of individuals in the family. The baseline for a long-stay visitor visa, without the ability to work, corresponds to net French minimum wage after social taxes, or SMIC, for 12 months, the length for which the visa is issued. In August 2024 as we are editing this edition, that net amount is €1400 per month, or €16.800 for 12 months for one adult.

To find the appropriate figure at the time of your application, you can do a quick google search for "net smic france (month in French) (year)" (e.g. "Net smic France avril 2025") to come up with the correct amount.

The exact amount you will have to demonstrate for a successful visa application will depend on your employment situation, your family size, and the different types of income you have. You do not have to show all of your bank accounts and financial resources as part of the application process, but rather, only show that you have at least the minimum amount in cash.

Work

Until you receive a resident card (10 year carte de séjour), a Vie Privée et Familiale (VPF) card, or are naturalized as a French citizen, the type of work you are allowed to do on each visa – and whether you are allowed to work *at all* is highly regulated. Salaried employees may not work as freelancers, and freelancers/self-employed people may not work as employees on standard work contracts. Salaried employees on salaried worker visas who want to change jobs must remain in their initial jobs for a certain length of time, or have their new employer sponsor them.

It is important not to rely on anecdotal and non-professional advice when choosing your visa type, and especially important not to assume that something not explicitly prohibited is allowed.

Do NOT assume that because one agency, or even one agent, tells you something is acceptable, that it is legal or even advisable. Work rights for foreigners fall under the jurisdiction of several agencies, none of which is equipped to completely advise you on your rights. Visa applications are collected by a private third party (VFS/TLS or TLS), visas are awarded by the consulates outside of France, and validated by OFII, an agency which integrates foreigners arriving in France to work and which ensures that taxes have been paid on all foreign hires. Approval of work contracts, however, is now overseen by DREETS, formally DIRECCTE, which evaluates the content of each contract and whether the hiring company has done their due diligence in trying to hire someone who *already* has the right to work in France before sponsoring a foreigner, and verifies the type of skilled immigration required regionally. That's already 4 different bureaucratic government agencies with different rules, and none of their employees are trained in how the other agencies apply their own rules to foreign workers.

DREETS also evaluates the viability of business plans of companies that want to open in France, and keeps track of workers on other visa types (student and au pair, for example) who have a work authorization based on their visa type, but who are restricted from full-time or self-employment.

Once you are a French tax resident (because you have a visa and spend more than 183 days in France in a calendar year), the local tax office will subject you to French taxation and determine how to apply the tax treaty between your home country and France to all of your income. All of these agencies will ultimately communicate with **URSSAF**, the Union de Recouvrement des cotisations de Sécurité Sociale et d'Allocations Familiales, and **CPAM**, the Caisse Primaire d'Assurance Maladie, to ensure you are paying social taxes appropriately in order to get universal health insurance coverage. (The "Universal" part means paying in is *not* optional.)

When you renew your visa, no matter what visa type you have, the préfecture is going to want to see your last bank statements from France and your home country, as well as your French tax declaration. While typically they ask for 3 months, you can be expected to show up to 12 months of statements. They, or the local tax office, can also ask for your tax declaration you made in your home country to ensure that all of your revenue has been properly reported and taxed, and so they can calculate that mandatory health insurance premium.

The fonctionnaires (public servants) at the préfecture and their superiors who process visa renewals are trained to notice discrepancies between your visa type and the types of income and deposits showing up in your bank account. They are trained to ask questions about where your money comes from and where you are paying taxes on it. And they are trained to apply the rules strictly, without regard for individual circumstance or, "but someone on the internet told me that his préfecture in (other city) told him to do it this way."

You do not want to get into a situation where you are fighting with the préfecture to renew your visa, or fighting with the tax office about how you declared income from work you weren't really supposed to be doing due to your visa type. You're better off paying protection money to the mob than trying to untangle a mess of fines and overdue social charges after you get hit by URSSAF. Believe us when we say it is cheaper and easier to do it right the first time, than to hire a lawyer to fix it down the line. It may take them a couple of years to process the information they share and to catch you, but if and when they do, you are going to regret all of your life choices.

All that to say, please heed what we tell you about the types of work you are allowed to do on each visa.

Taxation
Anyone who has a valid visa for France and who lives in France for more than 183 days out of 365 becomes a tax resident of France. Tax residency is based on a number of factors, including where you spend

most of your time, where your family lives, where you return, and where the center of your personal and economic interests lies.

You should not assume that because you spend less than 183 days in France, that you are not a French tax resident.

French tax residents are required to report their worldwide income as taxable in France. This includes declaring any bank accounts, businesses, and trusts held outside of France, and any income to these accounts. The tax treaty between France and the country where these assets or this income is located determines where the income is taxed, how it is taxed, and what foreign income tax credits it is subject to.

In our online program *Fast Track to France*, which has also been complete updated for 2024, we cover the different types of income you may have and where they are likely to be taxed based on the tax treaty between France and your home country, and we also identify the questions you should ask your accountant about the categories of income you earn. We think it's important to learn how your tax and financial situation will be affected by your move to France, ideally before you relocate.

As a general rule, while you are a French tax resident, your earned income – the income you earn through work, like salary or self-employment – will be subject to social charges and income tax in France first, and you will get credit in your home country (if you have to declare at all). Your passive income, from rentals, interest, dividends, capital gains, or pensions, will be taxed in the country where it is earned. Again, you should look to the specific agreements between France and your home country because each tax treaty is slightly different.

Maintaining & Renewing the Visa

If a particular visa type is renewable (all visa types except for "long séjour temporaire" can be renewed at least once, for part or all of a year), you are expected to continue to meet the visa conditions and to provide sufficient proof and documentation in order to renew. This comes in several stages.

First, your visa is validated or a carte de séjour is issued by the préfecture. Typically, visas issued for 1 calendar year will lead to a validation process through OFII (Office Français d'Immigration et d'Intégration) in your region. OFII will validate your work contract, or request proof of enrollment in your educational facility, or otherwise double-check whatever motive you have for obtaining your visa, and ensure that you've followed through with the original motive behind your relocation. Depending on your visa or carte de séjour type, you will resubmit documents online or to the préfecture and receive a multi-year carte de séjour.

When you renew your visa, you will receive a list of necessary documents, which tend to be the same documents you used to apply for your visa type in the first place. They will require proof that you have executed the terms of your visa for the previous year, and that you will continue to do so for the upcoming year. If you are a student, for example, they will want grade reports, attendance reports, and proof of enrollment for the upcoming year. If you are a salaried employee, for example, they'll want payslips for the past year, as well as an up-to-date copy of your work contract proving that you are still working in the same place.

If your situation changes during the year – you switch schools, or get let go from a job, or you get married or divorced – you'll have to provide documentation for your new situation and demonstrate that you still meet the requirements for a French visa. Depending on how it affects your visa, you'll also have to anticipate the change and potentially apply for a change of status. It's important to always inquire how such a change would affect your visa *before* you approach your visa renewal appointment, to avoid surprises and complications with processing your file.

One change being experimented in certain departments is requiring préfectures to evaluate your situation and suggest another carte de séjour type if you are no longer eligible for the one you previously had. This is not yet being widely implemented and will certainly take time and resources from the préfecture.

Paths to French Residency & Naturalization

While most work and family visa types can be renewed indefinitely until obtaining residency or being eligible for naturalization, some visas are not intended to establish residency or provide a long-term path to living sustainably in France. "Residency" is not just the fact of residing legally in France or even of being a tax resident. In this case, it is also the sense of having the right to renew your stay in France indefinitely, regardless of your work situation. French residency means having a 10-year carte de résident, which is distinct from "tax residency" which is far easier to establish. One indicator of whether you are on a path to long-term residency or naturalization is whether you sign a "Contrat d'Intégration Républicaine," which is covered in a later section.

Some visa options (student, au pair, travailleur temporaire) are considered temporary, which means they can only be renewed a limited number of times, and you can only convert them to certain other visa types. These visas are designed for people who want to spend a short time in France or those who want to study or participate in a youth work exchange. Study and work exchange visas were created to enable young people to spend time living and working in another country, but they do not allow the holder to get a permanent job contract (CDI – contrat à durée indéterminée), establish a career, or meet the requirements for financial stability required for residency and naturalization.

For each visa type, we have indicated whether there is a limit to how many times it can be renewed, and in what circumstances, and when holders of that particular status can expect to receive a 10-year resident card or submit a successful naturalization application. For the visa types that cannot be renewed, or that can be extended only briefly, we have also indicated what changes of status are possible. If you would like to remain in France indefinitely, you should aim to avoid visa types that do not enable you to apply for residency or naturalization.

The Importance of a Long-Term Plan

When we initially meet with our Your Franceformation clients, we stress the importance of envisioning a long-term plan for staying in France, and making visa and career decisions based off of that plan. The first few modules of our online program *Fast Track to France* covers this project development in-depth. The reason for creating a long-term plan and working backwards is that understanding your ultimate goals for your new life in France will help you to select the right visa type or understand what visa status changes you may need to make in order for your long-term vision to become possible. We coach our individual clients through this process as part of our client onboarding.

Selecting the wrong visa type from the beginning of the relocation process can jeopardize your goal of staying in France long-term or applying for naturalization. It's always possible to change your mind and leave France if you choose not to renew a visa, but it can be a long and difficult process if you decide you want to stay and have difficulty renewing the visa you've selected.

1.11 Helpful Vocabulary

The French visa process is complex, and requires a bit of specialized vocabulary to understand all of the concepts you need to know. In this section, Before we begin, please review the most useful vocabulary for the visa, carte de séjour, and renewal process, to help you understand each visa type and the administrative processes you'll have to go through.

We have also included a glossary of common terms, acronyms, and initialisms in the annex of this book.

Visa, Carte de Séjour, Titre de Séjour Vocabulary

"Tourist Visa"

People often say they are in France on a "tourist visa" when what they mean is that they are in France traveling on their passports under the visa waiver agreement. A "tourist visa" is a travel visa for a short-term stay, (Type "C" visa, commonly called a "visa de court séjour) and is usually required for people whose passports do not allow them to travel freely to France or Europe. Applicants must provide proof of resources and proof of work and strong ties to their home countries, to adequately demonstrate that they will return to their home countries and will not seek work in France, and must apply for the visa in their home country before departure. The visa is valid for a specific length of time (up to several years) but can only be used for individual trips up to 90 days in the respect of the 90/180 day Schengen travel rule.

A "Long Stay Visitor" visa is NOT a tourist visa. Americans, Canadians, and nationals from 60 other countries can travel to France without applying for a tourist visa. Starting in 2025, these travelers will have to apply for a Travel Authorization through the ETIAS system (See Section 1.6).

Travelers who are on passports, or who have a tourist visa, cannot apply for a long-stay visa in France. The ONLY exception is for spouses of French or EU nationals who do not apply for visas before arriving in France, and who can regularize their situation by paying a fee. Even in that situation, it is usually preferable to return to your home country for a long-stay visa, as the préfecture is not always aware of how to process these arrivals, and the timeline for receiving a carte de séjour and its accompanying work permit can extend to several months.

Long-Stay Visa, or Visa Long Séjour

A visa is a travel document issued by a consulate that allows you to spend a certain amount of time in a country. There are many different types of visas, but for the most part, we will be addressing the "Long Stay" or "Type D" visas, which are for people wanting to spend a year or more in France. A "Long séjour temporaire" is the only visa type that cannot be renewed or extended at all, under any circumstances, in France.

Because there are so many different types of "Long Stay" visas, saying "Long Stay" is not helpful to understanding what rights and obligations you have as a visa holder. Any visa you receive from the French consulate should indicate what type of visa it is, and what type of work it authorizes you to do, if your visa authorizes you to work at all. We will cover each type of Long Stay visa in this book.

Side note: Please do not write to us or post a question in the Americans in France Facebook group and tell us you're applying for a "long-stay visa." It means nothing until you tell us which type of long-stay visa you're applying for.

VLS-TS

This is short for a "Visa Long Séjour Valant Titre de Séjour." If you have a renewable long-stay visa (all D types except "Long Séjour Temporaire"), you have a VLS-TS. This means that you will complete the OFII validation procedures (discussed in Part 3) upon arrival, potentially completing a medical visit and integration visit (depending on your visa type) and receiving an OFII validation form for your records. After you have completed the OFII procedures, your visa is officially your "titre de séjour," or initial residency permit.

OFII Validation

OFII is the Office Français d'Immigration et d'Intégration, and the majority of foreigners arriving in France for immigration purposes are required to register with OFII within the first 90 days to validate their visas. In order to register your arrival and validate your visa you will need to provide a long term address to OFII.

As of 2019 the initial OFII procedure is started online on the ANEF (Administration Numérique des Étrangers en France) website. On the website you must validate your visa by entering certain information (arrival date, address, visa information) and paying the OFII tax. This tax is paid with a timbre fiscal (excise stamp). You can purchase a virtual timbre fiscal on the ANEF site. You will not need to bring any purchased stamps to any future appointments.

Once you have completed this step you will receive your validation document which will serve as your official 'titre de séjour' or legal proof of residency. This step also registers you with OFII and you will at some point be summoned for a medical visit, and depending on your visa type, you may also be summoned to a series of "integration days," where you learn about living in France and your rights and responsibilities as a French resident. The timeline for your appointment can be anywhere from a few weeks to several months after you register depending on the OFII office. You must keep all of the paperwork that OFII gives you for your renewal.

As soon as you validate your visa you will also be given login information to create an account on ANEF. You will need this account for renewing your visa as well as doing things like updating your address or applying for a DCEM (Document de Circulation pour Étranger Mineur).

Some visa holders, like students, passeport talent holders, and spouses of EU citizens, are not required to complete OFII procedures in-person. Students now validate their visas simply by purchasing the timbre fiscal and submitting the form online, while Passeport Talent holders and EU family members request a carte de séjour directly through different procedures.

PRO TIP: Save a scan or a copy of your visa showing your date of arrival in France, your OFII validation document, and passport ID page in case any of these documents are lost or stolen. We ask our Franceformation clients to send us visa scans as soon as the visa is issued.

Titre de Séjour or Carte de Séjour?

A titre de séjour is your legal proof of residency, and this can take the form of either your original visa that has been validated online, or a plastic card to carry in your wallet, issued after your first renewal, called a "carte de séjour."

The OFII validation process transforms your visa sticker into a titre de séjour, which can be renewed. Renewing your titre de séjour results in being issued a plastic carte de séjour card.

While technically a "visa" is only the initial sticker affixed in your passport, in this book, we will use the term "visa renewal" or "change of visa status" to refer to the process by which you extend your initial visa or get a new valid carte de séjour from the préfecture. The terms visa, carte de séjour, and titre de séjour can be used interchangeably throughout, as they all relate to the document proving your legal ability to reside in France and the type of work they enable you to do.

Passeport talent and famille accompagnante holders, as well as spouses of EU citizens, will have to resubmit certain documents through the ANEF platform to be issued a physical plastic carte de séjour before their visa expires. Passeport talent visas are typically issued for 3 months and require the online submission process to be finalized within that timeframe.

Préfecture Vocabulary

Récépissé or Prolongation
A récépissé is a paper receipt with your personal information and picture, which you receive when your titre de séjour is expiring. It extends the validity of your titre de séjour for a period of 3-4 months

while you await your renewal appointment or while your carte de séjour is being produced. It also enables you to continue working or to receive benefits from the government that require a valid titre de séjour (unemployment or CAF benefits). If it is a récépissé for a renewal (but NOT for a "première demande"), it also allows you to travel outside of France and return to the EU.

A récépissé should be given to you automatically at the end of your renewal appointment, to carry you through to when your new carte de séjour arrives. When you submit your application by mail, you typically receive a récépissé by mail several weeks after submitting your file. For online submissions, your application will be reviewed by an agent, and once the file is complete, you will receive a "Confirmation du Dépôt," followed by an "Attestation de Décision Favorable" when your renewal application is approved. If your file can not be examined by the administration before your visa or previous carte de séjour expires, you should be issued an "Attestation de Prolongation d'Instruction" which you will need to keep with your expired visa or carte de séjour.

If you make an appointment for a visa renewal, and the appointment falls *after* your titre de séjour expires, don't worry. It happens all the time. It is NOT required to get a récépissé if your titre de séjour is expiring or expired, provided that you have a convocation for a renewal appointment. If you are staying in France and do not plan on traveling between your card's expiration date and your renewal appointment, you can use the convocation along with your expired card to demonstrate your ability to stay in France.

However, if you prefer to have a récépissé to make things official, or if you need one for your employer, to travel outside of the EU, or to maintain certain benefits (CAF, unemployment), you can contact your local préfecture or sous-préfecture to learn how to obtain one a week or two before your card expires. For some préfectures, you need to make an appointment to get a récépissé or request one online. Most préfectures will only issue a new récépissé if the current one is expiring in a week or less.

Once you have renewed your titre de séjour and are awaiting your plastic card, you should receive notice to pick it up within the 4-month récépissé period. Occasionally, and in certain departments, card production can take longer than the 4 months, especially at certain busy times of the year.

A récépissé must always be carried with your expired carte de séjour or titre de séjour to be valid. You should also always make a copy or a scan of your titre de séjour (both sides) and your current récépissé in case either is lost or stolen.

Convocation

A convocation is an official invitation or summons for you to present yourself for an administrative appointment. It includes your name, visa number, and the date, time, and place of the appointment. You will receive several of these throughout your time in France. A convocation should be considered like a subpoena. You do not want to miss the appointments on it.

(You won't be arrested if you don't comply, but it won't be pleasant to try to sort out the mess of making new appointments you missed, and it may not be easy or possible to make new appointments.)

OFII Convocations: Once you submit your information to OFII for the OFII validation procedure, you will receive a series of convocations for the medical visit, integration day (if required), and the final validation of your visa.

Normally, you cannot choose the date and time of your convocation. If you MUST miss an appointment, because you're traveling, for example, you should go *in person* to your OFII office as soon as possible to make a new appointment. They will reschedule you one time. If you miss the second convocation for any reason, they will normally refuse to schedule you a third time, meaning that you must return to your home country and apply for a new visa.

You are typically not able to validate, extend, or renew your visa without completing the OFII validation procedure. However, if your regional OFII is so far behind on appointments that they do not summon you before your visa is due to be renewed, your renewal won't be jeopardized. In some cases, you may receive a 1-year card at renewal instead of a multi-year card if the OFII visits have not been completed.

Visa Renewal Convocations: When you make an appointment to renew your titre de séjour, you will receive a convocation (which you download when you make the appointment online, or which is emailed to you) with the date, time, and place of the appointment. When you arrive at your appointment, you will need to present the convocation along with your passport, titre de séjour, and other documents to receive a ticket to go to the guichet (window) and present your documents.

If your appointment is after your card expires, you can use the convocation as proof you are still in France legally, or use it to get a récépissé to extend the validity of your expired titre de séjour. It is very normal to have your visa appointment and convocation be *after* the expiry date of your visa, so don't worry if you're not able to secure an appointment within the recommended time frame. It is the date you make the appointment and the fact that you make it before your titre de séjour's expiration date that matters.

Première Demande versus Renouvellement

When you renew your visa status and keep the same status, the process is called a "renouvellement." It is administratively very simple, and you typically have to provide exactly the same documents that you provided during your initial visa request. You can refer to the checklists in each visa section, and you will be able to verify online what you will need for your type of renewal. You may receive this information by email or it may be downloaded from your local préfecture's website. Ensure that you use your own préfecture's list and forms in case they differ slightly from another department's. A récépissé for a renewal allows you to travel outside of the EU and to continue enjoying the same rights as your current visa type while you are waiting for your new card.

A "première demande" is the procedure for changing your visa type from one status to another, and is more administratively complex and time-consuming. The assumption under a première demande is that you maintain your former visa status until you are approved for the new type. Approval can happen on the spot during your appointment for some visa types, while other visa types require you to wait for notification from the préfecture that your request has been approved.

For example, a student who has been in France for several years and who marries a French person would request a "première demande" of a "vie privée et familiale" visa at her first appointment after the marriage. She would have to indicate that it was a change of status while making the appointment, which sometimes requires an in-person appearance, making a phone call, or submitting an application through a different online platform rather than using the automated appointment system some préfectures have instituted online. At the appointment, she would submit documents showing proof of her eligibility for the new visa type (marriage certificate, livret de famille, proof of common residence with her spouse, etc.). She would be issued a récépissé that continues her student status at the end of her appointment, and therefore would not receive full rights to work, start a business, etc. until her new carte de séjour has been approved.

Alternatively, a master's graduate on a Recherche d'emploi visa who would like to switch to a "profession libérale" visa in order to freelance may receive tentative approval for a change of visa status at the initial "première demande" appointment. In this case, the agent may approve a récépissé indicating the new status in order to enable the visa holder to formally register the business and to start having clients. She would then be invited back 2-3 months later with proof of the business registration and any contracts that have been established in order to get final approval of the new visa status.

Préfectures & Sous-préfectures

Upon arrival in France, the OFII validation process will be completed online with your visits being done at your regional OFII office and your renewal will be processed online or in the regional préfecture, which is a division of the police department. Depending on the size of your department and the number of foreigners living there, the préfecture may have certain procedures (renewal appointment requests, document lists) available online. It may also outsource certain renewals (récépissés, 10 year cards, naturalization requests especially) to a local "sous-préfecture" rather than processing them in the main building.

A **département** is a territory, similar to a county. Mainland France is divided into 96 departments. Corsica is divided into departments (2A and 2B, instead of 20) which is why the other departments are numbered 01 (l'Ain) to 95 (Val d'Oise). There are also 5 overseas departments (départements d'outre-mer): Guadeloupe, Martinique, la Réunion, Guyane, and Mayotte.

A **préfecture** is an administrative jurisdiction for a department, and the préfecture's headquarters is in the largest city of that department. All of your administrative requests will be handled by the préfecture of the department in which you live.

A **sous-préfecture** is a smaller administrative jurisdiction situated in and reporting to the main préfecture of the department. In *most* departments in France, immigration procedures are located in the main departmental préfecture, while the sous-préfectures process minor things like car registrations. There are some exceptions, like l'Hérault, where different towns' administrative procedures are divided between Montpellier and its two sous-préfectures.

It is important to know that different departments follow the same rules generally, but can have completely different procedures for making an appointment or submitting an application. Knowing or being able to research the rules and procedures for your specific department is essential to minimizing the stress of the bureaucratic process. We do this for our Franceformation clients prior to giving a fee quote for the renewal procedure.

An annex containing links to each préfecture's website as well as their contact information is at the end of this book. You will have to verify on your department's website whether your procedure is online or requires an in-person appointment, as many changes are currently being made in all departments.

Part 2: French Long-Stay Visa Types

There 29 situations for moving to France that we will be covering in this book. This includes the many different visas you can apply for in order to relocate to France, and several special programs (with overlapping visa types) to enable you to live and work in France temporarily. Whether you plan to relocate to France on a long-term basis or would simply like to try living and/or working in France for a short time, this section will help you to determine which visa type is the best for your situation, and what you are and are not allowed to do on each visa. We also cover how to move to France if you are already an EU citizen or are married to one.

Remember that while you are living in France as a foreigner with a visa, you are not a citizen, and you do not have the same rights that you do in your home country to find work, start a business, quit your job, or do whatever the heck you want. Each visa type has its own rules and regulations, and whatever is not specifically authorized should be avoided without clarification.

For each visa type, you should get a clear picture of what you are and are not allowed to do, what your opportunities for work, renewal, and naturalization will be, and whether or not that particular visa type will be a good fit for you. Keep in mind that no visa type will allow you to do EVERYTHING you want to do. But respecting your visa type's restrictions in the short-term will enable you to stay in France and gain permanent residency and the ability to do everything you want in the long term.

2.1 Non-Work Visas

The first types of visas we'll discuss are the "non-work" visas. They are the long-stay visitor and the temporary long-stay visa, both of which are designed for people who intend to live in France without working. The main difference between them is that the regular "visitor" visa allows you to continue to renew your stay in France, and most importantly, makes you a French tax resident. Conversely, the "temporary long-stay" visa is just that - temporary, without the option to renew or extend the length of time you're allowed to stay in France.

To successfully apply for these visas, you'll have to pay attention to how you assemble your application to ensure that you don't accidentally get a visa type you don't want. You don't want to end up with a "temporary stay" visa if you intend on staying in France for more than a year, and you don't want to end up with *either* of these types of visas if you actually want to work or do any income-producing activities. And neither of these visa types are ideal for getting on the path to French residency or naturalization, for reasons we'll explore in these sections.

Note: There is a visa type or carte de séjour called "retraité," but we are not going to cover it in this book. The retraité visa or carte de séjour is for a foreigner who has lived and worked in France long enough to receive at least a 10 year resident card, and who receives a French retirement pension. Other foreigners are not eligible for the "retraité" carte de séjour. This carte de séjour does not allow a spouse to permanently join the retired pensioner in France, but instead enables the spouse who had regularly resided with you in France during work years to regularly stay for durations of up to 1 year, while retired, without working, and without requesting a visa.

2.1-1 Long-Stay Visitor Visa

The visitor visa is designed first and foremost for retirees who can support themselves on their cash resources and pension income and who do not intend to work, and who will likely never gain the ability to work or be naturalized French. If this is you, you will gain access to a great (and inexpensive) healthcare system in a country with a relatively low cost of living, without paying too much in taxes. The long-stay visitor visa allows you to live in France without working for 12 months, and can be renewed yearly as long as you can continue to support yourself on your own cash resources or regular passive income.

Why should you avoid this visa type if you are not retired? Simply because it is very difficult to switch to another visa type. When allowed, changing your visa status from visitor to something else is a very long process that requires renewing your visitor status at least once for an additional year before you can apply or make an appointment to switch. During the change of status process, the préfecture will scrutinize your reasons for applying for the visitor visa in the first place, study whether you meet the criteria for the new status, and can revoke your status entirely if it finds that you were not abiding by the terms of your visa or that you came with fraudulent intentions that you did not declare to the consulate in your visa application.

Do not apply for a visitor visa with the intention of looking for a job. Do not apply for a visitor visa with the intention of taking time to start a business or a company. Do not apply for a visitor visa with the intention of working remotely. And do not apply for a visitor visa believing that you will be able to easily change statuses once you figure out what it is you really want to do. A visitor visa is not the first step in any plan to move to France long-term, unless you are retired. Carefully consider how a visitor visa would fit into your actual long-term plans before applying for one.

We once worked with a client for nearly 2 years to switch her status from visitor to profession libérale so she could be a photographer, and that was after she had already made the attempt to switch with another immigration professional. During that time, she was not able to work legally, which impacted her mental health and her ability to support herself. Part of the reason for the long timeline was her application's initial rejection when the préfecture suspected she had been working when it wasn't authorized. Fortunately, she is now thriving.

Visa Summary

On the France-Visas website, you select this visa by indicating Plans —> Visitor and Main Purpose of Stay —> Visitor. The Long-Stay Visitor visa is a VLS-TS which is validated online through OFII upon arrival and requires an OFII medical visit. It does not require a Contrat d'Intégration Républicaine (see section 4.2) and thus does not provide a path to naturalization.

Who is it for?

Anyone, of any age, who would like to live for one or more years in France without working.

VFS/TLS Appointment Fee: Approximately €30
Visa Application Processing Fee: €99
OFII fee: €200 in timbre fiscal upon OFII validation

Where to apply: In country of residence, at your local French consulate, VFS/TLS or TLS office.

Length of visa: 12 months
Validation: Within 90 days of the visa's start date, as soon as you have a long-term address.

Renewal: in 1 year increments, online through the ANEF platform.

Path to residency and naturalization:

After renewing for 5 years, you *MAY* receive a 10 year carte de résident, but it will very likely still have the mention "visiteur" and not enable you to work. This visa does not provide a clear path to full residency. Getting a 10 year card is subjective and depends on the area where you apply. You can apply for naturalization by decree after 5 years, but if you have not been paying French taxes (e.g. you do not have earned income which has been taxed in France totaling at least SMIC for 3 consecutive years), you are unlikely to be naturalized.

Health Insurance

As you will not be able to enroll in the French health system until you have been in France for more than 3 months, you will need a catastrophic coverage travel insurance policy in order to get your visa. The minimum coverage required for the visa is a long-stay visa policy for 12 months with €30.000 of coverage with no deductible, as well as repatriation insurance.

You can enroll in the French healthcare system under the PUMA scheme after living in France for 3 months on a valid visa. If you are not working in France and therefore contributing to the French system through employee social tax contributions, you will be assessed a roughly 6.5% tax called a PUMA cotisation (Protection Universelle MAladie) or health insurance premium. This will be on ALL income over approximately €10.000 *except* for government pensions. This means that if you are retired and receive US social security, it would not be included in the calculation of your healthcare premium, but income from IRAs, 401Ks, company pensions, rental income, other passive investments, etc. *would be* considered in the calculation of your French healthcare premium. PUMA cotisations are individual, so if you are moving with your spouse, you will be assessed and pay separately based on your individual incomes. If your PUMA-eligible income is very low, you may not pay for PUMA at all.

Note that maintaining private health coverage will NOT exempt you from paying the PUMA insurance premium, so it makes sense to cancel your private coverage once you are in the French system. It may take the better part of a year before you are assessed the PUMA fee.

US Medicare Part B: American retirees who are eligible for Medicare should carefully consider which "parts" they will sign up for before moving to France. Because you cannot use Medicare while living in France, this would mostly apply to any healthcare you expect to receive in the US, or whether you plan to move back to the US at some point later in life. Once you cancel certain "parts" of Medicare, if you plan to re-enroll for them, you will pay a penalty on your Medicare contribution each month that you are enrolled in that part, for the rest of your Medicare eligibility (the rest of your life.) Consider your likelihood of returning to the US and using Medicare and the cost of canceling Part B versus continuing to pay for it without using it in anticipation of your return.

Income & Savings Requirement

An adult on a long-stay visitor visa must have approximately net SMIC per month in cash resources, or about €16.800 total for the year. (These are July 2024 net French SMIC or minimum wage.) This amount must be in cash and cannot be in investments, CDs, or other inaccessible funds.

If you do not have sufficient resources for a full year, your visa will be limited to the number of months for which you have resources, and you will likely get a nonrenewable "long séjour temporaire" visa.

You are only allowed to count income from passive sources (pension income, interest and dividends, rental income) towards your means of financial support if you are officially retired. Otherwise, you can only count your cash resources.

Because you are not allowed to work in France, you should not plan on counting any business income or salary towards your financial resources. In fact, agents at your renewal appointment will request to see your French and US bank statements, and will pay special attention to any odd deposits that make it look like you are working for compensation. Be aware that even if the consulate waves it off, your income on this visa type could still be scrutinized at a later date by the préfecture or tax office.

Work

You are not allowed to work on a visitor visa. This means that you are not allowed to do any active income-producing activities for anyone, anywhere in the world. You cannot work remotely. You cannot work for clients outside of France, whether they are in your home country, in China, or on the Moon. It does not matter if the money is deposited from a non-French bank account into another non-French bank account. Please review the section on Working Remotely for more details.

If you are working in France, whether it's a salaried position or self-employment, and you do not have the appropriate visa status, you are violating the conditions of your visitor visa. If social taxes are not being paid on your income, you (and potentially your employer) are going to be in a world of trouble with URSSAF (French agency that collects taxes on earned income) when they find out.

Because you cannot easily change your visa status, you cannot look for employment or plan to switch from a visitor visa to any kind of work visa. You must be prepared to not do any income-producing activities while living in France on your visitor visa, and to maintain the visitor status for at least 2 years before you can consider requesting a switch to another visa type. Otherwise, you must return to your home country to apply for a new, different kind of visa after your current visa expires. Be aware that there are no advantages to applying for a change of status within France versus applying for a work visa type from outside of France, and in some cases, the change of status process can be longer and more complex.

Taxation

Having a visa to live in France for more than 183 days makes you a French tax resident, which means you will need to declare your worldwide income on your French tax declaration. However, this does not mean that you will necessarily pay French taxes.

You should also know that beginning in 2023, there is a new requirement for property owners in France to file a tax form specific to their property and to indicate the number of days it was owner-occupied, rented, or empty. This new form will assist the tax office in determining your tax residence as well as whether the property is your primary or secondary residence. Taxe d'habitation has being phased out for most primary residences, but taxes on secondary residences have increased.

For expats and dual citizens who have financial interests in multiple countries, where you pay tax and what you pay it on is largely governed by the tax treaty between France and your home country (or the country where you have your other financial assets.) As a general rule, EARNED income (e.g. salary or income from a business where you actively work) is taxed in the country where you live and are a tax resident. This is why residing in France but "working" remotely in another country does NOT exempt you from paying French tax on that income.

Conversely, income-producing property is generally taxed in the country where it is located. If you have two rental properties, one in France and one in the US, the French property would be taxed first in France, and income from the US property would be taxed first in the US. All income would need to be reported on both income tax declarations and the correct tax credits applied.

Depending on your country's tax treaty with France, you may get a French tax credit for *taxes* paid on the income in the other country, or you may get a French tax credit for *the amount of French tax you would have paid had the income been subject to tax in France.*

Finally, it's important to know that all of your worldwide income will "count" towards determining your French tax rate on the income that *is* taxed in France. So, for example, if you have pensions, interest and dividends from the US (which are not taxed in France) and ALSO have salary or autoentrepreneur income in France, you'll be in a higher tax bracket and pay a higher tax rate because of your untaxed income increasing your marginal tax rate.

Also note that income taxes are separate from social charges and the PUMA (health insurance) premium, and will be assessed independently. Exemption from paying French income taxes on non-French income does not exempt you from other kinds of French tax or from healthcare premiums.

Estate Planning
French laws about estates and successions are VERY specific, and you should take them into consideration before making France your residence. If you are retired or elderly, and there is a possibility that you

could die as a French resident, you should be aware that your residency will determine the laws that apply to your estate. Estate taxes are relatively high, and would apply to your worldwide estate and financial assets, except real property like houses.

The two main things you will have to consider are your marital regime (community property or separate property, and their derivatives) and your heirs. Unless you specifically declare otherwise, your marital regime is determined by your first marital domicile, meaning the state or country where you first lived with your spouse as a married couple. The laws of that jurisdiction will normally determine how you share property with your spouse and how it passes from one of you to the other (and whether there is gift tax between spouses). You should work with a French notaire experienced in international wills and estates to determine exactly what your situation is.

Similarly, unless you specify otherwise, and can legally specify otherwise with the help of a notaire, French law will apply to your estate. French residents who are nationals of other countries can now elect to have their home country's law apply to their estates, but this requires a formal declaration and filing a will officially with a French notaire. Even then, you may not be able to do certain things, like disinherit one of your children (not allowed in France in most circumstances) and you should plan with a notaire accordingly to ensure your wishes are respected. In 2021, there were significant changes to the French estate law which had previously enabled foreign citizens living in France to elect to apply another country's laws to their successions, so you'll want to consult with an experienced internationally-oriented notaire to review the issues.

As part of our online program *Fast Track to France*, we have assembled resources for you to understand how your estate may be affected after your death, and provided questions and resources for you to explore prior to consulting with a notaire about your situation. When you enroll in *Fast Track to France*, you'll gain a more thorough understanding about how French residency could impact your financial and estate planning.

Finally, you should make plans regarding burial or cremation, and whether you would want to have your body repatriated.

Timeline for Your Application

When we begin working with clients on their visitor visa applications, we typically start working together about 2-3 months before they intend to move. If you're sure that you're going to be getting a visitor visa, we recommend you schedule your consultation around 90 days before you want to arrive in France.

For the typical visitor visa application, the timeline will be as follows:
- 2-3 months before departure: begin working with Your Franceformation and have initial client call
- 6 weeks before departure: make visa appointment with VFS/TLS or your local consulate, for approximately 1 month before your departure date. Note that during the late spring and summer, peak periods for visa applications, we may want to start looking for visa appointments even earlier.
- 1 month before departure: attend visa appointment
- 2-3 weeks before departure: receive passport back in the mail

Maintaining and Renewing Your Visa

As long as you continue to abide by the terms of your visa (without working) and have sufficient financial resources, you should be able to continually renew your titre de séjour in France without returning to your home country. We keep track of renewal dates for all of our clients and will contact you just over 4 months before your visa expires, to assist you during the renewal process if you'd like to work with us again. We can also assist with the renewal process even if we did not complete the initial application.

If you previously worked with us on your visa application and would like our assistance in renewing, please email us at welcometo@yourfranceformation.com to receive a quote for the renewal process.

You may have challenges renewing if it is discovered that you are working or illegally operating a business from France, or if you do not establish a fixed residence while you are here. Moving around too much can also disqualify you from renewal, because you are supposed to have a permanent address, which you will need for all administrative procedures and the OFII and préfecture visits.

Changing Your Visa Status from Visitor

Changing your status from a visitor visa to something else is going to be quite difficult. Do NOT come on a visitor visa with the expectation of changing to another status, because you will not have a new status before you have been in France for at least two years.

If you arrive in France and decide you would like to have a different status, one option is to go home to your home country and apply for a new (different) kind of visa. Obviously you will have to meet the criteria for that new visa type, and you will lose any time you have accumulated in France towards residency. You will also have to wait until your current visa is expired prior to applying for a new visa.

Your other option is to ensure you have renewed your visitor visa at least once and received your new carte de séjour valid for one year. Once you receive the new card (you have picked it up from the préfecture and have it in your hand), you can make an appointment with the appropriate office and request a change of visa status, for example, from visitor to profession libérale.

The downside of this approach is that the process can take a VERY long time. If you arrive in France in June 2025 on a visitor visa, and you renew for June 2026, you might not receive your renewed carte de séjour until around September or October 2026. Once you have received the new card, you can THEN make an appointment or start the online process. Getting an appointment if necessary could take another 2-3 months, depending on availability or documents requested. This means that you might not be able to actually apply for your new status until around January 2027, and receive approval for your new status around March or April 2027. The complete change of status process can take up to 18 months after your arrival in France, so it is much quicker to return home and apply for a different visa unless you have already renewed your current status at least one time.

Establishing Residency

You'll establish tax residency during the first year, but getting an actual residency permit after living in France for 5 years will be discretionary and subject to approval by the préfecture. Some people seem to believe that someone can come to France, hang out for 5 years as a visitor, and then get a long-term residency card that affords full work rights, but that is rarely the case. It is very likely that you will receive a "visitor" residency card (if you even get a longer carte de séjour) which will not allow you to work. Better to come to France with a different status or change your status to get actual residency.

You will have a similar problem if you're considering naturalization. Although you will declare your worldwide income on your French tax return, you are unlikely to be paying much, if anything, in French income taxes if you do not have French salary or business income. Most retired expats in France pay zero income taxes. Because financial stability and your history of paying French taxes are taken into account during your naturalization application, it can be quite difficult to become French nationals if you have not paid income tax. (You will, of course, pay many other kinds of tax, like taxe d'habitation, VAT, and more.)

Family Members

An accompanying spouse or family members can get long-stay visitors visas and are subject to "regroupement familial" procedures. Note that if you have minor children, they will be subjected to the same work limitations as the adults. A child wouldn't be able to get an acting job, for example, if their parents were on visitor visas without the right to work.

Pros & Cons of the Renewable Visitor Visa
Pros:
- Enables you to live in France and to continue renewing your visa as long as you can continue to support yourself without working.
- Enables you to access French healthcare through the PUMA scheme

Cons:
- You must prove you can support yourself financially with €1.400 per month (net SMIC) of cash resources.
- You CANNOT work for anyone, anywhere. You cannot work in France, you cannot work remotely for a company abroad, you cannot work for clients on the moon, regardless of where the bank account and the clients are.
- Does not provide a clear path to residency or naturalization.
- Not easy to switch status in France; a switch is impossible before the first renewal.

Documents to Provide for Application
- ✓ Convocation for a visa appointment at consulate or VFS/TLS/TLS center
- ✓ A valid passport issued less than 10 years ago containing at least 2 blank pages
- ✓ A cover letter explaining the purpose of your move
- ✓ Long-stay visa application, completed through France Visas
- ✓ Place to stay for first several weeks upon arrival
- ✓ Proof of 12 months of catastrophic health and repatriation insurance for a value of at least €30.000, with no deductible
- ✓ Proof of financial resources of approximately €1.400 per month of your stay, for a total of around €16.800 for one year, in cash (July 2024 net monthly SMIC x 12)
- ✓ Signed statement saying you will not work or seek employment in France
- ✓ Name change and divorce/separation documents (if applicable)

Documents to Provide for Renewal

The process to renew your long stay visitor visa has completely gone online via the ANEF (Administration Numérique des Etrangers en France) website. You will need to complete the process no earlier than 4 months and no later than 2 months prior to your visa's expiration date. If you are a Your Franceformation client, we will remind you and provide a fee quote for assisting with this process.

After completing the renewal application, you will receive a document to show that you have filed your renewal. Once your file has been examined, if your renewal has been accepted, you will receive another notice, an "Attestations de décision favorable," which will give you the validity dates of your new carte de séjour. If the préfecture does not process your file on time or if your titre de séjour is approaching its expiration date, you will likely also receive a "Prolongation" document, which acts as a récépissé, extending your rights and enabling you to travel until you receive your new card. While your card is being fabricated, this paper along with your old visa will serve as your temporary residence permit and will allow you to travel outside of Schengen borders. You should be notified by text message to your French phone number when your card is ready for pick up at your local préfecture. You should not expect to receive your new card right away but if 2 months go by and you haven't heard anything, you should reach out to your préfecture.

You will need the following documents to renew:
- ✓ Access to your ANEF account, linked to a French phone number
- ✓ Attestation of OFII visit, and titre de séjour
- ✓ Copy of your passport
- ✓ Set of ePhotos for carte de séjour, available most Photomaton machines
- ✓ Proof of residence less than 3 months old (justificatif de domicile)
- ✓ Proof of health coverage (CPAM "Attestation de droits" or private health coverage)
- ✓ Proof of financial resources of net French minimum wage (net SMIC) per month of your stay, for a total of around €16.800 for one year, in cash, including all bank statements for your French and foreign bank accounts. The préfecture has been requesting French language documents, so make sure you open a French bank account in Euros during your first year and keep it funded.
- ✓ If married, copy of spouse's passport, place and date of marriage
- ✓ Name change and divorce/separation documents (if applicable)

- ✓ Most recent French tax declaration, and tax bill (avis d'impôts sur le revenu) if available
- ✓ A timbre fiscal of €225 will be required at the time you pick up your new card.

Note that the renewal process is now fully online and you will only need to go to the préfecture once the new card is ready. You must submit your renewal application online between 2-4 months prior to your previous card's expiration date, or you may be subject to a late penalty of €180.

2.1-2 Long Séjour Temporaire

The "long séjour temporaire" (LST) visa is the least flexible and possibly the least desirable visa type to get. It is also relatively new. The French consulates started issuing these visas unexpectedly to students planning to come to France for language classes and to retired people who didn't specifically request otherwise, without publishing any information about this nonrenewable visa type that has very few advantages aside from the simple fact of allowing the bearer to remain in France for a specific and non-extendable length of time.

Since its inception, we have mostly advised people on how NOT to get stuck with a long séjour temporaire visa, as we think it's better to plan for a longer stay and keep the option of renewing the visa. You can always decide to go home if you choose not to renew your visa in France. But with the Long Séjour Temporaire visa, you CANNOT opt to renew or extend your stay under any circumstances. Even during the pandemic, certain Americans in France group members were hopeful that they would be able to switch their "temporaire" visas to renewable long-stay visas due to the exceptional circumstances, and were unable to do so.

Occasionally people developing business ideas come to France for a year on a temporary visitor visa to develop their network and project so that they can have a successful business plan and future business visa application. This is especially true for people who need brick-and-mortar locations, like a purchased property with gîtes for retreats or seasonal rentals, or a storefront or restaurant, or who want to make contacts with local businesses and artisans. In this case, you won't be able to do paid work while you are in France, which means you will not be able to receive compensation for services. However, you can come to France to build those connections, start the process of establishing the business structure, and then return home to apply for the business visa.

The only advantage that comes to mind about the "long séjour temporaire" visa is the fact that it is exempt from the OFII visits, and it assumes you are going to be a tourist rather than a resident. Because you are not required to visit OFII and provide proof of long-term address, you will likely be issued an LST visa if you indicate that you plan to move around a lot within France and stay in different regions. If you're staying on a boat that moves around, or planning to spend a few months in a couple of different cities, an LST visa will prevent you from going through the complex change-of-address or change-of-department process each time you move.

There don't appear to be any advantages in terms of tax residency or ability to work, but we'll explore that in the "Taxation" section of this chapter.

Visa Summary

On the France-Visas website, you select this visa by indicating Plans —> Visitor and Main Purpose of Stay —> Visitor. The Long-Stay Visitor visa is a VLS-T which is validated online through OFII upon arrival and does not require any other visits or formalities after validation. It is not renewable under any circumstances and does not require a Contrat d'Intégration Républicaine (see section 4.2) and thus does not provide a path to naturalization.

Who is it for?

Anyone who wants to live in France temporarily, without working and who has the cash financial resources to be able to do so.

VFS/TLS Appointment Fee: Approximately €30
Visa Application Processing Fee: €99

Where to apply: In country of residence, at your local French consulate or VFS/TLS office.

Length of visa: up to 12 months
Renewal: None.

Path to residency and naturalization: None. Time spent in France on this visa will not count towards a residency or naturalization application.

Health Insurance

You will need a catastrophic coverage travel insurance policy in order to get your visa. The minimum coverage required for the visa is a travel policy with €30.000 of coverage with no deductible, valid for the duration of your stay in the Schengen space for up to 12 months, as well as repatriation insurance.

You will not be able to register on the French healthcare system with this visa type.

Income & Savings Requirement

This visa does not allow you to work, so any income you earn during your visa must be from passive sources, like investments or rental income, rather than from any type of work.

You will have to have savings of €1.400 per month for the entire length of your stay, or €16.800 in cash for a 12-month visa (Net French SMIC as of August 2024). If you do not have sufficient resources for a full year, your visa will be limited to the number of months for which you have resources.

Work

You are not allowed to do paid work with a long séjour temporaire visa. This includes any type of remote work as an employee or contractor for companies outside of France (See section 1.7 on Working Remotely). Because you cannot change your visa status, you cannot look for employment or plan to switch from an LST visa to any kind of work visa. You must not do any income-producing activities while living in France on your LST visa.

Taxation

If you don't really establish a permanent place to live, and are not working per the terms of your visa, your information will likely not be transmitted to the local tax office or relevant tax services. Therefore, while you could be present in France for more than 183 days during a given tax year, triggering tax residency, leaving at the end of your visa and not returning means that the tax services will not be looking for a French tax declaration from you.

This does NOT mean that you aren't *supposed* to complete a declaration if you meet the criteria for being a French tax resident. It simply means you may get away with not doing so if you leave and don't return to France. You could theoretically make the argument that the "temporary" status of this visa implies that you do not establish tax residency, but that would be a topic to discuss during a paid consultation with a certified accountant (expert-comptable) who can advise you appropriately.

Note that if you own a residence in France, you are now required to file a tax form indicating how many days out of the year the residence was occupied by you and by other tenants. If you have an LST visa and reside in your French home for enough days during the year, it may become your primary residence and trigger a tax filing requirement. Again, the best thing to do is consult with a French certified accountant.

Many people inadvertently get the LST visa while intending to prolong their stay in France and establish residency, and therefore return to their home countries at the end of their LST visa to reapply for another, more appropriate visa type right away. In that case, you should begin filing French tax declarations for the first calendar year during which you were in France for more than 183 days. Therefore, if you arrive in France with an LST visa in April, 2025, and return to your home country in March, 2026 to reapply for a new visa type, and return to France with a different visa in June, 2025, you should file a French tax declaration for 2025 and 2026, with your worldwide income from all sources.

Timeline for Your Application:
- For the typical temporary stay visa application, the timeline will be as follows:
- 2-3 months before departure: begin working with Your Franceformation and have initial client call
- 6 weeks before departure: make visa appointment with VFS/TLS or your local consulate, for approximately 1 month before your departure date. Note that during the late spring and summer, peak periods for visa applications, we may want to start looking for visa appointments even earlier.

- 1 month before departure: attend visa appointment
- 2-3 weeks before departure: receive passport back in the mail

Maintaining and Renewing Your Visa

The Long Séjour Temporaire visa is not extendable or renewable in France. The end date on your visa is the date by which you must leave French territory.

If you have been issued a temporary stay visa even though it was not the visa you requested, you may want to return to your home country, apply for a new visa, and immediately return to France. We have assisted several clients in this process, as they were unaware that they had received temporary visas prior to arriving in France. In 2020 during the Covid pandemic, we assisted a couple of American retirees who had worked with a different relocation agency. They went to renew their visas and were unaware that the ones they had were not renewable until after their appointment with the préfecture.

To maximize your chances of getting a renewable visa the next time, we encourage you to reach out to us for our assistance in preparing the renewable visa application.

Establishing Residency

Because you are required to leave by the end of your visa and must get a new visa in your home country to return to France, you will not be able to establish residency or count any time spent with a "Long Séjour Temporaire" status towards residency or naturalization. The clock on your continuous time spent in France will restart with each new LST visa, or with the new visa type you get after returning home after your LST status ends.

Family Members

An accompanying spouse or family members can get long-stay visitors visas of the same type.

Pros & Cons
Pros:
- Enables you to live in France for a set period of time, up to 12 months, without working.

- No need to establish a permanent address in France; you can move around.
- You likely won't be subject to French tax residency
- You do not have to worry about exchanging your driver's license

Cons:
- You must prove you can support yourself financially with €1.400 per month of cash resources or €16.800 total for the year (SMIC net).
- You CANNOT work for anyone, anywhere. You cannot work in France, you cannot work remotely for a company abroad, you cannot work for clients on the moon, regardless of where the bank account and the clients are.
- Does not provide a path to residency or naturalization.
- Impossible to switch status or extend the visa in France.

Documents to Provide for Visa Application
- ✓ Convocation for a visa appointment at consulate or VFS/TLS center
- ✓ A valid passport issued less than 10 years ago containing at least 2 blank pages
- ✓ A cover letter explaining the purpose of your move
- ✓ Long-stay visa application, completed through France Visas
- ✓ Place to stay for first few weeks upon arrival. (A long-term lease is not required if you have the financial resources to pay for housing.)
- ✓ Departure date (no plane ticket required)
- ✓ Proof of 12 months of catastrophic health and repatriation insurance
- ✓ Proof of financial resources of approximately €1.400 per month of your stay (about €16.800) in *cash*
- ✓ Name change and divorce/separation documents (if applicable)

As renewal of this visa type is not possible, there is no document list for renewal.

2.2 Student Visa Types

There are many opportunities to pursue higher education or enroll in quality French language programs in France. As a student in France, you can improve your language skills, develop international experience in your chosen career field, pursue a degree program that can cost *a lot less* than a degree in your home country. You'll also be able to take advantage of internships and network with the intention of finding jobs after graduation. As long as you pursue a field that will lead to interesting and lucrative job opportunities for you, and follow a coherent course of study that advances your skills in your chosen field, a student visa leading to work opportunities can be a great way to get your foot in the door in France.

The regular student visa does not technically have an age limit. 18-year olds can get the student visa for undergraduate or language studies, and a couple of our clients in their 60s or even their 70s who have pursued language classes or degree programs have gotten the student visa without issues. Similarly, 23-year olds who have *not* gotten the student visa because they made a few vital mistakes on their applications, the most common one being that they specify that they want the student visa so that they can work while they pursue their studies.

Pursuing a course of study in France does potentially give you the ability to work part-time, but you need to be aware that your options for such work are limited and cannot be seen as the primary reason for your relocation to France. Your work also can't factor into your visa application or means of support at all. You should not be providing documentation for any work contracts as part of a student visa application, with the exception of an internship.

You should also know that while student visas can provide a path to French residency and naturalization, you cannot become a naturalized citizen directly from a student visa. Because one of the main criteria of applying for naturalization by decree is your financial stability, and because students are only allowed to work part time, you must first switch to a work visa status enabling you to develop that financial stability. While your years as a student are taken into account in terms of the longevity of your time in France, that time is not sufficient for a successful naturalization application.

In this section, we'll cover the standard student visa, the internship visa, and the "Recherche d'Emploi Création d'Entreprise" visa which can be obtained after completing a master's degree or equivalent in France. While an "au pair" visa is not technically a student visa type, we have grouped it in here because au pairs are under 30 and are encouraged to take advantage of their time in France to learn French and experience French culture. Language classes used to be a formal requirement of the au pair status, whereas they are now simply recommended.

2.2-1 Student Visa

Students who are enrolled in full-time, accredited degree programs at the undergraduate or graduate level in French universities are eligible to receive long-stay student visas for the duration of their stay in France. Nontraditional students, including older students and professionals seeking a career change, can also apply. There is no age limit for enrolling in these programs or for receiving a student visa, but certain conditions make it more likely that your visa application will be successful, and you'll need to consider your options after your program ends.

Getting a regular student visa instead of a temporary one provides several advantages. It can be renewed in France without returning to your home country, and the years spent on a renewable student visa count towards eventual residency and naturalization requests. It also enables the student to work for up to 964 hours per visa year, which works out to about 20 hours per week.

The main barriers to successfully obtaining and renewing a student visa exist to prevent people from applying for student visas when their primary intention is to work instead of study. As the student visa does allow employment, it used to be fairly common for people to request student visas as a way to get to France, but then not attend classes or continuously enroll in (and fail out of) different unrelated academic programs. As a result, there is now a careful screening process to ensure student applicants are serious about their program of study and that it's not simply a shortcut to working in France without being sponsored. Similarly, renewal rules require you to attend and pass classes, and justify any significant changes to your course of study.

Minor students under 18 who are traveling to France alone to study can apply for long-stay student visas as well, in a specific category for minors. They will need parental authorization, and will be exempt from OFII procedures until they turn 18. As their 18th birthday approaches, they will have request an official titre de séjour. Note that children relocating to France with their parents do not apply for minor student visas.

Successfully getting a renewable student visa depends on the country where you're applying, your academic background and motives, and your financial resources, so you should make sure to develop and present a long-term plan for your academic career in France and how it relates to your career goals. Presenting a reasonable and well thought-out plan to incorporate your studies in French and take advantage of academic opportunities will maximize your chances of getting the renewable visa.

Visa Summary

On the France-Visas website, you select this visa by indicating Plans —> Study and Main Purpose of Stay —> Student. The Long-Stay Student visa is a VLS-TS which is validated online through OFII upon arrival and does not require any appointments after validation. It does not require a Contrat d'Intégration Républicaine (see section 4.2) and can provide a path to naturalization after you switch to another visa status at the end of your studies.

Who is it for?

Anyone, of any age, who wants to live in France while working on a serious, accredited, full-time course of study. For students enrolled in intensive language classes, this is at least 20h per week in a FLE Qualité accredited program, for at least 9 consecutive months, with gaps of no longer than 2 weeks between studies. Not all nationalities can get a student visa for language studies alone.

VFS/TLS Appointment Fee: Approximately €30

Campus France Etudes en France Fee: $270 or $430 for regular service (3 weeks, depending on program type), $430 for rushed service (3 business days)

Visa Application Processing Fee: €50 for students who go through the EEF process; €99 in countries where the EEF process does not apply.

OFII validation fee: €50.

Where to apply: In country of residence, at your local French consulate or VFS/TLS office. You can switch to this visa status from a visitor or au pair visa, but not from a work or family visa type.

Length of visa: 12 months

Renewal: typically in 1 year increments. You can get a multiyear visa "carte pluriannuelle" for 2-3 years if you are enrolled in a multi-year degree program like an undergraduate or graduate degree.

Program Application Deadlines: The Campus France platform opens on October 1, 2024 for the 2025-2026 academic year. Application deadlines start on December 15 for L1 (1st year license), PACES (1st year medical school), and all level of architecture (DAP). The deadline is January 1 for all other programs, including L2, L3, and Master's programs. These dates are for the current year, however, you can expect the timeline to be similar in future years. If you need to take a French language test like the TCF, DELF, or DALF prior to applying to your program, you should keep these dates in mind when researching available test centers and test dates, as you will need to receive your test results to submit the applications.

Program Types
French Language Classes
French language classes are the most common type of academic program that people enroll in to come to France, but the crackdown on student visas in the past few years has made it increasingly difficult to get an actual "long stay student visa" instead of a "long séjour temporaire" for language studies. While there's no guaranteed formula for getting the renewable visa, there are some things you can do to improve your chances of success.

As of 2019, it became more difficult for students in most countries to get a long-stay student visa for language studies. Consulates in Australia and India specifically advise that they will not issue student visas for these programs, so this advice applies mainly to Americans and Canadians.

To get a renewable student visa, you should first ensure that you enroll in intensive language classes for at least 20 hours per week, for 9 months (36 weeks), a full academic year. You can have a gap between periods of classes of no more than 2 weeks. If your first semester of classes is the spring semester, you will have to enroll in classes over the summer as well to ensure the continuity of your studies required to get a 12-month renewable student visa.

You are unlikely to get a renewable visa if you are a complete beginner in French, so try to have at least a B1 level before you apply. Include information about your previous French language studies and any ongoing tutoring or language classes you've taken as part of your application, so the consulate can see the seriousness and length of your studies. Taking an official French language test like the TCF (Test des Connaissances du Français) or passing a DILF/DELF/DALF (Diplôme Initial en Langue Française – levels A1/2, Diplôme d'Etudes en Langue Française – levels B1/2, or Diplôme Approfondi en Langue Française – levels C1/2) can help your case as well.

Enroll in a rigorous academic program in a university, or a program that meets the Qualité FLE requirements (Qualité Français Langue Etrangère) published by CIEP, the Centre International d'Etudes Pédagogiques, a French agency that accredits various academic programs. You should also look for programs that offer workshops and extracurriculars related to your other field of study, and favor schools that have small class sizes and offer individualized attention. Larger schools with cheap tuition are often magnets for less serious students who want to get the student visa to work rather than to attend class and improve their language skills. The consulates and préfectures are aware of such visa farms and subject those applications to more scrutiny.

Finally, you'll want to include as much information as possible in your application about how you will use the language studies as part of your ongoing personal and professional development. Including details in your cover letter about the academic and professional opportunities you'll want to take advantage of in France or around the world with the language skills you develop can be highly beneficial to your application.

The enrollment process for most language schools is very simple. For some of the more academically rigorous ones, you'll have to provide a diploma or transcript of your most recent academic degree, but in most cases, you'll simply submit an enrollment form and pay a deposit of up to 50% tuition. The school will provide you with a pre-enrollment certificate and receipt to send to Campus France and include with your visa application, and you will pay the remaining tuition and begin class once you arrive in France and validate your visa.

Undergraduate (Licence)

Undergraduate programs in France, or "licence" are 3-year intensive programs that train students in a particular field. Unlike US and Canadian universities, which often provide a generalized core in the humanities and sciences for all students, French universities are highly specialized, with a standard curriculum for all students and little room for electives and specializations. French university programs should be considered a full-time job, as most require students to take 7-8 classes per term.

The admissions process for French universities differs based on the level of study you'd like to enroll in, and where you are applying from. Students living in France – even foreigners – who have never begun university studies must submit an application identifying their top 3-5 university program choices in a selection process called Parcoursup. This process begins in the fall and has a deadline in early February/March for programs starting in September or October. High school graduates, or au pairs with a high school degree but no university coursework, should be prepared to submit high school transcripts and diplomas translated officially into French, and take the TCF - DAP exam, the Test des Connaissances du Français – Demande d'Admission Préalable. This exam will be required by the university for any student who has not completed their secondary education in French.

Students applying to French universities from abroad should expect to apply through Campus France, likewise submitting transcripts and diplomas, official TCF-DAP results, and a letter explaining their choices of university programs. As the majority of programs are taught in French, students should have a B2 or very high B1 level of French in order to gain admission.

VAE – Validation des Acquis et de l'Expérience

Students with previous academic coursework at the university level, or students with significant professional work experience, can apply for recognition and academic credit for those experiences through a process called "Validation des Acquis et de l'Expérience." This application allows students to skip one or more years of academic coursework, provided they meet the necessary prerequisites for enrolling in a later year of a program.

The university determines how much credit you receive for previous coursework and work experience by examining your CV, syllabi for courses taken in the field, and descriptions of your work duties and previous employment, all translated into French. Each department has its own deadline for VAE submissions, and they are usually early in the year.

If you intend to take advantage of a VAE to skip L1 coursework, keep in mind that you should probably *not* skip L2. In order to qualify for the Recherche d'Emploi / Création d'Entreprise visa, you must complete 2 years of a degree program and receive the degree. If you skip L1, you can still qualify for Recherche d'Emploi based on completing L2 and L3 coursework, which gives you the equivalent of a French bachelor's degree. Conversely, if you skip part or all of your program's L2 coursework, you would have to complete a master's degree, which is typically a 2-year program, before you can apply for Recherche d'Emploi.

DU – Diplôme Universitaire

Students or professionals who want to expand the education section on their CV can often enroll in complementary programs called a "diplôme universitaire." These programs are not state-sanctioned degrees like License/Master/Doctorat, but rather programs offered by universities that enable students to complement their academic track with a new area of interest or deepen their understanding of a particular niche topic.

For example, a bilingual student might pursue a DU in a third language in order to enroll in a rigorous translation and interpretation program that requires 3 or more languages, or to complement studies in political science. A law school may offer a DU in criminology or in legal English.

These programs generally cover a particular topic in a short period of time, but can be a great way to add to your CV. They don't necessarily have a prerequisite level of study, and you can register for them even alongside a License. DU are paid courses, which generate money for the university, and the fees are set by the school. They will not fulfil the student visa requirements on their own, but can be an intriguing option for complementary or continuing education.

Prépa

High school graduates who want to study at the "grandes écoles," or prestigious programs like Sciences Po often spend one to two years after high school in intensive programs to prepare them for entrance exams.

Graduate (Master)

Previously, candidates for master's programs in France could apply to M1 or M2 separately, but now, most programs are two full indivisible years and require 120 ECTS (credits). Foreign students' applications to most French graduate programs take place through Campus France, although some university departments can take applications through the platform Mon Master. Campus France requires students to select several programs and to upload transcripts and diplomas for all previous academic work, along with a cover letter, curriculum vitae, and results from a French language exam like the TCF or DELF. Universities accept students with a B2 or occasionally a high B1 level of French, but realistically you should aim for a C1 level in order to succeed at the master's level in France.

Over the past few years, there has been an increase in the number of programs offered in English, so you also have the option of looking for programs that do not require a particular level of French. But, if you do a program which is not taught in French, you'll have to determine whether it qualifies you to obtain a RECE status following your studies, and you'll also have to ensure that you study French alongside the program so you can eventually request a multiyear carte de séjour.

When you are applying to programs independently, you should submit your applications directly to the university or universities where you'd like to study. While French and other EU students use a platform called "Mon Master," this platform is not available to other international students. When you submit your master's application, you will need to provide your transcripts, cover letter, and other documents to the program you've selected. Some programs require an interview after the initial selection process.

Masters programs typically have a common core of coursework and are a continuation of the Licence curriculum, with little room for electives. Programs normally will require at least one short thesis, usually a minimum of 30-40 pages long. There will also be a required 6-month work experience or internship with a rapport de stage (internship report) upon completion.

Students who complete a 2-year master's program and who receive their degree can be eligible for the Recherche d'Emploi / Création d'Entreprise visa, which we will discuss in the next section. This can be advantageous to students who wish to find a job and work in France after completing their studies.

Doctoral programs usually require associating with a particular professor and research facility to complete a dissertation. Research and writing lasts 3 years, and a PhD program is likely to fall under the category "Passeport Talent – Chercheur Scientifique" rather than student.

Other Academic Programs

There are various other types of academic programs for subjects like art, cooking and baking, MBAs, programs on all subjects in English, exchange programs, and more, available in France. Prior to enrolling in one of these programs, you should carefully consider its accreditation to see if it will qualify you for a student visa and eventually Recherche d'Emploi / Création d'Entreprise. Similarly, if you would like to stay in

France after the degree program, ask the admissions office questions about internship and job placements, and whether the programs will qualify you for a work visa afterwards.

Some programs may not provide degrees that enable students to get student visas or apply for Recherche d'Emploi after the program ends. Being aware of the potential career paths and job opportunities that will arise from a program you complete is essential if you think you might want to stay in France after completing the program.

Internships

Students who are currently enrolled in accredited university programs in France can do internships for up to 6 months per year (12 months) while working full time at 35 hours per week in the internship, validated through a convention de stage. Students *must* be enrolled in a program of study and have a convention de stage signed by the company and their home university, regardless of whether the university is in France. A professor from your university should monitor the internship and help the student integrate it into her studies, and provide assistance, feedback, and a grade on the *rapport de stage*, or internship report, to be completed after the internship ends.

The internship should be a learning experience for the student and outline opportunities for learning skills that will advance the student's professional career. French law requires interns to be paid the 2024 intern minimum wage of roughly €4,35 per hour, starting with the 309th hour of work, which is after 2 months of full-time work. Internships of less than 2 months do not have to be paid, but will still need a convention de stage.

An intern can get a student visa for the length of the internship, by submitting the signed convention de stage to DREETS for approval.

Internships are considered part of the student's studies, and internship work does not count towards the 964 hour limit of student visa work, even if it's paid. Students who are hired for CDD or CDI jobs related to their studies can apply for an authorisation de travail if their job would take them beyond the 964 hour maximum.

Campus France - "Études en France"

Campus France or Études en France is an online portal that assists you with applying to French universities and validating your academic plans before you can obtain your student visa. Generally speaking, Campus France refers to the online platform where you can research different academic programs available in France, while Études en France refers to the platform through which you can apply directly to those academic programs and submit your student visa documentation for an initial review and interview by the EEF staff.

Citizens of 68 countries, including the United States, Canada, India, and many countries in Africa and South America must use the Campus France process. Citizens of other countries NOT concerned with Campus France, including Australia and New Zealand, can apply for student visas directly with their local French consulate or VFS/TLS office. A full list of countries using Campus France is available on their website.

No matter what type of academic program you apply for, you will have to go through Campus France if it's required for your country. There are two different procedures, depending on your level of study and whether the program itself participates in Campus France.

In one procedure, you apply to university programs that interest you directly through the Campus France platform, uploading your cover letter, résumé, French test results, transcripts, diplomas, and other required documents to the platform. You then select the universities and programs you would like to apply for, and Campus France will submit your application on your behalf. The university will communicate its admissions decision through the Campus France platform, and you will have to make your final selection prior to getting your student visa. Typically, university program applications are due between February and March for undergraduate and graduate programs, and decisions are made available in April and May. The Etudes en France application fee for this procedure is $430, and the procedure takes 3 weeks. It cannot be expedited.

In the second type of Campus France procedure, you apply directly to the university and submit your acceptance documents along with your diplomas, transcripts, and other documents to Campus France. This second procedure will be primarily for doctoral candidates, who will have to network and apply directly with their research advisors in French universities, and language schools, which do not have a formal application process but simply require an enrollment request and a paid tuition deposit. Programs to which you have already been admitted can be found online in the Campus France catalogue, and you will submit the school's acceptance letter directly to Campus France, along with payment.

For Independent and Doctorate students, plus students who submit their applications through the Campus France portal, the fee is $430.

Study abroad students and those who have received an acceptance from an undergraduate or graduate program outside of the Campus France program pay $270 for regular processing, which takes 3 weeks from the date of payment submission. If your visa appointment is quickly approaching, you can use their "rush" procedure by paying $430 and submitting your documents electronically. Rush service is only if you have been accepted to an academic program outside of the Campus France process and received an admission letter. This is not available to students in French language programs or culinary schools.

Recipients of France Excellence Eiffel, France Excellence Graduate Scholars, France Excellence Chateaubriand), Gilman Scholarship and Fulbright Scholarships are exempt from Campus France fees, as are students who have received a French baccalauréat in the 4 years preceding their application.

Application guide for students for the 2024-2025 academic year: https://www.usa.campusfrance.org/etudes-en-france-application-guide

Pay the Campus France application fee: https://www.usa.CampusFrance.org/pay-the-etudes-en-france-application-fee

Health Insurance

Student healthcare is now administered directly by Ameli, CPAM's website for managing French healthcare enrollees. All students, regardless of age, now register online for healthcare if they are not otherwise employed. You will need to provide proof of health insurance and Ameli registration in order to renew your visa.

To register, you will have to upload your academic enrollment, your passport and visa, your birth certificate, and your RIB (relevé d'identité bancaire). Here is the link: https://etudiant-etranger.ameli.fr/#/

Campus Life Fees

Enrollment in a French university now requires paying a CVEC fee for campus life and activities. See glossary for updated amount.

You will have to provide a receipt for the CVEC fee to complete your university enrollment. Link in the appendix.

Income & Savings Requirement

The financial requirement for obtaining the student visa is lower than for other types of visas, and requires a minimum of €615 per month for 12 months in order to qualify. This amount is what you'll need *after* your tuition is paid, so if you're going to a language school that costs €5.000 for the academic year, you'll need to factor that pricing in as well. Your total in savings would therefore need to be 12 x €615 + €5.000 = about €12.380.

When you initially apply for the student visa, you cannot be counting on work or planning to work in France, and you must have ALL of the financial resources available in cash in your personal account(s) or through a financial guarantee from a family member. The family member providing the financial guarantee would have to provide a notarized statement saying that they will provide you with €615 per month and help you to meet your financial needs if you are not able to do so.

Do NOT mention work or a plan to work on your visa application in the "means of financial support" section. Your means of financial

support should be your own personal financial resources, and, if necessary, financial assistance from your guarantor. Stating your intention to find work upon arrival (e.g. 'I'll babysit or teach English part-time to make extra money,') will likely result in your visa getting rejected.

Some family members are reticent about signing such a declaration, but the truth is that you may not need to take them up on their offer. Once you arrive in France, you can find part-time work that will likely meet the minimum income requirement, and you can use the proof of regular income during the renewal process, or you can use the financial guarantee. You should ensure that you open a French bank account upon arrival and make sure that you have at least €615 per month transferred into it during your first year. If you have provided a financial guarantee from a family member and intend to use the same guarantee at renewal, the préfecture will want to see evidence of regular monthly transfers from that person's foreign bank account into your French account. The préfecture may also request copies of the family member's bank statements and translations during the renewal process.

Work

Students are allowed to work up to 964 hours per year "à titre accessoire," meaning part-time. These hours must be part of a regular French employment contract (CDD or CDI) and declared to DREETS, which tracks foreigners employed in France and the hours worked. Student visas can be revoked if the student is not meeting the conditions for the student visa, and working too much or in the wrong type of work. As long as you remain within the limit of 964h per year or are doing an internship, you do not have to request any special work authorization.

This visa type's work restrictions also prevent you from working remotely or for companies outside of France to complement your income, as those income sources would be incompatible with your visa status.

Students who do not find a French job immediately can "save up" their hours and work full time in the summer, or for roughly 6 months of the year, rather than working 20 hours each week for the full year. If you are finishing a degree program and have the hours available, you can use them to begin a full-time salaried position while waiting for your change of status to Recherche d'Emploi or a Salarié status to be processed.

Students cannot be self-employed, work remotely as employees *or* contractors, or practice any type of regulated profession for which they do not have the necessary *French* qualifications. This includes students who would work for foreign companies and deposit the funds in a bank account outside of France. Any foreign degrees or qualifications should be converted and validated through ENIC-NARIC and the appropriate professional organization before they can be used in France.

Taxation

If you are employed, you are working in France, and you should therefore declare your worldwide earnings and pay French taxes from your date of arrival in France. You will contribute to French healthcare and retirement funds through social charges on your salary, and you should file a French tax declaration to reflect your worldwide earnings and to tax amounts earned in France.

Students who are less than 25 years old and who earn less than 3 times the minimum wage in one year (SMIC, roughly €1.767 per month in 2024) do not have to declare their income. This means students who worked full time for less than 3 months, or who earned less than about €5.100 total during the tax year, can declare €0 revenue on their French tax forms.

Internship gratification ("gratification de stage," which is not the same as salary, and comes from an internship approved through a university and officialized through a convention de stage) is tax exempt up to French minimum wage, or SMIC, which is €21.204 per year in 2024. Only the amount in excess of this ceiling needs to be reported; if a student intern earned €22.000 in a year from his internship, he would only need to report €792 in taxable income in France (Article 81bis du

Code Général des Impôts, 2014). There is no age limit for the tax exemption of this amount.

For US citizens, all income from all sources must be declared on a US tax return, including tax-exempt internship gratification and salary.

Maintaining and Renewing Your Visa

In order to remain in good standing with your visa, you should expect to provide proof of passing exams and most of your classes each year, along with attendance and grade reports, and proof of enrollment in the upcoming semester. You will have to provide ongoing proof of finances and bank statements, to show you meet the student minimum of €615 per month in income or resources in your French bank account.

At each renewal, you will be asked to provide an accounting of all of the academic programs you have undertaken since arriving in France, and any certificates or degrees earned. While it is normal and sometimes even expected to repeat a couple of classes or even a year from time to time, or to switch programs, you may be asked to account for any changes to your "parcours." If the préfecture sees that you have switched tracks several times (from biology to literature to political science to math), they may revoke your student visa on the grounds that you are not seriously pursuing your studies.

If you finish one degree and want to study a related field for a specific academic purpose, you can write a note to justify your choice. For example, Allison studied folktales in a comparative literature context before doing a master's in anthropology to study oral tradition, with the goal of applying to PhD programs in folklore and oral tradition. Even though the two fields were not strictly related, they made sense in relation to a plan she had at the time for my future. Studying science and translation, or science and law, can make sense if you want to become a scientific translator or a patent lawyer. It's also completely fine if you enroll in a program, discover you're in over your head or that you don't really like what you're studying, and switch to something else that makes sense. Just make sure you can justify any major changes and provide justification in the form of communications with your professors if you can.

Establishing Residency

You can't establish residency on a student visa, and you cannot go directly from a student visa to a ten year card or naturalization. If your visa status is that of a student, you will need to change your status to a work visa type prior to applying for naturalization. However, being a student for at least two years in a degree program can grant you certain benefits in applying for residency or naturalization.

After completing 2 years of study in an accredited program and earning a degree, you can apply for a Recherche d'Emploi visa, formerly known as APS. Recherche d'Emploi grants you the rights of your student visa for an additional year after the end of your degree program, without requiring you to be enrolled in studies. You can use this time to look for full-time employment.

While on Recherche d'Emploi, you can continue to work part-time (up to 964 hours per visa year or 20ish hours per week) at your student job, and look for a full-time position in a CDD or CDI. Once you are hired, your Recherche d'Emploi status means that the company hiring you does NOT have to prove they tried to hire a person who already has French or EU work papers. You have what is called a "situation de l'emploi non opposable," meaning that DREETS cannot veto your work contract unless there is dire unemployment in your field.

You must find a full-time job earning at least 1.5 times minimum wage, and that is related to your field of study. Once you have been hired, you can switch your visa status to Salarié (or Travailleur Temporaire if the contract is for less than 9 months). Your new employer will have to pay a tax of 55% of 1 month's salary for you to get your change of status approved, but they do not have to prove they tried to hire someone who already had the ability to work in France. The tax is paid by your new employer on its quarterly tax declaration.

If you are considering becoming a student in France as a non-traditional student, you'll want to be aware of your options in your field for after completing your program, as finding work may prove to be more challenging.

While on Recherche d'Emploi, you can also choose to develop a business and to apply for a profession libérale, entrepreneur (commerçant, artisan, industriel), profession artistique, or Passeport Talent – entrepreneur titre de séjour.

Several paths to naturalization that begin with a student visa are:
1. Student → Recherche d'Emploi → Salarié / Passeport Talent → Residency & Naturalization
2. Student → Passeport Talent Salarié or Carte Bleue Européenne → Residency & Naturalization
3. Student → Recherche d'Emploi → Profession Libérale / entrepreneur (commerçant, artisan, industriel) → Residency & Naturalization
4. Student → Chercheur / Scientifique → Passeport Talent → Residency & Naturalization

If you are not eligible for Recherche d'Emploi (because you have not completed a degree program or 2 years of study leading to a degree), do not apply for Recherche d'Emploi before you get a full-time salaried job (choosing instead to switch directly from student to salarié), or miss the deadline for your Recherche d'Emploi application, you do not gain any advantage while applying for jobs with French employers.

If you have a student status but do not have Recherche d'Emploi for whatever reason, your potential employer may still have to prove they tried to hire a French or EU person, which requires submitting the job description and all potential candidates to DREETS to prove that nobody else was able to take the job. This depends on your studies and diplomas but in general, it is quite difficult for a company to justify hiring you unless you have significant skills. In order to switch directly from student to another status, you will have to apply and meet the same conditions as if you were applying from your home country.

Applying for Naturalization After 2 Years

Theoretically, completing 2 years of study in France and earning a master's degree or higher reduces the time you must spend in France continuously to qualify for naturalization to 2 years. This means that upon completing your 2-year degree, you are technically eligible to apply for naturalization "by decree" almost immediately.

However, this eligibility comes with the caveat of proving your financial stability. As we explained in the section on Naturalization, you cannot apply directly from a student or Recherche d'Emploi visa; instead, you must first switch your visa type to one that enables you to work and meet the minimum financial requirements for being naturalized. Therefore, if you complete a master's degree and would like to become a French citizen as quickly as possible, you should opt to find a CDI in your field and begin the naturalization process as soon as your période d'essai (trial period, usually 3 months) has ended.

After completing 2 years or more in a degree program and earning an advanced degree in a French university (license or master's), you can apply for "Recherche d'Emploi," which enables you to spend an additional 1 year in France looking for a salaried job related to your field of study. You can then switch to a salaried worker visa if an employer will pay 1.5x SMIC and pay a tax on hiring foreign workers. They do not have to prove they tried to hire a French / EU citizen first.

If you complete a master's degree or higher, you can apply for naturalization after only 2 years of presence in France. However, since you must also show financial stability, you must first switch to another status (like salarié, profession libérale, or entrepreneur (commerçant, artisan, industriel)) to apply, and earn a regular income.

You cannot apply for naturalization while on a student visa, as students are not considered to meet the criteria of financial stability and integration without full time employment and salary. If you apply while on a student visa, even if you've been in France for 5+ years, your application will likely be adjourned for 2 years.

Family Members

An accompanying spouse or family members can get long-stay visitors visas and are subject to "regroupement familial" procedures.

Pros & Cons

Pros:
- You are allowed to work part time, up to 964h per visa year, on a student visa.
- Easily renewed as long as you are following a coherent plan of study.
- Financial resource burden is lower, and can be guaranteed by a family member.

Cons:
- You must prove you can support yourself financially with €615 per month of cash resources (preferably more), or have a notarized financial guarantee from a family member.
- If you want to work, you must work as a SALARIED employee (CDD or CDI) of a French company, and you cannot be self-employed. You cannot work remotely for a company abroad, you cannot work for clients on the moon, regardless of where the bank account and the clients are.
- Must switch visa types to get a path to residency or naturalization.

Documents to Provide for Campus France / Etudes en France application:
- ✓ Motivation statement of around 150 words
- ✓ Letter of acceptance from French university. Alternatively, some French university programs allow you to submit your application for admission and receive acceptances directly in your Campus France account.
- ✓ Pre-enrollment certificate from school and receipt for any tuition deposit paid.
- ✓ Résumé and cover letter explaining your academic path
- ✓ Transcripts and diplomas, officially translated into French
- ✓ Language test results from an official exam like the TCF, DELF, or DALF (TCF-DAP for students applying to L1, the first year of an undergraduate program.)
- ✓ Receipt for payment to Campus France/Études en France

Documents to Provide for Visa Application

- ✓ Complete the Campus France process prior to making the visa appointment and receive the Campus France attestation.
- ✓ Convocation for a visa appointment at consulate or VFS/TLS center
- ✓ Valid passport issued less than 10 years ago containing at least 2 blank pages
- ✓ A cover letter explaining the purpose of your move
- ✓ Long-stay visa application, completed through France Visas
- ✓ Proof of financial resources of €615 minimum per month (around €8.000 cash) plus tuition or notarized financial guarantee. Note that because of fluctuating exchange rates, we encourage students to show 3 months of bank statements with at least €650 per month in cash resources at the interbank exchange rate on the date of the application's submission.
- ✓ Letter of acceptance from school
- ✓ Pre-enrollment certificate from school
- ✓ Résumé and cover letter explaining your academic path
- ✓ Transcripts and diplomas, officially translated into French
- ✓ Receipt for payment to Campus France / Études en France
- ✓ Place to stay for first 90 days, unless you have more than the minimum amount of financial resources

Documents to Provide for Renewal

Note: The renewal process for student visas can now be completed entirely online.

You can create an online account and upload documents to renew your student visa here and select "Je renouvelle un titre de séjour." You will complete an online form and upload the following documents:

- ✓ Attestation of OFII validation, and titre de séjour
- ✓ Set of ANTS electronic signature passport photos (ePhoto), usually from a Photomaton machine
- ✓ Proof of residence less than 3 months old (justificatif de domicile)
- ✓ Proof of health coverage from Ameli
- ✓ Proof of financial resources, including bank statements for French bank account or bank account in your home country, and/or financial guarantee from a family member accompanied by your French bank statements
- ✓ Work contract and payslips for any jobs you've done
- ✓ Proof of enrollment, attendance, and grades from all classes taken the previous year, proving you enrolled, attended classes, and passed.
- ✓ Pre-enrollment certificate from school for the upcoming year, or proof of acceptance and enrollment
- ✓ Summary of all classes and academic studies undertaken in France since your arrival, and any diplomas or degrees earned in France

2.2-2 Internship Visa

Students who are currently enrolled in accredited university programs outside of France can apply for an internship visa to do an internship in France for a minimum of 3 and maximum of 6 months per year. You can apply for this visa by providing proof of your current enrollment in an academic program and can work full time at 35 hours per week in the internship, validated through a convention de stage.

Students must be enrolled in a program of study and have a convention de stage signed by the company and their home university, regardless of whether the university is in France. A professor from your home university should also sign the convention de stage and will be responsible for monitoring the internship and helping the student integrate it into her studies. The professor typically also provides assistance, feedback, and a grade on the rapport de stage, or internship report, to be completed after the internship ends. Your home university will set the requirements for completing the internship and signing off on it, and those modalities will be included in the convention de stage for it to be approved.

French law requires interns to be paid the 2024 intern minimum wage of roughly €4,35 per hour, starting with the 309th hour of work, which is after 2 months of full-time work. Internships of less than 2 months do not have to be paid. The "gratification de stage" or internship minimum wage, represents 15% of the social security ceiling, which is reevaluated on January 1 each year. Expect internship wages to rise with inflation on January 1, 2025.

An intern can get a visa for internships lasting 3-6 months, by submitting your passport and the signed convention de stage to DREETS for approval 2-3 months before the internship start date at this website: https://administration-etrangers-en-france.interieur.gouv.fr/immiprousager/#/information

You should expect approval of your convention de stage through

DREETS to take several weeks and prepare accordingly.

Note that in order to be validated and approved by DREETS, your convention de stage has to include certain information and respect all French laws regarding internships. If you are currently enrolled in a foreign university rather than a French university, you may ask the host company to draft the convention de stage, or find a model online, to ensure it includes all necessary details before having it signed by your home university.

Receiving Approval for the Convention de Stage:
At least 2-3 months before the internship's start date, submit a copy of your passport and the convention de stage through the DREETS portal. Once you receive approval from DREETS, you can apply for your visa.

Visa Summary
On the France-Visas website, you select this visa by indicating Plans —> Study and Main Purpose of Stay —> Student Internship. The Long-Stay Internship visa is a VLS-TS which is validated online through OFII upon arrival and does not require any appointments after validation. It does not require a Contrat d'Intégration Républicaine (see section 4.2) and can provide a path to naturalization if you switch to a student visa to pursue studies, followed by switching to a work status.

For an internship of more than 3 months you will be issued a Visa Long Séjour Stagiaire visa (VLS-TS) which is validated online through OFII. Please note that if your internship is under 3 months, you must apply for a Visa Court Séjour and the procedure will be different.

Who is it for?
Anyone who is not already on a student visa in France, who would like to complete an internship in France. Note that if you already have a student visa for France, you do not have to change your status to be able to do an internship, and you do not have to hold an "internship" visa. You can do your internship with your existing student visa.

VFS/TLS Appointment Fee: Approximately €30

Visa Application Processing Fee: €99
OFII validation fee: €75.

Where to apply: In country of residence, at your local French consulate or VFS/TLS office. If you are one of the countries subject to the Études en France procedure you may request your visa directly online through this procedure.

Length of visa: 3-6 months, as the maximum length of a legal internship in France is 6 months

Renewal: For internships set to last less than 6 months, the visa can be renewed if you submit an avenant to the original convention de stage, up to 6 months total. An internship visa can be renewed to a regular student visa if you enroll in a qualified academic program in France after your internship. Because internships in France are limited to 6 months per host organization and 6 months total per academic year, it is not possible to renew the visa solely to extend or take on another internship. It is also not possible to be hired into a full time position and switch your status to a salaried work visa type following an internship visa.

Health Insurance

Your employer will register you for French social security and pay social security contributions on your behalf, even if you have not previously been registered for French healthcare.

Income & Savings Requirement

The financial requirement for obtaining the internship visa is lower than for other types of visas and is the same as for the student visa. It requires a minimum of €615 per month for the length of your stay to qualify.

If your internship is paid, the amount of internship gratification (it's not called salary) can count towards your financial support in your visa application.

Work

Hours worked for an internship related to your studies are not subject to prior work authorization and can exceed the 964h/year.

Students cannot be self-employed, work remotely as employees *or* contractors, or practice any type of regulated profession for which they do not have the necessary *French* qualifications. This includes students who would work for foreign companies and deposit the funds in a bank account outside of France. Any foreign degrees or qualifications should be converted and validated through ENIC-NARIC and the appropriate professional organization before they can be used in France.

Taxation

If you are employed, you are working in France, and you should therefore declare your worldwide earnings and pay French taxes from your date of arrival in France. You will contribute to French healthcare and retirement funds through social charges on your salary, and you should file a French tax declaration to reflect your worldwide earnings and to tax amounts earned in France.

Internship gratification ("gratification de stage," which is not the same as salary, and comes from an internship approved through a university and officialized through a convention de stage) is tax exempt up to French minimum wage, or SMIC, which is set at €21.204 per year in 2024 (Article 81bis du Code Général des Impôts, 2014). Only the amount in excess of this ceiling needs to be reported; if a student intern earned €21.000 in a year from his internship, she would only need to report €492 in taxable income in France. There is no age limit for the tax exemption of this amount.

For US citizens, all income from all sources must be declared on a US tax return, including tax-exempt internship gratification and salary.

Maintaining and Renewing Your Visa

Internships in France, and therefore internship visas, are for a maximum of 6 months. However, you can extend your visa if you are enrolled in studies in France and want to apply for a regular student visa upon completing your internship.

Establishing Residency

You can't establish residency on a student or internship visa. You can switch to a student visa and then to another status. Alternatively, if you get hired by the company and you meet the professional qualifications and work contract requirements necessary, you can switch to a work visa type after the end of your internship. This is subject to meeting the requirements for sponsorship or for a passeport talent category.

Family Members

No family members can accompany the internship visa holder.

Pros & Cons

Pros:

- You can get a student visa to do an internship in France even if you are not enrolled in a French university (you must be enrolled in university somewhere in the world)
- Easily renewed as long as you are following a coherent plan of study. Can be switched to a regular student visa if you opt to stay in France after.
- Financial resource burden is lower, and can be guaranteed by a family member.

Cons:

- You must prove you can support yourself financially with €615 per month of cash resources, or have a notarized financial guarantee for this amount from a family member.
- Internships can only be done for up to 6 months per academic year
- Must switch visa types to get a path to residency or naturalization.

Documents to Provide for DREETS application:

- ✓ Your Passport and personal information
- ✓ Convention de stage signed by you, your university, and your future internship employer

Documents to Provide for Visa Application

- ✓ Convocation for a visa appointment at consulate or VFS/TLS center
- ✓ Valid passport issued less than 10 years ago containing at least 2 blank pages
- ✓ A cover letter explaining the purpose of your move
- ✓ Long-stay visa application, completed through France Visas
- ✓ Proof of financial resources of €615 minimum per month (around €3.690 cash for a 6 month internship) or notarized financial guarantee. Note that because of fluctuating exchange rates, we encourage students to show 3 months of bank statements with at least €615 per month in cash resources at the interbank exchange rate on the date of the application's submission.
- ✓ Letter of enrollment in your university
- ✓ Convention de stage approved by DREETS
- ✓ Résumé and cover letter explaining your academic path
- ✓ Transcripts and diplomas, officially translated into French
- ✓ Place to stay for first 90 days, unless you have more than the minimum amount of financial resources
- ✓ Proof of catastrophic health and repatriation insurance for the duration of the stage

Conditions for Renewal

If you would like to renew your visa beyond six months, you will only be able to do so by switching to a student visa and enrolling in an appropriate course of study. In this case, the renewal process can now be completed entirely online.

You can create an online account and upload documents to renew your visa here and select "Je renouvelle un titre de séjour." You will complete an online form and upload the following documents: https://administration-etrangers-en-france.interieur.gouv.fr/particuliers/#/

Note that you cannot switch to a work visa status directly from an internship visa.

2.2-3 Recherche d'Emploi / Création d'Entreprise Visa

Students who earn degrees from accredited academic programs after completing at least 2 years of study (Master's or Licence professionnel) in France are eligible for the status of "Recherche d'emploi / Création d'Entreprise," (Job Seeker/New Business Creator) formerly the status called "autorisation provisoire de séjour."

The RECE is technically a work visa status that allows qualified graduates who have earned degrees in France extra time to look for a job or start a business in their field so they may remain in France on a work contract. It is intended to help students who came to France to establish themselves and earn the ability to live in France indefinitely. Researchers (previously on a passeport talent chercheur visa) who have completed their research may also apply for this visa.

Recherche d'emploi status grants you the rights of your student visa for an additional year after the end of your degree program, including the right to work up to 964h per year, without requiring you to be enrolled in studies. You can use this time to look for full-time employment or to develop a business project.

When you find a job, you must meet all requirements in the job posting, and the company must be willing to pay the associated tax for hiring foreigners. They do not have to prove they tried to hire someone who already has work papers if you are on recherche d'emploi, but they do have to request work authorization on your behalf and demonstrate your qualifications for the job.

If you decide to register as autoentrepreneur or set up a company, it must be in your field of study or research. You can begin the AE or company registration process at any time during your RECE year, before pursuing your change of status.

In order to secure Recherche d'emploi status after completing your studies, you must have/have had a student visa/carte de séjour. You must also ensure you are/were in an accredited program that meets the préfecture's criteria. Any public French university will meet those criteria; if you are enrolling in a private school, you should check with that school's work placement office or the department where you will be applying, or inquire with the school's alumni in Facebook groups to verify that you will be able to receive this status upon completing your degree. Degree types that are eligible are specialized master's programs, licence professionnel (but not other types of license degrees), or "Master of Science" degrees, often used by the Grandes Ecoles but not by public universities. Graduates with any other degree at the master's level are also eligible. As previously mentioned, researchers who have completed their research may also apply for this visa as long as they have met the necessary criteria.

To apply for "Recherche d'Emploi" directly after your degree program without leaving France, you must apply before your current student visa expires. Most préfectures have simplified the application process to prevent people from being sent home. You should make sure to check your department's renewal procedures WELL in advance of your student visa's expiration date so you get an appointment in time and don't miss the deadline.

If you do choose to go home after you complete your degree, or if you miss the deadline, you still have up to 4 years to apply for RECE status after the date on your degree. However, if you do choose to go home and then return to France, you will lose your continuity and your years spent as a student will no longer count towards time spent in France for naturalization or residency purposes.

Visa Summary

If you are applying for a Recherche d'emploi / Création d'Entreprise visa, you will be doing so from your home country. On the France-Visas website, you select this visa by indicating Plans —> Business and Main Purpose of Stay —> Job Search Business Creation. The Long-Stay RECE visa is a VLS-TS which is validated online through OFII upon arrival and does not require any appointments after validation. It does not require a Contrat d'Intégration Républicaine (see section 4.2) and can provide a path to naturalization after you switch to another visa status to work or start a business.

Who is it for?

Anyone, of any age, who has completed 2 years of study in France and earned a master's degree, and who plans to remain in France to find a job.

Anyone, of any age, who has completed a graduate-level degree within the past 4 years in an accredited French university and who would like to spend a year in France looking for full-time employment or starting a business.

Anyone who had a passport talent chercheur visa and has completed their research and who would like to remain in France and look for a job or start a business in their field.

VFS/TLS Appointment Fee: Approximately €30
Visa Application Processing Fee: €99
Carte de séjour fee: €75 (€225 if you had a Passeport Talent-Chercheur visa)

Where to apply: You can switch to this visa status from a long-stay student visa while remaining in France. The procedure is done online through the préfecture. Alternatively, if you have returned to your home country after completing your degree, you can apply for a "Recherche d'emploi" visa in the 4 years following the end of your degree program at your local consulate or through VFS/TLS.

Length of visa: 12 months

Renewal: None. You must switch to a work visa with one of the following types: travailleur temporaire, salarié, Passeport Talent salarié or carte bleue européenne, profession libérale, entrepreneur (commerçant, artisan, industriel), profession artistique, or Passeport Talent entrepreneur. You could also switch directly to vie privée et familial. If you are not able to switch your visa type through qualifying for another visa within 12 months, you must leave France and return on a new visa; you will not be able to revert to student status.

Work

With the new "recherche d'emploi" status, you can continue to work within the limits of the student visa (964h/year in a CDD or CDI for a French company).

Once you are hired for your professional position, your status means that the company hiring you does NOT have to prove they tried to hire a person who already has French or EU work papers. You have what is called a "situation de l'emploi non opposable," meaning that DREETS cannot veto your work contract unless there is dire unemployment in your field. (If you do not apply for "Recherche d'emploi" first before switching to salarié, the company will have to go through the normal "salarié" hiring process with DREETS.)

You must find a full-time job for which you meet all of the posted job requirements, earning at least 1.5 x SMIC. Once you have been hired, you can switch your visa status to Salarié (or Travailleur Temporaire if the contract is for less than 12 months). Your new employer will have to pay a tax to DGFiP to get your change of status approved.

In order to switch to another salaried work status, you should check the requirements for that carte de séjour type and verify minimum income requirements.

Taxation

Because you are working in France, you should declare your worldwide earnings and pay French taxes from your date of arrival in France. You will contribute to French healthcare and retirement funds through social charges on your salary.

Maintaining and Renewing Your Visa

You cannot renew the "Recherche d'emploi" visa as it approaches its expiration date. Your only option is to switch to a work visa status before it expires. If you fail to do so, you will have to return to your home country.

Establishing Residency

Time spent on your student and RECE statuses counts towards

establishing residency in France, so if you have made it to this visa type, you are well on your way to becoming a French resident. You will have to switch your visa status to a permanent work status, which you will have to maintain for at least a year. Upon renewing your new work status (salarié, profession libérale, etc...) you should be eligible for a multi-year card. At the renewal of your multi-year carte de séjour, if you have not already been naturalized, you can request a 10-year resident card.

If you opt to go back to your home country and then reapply for Recherche d'Emploi within 4 years, your new visa will reset the clock on establishing residency, and your new "arrival date" in France will be the date you return with your Recherche d'Emploi visa.

Applying for Naturalization in 2 Years

Theoretically, completing 2 years of study in France and earning a master's degree or higher reduces the time you must spend in France continuously to qualify for naturalization to 2 years. This means that upon completing your 2-year degree, you are technically eligible to apply for naturalization "by decree" almost immediately. Your time spent on your Recherche d'emploi status will also count towards the 2-year minimum for being in France before your naturalization application.

However, this eligibility comes with the caveat of proving your financial stability. As we explain in the section on Naturalization, you cannot apply directly from this status; instead, you must first switch your visa type to one that enables you to work and meet the minimum financial requirements for being naturalized. Therefore, if you complete a master's degree and would like to become a French citizen as quickly as possible, you should opt to find a CDI in your field and begin the naturalization process as soon as your période d'essai (trial period, usually 3 months) has ended.

Family Members

An accompanying spouse or family members can get long-stay visitors visas and are subject to "regroupement familial" procedures.

Pros & Cons

Pros:

- You are allowed to work while you continue searching for full-time employment in your field.
- You can apply for RECE directly after the end of your student visa, or within 4 years of receiving your degree from France or your home country.
- You maintain your rights without having to be enrolled in a program of study.
- When you find a job, your employer does NOT have to prove they tried to hire someone who already had French work papers.
- You can easily switch to any work status, salaried or self-employed.

Cons:

- You must prove you can support yourself financially with €615 per month of cash resources, or have a notarized financial guarantee from a family member.
- If you do not apply for Recherche d'emploi before your student visa expires, you may have to return to your home country to apply for a new visa with the same name.
- You MUST switch your visa to a work visa type before it expires, or you will have to leave France.
- If you do not find a job or switch your status, you will have to leave France and start over.

Documents to Provide for Application at a Préfecture in France

You will have to submit your application to the préfecture at least 2 months before your student visa's expiration date. This procedure is sometimes done online and sometimes done through an appointment, depending on the préfecture.

- ✓ Personal information completed on the site or CERFA information form completed at the préfecture
- ✓ EPhoto for online submissions or set of photos for appointment submissions

- ✓ Proof of income or financial resources of €615 per month in a French bank account (around €7.380 cash annually) or notarized financial guarantee and proof of regular transfers of at least €615 per month to your French account
- ✓ Visa/Carte de séjour (still valid if you are still in France)
- ✓ Proof of residence (justificatif de domicile)
- ✓ Transcripts & proof of attendance from all courses taken during your time in France
- ✓ Certificate or attestation of completion from your school with the date you'll receive your transcript and diploma
- ✓ Diploma, if you have already received it
- ✓ Transcripts and diplomas from undergraduate / other studies undertaken before arriving in France
- ✓ Birth certificate with certified translation
- ✓ Proof of health coverage from Ameli (if you're changing status in France)
- ✓ If you intend to set up a business, you need to provide a business plan and evidence of your qualifications and the project's financial viability. You can set up your microentreprise before changing your status to "profession libérale" and begin invoicing clients so you have proof of income and invoices prior to the switch.
- ✓ Signed *Engagement à respecter les valeurs de la République*

Documents to Provide for RECE Visa Application within 4 Years

If you have returned to your home country after your studies, you can apply for a RECE within 4 years of completing your eligible program.

- ✓ France Visa application with photos and visa appointment confirmation
- ✓ Proof of income or financial resources of €615 per month (around €7.380 cash annually) or notarized financial guarantee
- ✓ Proof of housing upon return (reservation or justificatif d'hébergement)
- ✓ Copy of your previous visa/carte de séjour with the mention "student" or "student exchange program" which you held during your stay in France, or other proof you had this titre.

- ✓ Transcripts & proof of attendance from all courses taken during your time in France
- ✓ Certificate or attestation of completion from your school with your transcript and diploma
- ✓ Transcripts and diplomas from undergraduate / other studies undertaken before arriving in France
- ✓ 12-month catastrophic health insurance policy
- ✓ If you intend to set up a business, you need to provide a business plan and evidence of your qualifications and the project's financial viability. You can set up your microentreprise before changing your status to "profession libérale" and begin invoicing clients so you have proof of income and invoices prior to the switch.

2.3-4 Au Pair

An au pair visa is a temporary work visa that allows young adults between 18 and 30 years of age to learn French and have cultural exchange by living with and working for a family in France. At least one of the parents in the host family has to have a different nationality than the au pair, and the primary language practiced in the family should be French. The au pair cannot have family ties to the host family. Note that the requirements for the au pair visa have changed as of May 2019, and it is *no longer* considered a type of student visa, but a type of temporary work visa.

The au pair visa enables a young person to live in France for up to 2 years while working up to 25 hours per week doing childcare and light household chores for a host family in exchange for room, board, insurance, transportation, and pocket money (€320 minimum per month). It also allows her to take French classes throughout the academic year. Note that the maximum number of work hours is now 25 per week (down from 35 previously) which allows her time to take French class if s/he chooses to do so. In addition, au pairs must have a minimum of 1 day of rest (NO WORK!) during every 7 day period and the family has to make sure s/he has time to study if s/he has enrolled in French class.

Au pairs do not have to be non-EU citizens on a visa; they can also be EU citizens looking to live and work in another country and learn French. EU citizen au pairs must have contracts that meet the same requirements for an au pair position, or be employed as nannies with standard employment contracts.

The au pair visa is ideal for young people who have a lower level of French and who would like to improve their language skills before enrolling in a university program in France. It can also attract students or young people who don't have savings or a financial guarantor to qualify for the regular student visa. However, au pairs are no longer required to enroll in language classes in order to receive their visas but it is highly encouraged to do so.

Au pairs must pay for their own language classes should they choose to take classes and have a valid work contract, but they do not have to have significant financial resources or even a good working knowledge of French in order to apply, but a minimum of basic French such as having taken some French in school is officially required.

Visa Summary

On the France-Visas website, you select this visa by indicating Plans —> Other and Main Purpose of Stay —> Au Pair. The Long-Stay Au Pair visa is a VLS-TS which is validated online through OFII upon arrival and does not require any appointments after validation. It does not require a Contrat d'Intégration Républicaine (see section 4.2), but can provide a path to naturalization, if you switch to a student visa to pursue studies, followed by switching to a work status.

Who is it for?

Students between 18-30, who want to live in France while eventually taking French language classes and working around 25 hours per week for a French host family that provides room, board, and pocket money.

VFS/TLS Appointment Fee: Approximately €30
Visa Application Processing Fee: €99
OFII fee: €50 for validation
Préfecture: €75 for the card, if applicable

Where to apply: In country of residence, at your local French consulate or VFS/TLS office. You cannot switch to this status from another visa type.

Length of visa: 12 months

Renewal: once, for 1 year allowing for 2 years total. If you have successfully fulfilled your contract as and au pair, you can indeed request a change of status to a student status as long as you request the change between 2 and 4 months prior to the expiration of the au pair visa and you meet all of the requirements for a student visa.

Health Insurance

The host family is required to declare the au pair's work contract to URSSAF within 7 days of the start date and to pay all social charges on income. While you are not responsible for whether or not the family actually does this, it's a good idea to be aware of the requirement and to remind them. Please note, that the contract itself however needs to be completed before the au pair arrives in order to obtain the visa in the first place.

A few years ago, an au pair in the Americans in France Facebook group was hit by a motorcycle about 2 weeks after starting her au pair job, and the host family had to scramble because they had neglected to declare the start of her contract before the accident. This type of omission can cause a huge mess for both you and for your host family if there are accidents or injuries and the coverage was not properly established.

Income & Savings Requirement

Because your room, board, insurance, and pocket money are provided by your host family in exchange for your labor, there is no requirement to have a certain amount of savings to get this visa. However, you may want to have a certain amount saved up to ensure that you can pay for any travel or tourism expenses or find a place to live separately in case things with your host family don't go as planned. You don't want to be stuck in a bad situation with no money to get out.

The au pair contract must meet certain basic requirements, including that room, board, health insurance, and transportation (Pass Navigo in Paris, for example) are provided. Au pairs are paid pocket money, which is typically €80-100 per week in Paris, but can be as low as €320 per month.

Au pairs who wish to take language classes are expected to pay for their own language programs of 10 hours per week. Most private programs have 6 hours per week of class and 4 hours per week of homework and activities. An au pair can expect to pay around €1000 for 3 10-week trimesters of language classes during an academic year.

Work

When you have an au pair / 'stagiaire familial' visa, you are only allowed to work within the confines of your au pair contract and are not allowed to seek other employment. You do not have the legal ability to take on other jobs. This means you cannot work remotely or for companies outside of France to complement your income, as those income sources would be incompatible with your visa status.

The au pair visa is linked to the work contract signed with a host family. Because the host family can require you to work full time (now limited to 25 hours per week) with at least one day off out of 7, you are considered to be employed full-time and not allowed to take on additional employment outside of that contract. There have even been cases of people who have not had their visa renewed, or who have been denied for French nationality, for working too much. Working more than full-time hours is not recommended.

While many au pairs are paid in cash for extra hours of babysitting for the host family or other families, or for tutoring, such an arrangement is technically illegal and not without risk. While your insurance and your host family's insurance would cover any mishaps – injuries or accidents – that happen while you are watching their children, such insurance would *not* cover you if you are watching someone else's children in an undeclared work scenario. Caring for children outside of specific work contracts requires additional training and insurance under laws for French businesses, which you would not have. And both hiring someone without declaring the salary AND receiving income without declaring it and subjecting it to taxation can get you in trouble.

While hopefully nothing bad would ever happen while you were watching children that would trigger a review of your situation and your income, you should be aware of the risks before undertaking any additional paid work. Similarly, when you renew your visa, you will be required to show bank statements to agents at the préfecture, who may be suspicious of significant cash deposits outside of your pocket money. Your bank can also ask questions about regular deposits made to ensure you aren't money laundering or avoiding taxes, and French law typically prohibits payments of more than €1.000 in cash to merchants, all of which makes hiding undeclared income difficult.

If you choose to look for additional employment beyond what your visa allows, you should be aware of its risks and complications.

Leaving Your Host Family

If things with your host family are not going well, you can end your contract by giving the notice required in the work contract. You can also find a new host family to work for without having to leave France. Typically, this notice period for leaving your current host family is 7 days, and it will be indicated in your contract.

Similarly, your host family can terminate your contract if things are not working out, but they cannot kick you out of your accommodation immediately. They must also provide a notice period based on the contract of at least 7 days, and they must pay you through the end of the notice period. If they try to prevent you from accessing your belongings or your accommodation before the end of that period, you can go to the police to file a complaint.

Taxation

The host family is responsible for paying your insurance premiums and for paying all social charges on your pocket money and room and board. The amount you receive in cash should be considered a net amount after taxes.

Although you won't be required to pay taxes on the roughly €320 per month you receive, it is still a good idea to file a French tax declaration once you have been in France for 183 days. Declaring your income, however minuscule, will allow you to get an official "avis de non imposition," or zero tax bill, showing your official declared total income for the tax year and provide documentation that zero taxes are due. If you remain a student after your time as an au pair, this document can be used to request benefits like housing assistance from CAF (Caisse des Allocations Familiales) once you are paying for your own lodging. CAF usually bases its calculations on your income from 2 years prior, so benefits awarded in 2025 will be based on your overall 2023 income. Filing taxes before you need that document can be extremely useful.

If you are a US citizen, you must report your worldwide income on your US tax declaration, including income received as an au pair. This should include any amounts received as benefits in kind, like the value of your housing and transportation pass. To declare this income, you convert the total gross value in Euros to USD using the yearly average exchange rate.

Maintaining & Renewing the Visa

To maintain and renew your visa, you must continue to meet the conditions of an au pair work contract. To renew your au pair visa after the first year, you will have to provide an updated contract for the upcoming year.

You can renew your au pair visa once, to be an au pair for a total of 2 academic years. The au pair visa is formerly a type of student visa, but is now considered a temporary work visa. After the 2 years have expired, you may be able to renew as a regular student visa, which allows you to enroll in a full-time academic program (20 hours per week of language classes or a degree-issuing program) and to work part-time as an employee of a French company. However, it's possible that due to the change of classification, you will be required to return to your home country to seek a new visa and thus restart your time accumulated in France. If you meet all the requirements and request the change of status in advance, normally you should not have to return.

Establishing Residency

While you may become a resident for tax purposes, you will not establish residency or be eligible for naturalization for immigration purposes on an au pair visa. However, if you renew your au pair visa, then switch to another visa status without returning to your home country from France, the years you spend as an au pair can count towards the 5 year requirement for requesting a 10 year card or naturalization. This makes it even more essential to file your French income taxes even if you don't owe money.

You can potentially establish residency in France:
- Au pair → Student → Recherche d'Emploi → Any work or business

visa type
- Au pair → Student → Salarié / Passeport Talent Salarié
- Au pair → Salarié / Passeport Talent Salarié
- Au pair → Profession Libérale / entrepreneur (commerçant, artisan, industriel)

Naturalization

You cannot apply for naturalization while on an au pair visa, as au pairs and students are not considered to meet the criteria of financial stability and integration without full time employment and salary. You will need to switch your status at the end of your au pair contract to develop a path towards naturalization.

Family Members

Holders of au pair visas cannot bring dependant family members.

Pros & Cons
Pros:
- Has a low burden of financial resources since the family is covering most of your living expenses
- Your work for the family is capped at 25 hours per week, and they must ensure you get at least 1 day of rest per 7 day period, and that you can attend language classes if you wish to do so.
- There is no longer a requirement to take language courses, although most au pair language programs are for 10 hours of studies per week, which is typically 6 hours of classes and 4 hours of activities, in 10 week segments, and 3 trimesters. The cost of au pair language classes is lower.

Cons:
- You must pay for your own language courses, which are not covered by the family.
- You must switch to a standard student visa after 2 years if you are able, because the au pair visa will not be extended more than once.
- You can only work for the family hosting you, and are not allowed to take on other jobs, including babysitting.
- Must eventually switch visa types to get a path to residency.

Documents to Provide for Visa Application
- ✓ Passport
- ✓ Convocation for a visa appointment at consulate or VFS/TLS center
- ✓ A cover letter explaining the purpose of your move
- ✓ Long-stay visa application, completed through France Visas
- ✓ Proof of financial resources
- ✓ Au pair contract
- ✓ Show knowledge of French and any related professional qualifications

Documents to Provide for Visa Renewal (1 time only)
- ✓ Convocation for a renewal appointment at the local préfecture
- ✓ Attestation of OFII validation
- ✓ Passport and visa valant titre de séjour
- ✓ Set of ANTS standard passport photos or ePhotos, usually from a Photomaton machine
- ✓ CERFA form provided by the information desk when you arrive at your appointment
- ✓ Proof of residence less than 3 months old (justificatif de domicile)
- ✓ Proof of health coverage
- ✓ Birth certificate with certified translation
- ✓ Proof of financial resources, including bank statements for French bank account
- ✓ Au pair contract

2.3 Temporary Youth Work Programs

Like other countries, France recognizes the importance of allowing young people to develop international work experience and to have easier international mobility while improving their language skills. As a result, there are several programs that allow people, usually young people, to live and work in France for a limited time, with restrictions on the types of work they can do.

Special work and visa programs have been created with the explicit objective of promoting initial work experiences abroad for youth, and involve specific partnerships with various countries that participate in these exchanges. Whether or not you can participate in a specific work experience program will depend on your nationality (whether your home country participates) and if you meet the criteria for acceptance to the visa and work exchange program. In addition to meeting the minimum requirements, there are also quotas established for each country that participates, which are negotiated between France's Ministère de l'Intérieur and your home country's Department of State or Interior Ministry.

In this section, we will cover the programs that have been specially created to allow young people to live and work in France temporarily, almost always for less than one year. Note that for the most part, it is difficult to stay in France after one of these programs ends, and it is difficult or impossible to switch your visa status to something else. You will have to return home at the end of these programs.

Note that Work Holiday and the Franco-American Chamber of Commerce program are essentially the same visa type, but the latter is specifically for Americans, and the former is for citizens of countries participating in the Work Holiday program. Conversely, TAPIF and Lecteur d'Anglais are specific programs for hiring young foreigners to teach in France, but are not visa types unto themselves. However, the visa specifications for those two programs are discussed.

2.3-1 Working Holiday / Young Traveller* "Vacances Travail / Jeune Travailleur" Visa

Please note that this visa type is not available to American citizens; please refer to the Franco-American Chamber of Commerce program in the next section. We are therefore using the spelling of "Traveller" appropriate for Australian and Canadian applicants.

The Working Holiday / Young Traveller visa is a work exchange program for young people who would like to travel in France and discover French culture while having the ability to supplement their financial resources on-site. Nationals from 16 countries participate in the exchange, and the visa is relatively simple to get. It is a 12-month work visa that allows the bearer to work in a CDD or CDI contract, and some applicants (depending on nationality) can extend the initial visa for 6 additional months.

Young applicants with minimal financial resources can go to France without previously finding employment, and live and work in France for the duration of their visa, before returning to their home countries. There is no requirement to have a job prior to departure, to earn a certain minimum salary, or to work full-time or have a specific type of work contract. Any type of salaried work is authorized, although non-salaried work (freelancing and remote working) is disallowed.

This visa type is ideal for those who would like to spend a short time working in France, but it is discouraged for anyone who may want the ability to stay in France in the long-term.

Visa Summary

On the France-Visas website, you select this visa by indicating Plans —> Other and Main Purpose of Stay —> Working Holiday. The Visa Vacances Travail is a VLS-T which is validated online through OFII upon arrival and does not require any other visits or formalities after validation. It is not renewable under any circumstances and does not require a Contrat d'Intégration Républicaine (see section 4.2) and thus does not provide a path to naturalization.

Who is it for?

Individuals 18-30 with nationality from one of 16 countries who would like to discover French culture and who would otherwise need to be sponsored to work for a French company.

Citizens of Argentina (35 years), Australia (35 years), Brazil, Canada (35 years), Chile, Colombia, Ecuador, Hong Kong, Japan, Mexico, New Zealand, Peru, Russia, South Korea, Taiwan, or Uruguay.

VFS/TLS Appointment Fee: Approximately €30
Visa Application Processing Fee: €99

Where to apply: In country of residence, at your local French consulate or VFS/TLS office. You can switch to this status from a student status if you meet the criteria and don't have better more long-term options.

Length of visa: 12 months

Renewal: Some nationalities can extend one time for 6 months. Can NOT be renewed or extended beyond that, and you cannot switch to another status to remain in France.

Path to residency and naturalization: None, because you MUST leave after 12 months max and get a new visa in your home country if you would like to return to France. This resets the clock on your 5 years' continuous stay.

Eligibility

Applicants must be aged 18-30 (35 for Argentina, Australia, Canada) and hold the passport of one of the countries that has signed a bilateral agreement with France. Each individual can only participate once in France.

Applicants cannot bring dependent children and must submit a clean background and medical check in order to be approved.

Americans are eligible for a similar program through the Franco-American Chamber of Commerce, but not for this visa specifically.

There are quotas for visas in each country, with the most being awarded in Canada (7,050 visas per year) and the fewest being awarded in Mexico, Peru, and Uruguay (300 each per year.) There are no quotas for Australia or New Zealand.

Health Insurance

You will be required to get a catastrophic coverage and repatriation plan to qualify for the visa. Once you arrive in France and begin working, you will start the process to get your health insurance set up, but if you are job-hopping and have no steady address, your enrollment in the French healthcare system may not materialize before you leave.

Income & Savings Requirement

Depending on the applicant's nationality, personal financial resources between €2.000-€3.200 are required to purchase a return plane ticket and to pay for initial expenses upon arrival in France. You should check the program details on the website of the French embassy in your home country for details.

There is no particular requirement for the amount of income received from the job as long as you have the resources to support yourself for the duration of your stay.

Work

The Working Holiday visa simply requires around €2.000-€3.200 in personal financial resources, depending on your country of origin. You can apply for jobs in advance or upon arriving in France without going through a lengthy DREETS sponsorship and approval process. Once the visa is approved, you can arrive in France after your visa's start date and begin working at any time.

You can also change jobs at any time during the visa, or work multiple part-time jobs totalling 35 hours per week. For example, if you are a dance teacher, or an English instructor, you may have CDD contracts with limited hours with multiple agencies, as long as you do not exceeding the legal maximum work hours.

You cannot work as a self-employed person, freelancer, or autoentrepreneur, or start a business/company while on the Working Holiday visa. This includes remote work for companies outside of France who are not paying French social taxes on your income.

Taxation

Because you are working in France, you should declare your worldwide earnings and pay French taxes from your date of arrival in France. This means you cannot work remotely or for companies outside of France to complement your income, as those income sources would be incompatible with your visa status.

Maintaining and Renewing Your Visa

Certain nationalities can extend the visa for up to 6 months, but in most cases, the visa is for 12 months and non-renewable. Check your country's agreement with France to see if you'll be able to extend your visa or not.

You cannot change your visa status during the Working Holiday visa for any reason. You will be required to go back to your home country to apply for a new visa type if you want to remain in France.

Establishing Residency

Because you cannot renew or extend your visa, and must return to your home country at the end of your work holiday authorization, the time spent on this visa does not count towards establishing residency for the 10-year card or naturalization.

Family Members

Working holiday visa applicants are not able to bring dependent family members with them.

Pros & Cons
Pros:
- Your potential employer does NOT have to prove they tried to

hire a person with French work papers or pay the tax for employing foreign workers to DGFiP.
- It's an easy way to get a visa to find an initial work experience in your field or to live and work in France
- You can apply for this visa without already having a job lined up, and you do not need your contract to be approved by DREETS before getting your visa. This makes it easy for employers to hire you as you can be in France and readily available.
- Low burden of financial resources, since you can earn a salary upon arrival.
- No particular educational requirement
- Your carte de séjour is NOT linked to your employment, so if you leave your job voluntarily or get fired for just cause, you can find another job within that 12-month period.

Cons:
- You can ONLY do salaried work, and you are not allowed to freelance, be self-employed, or work remotely.
- Companies don't necessarily know about it, so if you are applying for positions before arrival you will need to inform them of the possibility and guide them through the administrative procedures.
- You CANNOT, under any circumstances, renew or extend your visa, or switch to another status. You MUST go back to your home country when your visa expires. Certain countries allow for a 6 month extension if you still have sufficient financial resources, but that depends on the country's agreement with France.
-

Documents to Provide for Application

The supporting documents required for your application, as well as the minimum bank balance you are required to show, may vary based on your country of origin and its agreement with France.

- ✓ Valid passport issued less than 10 years ago with at least 2 blank visa pages
- ✓ Convocation for a visa appointment at consulate or VFS/TLS center

- ✓ A cover letter explaining the purpose of your trip
- ✓ Long-stay visa application, completed through France Visas
- ✓ Proof of financial resources and bank account (amount to show varies depending on country of origin)
- ✓ Résumé and cover letter explaining your experience and qualifications
- ✓ Transcripts and diplomas for any degrees you may have
- ✓ Place to stay for first few weeks upon arrival
- ✓ Proof of 12 months of catastrophic health and repatriation insurance
- ✓ Confirmed return booking or commitment to leave France at the end of your stay
- ✓ Medical certificate stating that the visa applicant's health permits him or her to exercise a professional activity (depending on country of origin)
- ✓ Background check with proof of clean criminal record (depending on country of origin)

2.3-2 Franco-American Chamber of Commerce Temporary Work Visa

The Franco-American Chamber of Commerce sponsors young professional Americans for a 12-month entry-level work experience in France. The program is similar to the Working Holiday program (for 16 other nationalities) in that it provides a limited work visa and eases the requirements for a company to "sponsor" or hire an American worker.

Unlike the Working Holiday (vacances-travail) program, which does not require the applicant to have a job in advance, participants in the FACC program must find a job and get a work contract approved by DREETS prior to applying for their visa. The DREETS approval process can take up to 8 weeks, making this a lengthier visa application process than some other visa types. The advantage for the company is that the FACC takes care of sponsoring the visa and paying a lower OFII tax for the applicant's work visa, so the company does not have to prove they tried to hire an EU person or pay an extravagant tax to OFII.

Visa Summary

On the France-Visas website, you select this visa by indicating Plans —> Business and Main Purpose of Stay —> Recruitment or Posting Workers. The Visa Jeune Professionnel is a VLS-T which is validated online through OFII upon arrival and does not require any other visits or formalities after validation. It is not renewable under any circumstances and does not require a Contrat d'Intégration Républicaine (see section 4.2) and thus does not provide a path to naturalization.

Who is it for?

College students or graduates aged 18-35 with American nationality who would like to get an initial work experience in France and who need to be sponsored by the FACC to work for a French company.

FACC-NY Application fee: $250
    VFS Appointment Fee: Approximately €30
    Visa Application Processing Fee: €99

OFII fee: €200

Employer Tax: €72, paid by the French company

Where to apply: In the US, at a VFS office. You cannot switch to this status from another visa type.

Length of visa: 12 months

Renewal: Can be renewed for 6 months MAXIMUM, after which point you MUST leave France.

Path to residency and naturalization: None, because you MUST leave after 18 months max and get a new visa in your home country if you would like to return to France. This resets the clock on your 5 years' continuous stay.

Eligibility

American citizens are eligible for the FACC "jeune professionnel" visa if they meet the following criteria:

- ✓ Aged 18-35
- ✓ Some college experience or a college degree, or previous professional experience. The education and/or professional experience must relate to the job in France.
- ✓ Accepted for a full-time job (35 hours per week) on a CDD (contrat à durée déterminée) for 3-12 months
- ✓ The salary is at least French minimum wage (SMIC) before taxes, and the salary is similar to what an EU national would earn in the same role.
- ✓ You pay an application fee of $250 to FACC-NY.
- ✓ The company provides the contract and relevant documents, and agrees to pay the €72 tax.

The work contract must be sent to the FACC in New York, and they will obtain approval from DREETS. The process for getting the visa documents can take up to 8 weeks from the time the contract is submitted to DREETS.

Health Insurance

Your visa is tied to a specific job, which you will begin when you arrive in France with your visa. As such, you do not need to have a private health plan as part of your visa application.

Income & Savings Requirement

You will be paid a salary of at least French monthly minimum wage, or SMIC) for the duration of your contract, and as such, you do not have to have any particular amount of savings beyond what you will pay for a return plane ticket. It is helpful, however, to have additional savings to pay for your arrival costs, deposits on an apartment, etc.

Work

Because your FACC sponsorship is tied directly to your job and the contract that has been approved by DREETS, you are tied to your place of employment for the duration of your contract and visa. You cannot change jobs.

You cannot work as a self-employed person, freelancer, or autoentrepreneur, or start a business/company while on the FACC "jeune professionnel" visa. This includes remote work for companies outside of France who are not paying French social taxes on your income.

Taxation

Because you are working in France, you should declare your worldwide earnings and pay French taxes from your date of arrival in France until the date you return to the US. This means you cannot work remotely or for companies outside of France to complement your income, as those income sources would be incompatible with your visa status. You will pay taxes on your French salary to France first during the time you are working in France.

As a US person, you should declare all of your earned income on your US income tax declaration.

Maintaining and Renewing Your Visa

Normally, your initial visa will be issued for 12 months and you can extend the visa for up to 6 months. When your visa expires, you must stop working and return to the US.

You cannot change your visa status during the "jeune professionnel" visa for any reason or to any other visa status. You will be required to go back to the US to apply for a new visa type if you want to return to France.

Establishing Residency

Because you cannot renew or extend your visa and must return to your home country at the end of your work authorization, the time spent on this visa does not count towards establishing residency for the 10-year card or naturalization.

Family Members

You cannot be accompanied by dependent family members on this visa type.

Pros & Cons

Pros:

- Your potential employer does NOT have to prove they tried to hire a person with French work papers or pay a large tax on hiring a foreign worker. They only have to pay a €72 tax for the temporary visa.
- It's an easy way to get a visa to find an initial work experience in your field or to live and work in France.
- Low burden of financial resources, since you will be paid a salary upon arrival.

Cons:

- Companies don't necessarily know about it, so when applying for positions you will need to inform them of the possibility and guide them through the administrative procedures.
- You CANNOT, under any circumstances, renew or extend your visa, or switch to another status, beyond 18 months. You MUST go back to your home country when your visa expires.
- The minimum salary for this visa type is SMIC (minimum wage)
- Takes about 2 months to be processed through DREETS and the FACC.
- Your carte de séjour is linked to your employment, so if you leave your job voluntarily or get fired for just cause, you may lose your right to stay in France.

- Your employer knows those things, and they can take advantage of you.

Timeline for Application

Applying for jobs and getting an approved work contract can take time, so it's never too early to begin researching jobs in your field in France and submitting applications. At least 3 months before you intend to arrive in France, you should submit your work contract to DREETS and the FACC-NY office for approval with all of the documents listed below. Once you have received approval from the FACC-NY, they will inform you that you can make your visa appointment, which can be approximately one month prior to your departure. You should receive your visa within about 1-3 weeks after your VFS appointment.

Applicant Documents to Provide for FACC-NY Application
- ✓ Valid passport and any previous visas for France, along with a copy of the first 6 pages of the passport
- ✓ $250 processing fee paid through the FACC-NY website
- ✓ American Young Professional Request Form
- ✓ OFII Fiche de Candidature application form
- ✓ Passport photos
- ✓ A cover letter in French explaining the purpose of your move, your relevant education or work experience, and your interest in working in France
- ✓ Engagement de retour - promise to return to your home country at the end of your contract
- ✓ CDD work contract for a French company
- ✓ Fiche de poste (job description)
- ✓ Résumé or curriculum vitae in English and French
- ✓ Copy of your most recent degree and transcripts, and documents proving relevant work experience if applicable, with certified French translations

Host Company Documents to Provide for FACC-NY Application
- ✓ 4 original completed CERFA work contracts signed in pen (not scans or copies)
- ✓ Kbis - company's registration with their local Commercial Court

- ✓ Company's document proving social security contributions and tax payments (Bordereau de versement des cotisations et contributions sociales y compris les congés payés)
- ✓ Engagement to pay the €72 tax

One set of scans/copies must be sent to coordinator@faccnyc.org and one set of original documents must be sent by mail to:

FACC-NY American Outbound Program
c/o Massat Consulting Group
33 W 46th Street, Suite 800
New York, NY 10036

Documents to Provide for Visa Application
- ✓ Valid passport
- ✓ Convocation for a visa appointment at consulate or VFS/TLS center
- ✓ A cover letter in English explaining the purpose of your traineeship, discussing why you'd like to participate in the program, your relevant education and/or work experience, and the cultural aspects of wanting to work in France
- ✓ Long-stay visa application, completed through France Visas
- ✓ Proof of financial resources and bank account
- ✓ Work contract approved by DREETS and the FACC
- ✓ Engagement de retour - promise to return to your home country at the end of your contract
- ✓ CDD work contract for a French company
- ✓ Fiche de poste (job description)
- ✓ Résumé or curriculum vitae in English and French
- ✓ Copy of your most recent degree and transcripts, and documents proving relevant work experience if applicable, with certified French translations
- ✓ Place to stay for first few weeks upon arrival
- ✓ Certificate of visa health insurance policy

2.3-3 TAPIF Teaching Assistant Program in France Visa

TAPIF is the Teaching Assistant Program in France. It's a program run by the French Ministry of Education in conjunction with CIEP, The Centre International des Etudes Pédagogiques, and is designed to improve English language instruction in France by bringing hundreds of young native English-speakers to France each year to teach and work as language assistants. In recent years, there have been around 2,000 applicants for 1,100 spots. The program typically puts around 400 people on the waitlist and accepts the majority of them (around 300).

Applications are for TAPIF are typically open from October 15 January 15 each year for a program that runs for 7 months, from October 1 through April 30 of the following academic year. TAPIF Assistants work in elementary, middle, and high schools primaire, college, and lycée, sometimes in tandem with classroom teachers, and other times teaching sections or taking small groups of students. Candidates can select the regions they are most interested in working in, and whether they would prefer to be in a city, town, or a rural area. They can teach in up to 3 schools, for up to 12 hours per week, during the academic year. The weekly schedule is set by the school and with the agreement of the classroom teachers who require the language assistant's assistance, so the true schedule can be for much more than 12 hours per week.

As such, TAPIF assistants are discouraged from pursuing other projects and interests during their teaching time; and expected to focus solely on classroom duties and lesson preparation. Assistants are paid a salary of about €810 net per month and have all school vacations off for their zone, for an average of 2 weeks of vacation every 6-8 weeks.

It is difficult to supplement your income, especially given the visa restrictions.

A few things about the TAPIF program before you apply:
- While assistants can request regions, class levels, and city or rural, placement isn't determined until the summer and can be anywhere in the region or in France. They may not honor your

- request to be in a particular region and you are expected to go where you are placed.
- It is very difficult for the assistantship to lead to other ways to stay in France.
- You typically won't receive your acceptance to the program until April, your school placement until June, and your 'arrêté de nomination' for your visa paperwork until September. This makes it difficult to make other plans, reserve housing, and travel outside of the program.
- Currently, the program is open to Americans under age 35 and places about to 1600 Americans and green card holders. There are similar programs for other languages and other nationalities, although there are far fewer spaces.

The TAPIF visa is a "travailleur temporaire" visa, issued for slightly longer than the 7-month assistantship contract.

Timeline for Application:
Applications for TAPIF are due in mid-January for the academic year beginning in September.

You will typically receive the TAPIF contract, or Arrête de Nomination, during the month of September. It is very rare for schools to finalize the paperwork before the summer holidays, and they send the arrêté de nomination once classes have started again.

Therefore, you should not expect to have your visa appointment before September 10 at the earliest, as it will take time to receive the paperwork.

Make your appointment with your local VFS office for the second half of September, and expect to arrive at the end of September or early October.

Visa Summary
On the France-Visas website, you select this visa by indicating Plans —> Business and Main Purpose of Stay —> Recruitment or Posting Workers. The Visa Travailleur Temporaire is a VLS-TS which is validated

online through OFII upon arrival and requires an OFII medical visit after validation. It is not renewable under any circumstances and does not require a Contrat d'Intégration Républicaine (see section 4.2) and thus does not provide a path to naturalization.

Who is it for?

TAPIF is open to English-speaking US citizens and green card holders up to age 35, who have not participated in the TAPIF program more than three times. There is a similar mobility program for English teachers from other countries, including Canada.

While the application does not specifically state that a college degree is required, you are required to provide university transcripts for any studies as part of the application process, and you need to provide a recommendation and evaluation from a French teacher.

You need to have at least a B1 level of French.

The visa type you will receive is "travailleur temporaire," which is for workers with temporary salaried contracts (CDD) less than 12 months. To be accepted for a second or third consecutive year, you must apply for renewal through France Education International and receive a positive review from your host school. Even if you are accepted to participate in TAPIF for a second or third year, you will have to return to your home country to apply for a new visa with a new arrêté de nomination.

TAPIF application fee: There is a nonrefundable $90 fee to submit an application to TAPIF, which must be paid at the time of submission.
VFS Appointment Fee: Approximately €30
Visa Application Processing Fee: €0
OFII fee: €200
Where to apply: In country of residence, at your local French consulate or VFS office, or at the French préfecture in your region if you are switching from another status.

Length of visa: up to 10 months

Renewal: Cannot be renewed.

Health Insurance

Because you will be provided a salary and health insurance as part of your contract, you will not be expected to provide proof of a certain amount of financial resources or travel insurance, although temporary travel insurance can be a good idea. Once you arrive at your académie and complete your starting paperwork, you will be covered by French sécu and the process for getting your health insurance and carte vitale will begin.

Income & Savings Requirement

In the section that asks how you will support yourself in France, the appropriate answer is *only* your personal financial resources and TAPIF income. Do not make any mention of other sources of income, working other jobs, working remotely, or anything lest you risk your visa being rejected!

Because the TAPIF contract pays a salary (however meager at about €810 per month net – it was €780 per month net in 2007 when Allison was an assistant!), you do not need to have any particular amount of financial resources in order to receive the TAPIF visa. The TAPIF website claims that you can live comfortably in many regions of France, other than major cities, on that amount.

The TAPIF program suggests around $3,000 in personal funds to pay the costs associated with moving and your expenses for your first month or two in France until you begin receiving your income. You will also need to cover your visa application and travel expenses.

Work

The travailleur temporaire visa does NOT allow you to work additional jobs, to babysit, to work remotely, under the table, tutor, work remotely, freelance, or have any type of income or employment outside of the assistant position. While some assistants do find such work and are paid in cash, or have found additional part-time work for agencies, the visa technically does not allow it, and working under the table (*au noir*) is risky.

Taxation

In theory, you will be a French tax resident for the duration of your TAPIF contract, and you should declare your earnings on a French tax declaration.

In practice, the 7-month contract duration means that for one TAPIF contract, you will not be in France for more than 183 days in either calendar year. The amount you earn in each year would be below the threshold for taxation if you have no other income sources. If you don't declare your income on French taxes for one contract, you are unlikely to experience negative consequences.

However, if you do TAPIF for two consecutive years, or have another visa type before or after TAPIF to prolong your stay, or plan on staying in France, it is good practice to file a French tax return beginning with the day you arrive in France, or October 1, the date you start your TAPIF contract.

Maintaining and Renewing Your Visa

The TAPIF (travailleur temporaire) visa is typically issued for a few weeks beyond the end of the TAPIF work contract. The consulates tend to be generous in giving you a bit of time to travel or remain in France once your work contract ends, but this does not mean it can be renewed in France. If you are planning on doing TAPIF for a second year, you must return to your home country to apply for a new visa.

You cannot switch to student, au pair, or visitor status from the assistant visa. (Generally, you cannot switch from a work visa to a non-work visa). If you want one of those visa types, you MUST return home to receive a new visa.

Family Members

You are not able to bring dependent family members with you while you participate in the TAPIF program.

Pros & Cons
Pros:
- No cost to apply for the visa, since you will be an employee of the French government.
- Low burden of required financial resources, since you will be paid a salary upon arrival.
- Gives you a low-risk way to live and work in France, and to discover a new region you may not otherwise explore.

Cons:
- Salary is very low, has only been increased by €30 in 15+ years, and depending on your work hours, you may be making around hourly minimum wage.
- Application fee of $90 to apply for the program.
- The TAPIF program is only 7 months, which means you will have to return to your home country for a new visa if you want to participate for a second year and are accepted.
- Your carte de séjour is linked to your employment, so if you leave your job voluntarily or get fired for just cause, you may lose your right to stay in France.
- Little choice in where you are placed.
- Not typically a path that allows you to renew your visa and stay in France long-term.

Documents to Provide for TAPIF Application

Applications for TAPIF open on October 15 and are due by January 15 of each year for the academic year beginning in September.
- ✓ Motivation statement
- ✓ Attestations of your French language skills
- ✓ Recommendations
- ✓ CV or résumé for your work experience
- ✓ Degrees and diplomas received
- ✓ $90 application fee

Documents to Provide for Visa Application

You should make your visa appointment with VFS around late July for a date in early September.

- ✓ Convocation for a visa appointment at VFS center
- ✓ Valid passport issued less than 10 years ago with at least 2 blank visa pages
- ✓ Long-stay visa application, completed through France Visas
- ✓ Proof of financial resources and bank account (no particular amount required, but it's good to have enough for a plane ticket home.)
- ✓ Arrêté de Nomination provided by Education Nationale specifying the details of your employment
- ✓ Résumé and cover letter explaining your experience and qualifications
- ✓ Place to stay for first few weeks upon arrival
- ✓ Plane ticket & departure date

Applications open on October 15 and are due by January 15 at https://tapif.org/

2.3-4 Lecteur d'Anglais / Maître de Langue Visa

Lecteur d'anglais and maître de langue positions are one-year teaching positions in French universities. Graduate students who have a master's degree or higher can apply to teach at the university level, running discussion sections and sometimes individual classes in the foreign language departments. For the purposes of this book, which is in English, we'll call the position "lecteur d'anglais," but a "lecteur" can practice in any language that is offered at the university level. Therefore, you may also find lecteur positions available if you are a native speaker of Spanish, Italian, German, or another language.

Lecteurs de langue étrangère must have a master's degree or its equivalent, and teach for 300 total hours in the year of "travaux pratiques" which are similar to small discussion groups or language lab classes. Their teaching responsibilities can include up to 100 hours of teaching "travaux dirigés," which are discussion sections following the main lecture. Monthly gross salary for lecteurs de langue in 2024 is €1.486, or €17.836 annually.

Maîtres de langue must have completed at least one year of doctoral studies abroad or one year of higher education in France. Their course load includes 288 hours of a travaux pratiques, 192 hours of travaux dirigés or an equivalent combination of the two. They also participate in giving and grading exams and coursework, which does not reduce their teaching time nor increase their pay. Monthly gross salary for maîtres de langue in 2024 is €1.931, or €23.160 annually.

There is no overarching national program for recruiting lecteurs d'anglais for universities like there is for public schools through TAPIF. Lecteur d'anglais and maître de langue positions are available at the departmental level within French universities, which means that you must apply to each position individually. Some universities will even have multiple positions available through different schools: a business department, a science department, and an English department could each have distinct lecteur d'anglais positions available.

You will have to research each university and position individually and submit an application directly to the departments where you would like to work. This means that you will be able to choose your location much more precisely than with the TAPIF program, and you will very likely be in a major city, as that is where universities are located. You can apply specifically to programs in cities where you would like to live. The SAES, Société des Anglicistes de l'Enseignement Supérieur, lists available lecteur and maître de langue positions on its website, although it is not an exhaustive list:

https://saesfrance.org/carriere/postes-de-maitre-de-langue-et-de-lecteur/

Applications for lecteur d'anglais positions are usually due between February and April for positions beginning in September of the same year. Again, as each university does its own hiring, you will have to begin researching programs starting at the beginning of the year, and keep track of each department's deadline. If you miss the deadline by a few days, you can still apply, as these programs are not as widely known as the TAPIF program (meaning the universities get fewer applicants), and sometimes, the chosen applicant decides not to come to France, leaving an opening.

Contracts for lecteurs and maîtres de langue run from September to August, which means you are paid even during university vacations and the summer months during which you will not be teaching. It also means that your visa will be for one full year, and that you can renew your titre de séjour easily in France if you stay on with your school for a second year.

In addition, most universities have classes that can be taught by "vacataires," or adjunct professors, which are paid on a per-class basis. The fee for a class taught by a vacataire is paid 50% mid-way through the semester, and 50% after the class is complete. Most lecteurs d'anglais can pick up a couple of classes through their university or a partner university and end up with some extra income during the year. However, you should be aware that you cannot be a "vacataire" without another income source, and that it can take several months and significant hounding of the HR person to actually get paid, making it difficult to rely on the vacataire money for budgeting purposes during the academic year.

The disadvantage to the lecteur d'anglais position is that you can only do it for 2 years, and your school must sponsor you each year. This means that you are unlikely to be able to renew your titre de séjour for a third year without finding another job that can also sponsor you. However, there is some ambiguity in the statute that covers the "lecteur d'anglais" and "maître de langue" positions about whether you can do two years *total* in *either* of those types of job (e.g. one year as a lecteur d'anglais and one year as a maître de langue) OR if you can do two years of *each* position for a total of 4 years. A friend of Allison's who was well-liked at the university where she taught was able to make the case for them to hire her for two years at each job, and could renew her visa as such. Others at different universities have not been so lucky. It is up to you to make the case if you would like to stay, and of course, the longer you stay in France, the easier it becomes to renew your visa and to be able to stay permanently.

If you are not able to stay longer than 2 years in your university, you may be able to switch your status to "profession libérale" at the end of your contract in order to continue teaching and tutoring independently. While you would have to rely primarily on your independent teaching income to renew your visa and to prove you have a minimal amount of income, you may then be able to take on additional contracts as a vacataire in your university and others to complement your individual teaching and tutoring activity. Unfortunately, you cannot be a vacataire unless you also have additional income sources.

Visa Summary

On the France-Visas website, you select this visa by indicating Plans —> Business and Main Purpose of Stay —> Recruitment or Posting Workers. The Visa Travailleur Temporaire is a VLS-TS which is validated online through OFII upon arrival and requires a medical visit, and thus provides a path to naturalization if you are able to switch to another status.

Who is it for?
University graduates, usually with a master's degree or higher, who can teach English at the university level as a "lecteur d'anglais" or a "maître de langue" for one year. Unlike TAPIF, there is no age limit for a maître de langue or a lecteur d'anglais.

The visa type you will receive is "travailleur temporaire," which is for workers with temporary salaried contracts (CDD) less than 12 months.

VFS/TLS Appointment Fee: Approximately €30
Visa Application Processing Fee: €99
OFII fee: €200

Where to apply: In country of residence, at your local French consulate or VFS/TLS office, or at the French préfecture in your region if you are switching from another status.

Length of visa: 12 months

Renewal: Can be renewed once for the same position. There is some debate among préfectures about whether you can do 2 years TOTAL as a lecteur d'anglais OR maître de langue, or whether you can do 2 years of each position. Proceed with caution.

Health Insurance
Because you will be provided a salary and health insurance as part of your contract, you will not be expected to provide proof of a certain amount of financial resources or travel insurance, although temporary travel insurance can be a good idea. Once you arrive at your university and complete your starting paperwork, you will be covered by French sécu and the process for getting your health insurance and carte vitale will begin.

Income & Savings Requirement
In the section that asks how you will support yourself in France, the appropriate answer is *only* your personal financial resources and lecteur d'anglais income. Do not make any mention of other sources of income, working other jobs, working remotely, or anything lest you risk

your visa being rejected!

Because the lecteur d'anglais or maître de langue position pays a salary, you do not need to have any particular amount of financial resources in order to receive this visa.

Work

This salarié visa does NOT allow you to work additional jobs, to babysit, to work remotely, under the table, tutor, work remotely, freelance, or have any type of income or employment outside of the lecteur d'anglais position. However, you can sometimes supplement your income by teaching additional classes at your university as a "vacataire." These positions are paid on a per-class basis, and you receive 50% of the money during the semester and 50% at the end of the semester. Again, note that many universities do not pay their vacataires in a timely fashion, and so you should be cautious when budgeting that income.

Taxation

Because you are working in France, you should declare your worldwide earnings and pay French taxes from your date of arrival in France. This means you cannot work remotely or for companies outside of France to complement your income, as those income sources would be incompatible with your visa status.

Maintaining and Renewing Your Visa

Normally, your initial visa will be issued for 12 months and can be renewed. Because you will be working on consecutive 1-year contracts, you will not be able to renew at the end of the second year unless you have found another job that can and will sponsor you.

You can switch your status to another type of work visa or to take another job that can sponsor you at the end of the first year if you are not renewing your contract, or you can switch statuses after 2 years. You cannot switch from a salarié visa to a student or au pair visa.

Establishing Residency

You can easily renew your contract and therefore your visa for two consecutive years, and you can switch your visa status to another work visa type at the end of your two years as a lecteur d'anglais. If you switch to another salaried position, an employer will have to sponsor you again. You can also continue working as a vacataire and change to the "profession libérale" status so you can continue teaching at the university level.

Of course, the two years you spend teaching and declaring your lecteur d'anglais salary will count towards establishing residency as long as you do not leave France to get a new visa.

Family Members

An accompanying spouse or family members can get long-stay visitors visas and are subject to "regroupement familial" procedures.

Pros & Cons
Pros:
- A one-year contract that pays between €1.486-€1.931 per month, better than TAPIF, and allows you to choose the city and university where you want to work.
- Easily renewable for a second year without leaving France.
- Low burden of financial resources, since you will be paid a salary upon arrival.
- Easy to supplement your income by teaching additional classes as a "vacataire."

Cons:
- Lecteur d'anglais positions are for a maximum of 2 years, after which you will have to find another job that can sponsor you to stay in France and/or switch to another visa status.
- Some positions at certain universities are reserved for participants in specific international exchange programs, and are not open to the public.
- Your carte de séjour is linked to your employment, so if you leave your job voluntarily or get fired for just cause, you may lose your right to stay in France.

Documents to Provide for Job Application

Each university opens applications for lecteur d'anglais / maître de langue positions in late winter or early spring. Check each university's website starting in mid-February for details on how to apply. Hiring decisions are usually made in May or early June.

- ✓ Cover letter in French
- ✓ Résumé or CV in French
- ✓ Possibly, copies of your diplomas and transcripts, in French

Documents to Provide for Visa Application

Most universities will send your contract prior to closing for the summer, around July 14. You can therefore have your visa appointment any time in August and plan to arrive at the beginning of September.

- ✓ Convocation for a visa appointment at consulate or VFS/TLS center
- ✓ Valid passport issued less than 10 years ago with at least 2 blank visa pages
- ✓ A cover letter explaining the purpose of your move
- ✓ Long-stay visa application, completed through France Visas
- ✓ Proof of financial resources and bank account
- ✓ Work contract and authorization
- ✓ Letter of intent to hire
- ✓ Résumé and cover letter explaining your experience and qualifications
- ✓ Transcripts and diplomas
- ✓ Place to stay for first few weeks upon arrival
- ✓ Plane ticket & departure date

Documents to Provide for Renewal

You should make an appointment to renew your visa through your local préfecture's website at 2-4 months before your visa or carte de séjour is due to expire.

- ✓ Convocation for a renewal appointment at the local préfecture
- ✓ Attestation of OFII visit, and visa validation document
- ✓ Set of ANTS standard passport photos, usually from a

Photomaton machine
- ✓ Proof of residence less than 3 months old (justificatif de domicile)
- ✓ Proof of health coverage
- ✓ Birth certificate with certified translation
- ✓ Proof of financial resources, including bank statements for French bank account or bank account in your home country
- ✓ Work contract and payslips for any jobs you've done, including vacataire positions you've taken
- ✓ Work contract and authorization
- ✓ Letter of intent to hire
- ✓ Résumé and cover letter explaining your experience and qualifications
- ✓ Transcripts and diplomas with certified translation

2.4 Long-Term Work Visa Types

The long-term work visas in this section are for those who want to live and work in France long-term, and to establish their professional careers here.

The main differences between the visa types outlined here depend on:
how easy it is for the French company to sponsor you,
your education and experience,
your salary level,
the length of your work contract,
whether you have a path to long-term residence and naturalization.

The more experienced you are and the higher your salary, the easier it is for the company to sponsor you, because the easier it will be for them to prove you have specialized skills that can't be found elsewhere. The less experienced you are and the lower your job title, the more difficult it will be for the hiring company to justify employing you instead of someone who already lives and works in France.

For all of the visa types outlined in this section, your ability to live and work in France will remain tied to your employment for at least the first two years of your employment, even if you're switching from another visa status. Of course, the major downside to this type of setup is that your ability to find new employment or to leave an unhealthy work environment is limited, unless you find another company willing to sponsor you under the same conditions as your first job.

The good news is that French employment contracts are highly protected, and if you have a CDI (contrat à durée indéterminée), it is very difficult for the company to fire you once you have passed your période d'essai. In other words, If you can get through the challenges of being sponsored and of surviving your first few months in the French workplace, you will be able to stay in France and continue to renew your visa easily as long as you remain in the job. In fact, once you have a salaried position, it is wise to stay in the job for as long as possible, at least until you can receive a 10-year resident card and/or apply for naturalization, as having one of those statuses will make any subsequent job search that much easier. Furthermore, if you become pregnant and go on maternity leave or congé parental during your employment, or if you become injured or sick and unable to work, you will receive the same rights and protections as a French worker, and your job and immigration status will be protected during that time. All companies with employees in France are required by law to follow certain employment regulations, including vacation and sick time, parental leave, and dismissal, among other requirements.

If you have a visa or carte de séjour leading to naturalization, and you have been living in France for the requisite amount of time, having a CDI and being outside of the "période d'essai" are also the two main criteria for being considered financially stable and therefore a good candidate for naturalization as a French citizen "by decree." Once you have been in France for long enough, you should definitely apply if you are in a CDI, and remain in that job at least until your application is approved. If you have been employed full-time in France and paid taxes, speak French reasonably well, and are relatively integrated, your application should breeze through. Since the beginning of February 2023, all applications for naturalization by decree are submitted online through the NATALI platform.

While being downsized for economic reasons may protect your ability to remain in France and find a new job at least temporarily, being fired for "faute grave" (serious errors) or quitting your job could jeopardize your ability to stay in France. If you are considering changes in employment, or if the situation in your office becomes untenable, consult with a union representative based on your field's "convention collective" (collective bargaining agreement) and with an employment attorney to see how your rights can be maintained.

Any changes to your employment situation (like sudden job loss, even involuntarily) while you are going through the lengthy naturalization process can derail your application for at least 2 years, but once you have been naturalized, you gain all of the rights a French citizen has for seeking employment, starting a business, and more. If you want to start a business, for example, you may plan to complete the naturalization process before leaving your job to collect unemployment benefits from France Travail while setting up your business activity. Planning ahead for this type of situation will prevent you from having to change your visa status and will enable you to benefit from unemployment and other benefits granted to new business owners without jeopardizing your ability to live and work in France.

French Salary Reality Check
In our consultations and Q&As with people looking to move to France, we regularly speak with people who expect that they will easily be able to earn a salary high enough to receive a Passeport Talent Carte Bleue Européenne through an employer willing to sponsor them, with few issues. Their reasoning is generally that their salary in the US is over $100,000 annually, and therefore, a company will easily pay them at least €60.000 per year in France. Unfortunately, the math doesn't check out. If you are thinking about looking for a job in France and assume this will be your situation, we'd like to provide some perspective on what salaries actually look like in France, and how you can do some research before spending a lot of time on your job search.

It's also important to know that many companies, outside of large international corporations, aren't truly aware of the implications of hiring someone without a work visa, so you should know that many tentative job offers fall through once the company realizes what is required and begins to explore the visa process.

The gap between the highest and lowest salaries is not very wide in France. Salary data in France is collected by INSEE reveals that salaries in France are quite low compared to Anglophone countries, even among employees working for private companies. In 2021, the median net salary (net meaning after social charges but before income taxes) for all salaried employees in private companies in France was €2.012 per month. This corresponds to an after-income-tax monthly income of about €1.900, and a gross annual salary of €30.833. For women, the median net salary is €1.889 per month, which is an annual gross salary of €28.968.

See the 2021 data for salaries by percentile in private companies: https://www.capital.fr/votre-carriere/gagnez-vous-bien-votre-vie-comparez-votre-salaire-avec-celui-des-francais-1336109

A salaried employee earning the minimum salary required to obtain a Carte Bleue Européenne, €53.837 per year in gross salary, would receive a net monthly salary of €3.539, an after-income-tax monthly income of €3.030 per month, and earn more than about 85% of French salaried workers. And if you're a woman, then this salary would put you in the 90th percentile of female salaried employees, as there's approximately a 15% wage gap between male and female earners.

Note that updated data for these figures has not been released, and the salary minimum for the Carte Bleue Européenne has remained unchanged, despite increases in French minimum wage.

Despite the perception of "low" salaries in France, the cost of living in France is also quite low, and basic necessities, including housing, are relatively affordable. Even while earning the median French salary, it's possible to comfortably raise children and take the occasional paid vacation, all while knowing that you're fully covered by French healthcare in case of mishaps. If living and working in France has been your dream, don't allow the seemingly low salary offers to turn you off until you have actually run the numbers.

Understanding French Social Charges
One aspect of sticker shock with French salary amounts can be the difference between "gross" salary, which figures in your work contract, and "net" salary, which is the amount available to you to spend each month. These charges, which amount to approximately 22% for the employee and 23% for the employer, cover all of the important social protections that make France a great place to live: healthcare and sick leave, unemployment protection, retirement contributions, and housing or disability payments to those who qualify.

Paying these social charges provides an important safety net to anyone in the French system, and it's important to understand how vital they are to the culture here. Social charges fund everything from early childcare, to public transport, to back to school payments to families in need to purchase school supplies, and these programs ensure a smaller wealth gap than many other OECD countries. It's true that these charges can seem expensive, especially when you consider that basically half of the cost of employing you goes to the French government. But the employee also benefits from a robust protection system: ample vacation time that employees aren't discouraged from taking, state holidays, protection from unjust dismissal, and severance payments, among other things.

You will want to check out gross and net salary amounts so you fully understand the amounts listed in your contract and the amounts that will be paid out to you if you are a salaried employee in France. Note that theses amounts are estimates for salaried employees on French work contracts, and don't apply to business owners receiving compensation, or to self-employed individuals, all of whom pay different rates. Calculate gross and net salary and after-tax income using URSSAF's Charges Estimator: https://www.urssaf.fr/portail/home/utile-et-pratique/ estimateur-de-cotisations.html

You can also learn about what social charges pay for in France and how your contributions fund those program on the URSSAF website "À quoi servent les cotisations?":
https://www.aquoiserventlescotisations.urssaf.fr/

Work Contract Requirements for Salaried Worker Visas
In some Anglophone countries, especially the US, it is not common or required to have a written work contract, but in France, it is almost unheard of not to have a written contract. The contract covers many important aspects of your job and work conditions, and is an essential part, along with a "convention collective" (or collective bargaining agreement for your industry) of ensuring that your rights as an employee are protected. If someone does not have a written work contract when they begin a position, the law considers that they are employed on an indefinite basis with no trial period. But, for the purposes of a visa application, you will absolutely need a written job description along with a work contract that contains specific information relevant to your employment and the company.

CDD or CDI?
The default work contract in France is a CDI, a "contrat à durée indéterminée," which hires you on to a permanent position. A CDI usually has a trial period of 3 months, which can be renewed at the employer's discretion. During the trial period, it is possible for the employer to decide more easily to let you go, and it is also possible for you to decide the company isn't a good fit and leave the position before the end of the trial period. After the end of the trial period, it becomes much more difficult for the company to fire you, and you have to ensure you give appropriate notice if you'd like to leave. Typical notice periods are 1-3 months, depending on seniority and job level.

Conversely, a CDD is a "contrat à durée déterminée," which means that you have a work contract for a defined length of time. There are a few different kinds of CDDs, which are beyond the scope of this book, but usually, they are for 3-12 months and can be renewed up to 18 months total. In many cases, they are used to temporarily replace an employee on maternity, parental, or sick leave, or to work on a specific project for a short period. The reason for hiring someone on a CDD must be specified on the contract itself. For a CDD, the "trial period" is much shorter, and there are only some very specific instances which would allow you to quit or be fired once that period is over. In some cases, you may not be able to take your vacation time fully while on a CDD, and would have to have it paid out at the end. It's not typically possible to have multiple CDD contracts with the same company consecutively without having a gap between them, but in some cases, a CDD can ultimately lead to a CDI with the same employer.

Your Work Contract & Your Visa
Your work contract must demonstrate that the position meets the minimum requirements for issuing the type of visa that you are applying for, and will be necessary to get work authorization.

Here's what all work contracts must include by law:
- ✓ Contact information and legal details of the company, including the specific location and SIRET of where you will be working.

- ✓ Your name and address.
- ✓ Whether the contract is a CDD or CDI. If it's a CDD, the length of the contract and why the employer is opting for a CDD rather than a CDI.
- ✓ The contract's start date.
- ✓ The job description or "fiche de poste" describing the nature of the work and the qualifications required. Note that for some visa types, you will be required to demonstrate you meet all of the advertised job requirements to receive work authorization.
- ✓ Salary, other remuneration, and how salary is calculated. The method for determining pay, overtime, fixed or variable pay, and commissions, must be included. Note that for visas with a specific minimum salary, the requirement is for the base gross salary to meet or exceed that amount. Variable pay and commissions will not be taken into account for the visa requirements.
- ✓ The number of hours worked weekly. This determines whether the contract is part-time or full-time. For visa requirements, it should be a full-time position with at least 35 hours per week.
- ✓ Vacation days and how they are calculated. Typically, employees accumulate 2,5 vacation days per month, for a total of 5 weeks.
- ✓ Contact details for the company's social security and retirement affiliations.
- ✓ The convention collective: all companies have a collective bargaining agreement that applies to that particular industry, which outlines job hierarchies, minimum pay, vacation time, and things like bereavement leave or receiving additional vacation days for seniority. Your employer should be able to tell you which one applies (and it should be on your payslips when you receive them) and you can find the document online to understand it. If there is a convention collective agreement in place for your job, your minimum salary will be the salary amount specified in this document, rather than SMIC.

If the contract is a CDI, it must also include your qualifications, the job functions you'll fulfill, the trial period (if there is one) and how long it is, and the notice period you'll have to respect if you want to leave the position.

If the contract is a CDD, it will specify the person you're replacing and their qualifications, the minimum duration or length of the contract, the trial period, and the conditions for renewing the CDD.

To successfully receive a visa or carte de séjour, your work contract must contain all of the required elements above, plus meet the industry minimum requirements for the applicable convention collective.

2.4-1 Salarié/Travailleur Temporaire Visa

A salarié visa can be issued for a CDD (Contrat à Durée Déterminée) of more than 12 months, or for a CDI (contrat à durée indéterminée), which is an indefinite work contract, usually with a trial period of 3 months. A travailleur temporaire visa is issued if the work contract provided is a CDD of less than 12 months. The specific visa issued depends on the work contract you provide.

    A salaried worker visa is perhaps one of the most difficult visas to get, because in most fields of employment, the company has to get approval for your specific employment contract from DREETS, and your employment situation is considered "opposable."

    Note that for a small number of very specific types of short-term work contracts less than 90 days, DREETS authorization is not required to obtain the visa.

    If you have a "situation de l'emploi opposable," it means that DREETS can veto your work contract and its resulting visa. The company needs to prove they tried to hire someone who *already* has the right to work in France (vie privée visa, residency card, French/EU citizenship…) before they can hire you and sponsor your visa. This also means that they need to have a specific job description, advertise the job for at least 3 weeks with France Travail, and submit the information for candidates who were NOT retained along with your profile. They will need to make a compelling argument for why they hired you and why you are significantly more qualified than the un-retained candidates. Most companies are not willing and able to do this (even if they initially think they are).

    In contrast, having a "situation de l'emploi non opposable" means that DREETS cannot require the company to try to hire someone with French work papers before they try to hire you. There are a few fields with very high demand where work contracts are "non-opposable," (DREETS publishes a list each year per region), and jobs are also "non-opposable" for anyone on the Recherche d'Emploi status or the Passeport Talent – Salarié or Carte Bleue status, due to the skilled nature of those jobs and high salaries.

In both cases (opposable or non-opposable), the hiring company has to pay a tax to DGFiP. For CDD contracts 3-12 months long, the tax amount will be between €50 and €300, depending on your salary. For CDI contracts or CDD contracts of 12+ months, the tax will be 55% of one month's gross salary, up to a maximum tax amount of €2.427. Since 2024, the tax is paid to the Finances Publiques through an annex on the company's TVA declaration in the month the employee begins working, instead of via an annual declaration to OFII.

If you are applying for a salarié visa after obtaining a RECE status and after completing a degree program in France, your job situation is considered non-opposable if your salary is more than 1.5x SMIC (€31.800 gross per year, or €2.650 gross monthly salary), meaning the company doesn't have to try to hire a French person first. They DO, however, have to pay the tax on hiring foreign workers to DGFiP. To change your status from RECE, you must simply fulfil the requirements of the published job description. If you do not meet the job requirements or don't have the qualifications outlined in the job listing, your employment could be opposed by DREETS.

Visa Summary

On the France-Visas website, you select this visa by indicating Plans —> Business and Main Purpose of Stay —> Recruitment or Posting Workers. The Visa Salarié/Travailleur Temporaire is a VLS-TS which is validated online through OFII upon arrival and requires a medical visit as well as a Contrat d'Intégration Républicaine (see section 4.2) and provides a path to naturalization.

Who is it for?
Anyone inside or outside of France who has obtained work

authorization from DREETS for an employment contract with a company willing and able to sponsor you for a CDD of 3-11 months (Travailleur Temporaire) or a 12 month CDD or a CDI (Salarié).

The Travailleur Temporaire visa can also be requested for posted workers for international companies who have a foreign work contract if they are not eligible for "ICT Salarié Détaché" or "Salarié en Mission" status due to their seniority, the level of their position, or their mission.

VFS/TLS Appointment Fee: Approximately €30
Visa Application Processing Fee: €99
OFII fee: €200

Where to apply: In country of residence, at your local French consulate or VFS/TLS office. You can also switch to this status from another status if you have been in France for more than 1 year and already renewed your visa, or if you have a Recherche d'Emploi visa.

Length of visa: 3-11 months "Travailleur Temporaire" visa for a CDD of the work contract's duration, 12 months "Salarié" visa for a 12-month CDD or a CDI

Renewal: Can be a multi-year CDS (2-3 years) if you are in a CDI

Health Insurance

You will get health insurance through your employment, beginning from the start date of your work contract. You do not need a private health plan or travel coverage in order to get your visa.

Income & Savings Requirement

Because you will be provided with a salary, there is no minimum financial resources requirement for this visa beyond what you need to move yourself and your belongings to France. At this level, it is not reasonable to expect the company to pay moving or relocation expenses.

Work

Because your visa sponsorship is tied directly to your job and subject to work authorization, you are tied this work contract for the duration of your visa or CDS. It is not advisable to change employers within the first two years of being in France, and you would have to stay in the same general job title and same field. If you do change jobs within the first two years, your new employer will be required to seek a new work authorization and to pay the foreign worker tax again on your behalf.

If you are laid off from the company for financial reasons or are the beneficiary of a rupture conventionnelle, you can collect unemployment benefits until your visa expires. Receiving benefits from France Travail will allow you to renew your visa and seek other employment in your field, but you will still be subject to a new work authorization. If your période d'essai (trial period) is not validated, you can also seek new employment, but again, your new employer will have to pay the foreign worker tax for you.

You cannot work as a self-employed person, freelancer, or autoentrepreneur, or start a business/company while on the salarié visa, even if your work contract does not specifically forbid it. This includes prohibiting remote work for companies outside of France who are not paying French social taxes on your income.

Taxation

Because you are working in France, you should declare your worldwide earnings and pay French taxes from your date of arrival in France. You will contribute to French healthcare and retirement funds through social charges on your salary.

Maintaining and Renewing Your Visa

Normally, your initial "Travailleur Temporaire" visa will be issued for the length of your work contract if you have a CDD for 3-11 months, or, you will receive a "Salarié" visa issued for 12 months if you have a 12-month CDD or a CDI. These visa types can be renewed. If you are working for the same employer at the time of your renewal, and on a CDI contract, you can request a 4-year carte de séjour, which will carry you through until your request for a 10-year card and eligibility for naturalization.

You cannot change your visa status before you have renewed your visa at least once. You should not change jobs or employment before you have renewed your salarié visa at least once, as it could jeopardize your immigration status.

Establishing Residency

Assuming you stay with the same employer, you will receive a one-year visa, followed by a 4-year carte de séjour, followed by a 10-year residency card, at which point you will be able to apply for naturalization. If you have already been in France for several years prior to receiving the carte de séjour salarié, such as completing a degree and receiving RECE, you will be eligible to apply for residency and naturalization much sooner. Your years spent on other eligible visa types may count towards the 5-year minimum for residency and naturalization, as long as you do not return to your home country to get a new visa.

Family Members

An accompanying spouse or family members can get long-stay visitors visas and are subject to "regroupement familial" procedures. This is less advantageous than the visa for family members accompanying passeport talent holders.

Pros & Cons
Pros:
- If you are on RECE or have completed 2 years of higher education in a degree program in France, you meet the job requirements, and your salary exceeds 1.5x SMIC, your employer does NOT need to obtain work authorization from DREETS to prove they tried to hire someone who already has

French work papers.
- Once you have validated your "période d'essai" for your CDI, it is REALLY hard to fire you.
- If you are a salaried employee with a CDI when you apply for naturalization as a French citizen (after 5 years of being in France), it is relatively straightforward to get approved.
- Low burden of financial resources, since you will be paid a salary upon arrival.
- If you and your employer mutually agree to end your work contract through a process called a rupture conventionnelle or if you lose your job involuntarily (licenciement), you may be eligible to receive unemployment benefits from France Travail and assistance finding another job in your field. If you are receiving financial benefits or find another job, you can renew your visa or CDS while receiving those benefits.

Cons:
- Salaries are much lower in France than they are in the US and many Anglophone countries.
- If you do NOT have a Recherche d'emploi status or 2 years of higher education in France, your potential employer must prove they tried to hire someone who *already* has French work papers to get work authorization for you. This can be a lengthy and difficult process, which some employers are unwilling or unable to complete.
- Your employer must pay a tax to the DGFiP based on the length of your contract and your salary.
- You must stay in your job for at least 2 years, or your new employer will also have to pay the DGFiP tax again.
- Your carte de séjour is linked to your employment, so if you leave your job voluntarily or get fired for just cause, you may lose your right to stay in France.

Documents to Provide for Application

- ✓ Valid passport issued less than 10 years ago with at least 2 blank visa pages
- ✓ Convocation for a visa appointment at consulate or VFS/TLS center
- ✓ A cover letter explaining the purpose of your move
- ✓ Long-stay visa application, completed through France Visas
- ✓ Work permit and contract approved by DREETS
- ✓ Letter of intent to hire
- ✓ Résumé and cover letter explaining your experience and qualifications
- ✓ Transcripts, diplomas, and proof of qualifications or certificates of employment
- ✓ Place to stay for first few weeks upon arrival

Documents to Provide for Renewal

You should make an appointment to renew your visa through your local préfecture's website at least 3 months before your visa or carte de séjour is due to expire.

- ✓ Convocation for a renewal appointment at the local préfecture
- ✓ Attestation of OFII visit, and titre de séjour
- ✓ Set of ANTS standard passport photos, usually from a Photomaton machine
- ✓ CERFA form provided by the information desk when you arrive at your appointment
- ✓ Proof of residence less than 3 months old (justificatif de domicile)
- ✓ Proof of health coverage
- ✓ Birth certificate with certified translation
- ✓ Proof of financial resources, including bank statements for French bank account or bank account in your home country
- ✓ Work contract and payslips for any jobs you've done
- ✓ Work contract approved by DREETS
- ✓ Valid Recherche d'Emploi for a change of status, if

applicable
- ✓ Transcripts and diplomas with certified translations
- ✓ Signed "Engagement à Respecter les Principes de la République" form

2.4-2 Intra Corporate Transfer (ICT Salarié Détaché) Visa

An ICT visa is a temporary work visa valid for up to 3 years, for companies that want to send an employee with at least 6 months' seniority to France on a mission to hold a senior management position or provide expertise to their company or a company that belongs to the same group of companies in France, while maintaining them on a non-French work contract. It allows international companies (hotel chains, consulting firms, etc.) to move current employees internationally without having to go through the same onerous sponsorship process or provide a French work contract. This visa and carte de séjour type can be known as "intra-corporate" or "ICT Salarié détaché" on different French administration websites.

Typically, employees who are "seconded" to France must be employed by the company group in another country for a minimum period of time (at least 6 months) and then they are sent to the host country. This has interesting tax advantages for the company, because the employee's work contract is maintained outside of France, and French social charges are only paid if there is no "Social Security Totalization Agreement" between the home country and France.

This type of opportunity usually requires having employment in your home country for a company that also exists in France, like a large hotel chain (e.g. Hilton) or an international consulting firm (e.g. PwC). Occasionally, if you apply to companies already established in France, they may be able to arrange hiring you through a different country's office and sending you over after at least 6 months in an upper management or otherwise highly qualified position within the company.

There is a version of this visa that enables highly educated employees who are completing professional development, internships, or training in France with a valid "convention de stage" on an "ICT Stagiaire Détaché" visa for 12 months.

Companies that want to send other (non-senior, non-highly qualified) employees to France for specific missions can request work authorization and a Travailleur Temporaire visa for those workers.

Prior to sending you to France, the company will have to make an online declaration about your mission to SIPSI, the Système d'Informations sur les Prestations de Services Internationales.

Visa Summary
On the France-Visas website, you select this visa by indicating Plans —> Business and Main Purpose of Stay —> ICT Posted Employee & Professional Work Placement. The Visa ICT is a VLS-TS which is validated online through OFII upon arrival and requires a medical visit, and can provide a path to naturalization only if you are able to switch to a local French contract and different salaried visa type at the end of your 3 year mission without leaving France.

Who is it for?
Foreign employees with senior positions and a high level of qualification or education, who have worked for a company for at least 6 months prior to their relocation to France, and who are sent to France for a defined mission of up to 3 years total, with a monthly salary at least equal to what colleagues are earning in the host company in France.

VFS/TLS Appointment Fee: Approximately €30
Visa Application Processing Fee: €99
OFII fee: €200

Where to apply: In country of residence, at your local French consulate or VFS/TLS office. You cannot switch to this status from another visa type.

Length of visa: 1 year

Renewal: Renewable annually twice, but you cannot maintain this status for more than 3 years. At the end of your third year in France, you must either switch to a different salaried visa type on a local French work contract, or return to your home country. If you return to your home country and spend 6 months outside of the EU, you can request a new ICT visa and return to France for an additional 3 years. As long as you take a 6 month break from the EU between each 3-year stint, there is no limit on the number of ICT visas you can have, but you will never accumulate enough time for residency or naturalization without switching to a local contract and different status. A Certificate of Coverage exempting your employer from paying French social charges on your salary can only be valid for up to 5 years maximum.

Health Insurance

When you are on an ICT visa, your work contract remains attached to your home country, and your pay is managed by the company's office in your country, although you will be issued a French pay slip. Depending on what country the company is transferring you from, and if that country has a Social Security Totalization Agreement with France, they may have the option of maintaining your healthcare coverage and paying social charges in your home country instead of in France, which can be less expensive. If the company is not paying into the French healthcare system on your behalf, you will be required to purchase and maintain private health coverage and have a certificate of coverage from your home country's social security administration for the duration of your contract, and be able to show it to the French administration at any time. You will be able to get medical treatment in France, but it will be your private insurance that pays, rather than the French system.

France has signed bilateral Social Security coverage agreements with the following countries: Algeria, Andorra, Argentina, Benin, Bosnia and Herzegovina, Brazil, Cameroon, Canada, Cape Verde, Chile, Congo, French Polynesia, Gabon, Guernsey, India, Israel, Ivory Coast, Japan, Jersey, Korea, Kosovo, Madagascar, Mali,

Mauritania, Monaco, Montenegro, Morocco, Niger, New Caledonia, North Macedonia, Philippines, Quebec, San Marino, St-Pierre-et-Miquelon, Senegal, Serbia, Togo, Tunisia, Turkey, United States, and Uruguay.

If your country has not signed a bilateral social security agreement with France, you will be affiliated to French sécu and pay all obligatory social charges in France. Your company will have to determine whether they can opt out of paying social coverage in your home country, or whether they have to pay social charges on you in both places.

The Centre de Liaisons Européennes et Internationales de Sécurité Sociale has more information:

https://www.cleiss.fr/faq/accords_de_securite_sociale.html

Income & Savings Requirement

ICT jobs are typically very highly-paid and the compensation packages include moving expenses, visa consultation and relocation fees, international tax assistance from a reputable accounting firm, and more. For families, these packages can even include tuition for prestigious international schools.

Because you will be a salaried employee for the company and your salary is set by the contract, there is no particular savings or cash minimum for the visa.

Work

You will be a full-time salaried employee of the company in your home country that sends you to France, and your employment will be restricted to that employer. You cannot switch jobs, seek other employment, or be self-employed or a contractor while on this visa. If you want to change employers or switch to a different visa status, you will have to terminate your work contract and return to your home country to apply for a new visa type.

Note that even though your employment is through your home

country, the company still has to follow all French labor laws regarding your schedule, overtime pay, holidays, and dismissal, so ensure that you consult independently with someone to know your rights.

Taxation

As a French tax resident, you will declare all worldwide earnings in France and pay taxes on your salary (earned income) in France first. However, there are certain tax advantages to being on an ICT visa that can reduce your French tax liability.

If you have not been employed in France before, your sponsoring company can keep you on payroll in your home country for up to 5 years, and pay social charges there instead of in France. This significantly reduces your global cost to your employer and increases your potential salary. A salary of €50.000, for example, would cost your employer around €67.833 and the net amount in your pocket would be around €39.388 after French social taxes – healthcare, maternity care, retirement contributions, etc. – are accounted for. Conversely, if a company keeps you on American payroll, the employer taxes will be Social Security and Medicare, around 13%. The total cost to your employer would be €56.500, while the net amount in your pocket would be around €43.500. In the former case, you would be on French healthcare, receive French benefits like maternity and sick pay, and eventually receive a French pension for however many years you spend working in France. In the latter case, you would continue contributing to US Social Security and accumulating your quarters towards retirement in the US.

Impatriation and Expatriation tax regimes are two tax advantages for your *income* tax (not social charges) that can reduce the amount of your income subject to tax in France if you are seconded, based in France, and work part of the time outside of France. If you travel frequently for your employment, you will want to ask your French tax advisor about claiming tax exemption on the proportion of days spent working outside of France. Depending on the amount of travel you do and the tax regime you choose to apply to your income, you can exempt up to 50% of your income.

Maintaining and Renewing Your Visa

An ICT visa can be issued or renewed for up to 3 years, or the length of the mission. It cannot be renewed beyond 3 years in France, and if you would like to return to your position, you need to leave the EU for 6 months and then apply for a new visa in your home country. There is currently no limit on the number of consecutive 3-year ICT visas you can have as long as you respect the 6 month waiting period between each one, but your "clock" in France restarts each time you obtain a new visa.

Establishing Residency

Because the visa is for a maximum of 3 years and is not renewable, you cannot establish residency in France, or be eligible for naturalization unless your company enables you to switch to a local contract on a different salaried work status at the end of the 3-year mission. Each time you return to your home to get a new visa, your time in France will be reset to zero.

Family Members

The accompanying spouse or other family members can also receive "ICT Salarié Détaché" visas which enable them to work.

Pros & Cons
Pros:
- Your employer does NOT have to prove they tried to hire a person with French work papers nor pay a tax.
- Low burden of financial resources, since you will be paid a salary upon arrival.
- Salaries are usually very high for these types of positions.
- Your employer can potentially keep you on payroll in your home country, which can lower the burden of social taxes you pay and enable your employer to pay you a higher salary.

Cons:
- Only available for large multinational companies with subsidiaries in multiple countries.
- You have to show seniority in the group or company in your home country for a period of time, usually more than 6 months, before you can be eligible for this type of transfer. You cannot get hired to move to France directly.
- Most companies that offer internal transfers abroad have seniority criteria, especially for desirable locations like France.
- Your carte de séjour is linked to your employment, so if you leave your job voluntarily or get fired for just cause, you cannot stay in France.
- You have no path to residency or naturalisation unless your company is willing to switch you to a local contract and request a different CDS type at the end of your 3 year mission.

Documents to Provide for Application
- ✓ Valid passport issued less than 10 years ago with at least 2 blank visa pages
- ✓ Convocation for a visa appointment at consulate or VFS/TLS center
- ✓ A cover letter explaining the purpose of your move
- ✓ Long-stay visa application, completed through France Visas
- ✓ Work contract for country of origin with an addendum about your mission to France and your employer's obligations to abide by French employment law
- ✓ Declaration préalable de détachement to SIPSI
- ✓ CERFA form 15619*01 and required accompanying documents
- ✓ Certificate of coverage and comprehensive healthcare policy OR attestation of intention to register you with French social security (depending on your country of origin)
- ✓ Proof you have worked in the company for at least 6 months, such as payslips & tax documents

- ✓ Proof that your current company and the French company belong to the same group
- ✓ Letter of intent detailing your job functions, your mission in France, the duration of the transfer, the location of the company where you will be working,
- ✓ Proof you will occupy a managerial or expert position and that you will be able to return to a job in a different country at the end of your mission in France
- ✓ Résumé and cover letter explaining your experience and qualifications along with proof of qualifications
- ✓ Transcripts and diplomas of higher education degrees
- ✓ If applicable to your job, proof of ability to practice a regulated profession in France
- ✓ Place to stay for first few weeks upon arrival (your employer may set this up)
- ✓ Proof of financial resources and bank account

2.4-3 Passeport Talent Salarié en Mission Visa

A salarié en mission visa is a salaried work visa valid for one year, or a carte de séjour valid for up to 4 years, for companies that want to send an employee for a specific mission while employed on a local contract in France.

Employees who are sent to France must be employed by the company in another country for a minimum period of time (at least 3 months) and then they are sent to the host country to be employed on a local contract. In contrast with the ICT visa, Salarié en Mission workers are employed and paid by the host company in France, and are affiliated with French social security. There is no option to benefit from the tax advantages of staying on your home country's payroll.

Visa Summary
On the France-Visas website, you select this visa by indicating Plans —> Talent Passport International Talents and Main Purpose of Stay —> Employee on Mission / Talent. The Visa Passeport Talent Salarié en Mission is a 90-day visa which requires requesting a carte de séjour upon arrival through the online ANEF platform. As a Passeport Talent visa and CDS type, it does not require a medical visit or a Contrat d'Intégration Républicaine. The Salarié en Mission status does not lead to a French residency permit or naturalization path after 5 years, but you can switch to another salaried worker carte de séjour if you are eligible, which would put you on a path to residency/naturalization.

Who is it for?
Salarié en Mission is for foreign employees who are being sent to France to work in the same company or same international group of companies, who have worked for that company or group for at least 3 months prior to their relocation to France. They are sent to France for a defined mission with a French work contract paying a gross annual salary of at least €38.165 (2024). If the French contract is a

CDD of less than 12 months, a 12-month visa will be issued that requires validation. If the contract is a 12-month CDD or a CDI, a 90 day visa will be issued that requires requesting a multiyear carte de séjour upon arrival in France.

VFS/TLS Appointment Fee: Approximately €30
   Visa Application Processing Fee: €99
   OFII fee: €200 if you receive a 12 month visa to be validated as a VLS-TS; OR
   Carte de séjour fee: €225 if you receive a 90 day visa with "carte de séjour à solliciter dès l'arrivée" and receive a 4-year carte de séjour

Where to apply: In country of residence, at your local French consulate or VFS/TLS office. You cannot switch to this status from another visa type.

Length of visa: 4 years maximum, based on the duration of the work contract. You can either be issued a visa for 1 year, with a CDS at the end of the first year, or you can be issued a visa for 90 days and be able to request a 4-year CDS upon arrival in France.

Renewal: Can be renewed in France, but cannot be transformed directly into a residence card or lead to naturalization without switching status.

Health Insurance
You will get French health insurance through your employment, beginning from the start date of your work contract. You do not need a private health plan or travel coverage in order to get your visa.

Income & Savings Requirement
"Salarié en mission" jobs are paid at least 1.8x SMIC, which is gross annual compensation of €38.165 in 2024. Compensation packages can sometimes include moving expenses, visa consultation and relocation fees, international tax assistance from a reputable accounting firm, and more. For families, these packages

can even include tuition for prestigious international schools.

Because you will be a salaried employee for the company and your salary is set by the contract, there is no particular savings or cash minimum for the visa.

Work

You will be a full-time salaried employee of the local French company that employs you in France, and your employment will be restricted to that employer. You cannot switch jobs, seek other employment, or be self-employed or a contractor while on this visa. If you want to change employers or switch to a different visa status, you will have to terminate your work contract and return to your home country to apply for a new visa type.

The company has to follow all French labor laws regarding mandatory social charges, your schedule, overtime pay, holidays, and dismissal, so ensure that you consult independently with someone to know your rights.

Taxation

As a French tax resident, you will declare all worldwide earnings in France and pay taxes on your salary (earned income) in France first.

Maintaining and Renewing Your Visa

A salarié en mission visa or carte de séjour can be issued for up to 4 years, or the length of the mission. It may be renewed in France depending on the conditions of your employment.

Establishing Residency

With the salarié en mission status, you cannot establish residency in France, or be eligible for naturalization. You can become eligible if you switch to a different salaried work CDS.

Family Members

Accompanying family members can receive the "accompanying

family member of passeport talent" visa, meaning the accompanying spouse will have the right to work in France.

Pros & Cons
Pros:
- Your potential employer does NOT have to prove they tried to hire a person with French work papers nor pay a foreign employee tax.
- Low burden of financial resources, since you will be paid a salary upon arrival.
- Salaries are usually very high for these types of positions.

Cons:
- Only available for large multinational companies with subsidiaries in multiple countries.
- You have to show at least 3 months seniority in the group or company in your home country before you can be eligible for this type of transfer. You cannot get hired to move to France directly.
- Most companies that offer internal transfers abroad have seniority criteria, especially for desirable locations like France.
- Your carte de séjour is linked to your employment, so if you leave your job voluntarily or get fired for just cause, you cannot stay in France.
- You only have a path to residency or naturalization if you can switch your CDS status at some point.

Documents to Provide for Application
- ✓ Valid passport issued less than 10 years ago with at least 2 blank visa pages
- ✓ Convocation for a visa appointment at consulate or VFS/TLS center
- ✓ A cover letter explaining the purpose of your move

- ✓ Long-stay visa application, completed through France Visas
- ✓ CERFA form 15616*01 stamped by the employer and French work contract showing annual remuneration of at least 1.8 times SMIC.
- ✓ Up to date K-bis (less than 3 months old) for the hosting company or branch where the employee is being sent
- ✓ Certificate of company's up to date payment of social contributions, including paid leave
- ✓ Proof you have worked in the company for at least 3 months via payslips & tax documents
- ✓ If applicable to your job, proof the you are eligible to perform a regulated profession in France
- ✓ Letter of intent to hire detailing your job functions and the purpose of your mission to be carried out in France
- ✓ Résumé and cover letter explaining your experience and qualifications
- ✓ Transcripts and diplomas
- ✓ Place to stay for first few weeks upon arrival your employer may set this up
- ✓ Proof of financial resources and bank account
- ✓ Signed "Engagement à Respecter les Principes de la République" form

2.4-4 Passeport Talent Chercheur-Scientifique

The scientifique-chercheur status is a type of salaried worker visa for academics and researchers who are engaged in research with qualified French institutions. Researchers can have a master's or doctorate, or be working on studies at that level while completing research and/or teaching at the university level. In 2019, 7.150 Scientifique-Chercheur visas were issued, and a total of about 9.000 academics and researchers live and work in France with this status.

Visa Summary

On the France-Visas website, you select this visa by indicating Plans —> Talent Passport International Talents and Main Purpose of Stay —> Scientist-Researcher / Talent. The Visa Passeport Talent Chercheur is a 90-day visa which requires requesting a carte de séjour upon arrival through the online ANEF platform. As a Passeport Talent visa and CDS type, it does not require a medical visit or a Contrat d'Intégration Républicaine, it does provide a path to residency and naturalization.

Who is it for?

A researcher can be anyone who has the equivalent of a master's or doctoral programs or their equivalent, who is coming to France to participate in academic research or teaching at the university level or for a private research institution, who also has a signed convention d'accueil (hosting agreement) with an accredited academic institution or organization "agréé" (authorized) to host foreign researchers and scientists.

Chercheur-scientifique visa holders can be salaried doctoral students enrolled in a thesis (thèse) in France, or foreign doctoral students participating in doctoral research at the host institution in France without earning a salary from the French institution. PhD candidate researchers do not have to be salaried employees of the host institution to benefit from a convention d'accueil.

Postgraduate students, post-docs, foreign professors, and visiting foreign researchers must have a convention d'accueil from their French host institution, specifying how they are paid. They can be paid through foreign salary, grants, or salary from the host institution, depending on the specifics of their project.

A convention d'accueil is mandatory even for research stints less than 90 days long, if the researcher is salaried by the host institution.

Salaried researchers and doctoral students must have financing from that meets or exceeds the minimum pay for public doctoral contracts. In 2024, doctoral candidates will be required to have €2.100 gross remuneration per month, or €25.200 per year. In 2025, the required monthly gross salary will increase to €2.200, and in 2026, it will increase again to €2.300. If you do not have financing that meets this amount, you will instead be issued a student visa for your research contract.

The convention d'accueil can be completed as CERFA form 16079*03, and includes details about the research establishment and their focus, the guest researcher and their project, and the methods of financing the project. It must be signed and stamped by a representative of the host institution.

VFS/TLS Appointment Fee: Approximately €30
Visa Application Processing Fee: €99
OFII fee: €200 for a visa less than 12 months; OR
Carte de séjour fee: €225 if you receive a 90 day visa with "carte de séjour à solliciter dès l'arrivée" and receive a 4-year carte de séjour

Where to apply: In country of residence, at your local French consulate or VFS/TLS office. You can also switch to this status from another status if you have been in France for more than 1 year and already renewed your visa.

Length of visa: 12 months to 4 years, depending on the convention d'accueil. If your visa is issued for less than 12 months you must simply validate your visa within 90 days of your arrival. If your visa is for more than 12 months, within 90 days of arrival you must request a carte de séjour. Both of these procedures are online.

Renewal: Can be a multi-year visa (4 years), depending on the contract and research project.

Health Insurance

You will get health insurance through your employment, beginning from the start date of your work contract. You do not need a private health plan or travel coverage in order to get your visa.

Income & Savings Requirement

You will have to provide proof of financial resources requirement from a salary or grant for this visa. At this level, it is not reasonable to expect the company to pay moving or relocation expenses. The exact amount of your financial resources depends on the source of your income: financing from a scholarship or grant, or salary from a teaching or research position.

Work

Because your visa sponsorship is tied directly to your research and requires a convention d'accueil with your institution, you are tied to your place of employment and host establishment for the duration of your contract and visa. It is not advisable to change employers within the first two years of being in France, and you would have to stay in the same general job title and same field.

You cannot have supplemental employment activities outside of the organization that signed your original convention d'accueil. For example, if you are doing research with a particular institution, you cannot teach classes in another university without jeopardizing your visa status.

You cannot work as a self-employed person, freelancer, or autoentrepreneur, or start a business/company while on the salarié visa. This includes remote work for companies outside of France who are not paying French social taxes on your income.

Taxation

Because you are working in France, you should declare your worldwide earnings and pay French taxes from your date of arrival in France. You will contribute to French healthcare and retirement funds through social charges on your salary.

Maintaining and Renewing Your Visa

Depending on the length of your convention d'accueil, your initial visa can be issued for 12 months, validated as a VLS-TS and renewed. Alternatively, if your contract exceeds 12 months, you will be issued a 90-day visa with a multi-year carte de séjour to request upon arrival, valid for the length of your contract. If you are working for the same institution at the time of your renewal, and on a CDI contract, you can request a 4-year carte de séjour, which will carry you through until your request for a 10-year card and eligibility for naturalization.

You cannot change your visa status before you have renewed your visa at least once. Once you have completed your research you can apply for a 1 year Recherche d'Emploi / Création d'Entreprise visa, or another salaried visa type if you have secured full-time employment.

Establishing Residency

Assuming you have a multi-year contract with the same research institution, you will receive up to a 4-year carte de séjour. If you have already been in France for several years prior to receiving the carte de séjour salarié, such as completing a degree and receiving RECE, you will be eligible to apply for residency and naturalization much sooner. Your years spent on those other visa types will count towards the 5-year minimum for residency and naturalization, as long as you do not return to your home country to get a new visa.

You should try to apply for naturalization while on this status, or you may have to switch to another visa status (Passeport Talent salarié) at the end of your research contract.

Family Members
Accompanying family members can receive the "accompanying family member of passeport talent" visa, giving the accompanying spouse the right to work in France.

European Mobility
Holders of the "Scientifique-Chercheur" visa from another country can live and work in France and in a French institution for up to 3 months if required or allowed by their EU work contract. Scientifique-Chercheur holders who have been living in another EU country with a valid visa who would like to do research in France for longer than 3 months can relocate to France and apply for a French Scientifique-Chercheur status directly in their local préfecture, within one month of arriving in France, upon presenting a contrat d'accueil with a French agency.

French scientifique-chercheur holders who would like to go to other EU countries should check to see if the French status can easily be converted if they contract with a local university or research center in the new host country.

Pros & Cons
Pros:
- You are associated with a research institution and working towards research projects related to your academic or professional goals.
- Low burden of financial resources, since you will be paid a salary upon arrival.

- Easy mobility to other EU countries.
- Family members get Passeport Talent Famille Accompagnante visas

Cons:
- Academic salaries are much lower in France than they are in the US and many Anglophone countries.
- You must have at least a master's or PhD and be completing graduate level or post-graduate level research with an academic or private research institution to qualify.
- Your carte de séjour is linked to your employment, so if you leave your job voluntarily or get fired for just cause, you may lose your right to stay in France.

Documents to Provide for Application
- ✓ Valid passport issued less than 10 years ago with at least 2 blank visa pages
- ✓ Convocation for a visa appointment at consulate or VFS/TLS center
- ✓ A cover letter explaining the purpose of your move
- ✓ Long-stay visa application, completed through France Visas
- ✓ Proof of financial resources and bank account
- ✓ CERFA 16079*03: Signed convention d'accueil with a French university or research center. A convention d'accueil is a specific type of document outlining your status and describing your research and affiliation to the host institution.
- ✓ If you will be completing research in another EU country as part of your project, the convention d'accueil must specify your participation in an EU mobility program.
- ✓ Letter of intent to hire
- ✓ Résumé and cover letter explaining your experience and qualifications
- ✓ Transcripts and diplomas
- ✓ Place to stay for first few weeks upon arrival

Documents to Provide for Initial CDS Request & Renewal Online

- ✓ Access to your ANEF account
- ✓ Attestation of OFII visit, and titre de séjour
- ✓ Set of ANTS standard ePhotos, usually from a Photomaton machine
- ✓ Proof of residence less than 3 months old (justificatif de domicile)
- ✓ Proof of health coverage
- ✓ Birth certificate with certified translation
- ✓ Proof of financial resources, including bank statements for French bank account or bank account in your home country, and pay slips from your employment
- ✓ Signed "Engagement à Respecter les Principes de la République" form
- ✓ Signed convention d'accueil with a French university or research center
- ✓ Transcripts and diplomas

2.4-5 Passeport Talent Recrutement dans une Entreprise Innovante

The Recrutement dans une Entreprise Innovante is a visa type aimed at companies recruiting highly qualified individuals in specialized industries. The company must be recognized by the Ministry of the Economy and Finance as a being an innovative or a young innovative company (JEI).

The minimum salary requirement for obtaining this visa is at least two times the French minimum wage which would mean you would need a gross annual salary of at least €42.406 based on the 2024 SMIC.

Visa Summary

On the France-Visas website, you select this visa by indicating Plans —> Talent Passport International Talents and Main Purpose of Stay —> Employee recruited in an innovative enterprise / Talent. If you are given a contract for more than 1 year, the Visa Passeport Talent Recrutement dans une Entreprise Innovante is a 90-day visa which requires requesting a carte de séjour upon arrival through the online ANEF platform. As a Passeport Talent visa and CDS type, it does not require a medical visit or a Contrat d'Intégration Républicaine, but like other renewable work visa types, it does provide a path to residency and naturalization.

Who is it for?

The Passeport Talent Recrutement dans une Entreprise Innovante visa is specifically designed to encourage tech companies to recruit talent from abroad, and to make it easier for them to hire foreign talent. In order to more easily recruit foreign salaried employees, the hiring company must be on an approved "French Tech" list or have registered with the French government about an innovative project. It must specifically request JEI status from the Ministry of the Economy and pay a gross annual salary above €42.406. No particular level of education is required for the JEI visa, but the applicant must be working directly on the innovative aspects of the project, as justified in the hiring letter and job description.

VFS/TLS Appointment Fee: Approximately €30

Visa Application Processing Fee: €99

OFII fee: €200 if you receive a 12 month visa to be validated as a VLS-TS; OR

Carte de séjour fee: €225 if you receive a 90 day visa with "carte de séjour à solliciter dès l'arrivée" and receive a 4-year carte de séjour

Where to apply: In country of residence, at your local French consulate or VFS/TLS office. Alternatively, if you are in France on another visa type (student, Recherche d'Emploi, salarié) you can apply for a change of status directly in your local French préfecture.

Length of visa: 4 years maximum, based on work contract. You can either be issued a visa for 1 year, with a CDS at the end of the first year, or you can be issued a visa for 90 days and be able to request a 4-year CDS upon arrival in France.

Renewal: Can be a multi-year visa (4 years), depending on your work contract

Health Insurance

You will get health insurance through your employment, beginning from the start date of your work contract. You do not need a private health plan or travel coverage in order to get your visa.

Income & Savings Requirement

Because you will be provided with a salary, there is no minimum financial resources requirement for this visa beyond what you need to move yourself and your belongings to France. It is not reasonable to expect the company to pay moving or relocation expenses.

Work

Your visa sponsorship is tied directly to your job, so you are tied to your place of employment for the duration of your contract and visa. It is not advisable to change employers within the first two years of being in France, and you would have to stay in the same general job title and same field.

If you are laid off from the company for financial reasons, you can collect unemployment benefits until your visa expires. Receiving benefits from France Travail will allow you to renew your visa and seek other employment in your field. If your période d'essai (trial period) is not validated, you can also seek new employment, but again, but it must meet the same criteria as your initial position.

You cannot work as a self-employed person, freelancer, or autoentrepreneur, or start a business/company while on this Passeport Talent visa. This includes remote work for companies outside of France who are not paying French social taxes on your income. In order to be self-employed, you would have to switch your visa status to one of the self-employment types and leave your salaried position.

Taxation

Because you are working in France, you should declare your worldwide earnings and pay French taxes from your date of arrival in France. You will contribute to French healthcare and retirement funds through social charges on your salary. You cannot do any work outside of the salaried position that brings you to France.

Maintaining and Renewing Your Visa

Normally, your initial visa will be issued for 3 months, during which time you must request a carte de séjour from your local préfecture through an online procedure after arrival. The carte de séjour you receive will depend on the work documents you provide, and can be valid for up to 4 years. It can be renewed. If you are working for the same employer at the time of your renewal, and on a CDI contract, you can request a 4-year carte de séjour, which will carry you through until your request for a 10-year card and eligibility for naturalization.

Note that if you have a CDD of 3-12 months, you will instead be issued a 1 year visa to validate online and will not have to request a carte de séjour during the first year.

You cannot change your visa status during your first two years in France, and you must renew your visa with your current status at least once. In order to switch to another visa status, you must meet the requirements for the new status.

Establishing Residency

Assuming you stay with the same employer, you will receive a 4-year carte de séjour, which can be renewed, and you can then request a 10-year residency card at its expiration. You can also begin the process of applying for naturalization after 5 years total in France, potentially avoiding the need to renew the multiyear carte de séjour.

If you have already been in France for several years prior to receiving the carte de séjour Passeport Talent salarié, such as completing a degree and receiving RECE, you will be eligible to apply for residency and naturalization much sooner. Your years spent on those other visa types will count towards the 5-year minimum for residency and naturalization, as long as you do not return to your home country to get a new visa.

Family Members

Accompanying family members can receive the "accompanying family member of passeport talent" visa, giving the accompanying spouse the right to work in France.

Pros & Cons

Pros:
- Your employer does NOT have to prove they tried to hire someone with French work papers
- Easily renewed and provides an easy path to residency and naturalization.
- High salary and no proof of other financial resources required.
- You do not have to have a particular level of education or experience, as long as you are involved with the "innovative" aspects of the company's work.

Cons:
- Your carte de séjour is linked to your employment, so if you leave your job voluntarily or get fired for just cause, you may lose your right to stay in France.

- The company must officially be recognized by the Ministry of the Economy and Finance.

Documents to Provide for Application:

- ✓ Valid passport issued less than 10 years ago with at least 2 blank visa pages
- ✓ Convocation for a visa appointment at consulate or VFS/TLS center
- ✓ A cover letter explaining the purpose of your move
- ✓ Long-stay visa application, completed through France Visas
- ✓ Work contract justifying the required salary
- ✓ Letter of intent to hire
- ✓ Résumé and cover letter explaining your experience and qualifications
- ✓ Transcripts and diplomas with certified translations
- ✓ Valid RECE status, if applicable
- ✓ Place to stay for first few weeks upon arrival
- ✓ CERFA 15614*04 completed by the employer and required accompanying documents
- ✓ Company registration certificate (Kbis)
- ✓ Company's certificate of payment of social insurance contributions
- ✓ Company documents relative to the Innovative status: attestation from the Ministry of the Economy recognizing the innovative nature of the work, or tax document establishing the company as a young innovative company ("jeune entreprise innovante")
- ✓ Other documents from your employer

Documents to Provide for Initial CDS Request & Renewal Online:

- ✓ Access to ANEF account
- ✓ Titre de séjour
- ✓ Set of ANTS standard passport photos (ePhotos), usually from a Photomaton machine
- ✓ Proof of residence less than 3 months old (justificatif de domicile)
- ✓ Proof of health coverage
- ✓ Birth certificate with certified translation
- ✓ Proof of financial resources, including bank statements for French bank account or bank account in your home country
- ✓ Work contract and payslips
- ✓ Transcripts and diplomas
- ✓ Signed "Engagement à Respecter les Principes de la République" form

2.4-6 Passeport Talent - Salarié Qualifié Visa

The Passeport Talent Salarié visa type is for individuals holding a master degree or equivalent from an accredited French institution. The individual must have secured a work contract for a minumum of 3 months with the French employer.

The minimum salary requirement for obtaining this visa is at least two times the French minimum wage, which would mean you would need a gross annual salary of at least €42.406 (2024 SMIC).

Visa Summary
On the France-Visas website, you select this visa by indicating Plans —> Talent Passport International Talents and Main Purpose of Stay —> Qualified Employee / Talent. The Visa Passeport Talent Salarié Qualifié is a 90-day visa which requires requesting a carte de séjour upon arrival through the online ANEF platform. As a Passeport Talent visa and CDS type, it does not require a medical visit or a Contrat d'Intégration Républicaine, but like other renewable work visa types, it does provide a path to residency and naturalization.

Who is it for?
The Passeport Talent Salarié visa is for highly skilled workers who have a master's degree, or or its equivalent *from a French university or grande école*, and who earn at least €42.406 per year gross salary. Applicants who have received higher education outside of France are no longer eligible for this visa type.

VFS/TLS Appointment Fee: Approximately €30
Visa Application Processing Fee: €99
OFII fee: €200 if you receive a 12 month visa to be validated as a VLS-TS; OR
   Carte de séjour fee: €225 if you receive a 90 day visa with "carte de séjour à solliciter dès l'arrivée" and receive a 4-year carte de séjour

Where to apply: In country of residence, at your local French consulate or VFS/TLS office. Alternatively, if you are in France on another visa type (student, Recherche d'Emploi, salarié) you can apply for a change of status directly in your local French préfecture.

Length of visa: 4 years maximum, based on work contract. You can either be issued a visa for 1 year, with a CDS at the end of the first year, or you can be issued a visa for 90 days and be able to request a 4-year CDS upon arrival in France.

Renewal: Can be a multi-year visa (4 years), depending on your work contract

Health Insurance

You will get health insurance through your employment, beginning from the start date of your work contract. You do not need a private health plan or travel coverage in order to get your visa.

Income & Savings Requirement

Because you will be provided with a salary, there is no minimum financial resources requirement for this visa beyond what you need to move yourself and your belongings to France. It is not reasonable to expect the company to pay moving or relocation expenses.

Work

Your visa sponsorship is tied directly to your job, so you are tied to your place of employment for the duration of your contract and visa. It is not advisable to change employers within the first two years of being in France, and you would have to stay in the same general job title and same field.

If you are laid off from the company for financial reasons, you can collect unemployment benefits until your visa expires. Receiving benefits from France Travail will allow you to renew your visa and seek other employment in your field. If your période d'essai (trial period) is not validated, you can also seek new employment, but again, but it must meet the same criteria as your initial position.

You cannot work as a self-employed person, freelancer, or autoentrepreneur, or start a business/company while on the passeport talent salarié qualifié visa. This includes remote work for companies outside of France which are not paying French social taxes on your income. In order to be self-employed, you would have to switch your visa status to one of the self-employment types and leave your salaried position.

Taxation

Because you are working in France, you should declare your worldwide earnings and pay French taxes from your date of arrival in France. You will contribute to French healthcare and retirement funds through social charges on your salary.

You cannot do any work outside of the salaried position that brings you to France.

Maintaining and Renewing Your Visa

Normally, your initial visa will be issued for 3 months, during which time you must request a carte de séjour from your local préfecture through an online procedure after arrival. The carte de séjour you receive will depend on the work documents you provide, and can be valid for up to 4 years. It can be renewed. If you are working for the same employer at the time of your renewal, and on a CDI contract, you can request a 4-year carte de séjour, which will carry you through until your request for a 10-year card and eligibility for naturalization.

Note that if you have a CDD of 3-12 months, you will instead be issued a 1 year visa to validate online and will not have to request a carte de séjour during the first year.

You cannot change your visa status during your first two years in France, and you must renew your visa with your current status at least once. In order to switch to another visa status, you must meet the requirements for the new status.

Establishing Residency

Assuming you stay with the same employer, you will receive a one-year visa, followed by a 4-year carte de séjour, followed by a 10-year residency card, at which point you will be able to apply for naturalization.

If you have already been in France for several years prior to receiving the carte de séjour Passeport Talent salarié qualifié, such as completing a degree and receiving RECE, you will be eligible to apply for residency and naturalization much sooner. Your years spent on those other visa types will count towards the 5-year minimum for residency and naturalization, as long as you do not return to your home country to get a new visa.

Family Members
Accompanying family members can receive the "accompanying family member of passeport talent" visa, giving the accompanying spouse the right to work in France.

Pros & Cons
Pros
- Your employer does NOT have to prove they tried to hire someone with French work papers.
- Easily renewed and provides an easy path to residency and naturalization.
- High salary and no proof of other financial resources required.

Cons:
- Your carte de séjour is linked to your employment, so if you leave your job voluntarily or get fired for just cause, you may lose your right to stay in France.
- Foreign degrees are not valid for the PT-Salarié Qualifié visa; applicants must have a French master's degree or equivalent by an accredited institution in France.

Documents to Provide for Application:
- ✓ Valid passport issued less than 10 years ago with at least 2 blank visa pages
- ✓ Convocation for a visa appointment at consulate or VFS/TLS center
- ✓ A cover letter explaining the purpose of your move
- ✓ Long-stay visa application, completed through France Visas
- ✓ Work contract for a minimum of 3 months justifying the

required salary of at least 2x SMIC
- ✓ Letter of intent to hire
- ✓ Résumé and cover letter explaining your experience and qualifications
- ✓ Copy of your French master's degree or equivalent from an accredited French institution
- ✓ Transcripts and diplomas with certified translations
- ✓ Valid RECE status, if applicable
- ✓ Place to stay for first few weeks upon arrival
- ✓ CERFA 15614*04 completed and stamped by the employer and required accompanying documents
- ✓ Company registration certificate (Kbis)
- ✓ Company's certificate of payment of social insurance contributions

Documents to Provide for Renewal Online:

- ✓ Access to ANEF account
- ✓ Titre de séjour
- ✓ Set of ANTS standard passport photos (ePhotos), usually from a Photomaton machine
- ✓ Proof of residence less than 3 months old (justificatif de domicile)
- ✓ Proof of health coverage
- ✓ Birth certificate with certified translation
- ✓ Proof of financial resources, including bank statements for French bank account or bank account in your home country
- ✓ Work contract and payslips
- ✓ Transcripts and diplomas
- ✓ Signed "Engagement à Respecter les Principes de la République" form

2.4-7 Passeport Talent Salarié Hautement Qualifié / Carte Bleue Européenne Visa

The Passeport Talent Salarié Hautement Qualifié / Carte Bleue Européenne visa type is for highly qualified individuals holding a degree resulting in at least three years of higher education issued by an institution recognized by the state in which it is located or any document justifying at least 5 years of professional experience in a similar field. The individual must have secured a work contract for a minimum of 12 months with the French employer.

The minimum gross annual salary requirement for obtaining this visa is 1.5x the annual gross median salary, which established by French decree based on 2016 salaries and has not increased. In 2024, the actual required minimum gross annual salary for the Salarié Hautement Qualifié Carte Bleue Européenne card would be at least equivalent to €53.837.

The Salarié Hautement Qualifié visa, also known as the EU Blue Card, allows you to work in *any* EU country, to switch employment from one country to another easily by making a simple application locally with the immigration services in the new country. While each country sets its own minimum requirements for *eligibility* for the EU Blue Card in terms of minimum salary and educational requirements, once you have earned one, it is very easy to move from one EU country to another if you have spent at least 18 months working elsewhere in the EU.

Visa Summary

On the France-Visas website, you select this visa by indicating Plans —> Talent Passport International Talents and Main Purpose of Stay —> Highly Qualified Employee EU Blue Card / Talent. The Visa Passeport Talent Salarié Hautement Qualifié Carte Bleue Européenne is a 90-day visa which requires requesting a carte de séjour upon arrival through the online ANEF platform. As a Passeport Talent visa and CDS type, it does not require a medical visit or a Contrat d'Intégration Républicaine, but like other renewable work visa types, it does provide a path to residency and naturalization.

Who is it for?

The Passeport Talent Salarié Hautement Qualifié Carte Bleue Européenne visa is for employees with a gross annual salary over €53.837. Applicants must have at least 3 years of university education (from a university anywhere in the world) or 5 years of professional experience in the field. Applicants for this visa must have a work contract for at least 1 year.

VFS/TLS Appointment Fee: Approximately €30
Visa Application Processing Fee: €99
OFII fee: €200 if you receive a 12 month visa to be validated as a VLS-TS; OR
Carte de séjour fee: €225 if you receive a 90 day visa with "carte de séjour à solliciter dès l'arrivée" and receive a 4-year carte de séjour

Where to apply: In country of residence, at your local French consulate or VFS/TLS office. Alternatively, if you are in France on another visa type (student, Recherche d'Emploi, salarié) you can apply for a change of status directly in your local French préfecture. If you have been issued a Carte Bleue Européenne by another EU country and have resided in that country for at least 18 months, you may request French card directly through the ANEF website within 30 day of arriving in France.

Length of visa: 4 years maximum, based on work contract. You can either be issued a visa for 1 year, with a CDS at the end of the first year, or you can be issued a visa for 90 days and be able to request a 4-year CDS upon arrival in France.

Renewal: Can be a multi-year visa (4 years), depending on your work contract

Health Insurance

You will get health insurance through your employment, beginning from the start date of your work contract. You do not need a private health plan or travel coverage in order to get your visa.

Income & Savings Requirement

Because you will be provided with a salary, there is no minimum financial resources requirement for this visa beyond what you need to move yourself and your belongings to France. At this level, it is not reasonable to expect the company to pay moving or relocation expenses.

Work

Your visa sponsorship is tied directly to your job, so you are tied to your place of employment for the duration of your contract and visa. It is not advisable to change employers within the first two years of being in France, and you would have to stay in the same general job title and same field.

If you are laid off from the company for financial reasons, you can collect unemployment benefits until your visa expires. Receiving benefits from France Travail will allow you to renew your visa and seek other employment in your field. If your période d'essai (trial period) is not validated, you can also seek new employment, but again, but it must meet the same criteria as your initial position.

You cannot work as a self-employed person, freelancer, or autoentrepreneur, or start a business/company while on the Passeport Talent salarié or carte bleue européenne visa. This includes remote work for companies outside of France who are not paying French social taxes on your income. In order to be self-employed, you would have to switch your visa status to one of the self-employment types and leave your salaried position.

Taxation

Because you are working in France, you should declare your worldwide earnings and pay French taxes from your date of arrival in France. You will contribute to French healthcare and retirement funds through social charges on your salary.

You cannot do any work outside of the salaried position that brings you to France.

Maintaining and Renewing Your Visa

Normally, your initial visa will be issued for 3 months, during which time you must request a carte de séjour from your local préfecture through an online procedure after arrival. The carte de séjour you receive will depend on the work documents you provide, and can be valid for up to 4 years. It can be renewed. If you are working for the same employer at the time of your renewal, and on a CDI contract, you can request a 4-year carte de séjour, which will carry you through until your request for a 10-year card and eligibility for naturalization.

You cannot change your visa status during your first two years in France, and you must renew your visa with your current status at least once. In order to switch to another visa status, you must meet the requirements for the new status.

Establishing Residency

Assuming you stay with the same employer, you will receive a one-year visa, followed by a 4-year carte de séjour, followed by a 10-year residency card, at which point you will be able to apply for naturalization.

If you have already been in France for several years prior to receiving the carte de séjour Passeport Talent salarié, such as completing a degree and receiving RECE, you will be eligible to apply for residency and naturalization much sooner. Your years spent on those other visa types will count towards the 5-year minimum for residency and naturalization, as long as you do not return to your home country to get a new visa.

Family Members

Accompanying family members can receive the "accompanying family member of passeport talent" visa, giving the accompanying spouse the right to work in France.

European Mobility

Holders of the "Carte Bleue Européenne" from another country can live and work in France for up to 3 months if required by their EU work contract. CBE holders who have been living in another EU country with a valid CBE for more than 18 months can relocate to France and apply for a French CBE directly on the ANEF website, within one month of arriving in France. However, each EU country sets its own requirements for getting the Carte Bleue, and those relocating from other countries must meet France's requirements in order to maintain their CBE status. Holders of a French CBE for more than 18 months can also more easily relocate to other EU countries without submitting a visa application, by meeting the new host country's requirements.

Pros & Cons

Pros:
- Your employer does NOT have to prove they tried to hire someone with French work papers
- Easily renewed and provides an easy path to residency and naturalization.
- High salary and no proof of other financial resources required.

Cons:
- Your carte de séjour is linked to your employment, so if you leave your job voluntarily or get fired for just cause, you may lose your right to stay in France.
- You must meet the education or experience requirements.

Documents to Provide for Application:
- ✓ Valid passport issued less than 10 years ago with at least 2 blank visa pages
- ✓ Convocation for a visa appointment at consulate or VFS/TLS center
- ✓ A cover letter explaining the purpose of your move
- ✓ Long-stay visa application, completed through France Visas
- ✓ Work contract for a minimum of 12 months justifying the required salary
- ✓ Letter of intent to hire
- ✓ Résumé and cover letter
- ✓ Transcripts and diplomas with certified translations (Degree equivalent to Bac+3 or a Bachelor's degree)
- ✓ If you have professional experience, any document, such as payslips, employee tax documents, and professional licenses

justifying at least 5 years of experience
- ✓ Valid RECE status, if applicable
- ✓ Place to stay for first few weeks upon arrival
- ✓ If you had a European Blue Card from another country a front and back certified copy, or the card itself
- ✓ CERFA 15615*01, completed by the employer, along with the supporting documents from your employer
- ✓ Kbis less than 3 months old for hiring company
- ✓ Company's certificate of payment of social insurance contributions
- ✓ If applicable for your position, proof you are allowed to exercise a regulated profession in France

Documents to Provide for Initial CDS Request & Renewal Online:
- ✓ Access to ANEF account
- ✓ Titre de séjour
- ✓ Set of ANTS standard passport photos (ePhotos), usually from a Photomaton machine
- ✓ Proof of residence less than 3 months old (justificatif de domicile)
- ✓ Proof of health coverage
- ✓ Birth certificate with certified translation
- ✓ Proof of financial resources, including bank statements for French bank account or bank account in your home country
- ✓ Work contract and payslips
- ✓ Transcripts and diplomas
- ✓ Signed "Engagement à Respecter les Principes de la République" form

2.5 Independent Work Visa Types

Independent work visas are, in our opinion, the best and most flexible visa types that exist aside from the "vie privée et familiale" visas. This is because these visa types allow you to work as a self-employed person or to start a business (and to essentially sponsor your own work visa so you can live and work in France).

With one of the visa types in this chapter, you don't need an employer to officially sponsor you, and you don't need to prove you can do a specific job better than someone who already has EU work papers. You simply have to put together a project showing what type of work you will do and how you will make money. You'll have to set up a proper business structure, invoice, and pay French taxes, but you can work for clients anywhere: in France and the EU, in your home country, or on the moon.

The important thing to know for this chapter is that the vocabulary can be a bit confusing because it overlaps. The same words or phrases can refer to a type of *activity*, a type of *business structure,* and a type of *visa,* so you will have to be very clear about what you're referring to.

For example, if you are a graphic designer, you can have a visa type called "profession libérale", and a business structure called "autoentrepreneur," but have your activity be artisanal. Conversely, you could have your visa type be "entrepreneur (commerçant, artisan, industriel)," have your business structure be a company, and have your business's activity be consulting, which would technically fall under "profession libérale." See how confusing that is?

Types of Activities

All professions in France are clearly identified on a master list and fall into one of several categories. For the purposes of this book, We're just going to briefly define the types of activities related to running a business (excluding, for example, fonctionnaire or government positions, cadre/management positions in another company, etc.)

- **Commercial, artisanal, industrial:** activities involving the production, purchase, and resale of goods.

- **Profession libérale:** a "profession libérale" means that the activity is not regulated by the government, but can be regulated within the industry. Profession libérale can be "reglementée," meaning it is industry-regulated, or non-reglementée, meaning that there is no supervising body for professionals. A lawyer or a midwife would both be "profession libérale," and they would be regulated by the bar association and the midwifery association respectively, which sets the professional standards for those industries. A consultant would also be a "profession libérale," but consulting is an unregulated profession.

- **Artisanal:** Involves the making and selling of goods. Examples of artisanal activities would be upholstery, homemade jewelry or decorative objects, or even web and graphic design.

- **Artistic:** Can involve one of the following: the sale of individual works of art or prints, receiving royalties from art being used in a design (graphic design, stock photography and licensing photographs), receiving royalties for published works like books or recordings, receiving payment for performances. Participating in one of these activities usually requires registering with the Maison des Artistes or Agessa, depending on the activity category.

- **Agricultural:** Involves any type of outdoor activity related to landscaping or farming. These activity types usually have liability issues and cannot be invoiced with the "autoentrepreneur" business type. There is no specific visa for this type of activity, although workers may fall into "travailleur temporaire / saisonnier" categories in "métiers en tension."

Types of Business Structures

Note that this is a non-exhaustive list of ways to be self-employed, which I'm using to demonstrate the overlap in vocabulary for this section.

- **Autoentreprise / Microentreprise:** Two words for the same kind of business structure. A simplified self-employment structure that enables people to register and declare their gross income monthly, paying social taxes on the gross amount. An income cap of €77.700 per year for services and €188.700 per year for the sale of goods, along with a simplified accounting procedures and exemption from TVA for sales under €36.800 make this an ideal structure for someone with a small-scale activity or someone who is just getting started. All "microentreprise" businesses are "entreprises individuelles" since 2022.

- **Profession Libérale "frais réels":** A more complex self-employment structure that requires declaring income and business expenses, billing TVA, and undertaking a more complex accounting process.

- **Companies:** There are various types of limited liability companies (EURL/SARL, SAS(U), SA, SELARL, etc.) which each have different advantages for the owners, company directors, and investors. Depending on the company type, the director's status and benefits structure, investors' ability to resell shares, as well as the company's tax rates for social charges, company profits, and dividends paid to investors can all vary. The details of which company structure might be best suited for your activity is beyond the scope of this book, but can be discussed in a consultation.

Types of Visas

There are four possible visa types that can include self-employment, and all of these types are discussed in-depth in this chapter.

- **Profession Libérale:** for self-employed people who have a profession libérale or artisanal *activity type* and an autoentrepreneur or profession libérale *business structure*.

- **Entrepreneur (commerçant, artisan, industriel):** for self-employed people who have a commercial activity with an autoentrepreneur business structure, or who have a company with any category of business activity.

- **Passeport Talent - Entrepreneur:** for self-employed people who make a significant investment and have a company with any type of business activity.

- **Passeport Talent - Profession Artistique:** for artists and performers who may have a combination of the following: an artistic activity registered through Maison des Artistes and/or Agessa, an artisanal activity with an autoentrepreneur business structure, or a profession libérale activity with an autoentrepreneur business structure.

Our Franceformation Clients

We work with many talented self-employed people and entrepreneurs who have started businesses in France. Some of them have agreed to be interviewed for the *Profiles in Franceformation* podcast. If you'd like to learn about their moves to France and hear more about the process of working with us, you can listen to their stories here:

	Episode 43: Episode 43: Allez, viens! And take a page from Language curriculum creator Cherie Mitschke's French book; https://www.yourfranceformation.com/2022/10/12/episode-43/

[QR code]	Episode 44: Conjuring Dream Lives and Dream France Vacations, with Mallory Nettleton, Creator of France of a Lifetime Tours; https://www.yourfranceformation.com/2022/10/19/episode-44/
[QR code]	Episode 48: Living out a childhood dream with Vashti Joseph, an entrepreneur and small business owner; https://www.yourfranceformation.com/2022/11/16/episode-48/
[QR code]	Episode 51: Getting into the swing of things in Paris with Brian Bailey; https://www.yourfranceformation.com/2022/12/07/episode-51/

2.5-1 Profession Libérale ou Indépendante - Liberal or Independent Visa

The profession libérale visa is for people whose main source of income will be from self-employment, which is to say, work done for clients (and not salary or royalties). The profession libérale visa is our favorite type of visa to help people get, and it's the one we tend to work with the most with our Your Franceformation clients. Why? Because it allows people to essentially sponsor themselves for a visa that enables them to work, so they can create their own self-employment opportunities, work from anywhere, and find their own clients, in France and around the world.

It can also be a potential option if you don't want to commit to being in school, and you can't get sponsored by a company. Using the skills you already have and possibly jobs you've already done, you can weave your skills and experience into a unique offering and work for companies in both your home country (remotely) and in France and the EU as a contractor or freelancer.

You do not already have to have a working business to successfully get the visa. You can successfully obtain a Profession Libérale visa for a new business you are developing based on your contacts and previous professional experience if you have a good business plan and leads for potential clients in France and internationally. In previous years, we had clients who have become self-employed in their field after leaving a full-time position to move to France, as well as other clients who have changed industries completely, going from corporate jobs in finance to English tutoring.

We often advise people who want to work in France to go the route of getting the profession libérale visa, because it's relatively straightforward to put together a business plan and to begin finding clients for the skills you offer. Jobs like a photographer, or English teacher, or becoming a virtual assistant, have low barriers to entry, can draw on skills you've already developed during your higher education, and can be quite easy to run online, even if you find clients primarily in your home country at first.

France doesn't have a digital nomad visa, and while consulates do prioritize profession libérale applications from applicants who already have potential clients in France, it's one of the closest visa types for being a sort of digital nomad. While we often have people express a desire for France to create a digital nomad visa, the truth is that the existence of such a visa type would make it that much more difficult for people who want to live and work in France by being self-employed to do so.

We used to advise our clients that they could obtain a profession libérale visa with some clients in their home country and some ideas or networking possibilities for how to get clients in France. However, over the past 2 years, the French embassy has become more strict about wanting Profession Libérale visa applicants to have sources of income in France before awarding the visa. Now, we focus from the beginning on helping you to identify connections and potential clients in France who may be able to support your application.

Possible Changes to Profession Libérale Applications

Since 2022, there has been talk of a new approval procedure for the profession libérale activity whereas before applying for your visa, your business plan would be submitted to and evaluated by DREETS for an opinion on viability, prior to application through the French consulate. This procedure already applies to both Entrepreneur and Passeport Talent Entrepreneur business plans and visa applications, each through their respective platform. However, at the time this edition is being published, you do not have to submit your visa application and business plan for pre-approval online for profession libérale businesses.

Because this procedure has not yet been put in place, we don't yet know all the ways in which profession libérale visa applications might be limited or affected by the procedural change, nor do we have a good idea how long this process will take. We expect the validation process to add at least several weeks of time to the application process, but we won't be able to advise our clients until we have had a few data points come back. For reference, the Ministry of the Economy approval process for our Passeport Talent Enrepreneur clients typically takes around 3 weeks, and we would expect approval for Profession Libérale to take longer.

If and when this procedure gets put into place, we will be advising our clients to submit their projects entirely in French, and 8-10 weeks before their planned departure date (4-6 weeks before their visa appointment date) to receive their attestation on time.

Profession Libérale: Visa Type or Business Type?

The title "profession libérale" can be confusing because it refers to both a type of *visa* AND a type of *French business structure*. But, you can have a "profession libérale" visa without having a profession libérale business, and registering instead with a status called microentrepreneur or autoentrepreneur. (The name of autoentrepreneur changed to microentrepreneur in 2016, but most people still say autoentrepreneur. We use them interchangeably.) In many cases, the mention on your visa or carte de séjour will then be "profession libérale" or "independent profession."

Profession Libérale Business Ideas

If you're reasonably well educated, have hobbies and interests, are literate, and have basic computer skills, you have skills that you can share with others, and you have the ability to create a business you can run online. You have unique skills and knowledge that you can turn into a business. And if you're excited about something you can offer, a gift you have, and your ability to share it with the world, you can harness that enthusiasm and use it to create your own income and dream life.

Now, if you've never thought about starting a business before, you may be curious about what you can offer. Usually, the best business ideas come from combining something you're passionate about with skills that you already have, that you've learned through various other jobs or university clubs.

Everyone, including you, has skills you can turn into a business. And you can learn complementary skills easily to add to your repertoire. Some basic business ideas don't require a lot of equipment or expenses, but you just need to outline your idea very clearly and do some work on HOW you can help people and provide value by using your unique skills.

You have to have a really good idea. You have to have a plan to execute it. You have to have the skills to pull it off, and the money to support yourself while you're getting it up and running. And it certainly helps if you already have potential clients, including friends and acquaintances in your field who may hire you or recommend you to their networks..

But you don't have to have years of experience as a small business owner, and you don't have to make a huge amount of money in order to get the visa. The average income they look for by the end of your first year is just €1.767 brut per month, minimum wage in France (SMIC), and it's okay if it takes you a bit of time to build up to that amount.

Getting a profession libérale visa gives you the flexibility of working for yourself, of having multiple sources of income, and of setting your own schedule. It allows you to work for clients and companies around the world, including in France, while being covered by the French healthcare system and paying into retirement and maternity benefits. It means you're not relying on anyone else - a partner or an employer - to ensure you can stay in France and renew your visa. And as long as you can make it work financially, nothing is stopping you from staying in France on this visa type - forever. Or, until you get naturalized. If one client contract ends - you can get a new one without having to go through the trouble of getting sponsored again. If you want to expand or pivot your business idea, you can add secondary activities to your business declaration and create additional income streams. YOU decide: what you do, who you work for, how much you charge, and how much you make.

This works if you're working remotely or already running a small business that you want to be able to run from France, or if you're *just starting out* and want help getting your idea on paper and coming up with a plan to transition to being a small business owner. The main thing to focus on, especially if you're going to be "working remotely," will be that you'll technically need more than one client during the course of the calendar year, so your activity doesn't look like a disguised employment contract.

Over the years, we have helped many clients start a wide range of easy to start and run businesses with low start-up costs, including:
- Teaching English online and tutoring in person
- Managing social media for small businesses
- Being a virtual assistant or online business manager
- Freelance writing and editing
- College admissions counseling, academic tutoring, for SATs or a language
- Tutoring a skill you know well: a language, a computer program you're particularly good at using, etc.
- Coaching people at something you're good at
- Publishing consulting
- Digital marketing consulting
- Translating

A few other businesses might require a bit of equipment and developing your skills methodically so you can use them professionally, but you may already have some basic knowledge and a passion for the subject:
- Web or graphic design
- Photography
- Being an instructor in pilates, yoga, dance, or something else that requires experience and certifications
- Makeup artistry

Visa Summary

On the France-Visas website, you select this visa by indicating Plans —> Business and Main Purpose of Stay —> Liberal or Independent Profession. The Visa Profession Libérale is a VLS-TS which is validated online through OFII upon arrival and requires a medical visit as well as a Contrat d'Intégration Républicaine (see section 4.2) and provides a path to naturalization.

Who is it for?
Self-employed people, freelancers, and remote workers in professional service industries who would like to have French and international clients without establishing a full company structure. Those who want to work in France remotely for companies in France and elsewhere in the world as contractors.

VFS/TLS Appointment Fee: Approximately €30
Visa Application Processing Fee: €99
OFII fee: €200

Where to apply: In country of residence, at your local French consulate or VFS/TLS office. You can also switch to this status from another status if you have been in France for more than 1 year and already renewed your visa.

Length of visa: 1 year

Renewal: from 1-4 years, depending on your income

Path to residency and naturalization:
Normally, a 10-year card will be issued on the second renewal (following a 1-year and 4-year cartes de séjour, or 5 years total.) You can apply for naturalization by decree after 5 years of continuous residence on French soil.

Be sure to meet the requirements of financial stability before you apply for naturalization, as you will be held to an income standard of earning at least SMIC regularly for 3 years before your application will be approved.

Health Insurance
You will not need a travel insurance policy for the visa application, but it may be a good idea to maintain a private policy until you receive proof of coverage in the French system.

When you register your business in France, you will automatically begin the process to register with French social security and get coverage. It is as simple as checking a box on your business registration form and waiting for them to send you a letter in the mail. Since you will register your business shortly after arrival (as soon as you have secured long-term housing), you should be covered by the time you have been in France for 3-4 months. The process for getting your finalized social security number can take a few months, and it will take longer to be issued your carte vitale, but you will be able to be reimbursed for your medical expenses from the date your business is registered.

Income & Savings Requirement

We recommend having financial resources equal to net French SMIC when you apply - either by showing three months of bank statements with a balance of €16.800, or by showing passive income from other sources equal to €1400 per month. If you have lots of signed contracts or letters of support with stronger promises for payment, the more likely you are to get away with having less than a full year's worth of savings or income already in the bank. The consulate may take a few additional things into consideration when evaluating your application:

- ✓ Your savings
- ✓ Income you already have for your business (current clients and signed contracts)
- ✓ Income you expect to have for your business (potential clients and projected income)

The goal income for your first year is gross French minimum wage, or SMIC, which is about €1.767 per month (again, always check for the inflation-adjusted rate before you apply). Of course the consulates and préfectures understand that moving to a new country and starting a new business can be daunting, and it's understandable if you take the full year to build up to that amount.

You should also know that during your first year in France, you will have a lot of administrative obligations to fulfill, like the OFII medical visit, the 4 days of OFII Integration courses, and potentially 100-200 hours of French language classes if you don't test out of an A2 level of French at your OFII appointment. You will be fairly busy during your first year in France, and we advise prioritizing these administrative and residence obligations over any travel.

You should also be aware that unlike for some other visa types, you cannot have a financial guarantee for this kind of visa. The money must be your own, in your own account. Some clients who did not have quite enough savings on their own have taken out temporary loans from their banks or family members before applying for their visas, to show money in their own accounts, and paid it back soon after receiving their visas.

Work

The profession libérale visa allows you to be self-employed and to have a business activity in an unregulated profession as a freelancer. Your business status will either be the simplified business structure "autoentrepreneur" (sometimes called "microentrepreneur," which is the same thing) or "profession libérale," which is a self-employed business structure that is more complex in that it allows you to deduct business expenses and requires more complicated accounting practices.

When you register your activity, you will register a "main" business activity and can add related complementary activities and services that you also provide. For example, a web designer may add complementary activities of graphic design and administrative assistance. A Reiki healer may add complementary activities of "Shaman," EFT practitioner, or "witch." (Yes, those are all real activities that can be registered as microentrepreneur businesses, but we have not yet had the pleasure of writing a business plan for one of them!) In order to successfully obtain a visa for and register a business activity, you should be aware that it must be "unregulated" (i.e. not a "profession réglementée") and one that you are authorized to exercise in France. For example, you would not be able to register as a "psychologist" or an "architect", but you could register as a "coach," or "interior designer."

You will have to restrict yourself to working and invoicing on the activities you declare for your business. You want to avoid, for example, registering as a photographer and adding an irrelevant "secondary" activity like teaching English. It may help you to pay the bills in the short term, but to the préfecture, it's going to look like you don't know what you're doing and you can't make money from your main business. Of course, since you create your business plan and do the wording on your invoices, you have a lot of flexibility to come up with the ways in which your various talents relate to each other.

You will not be able to take on salaried work contracts, and you will have to have at least the appearance of multiple clients for your activity.

You can earn up to €77.700 per year on the simplified microentrepreneur status. Your earnings can be unlimited with a "profession libérale" business structure. In fact, once you reach €25.000-30.000 in annual income with a microentrepreneur scheme, you will want to determine when you should switch to a structure that allows you to deduct expenses. The break-even point will depend on your individual business and whether you have any expenses that could reasonably qualify as business expenses, and it's something we work on together as part of your business plan if you work with me in creating your visa application or use our *Complete French Business Incubator* to guide you through the process.

Taxation

Because you are working in France, you should declare your worldwide earnings and pay French taxes from your date of arrival in France. You will contribute to French healthcare and retirement funds through social charges on your business income.

With a microentrepreneur business status, you will pay about 23.1% of your gross earnings in social charges to cover your benefits. Your clients do not pay social charges on your behalf. Compare that to employees, for whom 45% of their total compensation goes to social charges. Note that social charges for microentrepreneurs with a liberal profession will increase to 24.6% in January 2025 and 26.1% in January 2026, to account for increased retirement contributions.

With a "profession libérale" business structure, you will pay about 40% in social taxes, but that amount is calculated *after* you have deducted business expenses. Once you have established a regular income, you will have to determine when it makes sense to switch to this more complicated business structure in order to claim expenses.

With the "microentrepreneur" business structure, you are exempt from billing and declaring TVA up to about €36.800 income. Taxe sur la Valeur Ajoutée, or VAT, is a 20% tax on goods and services.

Maintaining and Renewing Your Visa

Normally, your initial visa will be issued for 12 months and can be renewed. If you are reasonably successful and making a good income at the time of your renewal, you can request a multi-year carte de séjour at your renewal appointment. The préfecture can award anywhere from 1-4 years, at their discretion.

While there is no hard-and-fast rule for how long they will give you, you should expect to receive only 1-2 years if you are not fully attaining the target of €1.767 per month. If your income starts low when you arrive in France, but then you exceed the €1.767 per month target by the time you renew, and you have sufficient personal assets, you may be more likely to receive a multi-year renewal.

We advise clients to aim for €2.500-€3.000 per month in gross income for their activity by the end of the first year and to write a letter summarizing their income over the year and specifically requesting the 4-year card at their renewal appointment. To receive a 4-year card, they also have to complete all of their OFII obligations from their Contrat d'Intégration Républicaine and test out of the French language classes. When we work with our clients to develop their business idea and provide coaching on their services, fees, and packages, we focus on identifying how many clients they can reasonably expect to work with during their first three years, and what fees will meet these income goals.

You cannot change your visa status to anything else before you have renewed your visa at least once. If you do not make money from your business, and do not have sufficient personal financial resources, your visa may not be renewed. The sole exception would be if you decide not to pursue your business, you can change your status to "visitor" at your first renewal and close your activity.

Establishing Residency

Assuming you stay with the same business, you will receive a one-year visa, followed by a 1-4-year carte de séjour. After you have been in France for 5 years, you will receive a 10-year residency card and you will be able to apply for naturalization.

If you have already been in France for several years prior to receiving the carte de séjour profession libérale, such as completing a degree and receiving RECE, you will be eligible to apply for residency and naturalization much sooner. Your years spent on those other visa types will count towards the 5-year minimum for residency and naturalization, as long as you do not return to your home country to get a new visa.

You can change your visa status from "profession libérale" to another work visa type (for example, to salarié or passeport talent), but your employer will have to go through the same process to hire you as they would for another foreigner. Hiring you and switching your visa status will not be easier just because you are already in France, and the change-of-status procedure can be lengthy. Furthermore, if you do change your visa status to a salaried visa type, you will not be able to continue operating your freelance activity or business. You would have to close your business activity when your visa status switch is finalized so you can be a full-time salaried employee.

You can also switch your visa status from profession libérale to vie privée et familiale without issue. If you decide to end your business, you can also switch to a visitor visa through the online ANEF platform.

Family Members

An accompanying spouse or family members can get long-stay visitors visas and are subject to "regroupement familial" procedures, unless your spouse meets the eligibility requirements for another visa type.

Pros & Cons
Pros:
- You do not need to have extensive experience, advanced degrees, and a significant financial investment, just a viable

project and potential clients.
- You can work with clients both inside and outside of France.
- Microentreprise business structure is easier to register and to manage than other business types.
- Does not require a master's degree or minimum amount of experience in your field.

Cons:
- You must prove you can support yourself financially with your own personal financial resources, plus your revenue from your business.
- You must show that you have French potential clients and sources of income to be approved for your visa.
- You should show that you have at least 2 different clients throughout the year for your own security and to avoid a "disguised work contract" relationship with a client.
- You cannot supplement your income with a salaried job.
- Must be renewed after 1 year and show the project's financial health.

Documents to Provide for Application

We provide all business plans and documents to our VIP Concierge Entrepreneur Clients.

- ✓ Valid passport issued less than 10 years ago with at least 2 blank visa pages
- ✓ Convocation for a visa appointment at consulate or VFS/TLS center
- ✓ A cover letter explaining the purpose of your move and your plan
- ✓ Long-stay visa application, completed through France Visas
- ✓ Proof of financial resources of €16.800 (a year of net French minimum wage, or SMIC)
- ✓ RECE status, if you have it
- ✓ A detailed business and project plan for a viable business that meets the requirements of an autoentrepreneur activity
- ✓ Letters of interest from potential clients, collaborators, and supporters

- ✓ Diplomas and transcripts that support your project
- ✓ Résumé/curriculum vitae and cover letter explaining your training, experience, and any awards, especially in relation to your new business
- ✓ Choice of business structure (autoentrepreneur or frais réels)
- ✓ Detailed financial projections for the first 3 years in business showing income of at least gross minimum wage (2024: €1.767 per month)
- ✓ Place to stay for first few weeks upon arrival

Documents to Provide for Renewal

The most important thing to remember is that your renewal will be evaluated on you successfully starting and running your business activity during the first year, and the primary criteria for reviewing your file will be your income. This means that you want to register your activity relatively soon after you get settled in your new home (we do recommend waiting until you have your long-term address before registering as autoentrepreneur) and you want to make sure you have clients to invoice when you begin. Do not wait for months to begin earning an income, or you will have issues at renewal time.

As of 2024, this procedure is not yet on ANEF and renewal submission procedures will be by appointment, by mail-in, or through your préfecture's own online form, depending on your department's procedure.

- ✓ Convocation for a renewal appointment at the local préfecture
- ✓ Your passport, copy of your visa, and copy of your OFII validation (titre de séjour)
- ✓ Attestation of completion of OFII visits and CIR, and language classes
- ✓ Set of ANTS standard passport photos, usually from a Photomaton machine
- ✓ CERFA form provided by the information desk when you arrive at your appointment
- ✓ Proof of residence less than 3 months old (justificatif de domicile)
- ✓ Proof of health coverage

- ✓ Birth certificate with certified translation
- ✓ Proof of financial resources, including personal bank statements for French bank account or bank account in your home country
- ✓ Up-to-date INSEE business registration, less than 3 months old
- ✓ Full set of bank statements for the French bank account designated for your business use, notated with invoice numbers for deposited amounts
- ✓ Client contracts and full set of invoices issued for your activity since your previous renewal
- ✓ Up-to-date attestation with URSSAF, including an "attestation de vigilance"
- ✓ Full set of monthly income declarations to URSSAF with proof of payment of social taxes
- ✓ Most recent French tax declaration, and tax bill if available

2.5-2 Entrepreneur (artisan, industriel, commerçant)

An Entrepreneur visa is a visa that allows someone to start a business in France, whether it be as a craftsperson, manufacturer or retailer. We previously referred to this visa under its former name, the "commerçant," or commercial, visa. "Commerçant" can potentially refer any type of commercial activity registered with the Chambre de Métiers or Chambre de Commerce, even if it's run as an microentreprise, OR it can refer to the fact that ANY type of activity that is done through a company structure. Now, this visa type goes by "Entrepreneur," and we often call it "Classic Entrepreneur" to distinguish it from Passeport Talent Entrepreneur."

If you have a degree and experience, and your business does require a larger outlay of cash at the beginning to get started, it is more favorable to apply directly for a "Passeport Talent - Entrepreneur." Generic "Entrepreneur" visas are going to be especially for those in-between cases: small-scale commercial activities that don't require a lot of startup funding and aren't big enough to qualify for passeport talent.

An "Entrepreneur" visa which is not a "Passeport Talent" is going to be useful in a few main situations:
1. When the applicant does not have the professional experience or degree necessary for applying for a Passeport Talent Entrepreneur, but wants to open a French entity like an SAS or SARL.
2. When the applicant does not want to or cannot invest €30.000 in the social capital of the company required for the Passeport Talent.
3. When the applicant wants to register a microentreprise that falls under the activity categories typically registered with the Chambre de Métiers or the Chambre de Commerce.
4. When purchasing a small business that doesn't have €30.000 in social capital.

The difficulty with Entrepreneur visas is that in most cases, applications are going to go through two layers of an approval process.

First, you must have your project reviewed and approved by the "Plateforme Interrégionale de la Main d'Oeuvre Etrangère" in the region where your activity is planned. They may ask for additional documentation, especially about your finances. In addition, you will need to show proof that you have set up a company in France website as well as a letter of guarantee from a French-based credit institution or approved insurance company or proof of funds in a French-based credit institution in your name. None of this is easy to do or figure out if you are not already in France or don't have someone working with you on the documentation.

Commercial activities, whether as a craftsperson, manufacturer or retailer, necessarily require the purchase or production of goods for resale, and therefore imply significant start-up costs that are a barrier to entry, even at the "microentreprise" level. While microentreprise rules account for the cost of goods by charging a lower level of social charges (13% instead of 23.1% in 2024 on goods sold), you will still have to prove through your financing plan that you have the funds to ensure your business's success. Similarly, establishing corporate entities requires minimum payments for social taxes on your behalf and accounting services for the company. An activity like teaching English doesn't require much in the way of start-up costs or materials, but any type of retail activity for an Entrepreneur visa will have minimum required costs that you will need to consider.

If your activity type is "profession libérale" and you do NOT buy and resell goods, we would strongly recommend going for the profession libérale visa to begin with. Even if you eventually want to be running a company or agency, and have the funds available, it is easier to begin an activity in a microentreprise for a year or two and to calculate when switching to a company / commercial structure is prudent.

Note that multi-level marketing schemes (MLMs) are highly regulated in France and are not eligible for autoentrepreneur business status.

Finally, this classic Entrepreneur visa type is only valid for one year, which means that you have a very short time to establish the company and demonstrate that it is paying you a salary and turning a profit before it is time for the renewal. Because the costs associated with running a company are that much higher than for microentrepreneur activities, it's that much more difficult to get to this level. At least with a Passeport Talent Entrepreneur visa, you have the benefit of the 4 year carte de séjour to develop your activity.

Visa Summary

On the France-Visas website, you select this visa by indicating Plans —> Business and Main Purpose of Stay —> Entrepreneur (Craftsperson, Manufacturer, or Retailer). The Entrepreneur visa is a VLS-TS which is validated online through OFII upon arrival and requires a medical visit as well as a Contrat d'Intégration Républicaine (see section 4.2) and provides a path to naturalization.

Who is it for?

Business owners who are starting or purchasing an existing company (craftsperson, manufacturer or retailer) who may not have a master's or 5 years of professional experience, or who want to invest less than €30.000 each.

VFS/TLS Appointment Fee: Approximately €30
Visa Application Processing Fee: €99
OFII fee: €200

Where to apply: In country of residence, at your local French consulate or VFS/TLS office. You can also switch to this status from another status if you have been in France for more than 1 year and already renewed your visa.

Length of visa: 12 months

Renewal: for 1-4 years at your first renewal appointment, depending on your project's financial success and your company's ability to pay you.

Path to residency and naturalization:

Normally, a 10-year card will be issued on the second renewal (following two multi-year cartes de séjour) if you have been in France for at least 5 years.

You can apply for naturalization by decree after 5 years of continuous residence on French soil if you have three positive bilans (profitable balance sheets) paying you at least SMIC.

Health Insurance

You will not need a travel insurance policy as you will be required to show that the company is registered with URSSAF (if you are creating a company) or documents showing that URSSAF payments are up to date (for the purchase of an existing company).

The process for getting your finalized social security number can take several months, and it will take longer to be issued your carte vitale. We always recommend getting initial health insurance for the transition period.

Income & Savings Requirement

The income requirement for maintaining your visa is €1.400 per month in net remuneration to you, just like for profession libérale. However, that level of income can be more difficult to achieve within one year.

If you have a microentrepreneur business, the amount might not seem that high, but you do have to account for the fact that €1.767 represents gross income, before expenses and the raw materials you need to purchase. Depending on what you're selling, achieving that level of income could still be tricky.

If you are have purchased or are starting an actual company (SAS/SARL), however, the €1.767 per month must represent what the company pays to you in salary, owner's compensation, or dividends (which can't be paid out until the company's profit is reported and taxed). In other words, the company's income must be more than double that amount per month, to sustainably pay you at that level. Therefore, your visa application, business plan, and financial projections will be subject to a lot more scrutiny than for a profession libérale application. Typically, when we assist our clients with their visa applications, we do income calculations for both autoentrepreneur and for starting each type of company, and find the gross income amount needed for the creation of a separate entity to make sense. Comparing the numbers for each type of business structure will enable you to start the right type of business, or to know when to switch from an autoentrepreneur business to a company structure.

Work

If you are opening a business in France, you will be able to work full-time for that business only. You will not be able to have any type of supplemental income or activity while your business gets off the ground.

Taxation

Because you are working in France, you should declare your worldwide earnings and pay French taxes from your date of arrival in France. You will contribute to French healthcare and retirement funds through social charges on your business income.

If you set up a French company, you will have the company's income, minus the company's expenses, equals the company's profit. One of the company's expenses will be your salary or your director's remuneration. (The name, and the rate of social taxes, is dependent on the type of company you set up.) The company's profits will be taxed, and the remainder of the profit can be reinvested in the company, or paid out to the shareholders as a dividend. In addition, your salary/director's remuneration will be considered an expense to the company, and both you and the company will pay social taxes on it. You will also pay income taxes on the amount of salary paid out directly to you, and on any dividends you receive. The amount of social charges paid on your compensation as a business owner will depend mainly on the type of business structure you choose (SARL or SAS) and is covered more in-depth, along with comparison spreadsheets, in The Complete French Business Incubator. Again, note that if you are a US person, owning part or all of a company in France will lead to additional tax filing requirements, such as form 5471, which translates your foreign balance sheet onto your US tax declaration.

We strongly discourage you from applying for this visa to create a microentreprise for a commercial activity. However, if you do have "microentrepreneur" status for a commercial activity, meaning you are buying and reselling items, you will pay 13.1% of your gross sales in social chargers. You will not be able to claim deductions or business expenses to reduce the amount of your income that is subject to social charges. Then, 29% of your gross income will be subject to income taxes. In 2024, commercial microentrepreneur activities are limited to €188.700 per year in sales. If you cumulate multiple autoentrepreneur activities, including sales of goods and services, the service portion remains limited to €77.700 in income per year and the total income is capped at €188.700.

An example of this would be a client who set up a business selling wine baskets and doing wine tours. The portion of her business related to giving the wine tours is capped at €77.700 per year in income and is subject to tax as services, thus subject to 23.1% social charges. The portion of her business related to selling wine and wine baskets is subject to the 13.1% social charges for the sale of goods, and her overall income is capped at €188.700 per year. She tracks her expenses so she knows when to begin considering creating an actual company structure.

Maintaining and Renewing Your Visa

Your initial visa will be issued for 12 months and can be renewed. If you are reasonably successful and making least SMIC at the time of your renewal, you can request a multi-year carte de séjour at your renewal appointment. The préfecture can award anywhere from 1-4 years, at their discretion.

While there is no hard-and-fast rule for how long they will give you, you should expect to receive only 1-2 years if you are not fully attaining the target of paying yourself gross minimum wage (SMIC) per month. If your income starts low when you arrive in France, but then you exceed the SMIC target by the time you renew, and you have sufficient personal assets, you may be more likely to receive a multi-year renewal.

We advise our clients to aim for €2.000 per month in gross income paid to them personally by the company for their activity and to write a letter summarizing their income and specifically requesting the 4-year card. Remember that you will need an accountant to assist you in determining the social charges that apply to the compensation the company pays you, with reporting your earnings to URSSAF, and with establishing pay slips if necessary. We go into more detail on comparing owner's compensation depending on company structure in the Finances module of the Complete French Business Incubator.

You cannot change your visa status to anything else before you have renewed your visa at least once. If you do not make money from your business, and do not have sufficient personal financial resources, your visa may not be renewed.

Establishing Residency

Assuming you stay with the same business, you will receive a one-year visa, followed by a 1-4-year carte de séjour. After you have been in France for 5 years, you will receive a 10-year residency card and you will be able to apply for naturalization.

If you have already been in France for several years prior to receiving the carte de séjour profession libérale, such as completing a degree and receiving RECE, you will be eligible to apply for residency and naturalization much sooner. Your years spent on those other visa types will count towards the 5-year minimum for residency and naturalization, as long as you do not return to your home country to get a new visa.

You can change your visa status from "Entrepreneur" to another work visa type (for example, to salarié), but your employer will have to go through the same process to hire you as they would for another foreigner. Hiring you and switching your visa status will not be easier just because you are already in France, and the change-of-status procedure can be lengthy. Furthermore, if you do change your visa status to a salaried visa type, you will not be able to continue operating your business. You would have to close your business activity when your visa status switch is finalized so you can be a full-time salaried employee.

You can also switch your visa status from entrepreneur to vie privée et familiale without issue, or you can switch to visitor if you close the company and can financially support yourself without the business income.

Family Members

An accompanying spouse or family members can get long-stay visitors visas and are subject to "regroupement familial" procedures. This is less advantageous than family members of Passeport Talent - Entrepreneur visa holders, who can get accompanying family member of passeport talent status which enables them to work.

Pros & Cons

Pros:

- You can invest any amount of money in the business's social capital, without making a €30.000 investment.
- You do not have to have an advanced degree or 5 years of professional experience in your field.

Cons:

- The company has to begin paying you at least SMIC quickly after being created, which is difficult for a new company.
- Must be renewed after 1 year and show the project's financial health.
- You have to register the company and deposit money in French accounts prior to requesting the visa, which can be difficult if you do not already have French residency.
- Project and plan is evaluated for viability by the Plateforme Interrégionale de la Main d'Oeuvre Étrangère through DREETS, meaning the approval process can be long.
- You must prove you can support yourself financially with your own personal financial resources, plus your revenue from your business. You cannot supplement your income with a salaried or other freelance job.
- Starting a company is costly and comes with legal, registration, and accounting fees, along with social charges.

Documents to Provide for Application

Note that all of the following documents should be prepared in French. Your Franceformation provides all of our documents in French to our Entrepreneur Concierge package clients.

- ✓ Valid passport issued less than 10 years ago with at least 2 blank visa pages
- ✓ Convocation for a visa appointment at consulate or VFS/TLS
- ✓ A cover letter explaining the purpose of your move
- ✓ Long-stay visa application, completed through France Visas, with Registration Receipt
- ✓ Proof of financial resources of €1.767 per month
- ✓ A detailed business and project plan
- ✓ Detailed financial projections for the first 3 years in business
- ✓ Letters of engagement from accountant, real estate agent, lawyer (where applicable)
- ✓ Letters of interest from potential clients and supporters
- ✓ Diplomas and transcripts (no requirement for a particular degree)
- ✓ Pay slips, previous business or professional licenses, or work documents demonstrating any professional experience (no minimum requirement)
- ✓ Any professional certifications or licenses required to run your particular business
- ✓ Résumé/curriculum vitae and cover letter explaining your training, experience, and any awards or professional certifications
- ✓ Company statutes
- ✓ Kbis (company registration document)
- ✓ Attestation de non-condamnation
- ✓ Attestation de nomination du gérant
- ✓ Proof of a social capital deposit in an escrow account designated for the business, for any amount (no minimum requirement)
- ✓ CERFA form for "Commerçant, Artisan, Industriel"
- ✓ Company lease agreement or company domiciliation for the business address
- ✓ Any documents related to financing, business loans, or

company bank accounts
- ✓ Approval of the company creation project from the Plateforme Interrégionale de la Main d'Oeuvre Étrangère through DREETS
- ✓ Place to stay for first few weeks upon arrival
- ✓ FBI or other police background check

Documents to Provide for Renewal
- ✓ Convocation for a renewal appointment at the local préfecture
- ✓ Titre de séjour
- ✓ Proof of completion of OFII formalities and the Contrat d'Intégration Républicaine
- ✓ Set of ANTS standard passport photos, usually from a Photomaton machine
- ✓ CERFA form provided by the information desk when you arrive at your appointment
- ✓ Proof of residence less than 3 months old (justificatif de domicile)
- ✓ Proof of health coverage and social charge payments made on your behalf
- ✓ Birth certificate with certified translation
- ✓ Proof of financial resources, including personal bank statements for French bank account or bank account in your home country accompanied by certified translation
- ✓ Up-to-date K-bis less than 3 months old
- ✓ Full set of bank statements for your French business account, notated with invoice numbers for deposited amounts
- ✓ Client contracts and full set of invoices issued for your activity since your previous renewal
- ✓ Full set of income declarations to URSSAF with proof of payment of social taxes
- ✓ Most recent French tax declaration, and tax bill if available
- ✓ Most recent business tax declaration form and tax bill, if available, along with tax status certificate for the company (P237)
- ✓ Payslips with salary info for the director, or attestation of director's remuneration, showing at least SMIC
- ✓ Contrat d'Engagement à Respecter les Principes de la République

2.5-3 Passeport Talent - Profession Artistique Visa or Renommée Nationale ou Internationale Visa

A "profession artistique" passeport talent is designed for artists and performers whose primary purpose for being in France is pursuing their artistic career. Artists in France are not tied to one specific kind of revenue or income source, but rather, to an artistic project that can have multiple income streams. The most important thing about the artistic visa is to have an overarching mission of how you will develop your artistic skills, be involved in the artistic community for your art form, and finally, how you will make money. Because the art and your participation in cultural exchange is the most important, the financial burden for this visa type is lower than for "profession libérale" or salaried worker visas.

In order to get the profession artistique visa, you'll have to put together a project plan outlining your skills and your intended participation in the arts community, and provide an overview of your planned income sources. You may potentially earn income from performing, selling art (prints/designs/licensing) or recordings, royalties from publications, or freelance income teaching your activity. It will be up to you to register these various activity types with the appropriate agencies.

In most cases, writers are not going to qualify for the "profession artistique" visa unless they have a publishing contract with a French publishing company or some type of artist-in-residence award in France. Writers should instead consider the "Profession Libérale" visa type.

The types of income possible on an Artist visa:
1. Salary from a CDD d'Usage (CDDU) for one-time performances.
2. Salary from a CDD or CDI for long-term projects like teaching in a music / art / dance school.
3. Royalties from licensing or recording of art or music or from publications.

4. Self-employment income from teaching music or art, or from selling art, or running workshops, or freelance art or writing for hire.
5. Intermittent du Spectacle - unemployment income from France Travail, to stabilize income for performing artists.

It is not possible to register a company on a Profession Artistique visa and any employment or work must be related to the overall artistic project.

In the past, clients of ours who have had this visa type have been a violinist who performed with orchestras and taught violin lessons, a model/photographer who had income from advertisements and sold individual art prints of her photography, and a stand-up comic who performed in various venues in Paris. We have had a client who is a visual artist, who sells paintings, and her wife is planning to start a gardening and horticulture business under her own Passeport Talent Famille Accompagnante visa. We've also worked with multiple painters, an actor, and a voiceover performer to obtain their visas.

If you are on a profession artistique visa, you can have several different income types, but they all must be related to your overall project proposal that you present to the consulate or the préfecture when you initially apply for this visa. It is possible to have several different *types* of income streams, but they must all be related to the same activity. The violinist or the model would not be able to have a supplementary income from teaching English or web design in case they weren't making enough money from their art. But teaching violin or photography as freelancers would be acceptable activities related to their main projects.

Because of the many different options for receiving income with this visa type, we highly encourage you to explore all of your options and to consult with a professional to understand how you can earn money and what types of registrations you'll have to do for your taxes. Each type of income (salary/freelance/royalty/etc.) has a different agency to register with and different ways to declare your income and pay taxes, so this visa type can be one of the most administratively complex to navigate.

We assist with the registration process with all of these different agencies for all of our clients in our Artist Concierge package.

Renommée Nationale ou Internationale

A variation of the "profession artistique" visa type is the "renommée nationale ou internationale," which is for famous or well-known and established people in various fields. For the purposes of this guide, we've grouped it in with the artistic visa because it requires less in terms of proving you can make money, and more in terms of proving your level of expertise in your field and having a specific project to develop while you are in France, with planned projects, events, or contracts on French territory.

However, you should be aware that "Personne de Renommée" is not solely for artists, and in many cases, the consulate sticks with granting "Profession Artistique" visas regardless of how "renowned" you may be. "Personne de Renommée" is more geared towards professional athletes and others who are professionally well-known outside of the arts.

If you're an artist who feels like you are renowned enough to qualify for the "Personne de Renommée" status, you can also specify in your cover letter that if the consulate feels like "profession artistique" is a better fit, you would like your application to be considered for that status as well. You do have to have official documents establishing reputability in your field and attesting recognition by the relevant professional sphere.

Visa Summary

On the France-Visas website, you select this visa by indicating Plans —> Talent Passport International Talents and Main Purpose of Stay —> Artistic & Cultural Profession / Talent (or Person with a National or International Reputation / Talent). The Visa Passeport Talent Profession Artistique is a 90-day visa which requires requesting a carte de séjour upon arrival through the online ANEF platform. As a Passeport Talent visa and CDS type, it does not require a medical visit or a Contrat d'Intégration Républicaine, but like other renewable work visa types, it does provide a path to residency and naturalization.

Who is it for?
- Creators and performers who would like to develop their skills while performing and working in France.
- Creatives who will have multiple sources and types of income from their professional artistic endeavours.
- NOT for technicians in the arts, who should request a regular "salarié" visa.

Since 2021, reviewers processing applications for the Passeport Talent Profession Artistique and Renommée Nationale ou Internationale visa types have been focusing on making sure applicants had contracts to exhibit and sell their work in France, or that performances and recording contracts were tied to income sources in France. In other words, we emphasize our clients' contacts and relationships in France and provided evidence that they were going to be receiving money for work in France from French and EU sources to successfully obtain their visas.

VFS/TLS Appointment Fee: Approximately €30
Visa Application Processing Fee: €99
OFII fee: €200 for a visa less than 12 months; OR
Carte de séjour fee: €225 if you receive a 90 day visa with "carte de séjour à solliciter dès l'arrivée" and receive a 4-year carte de séjour

Where to apply: In country of residence, at your local French consulate or VFS/TLS office. You can also switch to this status from another status if you have been in France for more than 1 year and already renewed your visa.

Length of visa: 12 months to 4 years, depending on if you have any sort of work contract showing longtime work. If your visa is issued for less than 12 months you must simply validate your visa within 90 days of your arrival. If your visa is for more than 12 months, within 90 days of arrival you must request a carte de séjour. Both of these procedures are online.

Renewal: Can be a multi-year visa (4 years), depending on your work contracts and financial resources.

Path to residency and naturalization:
You can receive a 10-year resident card after renewing your carte de séjour at least once for total 5 years. You can apply for naturalization by decree after 5 years of continuous residence on French soil.

Health Insurance
You will not need to show a travel insurance policy however you may choose to purchase a policy for coverage during your first few months in France.

As an artist, you have the potential to work in several different kinds of jobs, and you will pay social taxes slightly differently through each type of employment you have. For health insurance purposes, certain programs like Maison des Artistes will not allow you to register until you have achieved a certain income level, and you will have to have a supplemental source of income to enable you to pay social taxes and properly register for French healthcare. Alternatively, you can enroll with CPAM after 3 months on a valid visa through PUMA if you are not yet able to register with the government agency that oversees your activity type.

Income & Savings Requirement
The minimum monthly income for a profession artistique is much lower than for a profession libérale. It is currently set at 70% of SMIC, which works out to about €1.237 per month in gross income from your professional activities related to your project for every month you stay in France.

If you are applying for the Renommée visa you will need to prove you have financial resources of at least SMIC, which can include your cash resources or income you will be generating during your séjour in France. This amount for 2024 is €1.767 per month or €21.204 per year.

One word of caution: certain schemes for artists' income, like the Maison des Artistes/Agessa (for royalties and sale of works of art) and "intermittent du spectacle" through France Travail require minimum numbers of hours worked or amounts of income earned before you can formerly enroll. Intermittent du spectacle, for example, requires 507 hours of salaried performance work before you can sign up, and MDA similarly requires at least €8.000 in income over the course of a calendar year to enroll with them. If your primary sources of income are through royalties, the sale of artwork, or performance with groups and venues, you will need to keep track of your hours and income so that you can register properly when you meet the limit.

Work

The profession artistique and personne de renommée visas both allow you to do multiple types of work as long as they are in relation to the project you proposed. You may end up having several different types of revenue to declare, which would require registration with various government agencies. You are not restricted in the type of work contract that you accept, but rather, by its coherence with your overall project.

For example, a musician may have salaried income from being a member of a professional orchestra, intermittent du spectacle income from a France Travail scheme to compensate performers for erratic income, autoentrepreneur income from teaching music lessons as a freelancer, and royalty income through the Maison des Artistes for musical recordings. Registering for these four types of programs (the taxes and reporting requirements vary for each) would be allowed, but adding a supplemental autoentrepreneur activity like "teaching English" would be strongly discouraged.

As part of your project plan, you should consider the different types of income you will have and the different entities ("intermittent du spectacle" through France Travail, URSSAF, Maison des Artistes/Agessa) along with the possibility of freelance income as an autoentrepreneur (usually from teaching your activity.) Together, we can strategize about what types of income and opportunities you will prioritize to ensure you can meet the minimum income requirements.

Taxation

Because you are working in France, you should declare your worldwide earnings and pay French taxes from your date of arrival in

France. You will contribute to French healthcare and retirement funds through social charges on your various activities.

For each activity type, you will pay a different percentage of your income in social charges. For salaried performances (usually a one-day CDD or multi-day CDD), social charges will be withheld directly from your salary. For autoentrepreneur income through teaching, you will pay a percent of your gross income in taxes. For income through the Maison des Artistes or Agessa, they will calculate a monthly amount and send you a bill after you have enrolled with them, but your enrollment will not happen until at least the end of your first calendar year in France.

Maintaining and Renewing Your Visa
If your artistic profession is primarily short contracts and self-employment, your initial visa will likely be issued for 12 months and can be renewed. If you have a longterm contract from the start, the length of stay permitted will most likely correspond to the length of your contract up to 4 years. If you are not on a contract but are reasonably successful and making a good income at the time of your renewal, you can request a multi-year carte de séjour at your renewal appointment. The préfecture can award anywhere from 1-4 years, at their discretion.

The minimum income for renewal is €1.237 gross income per month of income related to your activity (or SMIC of €1.767 for the Renommée visa). You will have to exercise only the activity you specify in your project proposal, and count only that income towards your visa renewal.

We advise our clients to aim for €1.500-€2.000 per month in gross income for their activity and to write a letter summarizing their income and specifically requesting a multi-year card.

You cannot change your visa status to anything else before you have renewed your visa at least once. If you do not make money from your combined artistic activities, and do not have sufficient personal financial resources, your visa may not be renewed. This has never been an issue with our clients.

Establishing Residency

Assuming you stay with the same activity, you will receive a one-year visa, followed by a 1-4-year carte de séjour. After you have been in France for 5 years, you will receive a 10-year residency card and you will be able to apply for naturalization.

If you have already been in France for several years prior to receiving the carte de séjour profession artistique, such as completing a degree and receiving RECE, you will be eligible to apply for residency and naturalization much sooner. Your years spent on those other visa types will count towards the 5-year minimum for residency and naturalization, as long as you do not return to your home country to get a new visa.

You can change your visa status from "profession artistique" to another work visa type (for example, to salarié or Passeport Talent), but your employer will have to go through the same process to hire you as they would for another foreigner. Hiring you and switching your visa status will not be easier just because you are already in France, and the change-of-status procedure can be lengthy. Furthermore, if you do change your visa status to a salaried visa type, you will not be able to continue certain aspects of your artistic career, like any freelance teaching you might do or any other salaried positions you may have for performances. You would have to close your business activity when your visa status switch is finalized so you can be a full-time salaried employee.

You can also switch your visa status from profession artistique to vie privée et familiale without issue and can continue exercising all of your activities. You can also cease your activities and switch to visitor if you have the passive financial resources to support yourself.

Family Members

Accompanying family members can receive the "Passeport Talent - Famille Accompagnante" visa, giving the accompanying spouse the right to work in France.

Pros & Cons
Pros:
- You are allowed to work as a salaried worker, self-employed, or

intermittent du spectacle as long as all income sources are related to your project. (For example, a musician could receive a regular salary from a music school, teach music lessons independently, and receive salary for an "intermittent du spectacle" status, which are all different.
- Lower income barrier than other types of carte de séjour unless you have Renommée visa (approximately €1.237 per month for profession artistique rather than €1.767 or more in gross income for renommée)
- Provide proof of performances and non-paid activities to boost your application, along with paid work.
- Intermittent du spectacle status helps you to stabilize your income when you go through the uncertain feast-then-famine cycle of the arts.

Cons:
- You must support yourself *only* using income sources related to your project. (e.g. a musician can't take a part-time job at Starbucks)
- Income of only €1.237 per month might not be sufficient for your living expenses.
- Provide proof of performances and non-paid activities to boost your application, along with paid work.
- Must exceed minimum income requirements for the visa to eventually become a resident or be naturalized.

Documents to Provide for Application
- ✓ Valid passport issued less than 10 years ago with 2 blank visa pages
- ✓ Convocation for a visa appointment at consulate or VFS/TLS center
- ✓ A cover letter explaining the purpose of your move and your plan
- ✓ Long-stay visa application, completed through France Visas
- ✓ Proof of financial resources of €1.237 per month (or €1.767 depending on visa)
- ✓ A detailed project plan outlining your activities, experience, training, and sources of income, similar to a business plan for

your art.
- ✓ Letters of interest from potential clients, collaborators, and supporters, any contracts for projects to be undertaken in France for artistic projects. Ideally some of these letters or contracts will specify ways that you will earn income in France from your artistic activity and be tied to specific events physically happening in France.
- ✓ Any work contracts that you already have with employer documents (ex: Kbis and proof of payment of social charges and cerfa form n° 15617*01)
- ✓ Diplomas and transcripts
- ✓ Résumé/curriculum vitae and cover letter explaining your training, experience, and any awards
- ✓ Copies of brochures, flyers, programs, newspaper articles, press releases, publications, recordings, portfolios, etc. to demonstrate your status as a professional artist and especially to demonstrate "renowned person" status
- ✓ Choice of business structure or knowledge of the types of income reporting you will have to do
- ✓ Detailed financial projections for the first 3 years of your activity in France
- ✓ Letters from accountant, real estate agent, lawyer (where applicable)
- ✓ Place to stay for first few weeks upon arrival

Documents to Provide for CDS Request (if applicable) and Renewal Online
- ✓ Access to ANEF account
- ✓ Titre de séjour
- ✓ Set of ANTS standard passport photos (ePhotos), usually from a Photomaton machine
- ✓ Proof of residence less than 3 months old (justificatif de domicile)
- ✓ Proof of health coverage
- ✓ Birth certificate with certified translation
- ✓ Proof of financial resources, including personal bank statements for French bank account or bank account in your home country with certified translations

- ✓ Up-to-date INSEE business registration or K-bis if applicable
- ✓ Full set of bank statements for your French business account, notated for deposited amounts
- ✓ Client contracts and full set of invoices issued for your activity since your previous renewal
- ✓ Up-to-date attestation with URSSAF or Maison des Artistes / Agessa, including an "attestation de vigilance"
- ✓ Full set of income declarations to URSSAF / Maison des Artistes / Agessa with proof of payment of social taxes
- ✓ Full set of payslips for any salaried work completed (performances, teaching, etc.)
- ✓ Attestations from France Travail for any intermittent du spectacle compensation
- ✓ Programs, flyers, ticket stubs, publications, and other proof of performances, gallery showings, etc.
- ✓ Most recent French tax declaration, and tax bill if available
- ✓ Copies of future contracts for the upcoming year
- ✓ Copies of brochures, flyers, programs, newspaper articles, press releases, etc. for any events you've done in France related to your project.
- ✓ Contrat d'Engagement à Respecter les Principes de la République

2.5-4 Passeport Talent Entrepreneur or Passeport Talent Investor

These two visas are quite similar and the main distinction is the amount of money that you will invest into the French entity. For this reason, we have described the Passeport Talent Entrepreneur and the procedure for registering a company in detail, and then specified the additional requirements for the Investisseur visa type later in this section.

The Passeport Talent Entrepreneur visa is for serious self-employed business owners who would like to open larger-scale businesses in France requiring a significant cash investment. While the PT-E visa is quite similar to the "profession libérale" or "entrepreneur (commerçant, artisan, industriel)" visas, there are two requirements that set it apart: the requirement to have either a master's degree or 5 years of professional experience in the field where you will be opening the business, and the requirement for each investor to invest at least €30.000 cash in the start-up capital of the business you are forming. The start-up investment requirement precludes PT-E holders from starting autoentrepreneur businesses.

Aside from the more stringent start-up requirements and the committee-level approval of your visa application (leading to a longer processing time than profession libérale and entrepreneur (commerçant, artisan, industriel) visas), there are also several advantages to this visa type. Its initial length of up to 4 years allows business investors time to build up their business activity and begin making money before having the business's finances and salary payments to the director subject to review by the préfecture.

The initial €30.000 investment is in what's called the social capital of the company. Social capital is the financial investment from the owners, which is the total amount of liability the company has. Companies can theoretically be started with as little as €1 in social capital, and having a higher social capital amount doesn't necessarily provide any benefits. Higher social capital is primarily useful when working with larger companies in B2B industries. Investing the €30.000 creates shares, in the number and initial value you choose. While steep, this initial investment can be used for business expenses that enable the business to function, like salary to employees, purchase of equipment and materials, or payment of rent. One client earmarked her investment for the purchase of a property where she plans to host retreats. Other clients have started a digital marketing company, a yoga retreat business, a human resources consulting firm, an organic cosmetics brand, a tour company in the Loire valley, to name a few.

One main advantage of the Passeport Talent Entrepreneur is that the PT-E visa enables both the visa holder and the spouse to work. The primary visa holder must work full-time on the established business, but the accompanying spouse can choose to work another type of job. If both partners want to come to France and work, it can be advantageous to invest in this visa type to get several years at a time and to get a work visa for the accompanying spouse, who could work in the business, or pursue other employment while waiting for the business to become profitable.

There are three main considerations for the financial investment aspect of the Passeport Talent Entrepreneur visa. First, *each* investor in the company must contribute €30.000. It cannot be a joint investment. So, a couple starting a business would either have to invest €30.000 each, or the company would have to be solely owned by one person. You should discuss the implications of this ownership with a notaire, lawyer or accountant. Second, at the end of each fiscal year of your company, the company's accounts must retain at least half of the social capital. For the first year in business, your company can have a longer fiscal year, which can include the remainder of the current calendar year plus the entire following year. A company opened on January 2, 2022, can have a first fiscal year which ends on December 31, 2023. Finally, the company must actually be profitable and be paying you at least SMIC (French minimum wage) before you renew your carte de séjour. You cannot keep injecting cash and owner's loans into the company and expect your carte de séjour to be renewed.

The main challenges people have when preparing an application for the Passeport Talent Entrepreneur visa is that when they attempt the application themselves, they don't fully understand all of the accompanying documents they need to prepare to go along with their business plan, and they end up submitting a partial application. In many cases, EU banking regulations mean that potential PT-E applicants can have major difficulties opening a French bank account and making the €30.000 investment if they do not already have a valid visa for France. Working with a professional to guide you through the process can facilitate the process of developing the proper documents, ensuring the business plan and business documents accurately reflect your project and meet the requirements of the Passeport Talent.

When we work with clients on their Passeport Talent Entrepreneur applications, we work with qualified professionals in our network, including accountants, notaires, lawyers and currency transfer specialists who can facilitate the company setup process. Working with companies like us can therefore ease the process of opening accounts and making your investment through these professional connections.

Beware of anyone who advises you that you can get a Passeport Talent Entrepreneur visa without making the required minimum investment. We were previously contacted by someone from our Americans in France Facebook group who had chosen to work with an immigration law firm promising to set up a Passeport Talent Entrepreneur business for them. The attorney in question told them they only needed to invest €500, then €5.000. They made the investment, and of course the consulate then requested proof of the €30.000 investment, which they didn't want to make. Instead of admitting their error and completing the paperwork to switch their visa application to a *entrepreneur (commerçant, artisan, industriel)* visa type, the firm wanted to charge them a new fee for an entirely separate visa application.

Of course, the client was not entirely without fault either, because the €30.000 investment requirement is clearly stated on any and all documentation about the Passeport Talent Entrepreneur, and it is ultimately your responsibility to know the requirements of the visa you're applying for.

At Your Franceformation, we explain the requirements for their visa type before we sign them up as clients and provide extensive written materials describing each step in the process. We also commit to revising and resubmitting the application at no additional charge if the application is rejected the first time, which is extremely rare.

How a French Company is Created

We want to give a brief overview of how a French business is developed and registered, because parts of this process will be completed before you even submit your visa application, and the business must be registered shortly after your arrival in France.

1. We work with you to develop the business plan, assist in drafting company creation documents like company statutes through collaboration with our partners, and secure a business address for registering the company.

2. We assist with you making the €30.000 investment in the startup capital of your company through our professional contacts. You transfer the money to the financial institution using a currency transfer service.

3. The financial institution creates a Certificat de Dépôt des Fonds, which attests that you have deposited the funds required for starting the business.

4. We submit the Certificat de Dépôt des Fonds, along with the business plan and other company creation documents, to the Ministère de l'Economie, which studies your project and issues a certificate "attesting to the real and serious nature of the project" to confirm your project is well-developed and acceptable for issuing a visa.

5. You attend a visa appointment to submit your business creation documents along with the certificate of viability from the Ministry of the Economy, and the French consulate issues your visa.

6. You arrive in France and find long-term housing.

7. Once you have secured a long-term address in France, we submit the business creation documents and other important documents to the préfecture through their online portal to request your carte de séjour. When the préfecture reviews your file (usually 7 days to 7 months), your online account is created and we can submit your spouse's CDS application as well.

8. Within an amount of time known only to préfectural beings who exist beyond time and space and who cannot be bothered with such mundane trivialities, you receive an approval for your CDS request.

9. Your accountant reviews the company registration documents and registers the business. S/he can normally use the approval of your CDS to accompany the application, although sometimes the accountant or the greffe wants you to have the physical carte de séjour before registering the company.

10. INPI processes your business registration and issues a document called a Kbis, which is the birth certificate of your company and contains its important information, such as your APE code (activité principale exercée), SIREN and SIRET numbers, and business address, and identifies you as the owner and director of the company.

11. The préfecture produces your carte de séjour and notifies you by email or text that it is available for pickup. It is typically valid for 4 years, although sometimes they award 2 years initially.

12. You forward the Kbis to your bank, which finalizes the bank account setup.

13. The financial institution holding the funds deposits the social capital into your business bank account.

13. You happily and successfully operate your business in France!

Visa Summary

On the France-Visas website, you select the Passeport Talent Entrpreneur visa by indicating Plans —> Talent Passport International

Talents and Main Purpose of Stay —> Business Creator / Talent, or Investor/Talent for the Investisseur. The Visa Passeport Talent Entrepreneur and the Visa Passeport Talent Investisseur are normally 90-day visas which requires requesting a carte de séjour upon arrival through the online ANEF platform. Occasionally, the consulate issues a 12-month visa to validate within 90 days as a "VLS-TS." As a Passeport Talent visas and CDS types, they do not require a medical visit or a Contrat d'Intégration Républicaine, but like other renewable work visa types, they do provide a path to residency and naturalization.

Who is it for?

The Passeport Talent Entrepreneur visa is for serious, experienced business owners who are starting a company in France that requires a significant financial investment. Applicants should have at least a master's degree and/or 5 years of professional experience in their field, and plan to make a €30.000 investment each in the start-up capital of their company for starting their business. We don't recommend applying for a Passeport Talent Entrepreneur visa if your business doesn't require capital or have significant start-up expenses.

The Passeport Talent Investisseur visa is for investors who want to create or direct companies and make an investment of more than €300.000 in the company's capital. The €300.000 investment must represent at least 30% of the company's total capital, and the investor must be involved in running the company and plan to create or save jobs as part of running the business. For purchasing an existing company, or investing the €300.000 in a company for the Passeport Talent Investisseur, the company's accountant will work with you to infuse the money into the business account and do an "augmentation de capital" or transfer of shares. If the company already exists, depositing the money you invest will be easier.

VFS/TLS Appointment Fee: Approximately €30
  Visa Application Processing Fee: €99
  Carte de séjour fee: €225

Where to apply: In country of residence, at your local French consulate or VFS/TLS office. You can also switch to this status from another status if you have been in France for more than 1 year and already renewed your visa.

Length of carte de séjour: 2-4 years. Typically, the Talent Passeport Entrepreneur is issued for multiple years, but we have occasionally seen the case of the consulate issuing a 12-month visa to validate. This isn't necessarily a bad thing, as then there is no waiting for a carte de séjour to be issued by the préfecture before completing certain administrative procedures.

Renewal: in multi-year increments, provided that the company is paying you at least SMIC.

Change of Status to PTE

For a significant project like starting a Passeport Talent Entrepreneur business, many people like to travel to France to make business connections before their move, especially if they have to scout out business locations prior to their application. In some cases, being in France can be useful, and if you spend a year in France on a visitor visa, you can network with potential clients and set up bank accounts for your future business activity prior to applying for your visa. You will not, however, be able to register your business without obtaining the Passeport Talent Entrepreneur carte de séjour first. You will also not be able to open the bank accounts if you are simply on a tourist status, without a long-stay visa or carte de séjour.

Path to residency and naturalization:

You will have to pay yourself a salary of at least French minimum wage (SMIC) from the company and the company will have to be viable in order to renew your carte de séjour.

Normally, a 10-year card will be issued on the second renewal (following two multi-year cartes de séjour.) You can apply for naturalization by decree after 5 years of continuous residence on French soil.

Be sure to meet the requirements of financial stability before you apply for naturalization, as you will normally have to show income from your company exceeding SMIC for 3 consecutive fiscal years to be naturalized.

Health Insurance

After you register your business in France, you will be able to submit your healthcare registration documents to CPAM even if you do not plan to immediately pay yourself a salary through your company. The process for getting your finalized social security number can take several months, and it will take longer to be issued your carte vitale, but you will be able to be reimbursed for your medical expenses from the date your business is registered. Your company will make minimum monthly payments to insure you until you are earning an actual salary from the business.

Income & Savings Requirement

The income requirement for maintaining your visa is SMIC, or around €1.767 gross income per month in remuneration to you, just like for profession libérale and entrepreneur (commerçant, artisan, industriel). You will also have to have cash resources and savings for your moving expenses while you are getting your business up and running.

If you are starting an actual company, the €1.767 per month must represent what the company pays to you in salary or owners' compensation (and what we call it depends on the type of company you register). In other words, the company's income must be at least €3.000 per month, if not more, in order to pay you at that level, with no other expenses. Therefore, your visa application, business plan, and financial projections will be subject to a lot more scrutiny than for a profession libérale application.

To qualify for this visa, you must make a minimum €30.000 investment in the start-up capital of the business. You will have to block these funds in an approved bank account while you are waiting for your visa to be approved. However, once you have your visa in hand and finalize your business's registration, you will be able to use those funds for your business's expenses, including for salary payments to you. In many cases, making this investment from abroad can be one of the most difficult parts of creating a Passeport Talent Entrepreneur.

Keep in mind that you will have several years before you have to prove that your company is able to pay you, so you don't have to worry about being paid a salary immediately. Better to invest in getting the company up and running until you are able to have the company pay you.

Work

If you are opening a business in France, you will be able to work full-time for that business only. You will not be able to have any type of supplemental income or activity while your business gets off the ground.

If your spouse is coming with you, s/he can be an employee in the business, or work on the "Passeport Talent Famille Accompagnante" CDS provided.

Taxation

Because you are working in France, you should declare your worldwide earnings and pay French taxes from your date of arrival in France. You will contribute to French healthcare and retirement funds through social charges on your business income.

If you set up a French company, you will have the company's income, minus the company's expenses, equals the company's profit. One of the company's expenses will be your salary or your director's remuneration. The company's profits will be taxed, and the remainder of the profit can be reinvested in the company, or paid out to the shareholders as a dividend. In addition, your salary/director's remuneration will be considered an expense to the company, and both you and the company will pay social taxes on it. You will also pay income taxes on the amount of salary paid out directly to you, and on any dividends you receive.

Note that for US persons, owning a French entity will trigger additional US tax reporting obligations, such as filing form 5471. You will want to ensure your CPA is well-versed in US tax law for Americans overseas. We can direct you to accountants familiar with these forms and associations that assist with tax issues for Americans residing abroad.

Maintaining and Renewing Your Carte de Séjour

Normally, your initial carte de séjour will be issued for 4 years initially and can be renewed. If you are reasonably successful and making a good income at the time of your renewal, you can request a multi-year carte de séjour at your renewal appointment.

You cannot change your visa status to anything else before you have renewed your visa at least once. If you do not make money from your business, and do not have sufficient personal financial resources, your visa may not be renewed. This has never been an issue with our clients.

Establishing Residency

As the holder of a Passeport Talent visa type, you will be exempt from OFII arrival procedures. Instead, you will solicit a carte de séjour immediately upon arrival. After you have been in France for 5 years, you will receive a 10-year residency card and you will be able to apply for naturalization.

If you have already been in France for several years prior to receiving the carte de séjour Passeport Talent Entrepreneur, such as completing a degree and receiving Recherche d'Emploi Création d'Entreprise, you will be eligible to apply for residency and naturalization much sooner. Your years spent on those other visa types will count towards the 5-year minimum for residency and naturalization, as long as you do not return to your home country to get a new visa. However, you will still have to meet minimum income requirements for being naturalized by decree.

You can change your visa status from passeport talent entrepreneur to another work visa type, but your employer will have to go through the same process to hire you as they would for another foreigner. Hiring you and switching your visa status will not be easier just because you are already in France, and the change-of-status procedure can be lengthy. Furthermore, if you do change your visa status to a salaried visa type, you will not be able to continue operating your business. You would have to close your business activity when your visa status switch is finalized so you can be a full-time salaried employee.

Family Members

Accompanying family members can receive the "Passeport Talent Famille Accompagnante" visa and carte de séjour, giving the accompanying spouse the right to work in France. For example, the spouse could work as a salaried employee of the company, or have another job to help support the family as the business activity builds. The spouse's carte de séjour will be tied to the main visa holder's CDS, however, so if the business closes or the main card holder's visa is not renewed, the spouse will lose his/her status in France also.

Pros & Cons

Pros:

- You can get more than 1 year on this visa.
- You do not have to prove your business's financial success (or your income from your business project) within the first 2-3 years while your business is growing.
- If you bring your spouse, s/he gets a "Passeport Talent Famille Accompagnante" visa, which allows its holder to work.

Cons:

- Must have extensive professional experience and advanced degrees, with documentation to prove it.
- Project and plan is evaluated for viability by the Ministère de l'Economie. The plan is subject to quite a bit of scrutiny and the approval process adds additional time to the visa application process.
- You must prove you can support yourself financially with your own personal financial resources during the startup phase, plus your revenue from your business. You cannot supplement your income with a salaried or other freelance job outside of the company.
- You must have ample financial resources and each investor must make an investment of at least €30.000 in starting the business.
- It can be quite difficult to successfully obtain this visa without professional support in setting up the business and making the investment before requesting the visa.
- VFS is not familiar with this visa type and does not understand

the documents provided. The process of applying for this visa tends to be stressful because they have difficulty matching the documents provided to the checklist.

Documents to Provide for Request of Viability Certificate from the Ministry of the Economy

Note that all of the following documents should be prepared in French. Your Franceformation provides all of our documents in French to our Entrepreneur Concierge package clients.

- ✓ Proof of financial resources of €1.767 per month (equivalent to French SMIC at the time of application)
- ✓ A detailed business and project plan
- ✓ Detailed financial projections for the first 3 years in business
- ✓ Thoughtfully prepared answers to questions on Ministry of the Economy application
- ✓ Letters from accountant, real estate agent, lawyer (where applicable)
- ✓ Diplomas and transcripts, ideally showing a master's degree or higher. (If you don't have a master's, you will have to demonstrate 5 years of professional experience)
- ✓ Pay slips, previous business or professional licenses, or work documents proving at least 5 years of professional experience (this is required if you do not have at least a master's degree and can supplement your application if you do)
- ✓ Any professional certifications or licenses required to run your particular business
- ✓ Résumé/curriculum vitae and cover letter explaining your training, experience, and any awards or professional certifications
- ✓ Choice of business structure and proposed company statutes, with accompanying attestations
- ✓ Attestation de non-condamnation
- ✓ Proof of a €30.000+ deposit in an escrow account designated for the business, for each investor
- ✓ Company lease agreement for the business address
- ✓ Any documents related to financing, business loans, or company bank accounts

- ✓ If the company is already registered, a Kbis

Documents to Provide for Visa Application

All documents required for the Ministry of the Economy certificate request, plus:

- ✓ Passport issued less than 10 years ago with at least 2 blank visa pages
- ✓ Convocation for a visa appointment at consulate or VFS/TLS
- ✓ A cover letter explaining the purpose of your move
- ✓ Long-stay visa application, completed through France Visas
- ✓ Certificate of business viability from the Ministry of the Economy
- ✓ Cerfa for Commercial, Industrial, Artisanal activities
- ✓ Proof of personal French bank account (often, but not always, requested)
- ✓ Place to stay for first few weeks upon arrival (justificatif de domicile for your long-term address for CDS request in France)
- ✓ FBI or other background check

Documents to Provide for CDS Request and Renewal Online

- ✓ Access to ANEF account
- ✓ Titre de séjour (normally exempt from OFII procedures)
- ✓ Set of ANTS standard passport Ephotos, usually from a Photomaton machine
- ✓ Proof of residence less than 3 months old (justificatif de domicile)
- ✓ Proof of health coverage and social charge payments made on your behalf
- ✓ Birth certificate with certified translation
- ✓ Proof of financial resources, including personal bank statements for French bank account or bank account in your home country with certified translations
- ✓ Up-to-date Kbis less than 3 months old
- ✓ Full set of bank statements for your French business account, notated with invoice numbers for deposited amounts
- ✓ Bilan / Balance sheet for each fiscal year the company has been operating
- ✓ Full set of income declarations to URSSAF with proof of payment of social taxes
- ✓ Most recent personal French tax declaration, and tax bill if available
- ✓ Most recent business tax declaration form and tax bill, if available
- ✓ Payslips with salary info for the director, or attestation of director's remuneration, showing at least SMIC
- ✓ Signed Engagement à Respecter les Principes de la République

2.6 Family Member Visas

All of the visa types we have discussed so far have a very specific purpose: to enable you to study or work in France because it furthers your academic or professional goals. However, many people also move to France to be with a French partner, or, once in France, meet someone and start a relationship while here on another visa type, start a family, or move to France in order to accompany someone coming for a job or business opportunity.

In this section, you will learn about the different ways you can live and work in France if you are the family member of a French citizen, or, in the case of the final chapter, if you are eligible for EU citizenship through your family. Aside from having EU citizenship, the "vie privée et familiale," or private life visas, are the best and most flexible visa types for living in France. They allow you to exercise any profession that you are legally qualified to do, and they are among the most desirable because your employment is unrestricted and uncoupled from your visa.

With a family life visa, you are more attractive to employers who do not have to sponsor you, and you are not tied to a job you don't want or to a particular type of employment contract. Instead, your visa type is tied to your French family member.

There are a few reasons to be cautious. First, you have to consider that if your relationship ends within your first few years in France, of if the situation becomes unliveable (due to abuse or extreme conflict) you will struggle to find a way to remain legally and to continue to work in whatever job you have. If you do not work, your situation will be even more precarious if the relationship is in jeopardy. We always advise people to consider the relationship carefully and to look out for any red flags, and to seek another visa type if they have any doubts about the relationship.

Second, entering a relationship for the visa, a "mariage blanc" (literally, "white marriage") is illegal. While there may be a fine line between "getting married slightly before you might otherwise since it makes the visa process so much easier," and "getting married for the visa," be advised that the police can and will investigate if they suspect marriage fraud. If you've had a whirlwind relationship or marry or PACS your partner close to an expiring visa's deadline, expect some extra scrutiny. Do not suggest to anyone at the mairie's office or the préfecture that you might get married or PACSed to resolve visa issues.

Despite these caveats, the vie privée visa remains the most desirable visa type for its simplicity and its flexibility. It is also the *only* visa type for which the consulate or préfecture has to justify *not* giving it to you. A refusal, while rare, would allow you to prepare a "recours" with an attorney who understands the laws and the case law and who can help you to submit an appeal.

Here's something Allison sees far too often as an administrator of a large Facebook group: whatever your situation, PLEASE don't brag on social media about formalizing your relationship so that you can get a visa. Allison sees too many posts from happy young long-distance couples planning to get married or PACSed with the express purpose of getting the visa and moving to one country together. Taken out of context and seen by the wrong person, these posts could make it seem like you are engaging in a "mariage blanc" or formalizing your relationship with the intended result of the visa, rather than of the relationship and your future. Under scrutiny by immigration officials, this could raise a red flag that will cause you an administrative headache, cost you time and money in immigration attorney fees, and delay your ability to live and work in France. (Or in any country where you may want to establish yourselves.) The internet is not private, and even the most innocent post about a tested and true relationship can potentially cause problems. Social media posters, beware.

The final and most important thing to know before getting one of these visas, especially if you are moving with children, is that doing so **will make you a French resident and will mean that you and your children are subject to French law, and particularly, French family and inheritance law.** Moving children internationally after establishing residence here would be subject to family court rulings and the Hague

Convention. You want to ensure that you fully understand the implications of this before moving. We have witnessed unfortunate situations where a French partner convince their non-French partners to move to France with their children, only to request divorce and custody soon thereafter. We strongly encourage you to research the implications of moving your family to France, so you can hopefully avoid experiencing any similar situation yourself.

Even if you are blissfully happy in your relationship, please do your due diligence before moving in some of the following ways:

- ✓ Understand the signs of coercive control and assess your relationship for it. In many cases, overt abuse doesn't begin until the victim is in a precarious situation, such as residing in a new country, without speaking the language, with her children, and financially dependant.
- ✓ Consult independently with an attorney before agreeing to move to understand how a move to France with your partner will affect your personal situation. We recommend speaking with a French attorney specialized in international family law if you have questions about how a move would affect potential divorce or custody issues.
- ✓ Check out the English language resources on Women to Women France (https://womenforwomenfrance.org/) to understand how the legal system and family court work and how they can disadvantage immigrant non-Francophone women. Forewarned is forearmed.

	Listen to Allison's podcast interview with Sarah McGrath, founder of Women for Women France: https://www.yourfranceformation.com/2023/03/07/episode-60-sarah-mcgrath-of-women-for-women-france-helps-when-the-dream-becomes-a-nightmare/

2.6-1 Vie Privée et Familiale: Spouse of a French Citizen

Marrying a French citizen gives you the virtually incontestable right to live in France with your French spouse. In fact, if the consulate or préfecture does *not* grant your "vie privée et familiale" visa, you can ask for them to justify their refusal, and challenge it. The administation would have to present evidence that the marriage was fake or that you're a menace to the public order to refuse the request.

In order to receive a visa vie privée et familiale, or to switch your status from a different visa to VPF, you have to show that 1) you are married and 2) you have been living together for 3 months (or intend to live together upon arrival in France.) If you are married before applying for the visa, you will have to go through the OFII process and integration appointments and prove your common residence through common bills at a shared address. Technically, the police can drop by to verify you are living together or to interview you; in practice, this doesn't happen often, and usually happens only if someone suspects marriage fraud, e.g., marrying to get a visa.

Getting married can actually be a bit more complicated than it sounds.

If you are getting married in France, the non-French partner will have to provide a "certificat de coutume" from their home country's embassy or consulate. It is a document to state that you are not already married. If you are an American citizen, you can self-certify a document downloaded from the US Embassy website, since the US does not have a common registry of marriages and divorces, then have it legalized by your local mairie in France. If the mairie insists on having it notarized by the US, you can do this at the US Embassy or Consulate in Strasbourg or Marseille for $50 with an appointment, but in many cases they will accept a witnessed signature from a local official. There are also some notary services available online in the US, but be sure that this type of notarized document will be accepted before paying for the service. Similarly, if you are a national from another country, you will have to check with your country's embassy in France to determine how to obtain this document.

Other documents for marrying in France will include both of your birth certificates (less than 3 months old for a French birth certificate; less than 6 months for an official copy of a foreign birth certificate, with an apostille, translated by a court-certified translator), a proof of residence for each of you, your passport and carte de séjour, and the French partner's national ID card. After submitting your documents to the local mairie where you will be married, they will publish a *bans* advising the public of your upcoming marriage. The bans publication is the old-fashioned custom of publicizing the union to see if anyone would object. Hopefully, they won't!

When you are married in France, the mairie will issue your livret de famille and a marriage certificate on the date of your marriage, and you will be able to get subsequent copies of your marriage certificate from the mairie directly. In some cases, they can even be ordered online. You will need both of these documents for your change of status appointment or your initial visa application, and you will need to order a new copy of your marriage certificate for each renewal, as it must always be less than 3 months old. French documents like birth certificates and marriage certificates are "living," meaning that they are updated with information about death and divorce – hence why they always have to be relatively new.

If you are getting married outside of France, you will have to go through the local French consulate to register your marriage. The French partner will have to contact the French consulate for their jurisdiction to ask what documents need to be provided for the *inscription de l'acte de mariage à l'état-civil des Français à l'Etranger de Nantes*. Typically, this will be a certificat de coutume for the French spouse (who will be a foreigner where the marriage occurs), birth certificates for both of you, proof of residence, and your ID documents. You will submit these documents in advance to the French consulate for the jurisdiction where the marriage is celebrated, and then you will submit the marriage certificate after the wedding occurs. The consulate will process your paperwork and issue your livret de famille and provide a French version of the marriage certificate following its registration in Nantes with the état-civil service. You will need to order the French version of your marriage certificate for each renewal. If you are applying for a French visa immediately, the consulate should be able to issue it at the same time as they are processing your marriage certificate and producing your livret de famille.

In the event that you have already been married to a French person for several years and your partner never registered the marriage with France, s/he will have to submit the paperwork for the marriage certificate and livret de famille, along with the birth certificates for any children you may have together, before you can apply for your VPF visa. This process can take 6-8 weeks from start to finish, so plan to do it well in advance of applying for the visa.

It's rare for a VPF visa to be challenged, but if it does happen, it's usually because there is some doubt about the true nature of your relationship. If they have any suspicions that you are marrying *for* the visa, they can refuse, or require you to jump through hoops to get it. For example, if your current visa or titre de séjour is expiring and you are not able to renew it or switch to another status, or if you have previously been refused for a renewal or change of status, applying through marriage can appear suspicious. Getting PACSed, realizing you won't get a work visa through PACS, then annulling the PACS to get married will throw up HUGE red flags, so beware.

Vie Privée et Familiale Visa Summary
On the France-Visas website, you select this visa by indicating Plans —> Family or Private Settlement and Main Purpose of Stay —> Spouse of a French National. The Visa Vie Privée et Familiale is a VLS-TS which is validated online through OFII upon arrival and requires a medical visit as well as a Contrat d'Intégration Républicaine (see section 4.2) and provides a path to naturalization.

Who is it for?
Individuals married to a French citizen.

Appointment Fee: Approximately €30
Visa Application Processing Fee: $0
OFII fee: €200 to validate your visa

Carte de séjour fee: if you get married in France without a visa and manage to apply directly, you will pay €405, which corresponds to €225 for the CDS and €180 in a "régularisation" fee.

Where to apply: In country of residence, at your local French consulate or VFS/TLS office. You can also apply in France if you have been living there for at least 3 months with a French partner, or switch from another status.

Applying for a VPF carte de séjour without a visa: IF you got married *in France* as a tourist, without applying for a visa before arrival, you can apply for a carte de séjour directly at your local préfecture without returning home to get a visa. You will have to pay an additional fee of approximately €180 to regularize your situation. This process can be long and tedious, and if successful, it will take at least several months and multiple documents proving you live together in France before you can receive a récépissé and have the ability to work and do other administrative procedures. Because this process can drag on for so long, we do not recommend this option. Instead, if you marry in France, you will receive the livret de famille and marriage certificate which enable you to return to your home country and apply for the proper visa immediately, which you will validate with OFII through the ANEF platform upon your return.

Important: If you got married to a French citizen outside of France, you MUST register the marriage with the French consulate AND apply for a visa in your home country BEFORE arriving in France. If you arrive in France already married, even with the French marriage certificate and livret de famille, you will NOT be able to apply for a carte de séjour in France. The préfecture will send you back to your home country to apply for a visa before you can return.

Length of visa: 12 months

Renewal: can be renewed for a 2 year carte de séjour, then 10 years.

Path to residency and naturalization:
After the 2 year card, you can expect to receive a 10 year carte de

résident.

You can apply for naturalization by marriage after 4 years if you have lived for at least 3 years consecutively in France, or after 5 years of marriage if part of that time was spent living outside of France.

Applying for French nationality without living in France:
As the spouse of a French citizen, you can apply for French nationality after 5 years of marriage, even if you have been living outside of France for the duration of your marriage. You are required to have registered the marriage through the French embassy in your home country, and you'll have to provide TCF-ANF results or another attestation of your French language level.

As of 2020, there are no longer any age-based exemptions for French language requirements for candidates for French naturalization.

You can apply through your local French consulate by providing the necessary documents, and requests are typically processed faster for people living outside of France. Obtaining French nationality before moving to France with your French spouse will facilitate many of your administrative procedures in France, and you will not have to apply for visas or renew a carte de séjour.

Health Insurance
You will not be required to purchase a visa health insurance policy in order to obtain your visa, but we recommend doing so because it will take several months to be registered in the French healthcare system. If you find work after getting your visa, you will get access to French healthcare through your employment, or if you are already working in France at the time of the marriage, you will continue on the same healthcare plan. You have the option of using your spouse's mutuelle for complementary health coverage.

If you are not working right away, you can apply for PUMA after living in France for 3 months.

Income & Savings Requirement

There is no minimum savings requirement or minimum income requirement for the non-French spouse on a VPF visa. You will have to show that your finances are somewhat combined and that you have common bills and a common residence as part of your visa application or renewal.

If one of you has significantly more income or assets than the other, you may discuss contrats de mariage with a French notary to declare your marital regime. You can do this prior to the marriage, or change it at any time after the marriage. The default marital regime is communauté de biens réduite aux acquêts, meaning that anything acquired during the marriage is community property to be split 50-50 in the event of a divorce.

If you or your spouse has significant assets, you should discuss the options individually with two different qualified notaires to make sure you both understand the impact of your decision. Note that prenuptial agreements regarding child custody are typically not valid in France.

Work

If you are on a Vie Privée et Familiale visa, you have the right to work in any profession in France that you are legally qualified to do. You can work on a short-term or indefinite contract, part-time or full-time, or be an autoentrepreneur.

Taxation

Because you are working in France, you should declare your worldwide earnings and pay French taxes from your date of arrival in France. You will contribute to French healthcare and retirement funds through social charges on your salary. You will file French taxes jointly with your spouse.

Maintaining and Renewing Your Visa

After you have been in France for one year and have proof of still being married (recent French marriage certificate) and of living together, you will get a 2-year carte de séjour at your first renewal, provided that you have also completed all of your OFII appointment obligations and any mandatory language classes you have been assigned. At your second renewal, after 3 years of marriage, you should receive a 10-year carte de résident.

In order to renew your visa, you do not have to provide any proof of income or savings above a certain amount. You merely have to show multiple examples of sharing a common residence and common bills. This can take the form of tax bills, a shared bank account, electricity bills, rent receipts along with a common lease, or other documents.

You also must sign an attestation that you are married, living together, and are not married to other people.

Divorce and Custody
If you divorce your spouse within the first 2-3 years of being in France, you will lose the right to the carte vie privée et familiale through marriage, although you may be eligible to it based on having minor children who are French (see Section 2.6-3, Having a Minor French Child). In the case of domestic violence or abuse, having ample evidence by filing a "main courant" for each incident can help an attorney build a case for why you should be able to remain in France. (Filing a "main courant" is not the same thing as "porter plainte," – pressing charges – but it documents certain criminal activities for legal reasons.) Unless you are in danger, you do not want to abandon the marital home, because that can be held against you in divorce proceedings.

The divorce process can be long in France even if it's amicable, but being in the middle of a divorce can complicate your ability to renew your carte de séjour, especially if you cannot provide proof of living together, or your soon-to-be-ex spouse is uncooperative. If you are working and not yet on a 10-year resident card, you will want to discuss your visa situation with your attorney and attempt to change your visa status in anticipation of the divorce. In France, administrative abuse - withholding of documents necessary for your visa or carte de séjour renewal - is not recognized in law.

If you have minor children, the children will be considered residents of

France during divorce and custody proceedings, and the French spouse will be at an advantage, especially if you do not speak French well and are not working. You will not be able to leave the country with the children while the divorce is ongoing without your spouse's permission, and it is unlikely the children will be authorized to leave France permanently. It is possible you will have to stay in France until they turn 18 to be with them, or leave France and give up custody to the French parent.

Women experiencing domestic violence from a French partner or who want to leave their marriage but aren't sure of their rights can contact CIDFF (Link & details in the appendices.) The organization Women for Women France also provides a multilingual resource portal for women experiencing coercive control, financial and administrative abuse, or physical abuse to provide assistance with reporting abuse to the authorities and with navigating the French legal system for criminal, divorce, and custody issues.

Death of the French Spouse

If your French spouse dies before you receive your 10-year card, you can still maintain your residence in France. You will want to consult with an attorney for assistance to ensure the process goes smoothly while you are grieving.

Note that if you or your spouse dies while residents of France without a French will, the default French inheritance laws will apply, which are not generous to the surviving spouse. Therefore, you will want to ensure you have a French will registered with a notaire, especially if you have children (adult or minor children). It is a good idea to understand how inheritance will work prior to becoming French residents, especially if you have a blended family.

Establishing Residency

After 3 years of marriage to a French citizen, you are eligible to receive a 10-year resident card. This card is irrevocable, even if you separate or divorce.

Once you have been married for 4 years, and living in France continuously for this entire period of time, you can apply for naturalization by marriage. This process is very simple and does not require any proof of finances or a particular salary level. Once your French naturalization request has been processed, you must remain married for at least 2 years after receiving your nationality, or it could be revoked if you get divorced.

If you have not been living in France with your spouse, you can still apply for naturalization through marriage after being married for 5 years, through the French consulate or embassy where you reside with your spouse.

Pros & Cons
Pros:
- Enables you to exercise any profession and any type of work. You can be self-employed or work in a CDD or CDI.
- Does not require proof of financial resources for application.
- Processes relatively quickly once you have a livret de famille.
- One of the only visa types you can apply for directly in France, after you get married in France, but the process is long and onerous.

Cons:
- Your visa is tied to your spouse. If the marriage ends, you will have to change your visa status to remain in France. If there are ANY red flags in your relationship... beware.
- If you have children, their residence will become France. Any custody issues in the case of divorce will keep the children as residents of France, and the French parent will likely get preferential treatment even in cases of abuse. You may be stuck in France until the children turn 18.
- Getting married as another visa is expiring (and can't be renewed) can subject you to increased scrutiny, as the authorities may believe you got married to facilitate the visa process.

Documents to Provide to Get Married

Getting married in France: This list will be provided by your town hall when you get the dossier from the état-civil office in the mairie where you will be getting married. Marriages in France only take place at the town hall, and any religious ceremony can take place after the official secular ceremony. When you submit the documents, you will have to go to the mairie together and discuss your marriage with a representative from the mairie. If your level of French is not very good, the mairie may require you hire an interpreter for the event, to ensure you fully understand the proceedings.

Getting married outside of France: You will provide these documents to the French consulate for your jurisdiction if you are getting married outside of France. All documents should be provided in French or with a certified translation if they are being provided in France. They will have to be provided a certain number of days in advance of the ceremony. After the ceremony, you will provide a copy of the marriage certificate, and you will receive the French transcription of your marriage certificate along with your livret de famille 6-8 weeks later at your home address. You will need to order a new *French* copy of the marriage certificate and provide the livret de famille for many administrative procedures in France.

- ✓ French partner's French ID or passport
- ✓ French partner's birth certificate, less than 3 months old
- ✓ Non-French partner's passport and visa or carte de séjour
- ✓ Non-French partner's birth certificate, with an apostille, and a certified translation, usually less than 6 months old
- ✓ At least 2 bills demonstrating common residence
- ✓ A "certificat de coutume" for the non-French partner, an attestation stating that the partner is not already married

Documents to Provide for Visa Application
- ✓ Valid passport issued less than 10 years ago with at least 2 blank pages
- ✓ Convocation for a visa appointment at consulate or VFS/TLS

center
- ✓ Long-stay visa application, completed through France Visas
- ✓ French marriage certificate registered at the town hall, or the transcription of the foreign marriage certificate through Nantes
- ✓ Livret de famille
- ✓ Proof of common residence of at least 3 months (for marriage) or 12 months (for PACS) (bills with both names and common address), especially if applying in France
- ✓ Birth certificate with certified translation

Documents to Provide for Visa Renewal
Typically the French spouse must accompany the non-French spouse to the visa renewal appointment at the préfecture.

- ✓ Convocation for a renewal appointment at the local préfecture
- ✓ Attestation of OFII visits, and titre de séjour
- ✓ Set of ANTS standard passport photos, usually from a Photomaton machine
- ✓ CERFA form provided by the information desk when you arrive at your appointment
- ✓ Proof of residence less than 3 months old (justificatif de domicile)
- ✓ Recent French marriage certificate (less than 3 months old) from the mairie where the marriage was registered, or the transcription of a foreign marriage delivered by Nantes
- ✓ Livret de famille
- ✓ At least 2-3 kinds of proof of common residence (bills with both names and same address, like insurance policies, joint bank accounts and statements, joint tax bills, joint utility bills)
- ✓ Proof of health coverage
- ✓ Birth certificate with certified translation
- ✓ Proof of financial resources, including bank statements for French bank account or bank account in your home country with certified translations
- ✓ Work contract and payslips for any jobs you've done
- ✓ Signed Engagement à Respecter les Principes de la République

2.6-2 Vie Privée et Familiale: PACSed with a French Citizen

French people tend to think that PACS is just like marriage, but easier, and for many French couples, it is. Originally developed as alternative to same-sex marriage (officially recognized in France beginning in 2013), many heterosexual couples also opted for the simplified administrative procedures, more straightforward breakup options, and distinct tax and inheritance rules.

A PACS with someone who is not French has zero impact on successfully obtaining a visa, and as a result, we will not be addressing that situation in this book. We also can't comment on whether France would recognize a civil partnership from another country as equivalent to a PACS for the purposes of visas. If you are partnered with a French person in another country, it is possible to conclude a PACS through the French consulate. However, it is unclear whether being PACSed for a year and residing together outside of France would assist with requesting a vie privée visa directly without waiting. In most cases, these applications are evaluated subjectively on a case-by-case basis at the consulate.

However, if you are a foreigner who needs a visa to live and work in France, it's not easier unless you are already here and well-established. That is because a PACS in itself does not award foreigners any rights to residence in France, aside from as a "visitor" without the ability to work, and only if you can justify sufficient resources for the visitor visa application, or if the French partner can show income sufficient to sponsor the foreign partner. A PACS is merely a single piece of evidence of your ties to France, but other elements are necessary to successfully obtain a family visa or titre de séjour.

A PACS, or a "pacte civil de solidarité," is a type of civil union that is an "element of consideration" in your visa or carte de séjour application, but it is not sufficient for a visa on its own. If you do not already live in France, the best you could hope for by being PACSed to a French citizen is a long-stay visitor visa. Depending on your jurisdiction, you may then be entitled to request - not necessarily to receive - a carte de séjour vie privée et familiale after one year of being PACSed AND living together *in France.* Applying for a "vie privée" visa prematurely after a PACS and without meeting the minimum requirements can cause the préfecture not only to reject your application, but also to remove your existing visa if they think you were PACSing *for* the visa.

Since the first edition of *Foolproof French Visas* in 2019, the requirements for obtaining a vie privée et familiale CDS through PACS have mostly been standardized. Do not take advice from random people on the internet who have "done it before," because they were 1) not necessarily living and applying for a carte de séjour in your region, and 2) did it several years ago when the requirements were different and more loosely applied, or varied between regions and among préfectures.

Even if you come to France on a student visa (or visitor visa), PACS immediately, and are living together for the whole year of your visa, it would *still* be a better idea to renew your initial visa and wait to change your status until your second renewal (after 2 years in France.) Similarly, if you have had a series of visas, but have had to go home for a new visa more than once, the "living together" requirement will be interrupted as well. How can you have lived together for longer than 1 year if your current visa has only been for 8 months? You will have to provide extensive documentation to show the continuity of your PACS and your cohabitation.

For example, a student who gets PACSed and lives with her partner for 6 months, then goes back to the US to get the FACC "jeune professionnel" visa for 18 months will arrive at the end of the FACC program with 2 years of common residence and PACS - but will still be unable to change her visa status to VPF due to restrictions on changing from the FACC visa type to something else. The resets in her visa situation and cohabitation, due to leaving France multiple times, means the PACS may not be sufficient for a vie privée visa. She'll likely have to return to France a third time with a visitor visa and only THEN be able to switch to VPF status. It is a long wait on that visa to be able to work, and if your relationship ends (getting un-PACSed is relatively straightforward), you are in France without any way to support yourself.

The most important thing to understand is that the préfecture will have reasons to suspect if you have gotten a PACS specifically to get a carte de séjour. If you are on another kind of visa that is expiring and cannot be renewed (a student or travailleur temporaire or "jeune professionnel" visa, for example), a PACS as your visa draws to a close with the intent of switching will look *very* suspicious. If they catch it, they can and they will give you a hard time, and they can refuse your visa or give you a non-working visa.

The worst thing you can do if you get PACSed and start to have problems with the préfecture is to get married. Getting married will NOT solve your problems; it will make them a thousand times worse. To the préfecture, that would practically *prove* you merely wanted the PACS for visa purposes, and that you are trying to circumvent their scrutiny of your PACS to get the visa more easily. Many couples have ended up with expensive and complex legal messes because they got denied a VPF visa for their PACS and then immediately got married to rectify the situation. If you get rejected for a visa based on PACS and want help fixing it, we would recommend going straight to your nearest immigration attorney. (Not us - we are not qualified to give you the legal advice you'd need to sort this one out. We are happy to provide a recommendation if necessary.)

As professionals, we would ONLY recommend a PACS if you are already on a multi-year carte de séjour linked to your employment or if you already have a 10-year resident card or French nationality, and not if you would prefer to have a "vie privée et familiale" visa.

Visa Summary

There is no one particular visa type when you first obtain a PACS, and you will likely remain on your previous visa status or get a long-stay visitor visa for the first year of your PACS.

If you are in an established partnership and living together, in France, with proof of common residence, for at least one year, you may be eligible for a Vie Privée et Familiale visa. It largely depends on your individual situation. How long you have been PACSed with your partner and how long you have been living together, and how long you have been in France prior to the PACS are taken into account when applying for the VPF visa.

If you are thinking about getting a PACS to make getting a visa easier, DON'T.

Health Insurance
If you arrive in France on a visitor visa to live with your PACS partner, you will have a catastrophic healthcare policy consistent with the visitor visa requirements, and can apply to PUMA after 3 months. Otherwise, if you are employed, your healthcare will be covered through your job or self-employment contributions.

Income & Savings Requirement
The income and savings requirement depends greatly on whether you are applying for a "visitor" visa, or you are switching statuses and requesting a "vie privée et familiale" status. In either case, you will have to show that your finances are somewhat combined and that you have common bills and a common residence as part of your visa application or renewal.

PACS rules related to shared assets differ significantly from rules for married couples, so you should consult a notaire to see how you will both be affected.

Work
Once you have a Vie Privée et Familiale visa, you will have the right to work in any profession in France that you are legally qualified to do. You can work on a short-term or indefinite contract, part-time or full-time, or be an autoentrepreneur.

If you are on a visitor visa, the visitor restrictions will apply, and you will not be able to work until you have been PACSed and living together long enough to switch to VPF status. You can also apply for or remain on any other type of visa in this book (except salaré en mission, work holiday, or jeune professionnel) and retain the work rights associated with that visa type until you are eligible for VPF.

Taxation
Because you are working in France, you should declare your worldwide earnings and pay French taxes from your date of arrival in France. You will contribute to French healthcare and retirement funds through social charges on your salary. You will file French taxes jointly with your partner.

Maintaining and Renewing Your Visa
In order to renew your VPF status, you will have to provide ongoing proof of living together and remaining PACSed. You will also have to show your work situation, income and savings, and other ties to France. If your partnership ends, and you de-PACS, you will have to change your visa status to something else. You should begin the change of status process *before* the un-PACSing is begun.

Establishing Residency
After 12 months of PACS to a French citizen, you are eligible to request a vie privée et familiale card at your visa renewal. After living in France for 5 years, you can request a 10-year resident card, which will allow you to stay in France, regardless of any changes to your relationship status.

Once you have been living in France for 5 years, you can apply for naturalization by decree. It is not the same as applying through marriage, and will require proof of all of your various activities and ties to France, including your work and financial stability.

Pros & Cons
Pros:
- ✓ Once you have received VPF status, it enables you to exercise any profession and any type of work. You can be self-employed or work in a CDD or CDI.
- ✓ A PACS is not as legally complex as marriage, and can be easily dissolved. In certain (non-visa-related) circumstances, it could be more advantageous to be PACSed than married.

Cons:
- ✓ Your visa is tied to your partner. If the partnership ends, you will have to change your visa status to remain in France. If there are ANY red flags in your relationship... beware.
- ✓ PACS is NOT sufficient on its own to get a Vie Privée visa. It will only allow you to get a "long séjour visiteur" visa if you are applying from your home country. You may be able to get a VPF if you are currently in France on another type of visa and have additional positive elements in your file.
- ✓ Getting PACSed as another visa is expiring (and can't be renewed) can subject you to increased scrutiny, as the authorities may believe you got married or PACSed to facilitate the visa process.
- ✓ Unlike with marriage, if your relationship ends in separation or the death of your partner you will not be able to keep your visa status.

Documents to Provide for Change of Status Application
(An initial visa application will always be a "visitor" or other visa type)

- ✓ Convocation for in-person appointment for a change of status
- ✓ CERFA form provided
- ✓ PACS certificate less than 3 months old
- ✓ Proof of common residence of at least 12 months (multiple bills for different utilities with both names and common address, over the 12-month period), especially if applying in France
- ✓ Birth certificate with certified translation
- ✓ Other proof of relationship and living together
- ✓ Proof of other ties to France (job, studies, pay slips, tax documents, etc.)
- ✓ Signed "Engagement à Respecter les Principes de la République"

2.6-3 Vie Privée et Familiale: Parent of a Minor French Child

If a minor child with French nationality resides regularly in France for more than 1 year, the non-French parent has the right to a Vie Privée et Familiale carte de séjour. This means that a non-EU citizen cannot immediately obtain a visa with full work rights by moving their French national child to France but would be eligible for VPF after residing in France with that child for more than 12 months. Children have French nationality if one of their parents is French when they are born, or they can obtain nationality if one of their parents is naturalized while they are minors.

Note that France does not have birthright (*jus solis*) citizenship, so children born in France are not automatically French citizens unless they would otherwise be stateless, or unless they are born to a non-French parent who was also born on French soil (*double droit du sol*). They must live and be educated in France until early adolescence and can request French naturalization as teenagers. The requests made by these children are granted virtually automatically, unless there is a criminal record. The 2024 immigration law did impact the process and we will begin to see the results of those changes in the coming years.

A French child can provide a path to residency in France in several ways. If a couple living in France divorces (or the French partner passes), the non-French parent would retain his or her right to a VPF visa and therefore full work authorization through the child, as long as they continue to provide financial support to the child. Even if the couple were never married, the non-French partner could arrive with a different kind of visa (student, visitor, salarié, etc.), and could switch visa statuses to VPF after 1 year of providing financial support.

If the parent of a French child lived outside of France, and wanted to move to France, the situation would be a bit more complicated. First, the parents should ensure that the child's birth was properly registered with the local French consulate and the list of Étrangers Établis Hors de

France in Nantes. This process ensures that the child's French nationality is recorded, and the child can get a French passport and ID card, and the parents can get a livret de famille.

If the parents (non-French partner and French partner) are married, the non-French partner would arrive with the visa for being the spouse of a French citizen. If the parents are not married, or if the non-French parent wants to move to France with the French child but not the French parent, the non-French parent would have to apply for another visa type, live in France for one year to establish the child's residence, and then switch to VPF. This will only work until the child turns 18. If the child has her own French passport, she won't need a visa. However, the non-French parent should ensure she has sole legal custody or permission from the other parent to move the child to France, to avoid international custody battles and to facilitate various administrative procedures in France.

Note that this information applies to the non-French parent when:
1. both parents are the biological parents of the child;
2. the biological mother gave birth to the child (surrogacy is complicated as it is illegal in France);
3. the child's French biological parent recognizes and partially supports the child;
4. the non-French parent provides regular financial support to the child; and
5. both parents wish to move to the child to France.

The parents do not have to be currently or previously married or PACSed for these conditions to be met. The French parent can also be deceased provided that s/he recognized the child. If the French parent did not recognize the child prior to death, you may have to consult an attorney to determine whether it's possible to have the child's French nationality recognized.

In situations where there is an adoption, a birth using donor eggs or sperm, or use of a surrogate, the visa documentation becomes more complex and may also require an attorney.

Visa Summary
On the France-Visas website, you select this visa by indicating Plans —> Family or Private Settlement and Main Purpose of Stay —> Parent of French Minor Child.

You will be issued a visitor visa for the first year if your child has not been regularly residing in France. After the first year, you can request a Visa Vie Privée et Familiale from your préfecture, which will require a Contrat d'Intégration Républicaine (see section 4.2) and provides a path to naturalization.

If the child was living in France with their French parent, and you as the non-French parent can prove you've been providing support from outside of France for more than one year, you can potentially request a Vie Privée from the start.

Who is it for?
A non-French adult who has a biological child with French nationality passed by the other parent, and who has contributed financially to supporting the child.

VFS/TLS Appointment Fee: Approximately €30
Visa Application Processing Fee: None.
OFII fee: €200

Where to apply: You need to already be living in France with your French minor child, so you must apply for a change of status directly in France at your local préfecture.

Length of visa: 12 months
Renewal: eligible for multi-year visa upon renewal.

Path to residency and naturalization:
After 5 years, you can expect to receive a 10 year carte de résident. You can also apply for naturalization if you meet the financial requirements.

Health Insurance
A travel health plan is not required to apply for or to renew a VPF visa. The parent of a French child will get access to French healthcare based

on employment, or through PUMA (Protection Universelle MAladie).

Income & Savings Requirement

There is no minimum income or savings requirement for the VPF visa based on having minor children residing in France, but you must demonstrate that you contribute to your French child's support by providing receipts for essential items like rent where the child lives, grocery bills, clothing receipts, or child support if you are separated from the child's other parent.

Work

The vie privée et familiale status allows you to do any type work you are legally authorized to do (unregulated professions). You can work on a short-term or indefinite contract, part-time or full-time, or be an autoentrepreneur.

Taxation

Because you are working in France, you should declare your worldwide earnings and pay French taxes from your date of arrival in France. You will contribute to French healthcare and retirement funds through social charges on your salary.

Maintaining and Renewing Your Visa

You can continue to renew a vie privée visa based on minor children in France indefinitely, as long as you can prove you support them and maintain a relationship with them.

Establishing Residency

Once you have been in France for 5 years continuously, you are eligible to receive a 10-year resident card and to apply for naturalization as a French citizen.

Pros & Cons

Pros:
- Allows you to live and work in France while supporting your minor child who has French nationality.
- Allows you to remain in France and continue to work if you have (a) French child(ren) who reside(s) in France for more than a

year. This means that if you are divorced or separated from your spouse, or were never married but share a biological child, you can maintain a vie privée visa status.
- Renewable indefinitely and can lead to residency and naturalization.
- Allows you to do any type of work (CDD, CDI, part-time, full-time, owning a business) with no minimum income requirement.

Cons:
- Requires having a child. Don't have a child specifically for visa obtention purposes.
- The child's French parent has to recognize the child and register the child's birth through the consulate abroad or be on the birth certificate and livret de famille.
- Having a French child isn't sufficient for getting the visa with the ability to work. If you do not already live in France with the child, you would have to get another visa type and live in France for 1 year or more before you could transition to VPF status, and financially support the child during that year.
- Once the child's residence is established in France, any custody hearings would go through the French court system until the child is an adult or you get permission to change the child's country of residence. This could be a disadvantage to you if you do not have French nationality, as the courts may favour the French parent.
- Similarly, your ability to travel outside of France or move away from France with your French child may be affected by court decisions or custody agreements.

Documents to Provide for Visa Application if your child is not yet living in France
See the Visitor list or determine if you are eligible for a different visa type.

Documents to Provide for Change of Status Application
or for Initial Visa Application if your child is already residing regularly with their French parent in France and you are financially supporting them.
- ✓ Convocation for appointment at préfecture

- ✓ CERFA from the préfecture
- ✓ Marriage & divorce certificate(s) if previously married to French partner, or PACS documentation (all less than 3 months old); death certificate if the child's French parent is deceased
- ✓ Livret de famille
- ✓ Child's birth certificate, from the French mairie if born in France, or the Etat-Civil service in Nantes if born and declared abroad
- ✓ Child's proof of French nationality (passport or ID card)
- ✓ Proof of custody of the minor child and proof of providing support to minor French child
- ✓ Child's proof of living in France: school or childcare enrollment, attestations from friends and family members, medical records... this can be more difficult if the child is not yet school age.
- ✓ Financial resources & French bank statements, or foreign bank statements with translation
- ✓ Birth certificate with certified translation
- ✓ Signed "Contrat d'Engagement à Respecter les Principes de la République"

Documents to Provide for Visa Renewal
- ✓ Convocation for a renewal appointment at the local préfecture
- ✓ Attestation of OFII visit, and titre de séjour
- ✓ Set of ANTS standard passport photos, usually from a Photomaton machine
- ✓ CERFA form provided by the information desk when you arrive at your appointment
- ✓ Proof of residence less than 3 months old (justificatif de domicile)
- ✓ Recent French marriage certificate (less than 3 months old) if married
- ✓ Livret de famille
- ✓ Child's birth certificate, from the French mairie if born in France, or the Etat-Civil service in Nantes if born and declared abroad
- ✓ At least 2-3 kinds of proof of supporting child, proof of school enrollment or childcare in France

- ✓ Proof of health coverage
- ✓ Birth certificate with certified translation
- ✓ Proof of financial resources, including bank statements for French bank account or bank account in your home country with translations
- ✓ Work contract and payslips for any jobs you've done

2.6-4 Vie Privée et Familiale Visa: Spouse of an EU citizen (not French)

Marrying an EU citizen does not give you the same rights as marrying a French citizen does. The spouse of a French citizen can very easily get a vie privée et familiale visa from any French consulate, arrive in France, and begin to integrate and work almost immediately (See section 2.6-1). Conversely, the spouse of an EU citizen exists in a legal grey area, because they are only allowed to freely live and work in France if the EU spouse is exercising his or her EU treaty rights. That means that the non-EU spouse cannot apply for a visa, but instead applies directly for a 5-year carte de séjour in France. This can only happen once the EU spouse proves that she has been living and working in France and either has resources amounting to or is currently earning at least French minimum wage (SMIC).

Note that this same procedure can apply to the parent of an EU citizen child regularly residing in France, in which case the non-EU citizen parent will need to be supporting the child, and the family will need to have private health coverage until they get on the French healthcare system.

To establish yourself in France as the spouse of an EU citizen and receive a carte de séjour, you must request a carte de séjour for the non-EU spouse within 90 days of arrival. Since 2023, this procedure is done online through the ANEF website, and you do not need to have a visa or foreigner ID number in order to do so.

You will need to provide your marriage certificate (and a certified translation), birth certificates, passports, proof of residence in France, proof of common residence with bills in both names, and documents related to your EU spouse's work in France. You will also need to establish a long-term address and begin setting up your residence. The EU spouse can do any type of work, part-time, full-time, CDD or CDI, or freelance – but in order to "sponsor" you, s/he MUST be earning at least SMIC per month for at least 3 months. Alternatively, you may show combined bank accounts with the cash equivalent of SMIC each per month for 1 year.

It will take some time to secure an appointment and to receive official paperwork and documentation that enables you to legally reside in France and cross borders. During this time, you should not plan to travel, and you will not be able to work. However, you are not subject to the 90/180 day Schengen travel rules and you should not leave the Schengen space while waiting for your appointment or for your CDS to be approved. Upon submitting your file through ANEF, you will get a receipt, but you will not get the right to work in France until your application is approved by the préfecture and your official titre de séjour for "membre de famille EU" is issued, which means you may be in France without proper work papers for up to 4-5 months after you submit your application. During this time, you will not be able to submit an application to the French healthcare system, so you will need to be covered by a private insurance policy.

In some cases, if the EU citizen will not be working right away, or if the non-EU spouse wants to be able to work immediately, we would advise you to ensure you have sufficient financial resources to apply as the "spouse of an EU citizen" as soon as possible after arriving, and try to secure a long-term lease so you can request the carte de séjour as soon as possible.

Visa Summary
There is no visa to request unless you require a short-stay visa to travel as a tourist into France. Upon arrival in France, you request a carte de séjour from the local préfecture within 90 days. This carte de séjour does not require a medical visit or CIR per European regulations, but can lead to residency and naturalization if you live and work in France for more than 5 years.

Who is it for?
Individuals married to EU citizen (other than French nationality)

VFS/TLS Appointment Fee: Not needed if you are not required to have a short-stay visa to travel to France.
Visa Application Processing Fee: None.

OFII fee: Not applicable.

Carte de séjour fee: €50 in timbre fiscaux to submit the application

Where to apply: Directly in France through the ANEF website. You cannot apply before arriving in France.

Length of carte de séjour: 1-5 years, depending on the whims of the préfecture. It appears that spouses of inactive or retired EU citizens are first being issued a 1-year card by many préfectures.

Renewal: yes, for 1-5 years

Path to residency and naturalization:
After the 5 year card, you can expect to receive a 10 year carte de résident if you can demonstrate that you have maintained residence in France. You can apply for naturalization by decree after 5 years if you meet the financial stability criteria and speak French at a B1 level.

Health Insurance
For the first several months, you will not be in France on a valid visa, and as a result, you will not be able to work, and you will not be able to apply to PUMA. Therefore, you should get a private policy or catastrophic coverage while you are waiting for your carte de séjour to be issued.

Income & Savings Requirement
In order to be legally "exercising their treaty rights" and eligible to living in France full-time with their family, the EU citizen spouse will have to be working and earning at least SMIC for at least 3 months, or have sufficient financial resources to support your family without working. They will need to continue doing so at least until the non-EU spouse gets their carte de séjour. After the non-EU spouse obtains the ability to work, it is possible for the non-EU spouse to become the primary breadwinner for the family, with the EU spouse earning less or choosing not to work outside the home.

Work
As the non-EU partner, there is no family visa that you can apply for that would enable you to work upon arrival in France. If you are *only* going to

France based on your spouse's EU citizenship, you will have to wait a minimum of several months before you are able to legally work.

If you want to work, and you can meet the eligibility requirements for another visa type, it may be advisable to apply for a different kind of French visa for one year. You will be restricted to whatever work can be done on that visa, but you will still be able to work while waiting for your spouse to establish French residency and provide the necessary documents for getting your EU spouse carte de séjour.

Once you have received your carte de séjour based on your partner's EU citizenship, you will have the right to work in any profession in France that you are legally qualified to do. You can work on a short-term or indefinite contract, part-time or full-time, or be an autoentrepreneur.

While you are waiting for your carte de séjour, you are not allowed to work in France, nor can you work remotely for a foreign employer from France. Once you have received your carte de séjour, you can set up a proper business structure in France if you would like to work remotely or as a contractor.

Taxation
Because you are residing in France, you should declare your worldwide earnings and pay French taxes from your date of arrival in France, even if you are not technically working and do not have an official residency permit. Your spouse working in France and "sponsoring" you establishes your family's tax residency in France. You will file French taxes jointly with your spouse.

Once you begin to work, you will pay social charges from your salary or business income.

Maintaining and Renewing Your Visa
Normally, as the spouse of an EU citizen, you will get a multiple-year carte de séjour within 4-5 months of your arrival. You will also be exempt from the OFII integration process. However, while France previously issued 5-year cards automatically to all spouses of EU citizens, they have recently begun issuing cards for "up to 5 years," at the discretion

of the préfecture. If your EU spouse is not working when you request the card, you may receive a 1-year card and have to renew at the end of the first year.

Establishing Residency
The date your carte de séjour is approved will be your official start date in France for obtaining residency. At the end of your 5-year carte de séjour, you can be issued a 10-year resident permit. After 5 years of continuous presence in France, working, and declaring and paying taxes, you can apply for naturalization as a French citizen "by decree."

Pros & Cons
Pros:
- Enables you to exercise any profession and any type of work. You can be self-employed or work in a CDD or CDI.

Cons:
- Residence for the EU spouse is established by having a permanent place of residence, proven by a long term lease or utility bills.
- Your CDS is tied to your spouse. If the marriage ends, you will have to change your visa status to remain in France. If there are ANY red flags in your relationship… beware. Any children also become residents of France.
- Requires EU spouse to be exercising their treaty rights: meaning they can fully support themselves with their own financial resources, or they are working full time for at least 3 months while earning at least minimum wage.
- You will not be entitled to any benefits (CAF, RSA) in France for the first 5 years.
- It will take at least 4-5 months of being in France before the non-French spouse receives a carte de séjour and is able to work.

Documents to Provide for Application in France
- ✓ Valid passport
- ✓ Set of ANTS standard ePhotos, usually from a Photomaton machine
- ✓ Marriage certificate less than 3 months old, with certified

translation into French. If the EU country transcribes the marriage and issues their own marriage certificate, provide the EU version.
- ✓ Livret de famille if your EU country issues them
- ✓ Proof of common residence, such as multiple bills with both names and common address
- ✓ Birth certificate from EU country for EU citizen partner
- ✓ Birth certificate with certified translation for non-EU partner
- ✓ Proof of financial stability or of the EU partner working for at least 3 months at SMIC. This could include a work contract and payslips, business registration, or bank statements showing financial resources
- ✓ Proof of temporary health coverage for you and EU spouse
- ✓ €50 in fiscal stamps for application submission

Documents to Provide for Renewal
- ✓ Set of ANTS standard passport photos, usually from a Photomaton machine
- ✓ CERFA form provided by the information desk when you arrive at your appointment
- ✓ Marriage certificate less than 3 months old, with certified translation into French
- ✓ Livret de famille if applicable)
- ✓ Proof of common residence of at least 6 months (for marriage), such as multiple bills with both names and common address
- ✓ Proof of financial stability or of the EU partner working for at least 3 months at SMIC
- ✓ Proof of health coverage for you and EU spouse (can be CPAM Attestation des droits)
- ✓ Birth certificate from EU country for EU citizen partner
- ✓ Birth certificate with certified translation for non-EU partner
- ✓ Bank statements for French bank account and other jointly held bank account.

2.6-5 Passeport Talent Famille Accompagnante Visa: Spouse of a Passeport Talent Visa Holder

The spouse (married - not PACSed) of someone who holds a Passeport Talent visa type can accompany the working spouse and live in France with the ability to work, for the duration of the spouse's valid Passeport Talent.

Visa Summary
On the France-Visas website, you select this visa by indicating Plans —> Family or Private Settlement and Main Purpose of Stay —> Accompanying Family of Beneficiary of the Talent Passport. The Visa Passeport Talent Famille Accompagnante is a 90-day visa which requires requesting a carte de séjour upon arrival through the online ANEF platform. As a Passeport Talent visa and CDS type, it does not require a medical visit or a Contrat d'Intégration Républicaine, but like other renewable work visa types, it does provide a path to residency and naturalization.

Who is it for?
Married to the holder of one of the Passeport Talent visa types previously outlined in this book.

VFS/TLS Appointment Fee: Approximately €30
Visa Application Processing Fee: €99
Carte de séjour fee: €225

Where to apply: In country of residence, at your local French consulate or VFS/TLS office. You can also apply in France if you have been living there for at least 3 months with a French partner, or if you are switching from another status.

Length of carte de séjour: the same length as the visa of the primary passeport talent holder

Renewal: yes, for 1-5 years, unless your spouse has a Salarié en Mission carte de séjour.

Path to residency and naturalization:
After the 5 year card, you can expect to receive a 10 year carte de résident. You can apply for naturalization by decree after 5 years if the primary Passeport Talent's status allows you to do so, provided that you meet the financial stability criteria and speak French at a B1 level.

Health Insurance
You will be able to register for PUMA after living in France for 90 days on a valid visa and receiving your carte de séjour, regardless of whether or not you begin to work within that time period. You can get a private policy or catastrophic coverage while you are waiting for your carte de séjour to be issued.

Income & Savings Requirement
For any of the Passeport Talent visa types attached to a salaried position, there is no particular income or savings requirement, because the salary is sufficient to cover a couple's expenses, even with children.

For self-employment Passeport Talent types, including Profession Artistique, Personne de Renommée, Entrepreneur, or Investisseur, you as a couple will have to prove joint financial resources about 25% higher than for a single person to ensure you can cover two people's expenses.

Work
If you are on a Passeport Talent - Famille Accompagnante visa, you have the right to work in any profession in France that you are legally qualified to do. You can work on a short-term or indefinite contract, part-time or full-time, or be an autoentrepreneur. You can also work as a "conjoint collaborateur" in a business owned by your spouse. You cannot register your own company.

Taxation
Because you are working in France, you should declare your worldwide earnings and pay French taxes from your date of arrival in France. You will contribute to French healthcare and retirement funds through

social charges on your salary. You will file French taxes jointly with your spouse.

Maintaining and Renewing Your Visa

To renew your visa, you have to prove that you are still married and that your spouse maintains his or her passeport talent status.

In order to renew your visa, you do not have to provide any proof of income or savings above a certain amount. You merely have to show multiple examples of sharing a common residence and common bills. This can take the form of tax bills, a shared bank account, electricity bills or attestations, rent receipts along with a common lease, or other documents.

Pros & Cons

Pros:
- Enables you to exercise any profession and any type of work. You can be self-employed or work in a CDD or CDI.

Cons:
- Many préfectures do not process the "Famille Accompagnante" titre de séjour very quickly. The main Passeport Talent visa holder's carte de séjour has to be approved before the spouse can apply, and the waiting period for approval can be long. If the préfecture approves the main applicant's carte de séjour close to the expiration date, the spouse can have difficulty creating an ANEF account and submitting an application.
- Your visa is tied to your spouse's carte de séjour. If the marriage ends or your spouse's eligibility for the carte de séjour category ends, you will have to change your visa status to remain in France.

Documents to Provide for Visa Application
- ✓ Valid passport issued less than 10 years ago with at least 2 blank pages
- ✓ Convocation for a visa appointment at consulate or VFS/TLS center

- ✓ Long-stay visa application, completed through France Visas
- ✓ Marriage certificate
- ✓ Joint bank statements
- ✓ Proof of address in France upon arrival
- ✓ Submission along with the spouse's application for a Passeport Talent category visa

Documents to Provide for Online Carte de Séjour Application
- ✓ Copy of spouse's passport
- ✓ Spouse's ANEF account details, AGDREF number, and approval for the main Talent Passport application
- ✓ Marriage certificate
- ✓ Set of ePhotos
- ✓ Justificatif de domicile with both spouses' names on the bills
- ✓ Signed Contrat d'Engagement à Respecter les Principes de la République

Documents to Provide for Visa Renewal
- ✓ Access to online ANEF account
- ✓ Titre de séjour
- ✓ Valid titre de séjour in one of the Passeport Talent categories for your spouse
- ✓ Set of ANTS standard passport ePhotos, usually from a Photomaton machine
- ✓ Proof of residence less than 3 months old (justificatif de domicile)
- ✓ Marriage certificate with certified translation
- ✓ At least 2-3 kinds of proof of common residence (bills with both names and same address, like insurance policies, joint bank accounts and statements, joint tax bills, joint utility bills)
- ✓ Birth certificate
- ✓ Proof of financial resources, including bank statements for French bank account or bank account in your home country with translations

2.6-6 Vie Privée et Familiale Visa: Regroupement Familial for Spouse of a CDS Holder

The spouse (married - not PACSed) of someone who has held a work visa type for France for longer than 18 months can request a "vie privée et familiale" carte de séjour to continue to live in France, while gaining the ability to work, for the duration of the spouse's valid CDS. For example, if a couple arrives in France and one spouse has a "salarié" carte de séjour while the other maintains a "visitor" carte de séjour, the "visitor" spouse can request "regroupement familial sur place" to receive a "vie privée et familiale" carte de séjour after 18 months of residence in France.

The regroupement familial procedure can also work in other scenarios:
If a >18m CDS holder or long-term resident holder marries someone without a visa, or with a temporary CDS such as visitor or student.
For children who arrive in France as minors with their parents and wish to remain in France long-term, so that they can begin working at age 18 and have a better status than student.

If someone residing and working in France for more than 18 months came to France alone (leaving a family in their home country) or marries someone living outside of France, they can begin the process of regroupement familial to request visas for the spouse and children living outside of France.

Note that "regroupement familial" only applies to the spouse and minor children, and does not apply to parents or elderly family members. Elderly family members would be able to apply for visitor status if they have sufficient financial resources or the family can support them.

Visa Summary
On the France-Visas website, you select this visa by indicating Plans —> Family or Private Settlement and Main Purpose of Stay —> Family Reunion. As a VLS-TS visa and CDS type, it requires a medical visit and

a Contrat d'Intégration Républicaine, and like other renewable work and family visa types, it does provide a path to residency and naturalization.

Who is it for?
Married to the holder of one of the VLS-TS work visa types previously outlined in this book. The main CDS holder must have lived and worked in France for more than 18 months.

Carte de séjour fee: €225

Where to apply: In France, after your spouse has held a work visa with a "Contrat d'Intégration Républicaine" for 18 months or more, while earning the minimum financial resources based on family size

Length of carte de séjour: 1 year

Renewal: yes, for 1-4 years in a multiyear card, with multiple years possible if you have completed all of your OFII requirements

Path to residency and naturalization:
After the 5 year card, you can expect to receive a 10 year carte de résident. You can apply for naturalization by decree after 5 years of continuous residence, provided that you meet the financial stability criteria and speak French at a B1 level.

Health Insurance
Arriving spouse: If the working spouse moved to France first and has lived there for more than 18 months, the arriving spouse will need a temporary healthcare policy for one year that meets the minimum requirements in order to receive the visa for France.

Regroupement familial sur place when both spouses already live in France: You will be able to register for PUMA after living in France for 90 days on a valid visa, so you should already be covered by French healthcare by the time you begin this procedure.

Income & Savings Requirement
The main CDS holder's salary or business income must be equal to at

least SMIC to be considered sufficient to cover a couple's expenses. The income requirement increases slightly for additional family members.

Work

If you are on a Vie Privée et Familiale visa, you have the right to work in any profession in France that you are legally qualified to do. You can work on a short-term or indefinite contract, part-time or full-time, or be an autoentrepreneur. You can also work as a "conjoint collaborateur" in a business owned by your spouse. You can register your own company.

Taxation

Because you are working in France, you should declare your worldwide earnings and pay French taxes from your date of arrival in France. You will contribute to French healthcare and retirement funds through social charges on your salary. You will file French taxes jointly with your spouse.

Maintaining and Renewing Your Visa

To renew your visa, you have to prove that you are still married and that your spouse maintains his or her work CDS status.

In order to renew your visa, you do not have to provide any proof of income or savings above a certain amount. You merely have to show multiple examples of sharing a common residence and common bills. This can take the form of tax bills, a shared bank account, electricity bills or attestations, rent receipts along with a common lease, or other documents.

Pros & Cons

Pros:
- Enables you to exercise any profession and any type of work. You can be self-employed or work in a CDD or CDI.
- You can also request regroupement familial for children over 16 so they can receive a titre de séjour and have the right to work.

Cons:
- Your CDS is tied to your spouse's carte de séjour. If the marriage ends or your spouse's eligibility for the carte de séjour category ends, you will have to change your visa status to remain in France.

Documents to Provide for Regroupement Familial Submission
- ✓ Convocation for a visa appointment at your local préfecture
- ✓ Titre de séjour
- ✓ Valid titre de séjour for your spouse who has been present in France more than 18 months
- ✓ For your spouse's work activity: contract and pay slips, or business registration and business income documents
- ✓ CERFA 11436*05 (https://www.formulaires.service-public.fr/gf/cerfa_11436.do)
- ✓ Set of ANTS standard passport ePhotos, usually from a Photomaton machine
- ✓ Proof of residence less than 3 months old (justificatif de domicile)
- ✓ Birth certificate with certified translation
- ✓ Marriage certificate with certified translation
- ✓ Children's birth certificates, with certified translations
- ✓ At least 2-3 kinds of proof of common residence (bills with both names and same address, like insurance policies, joint bank accounts and statements, joint tax bills, joint utility bills)
- ✓ Proof of financial resources, including bank statements for French bank account or bank account in your home country
- ✓ Joint French income tax declaration for years you have been in France
- ✓ Children's residency in France: certificats de scolarité
- ✓ Signed Contrat d'Engagement à Respecter les Principes de la République

2.7 Getting EU Citizenship through Ancestry

Certain countries allow descendants of their citizens to claim citizenship and get the coveted EU passport. Grandchildren of Irish citizens, for example, can file for Irish citizenship in some cases, and Spain and Italy also make it relatively easy for their citizens' family members to get citizenship, as long as the citizens did not renounce their citizenship. If you have recent ancestry from one of those countries, you can check with family members and your local consulate for that country to see how to complete the process.

The only downside is that sometimes tracking down the necessary paperwork for the citizenship application and waiting for it to be processed can take several months or even more than a year. France's bureaucracy (which takes 18 months to process a naturalization application) is nothing compared to Italy's bureaucracy, so you could wait quite a long time for everything to go through, and you may have to hire a local attorney to facilitate or expedite the processing.

While you wait for your citizenship to go through, nothing is preventing you from applying for another one of these visa types to allow you to live in France while you await your EU citizenship approval. We worked with several clients this year who were in the process of obtaining EU citizenship through another country, and who moved to France with one of the visa types in this book while waiting for their citizenship applications to be validated. You will, of course, have to meet the same conditions as other visa applicants, but it means you can arrive in France earlier, without waiting for your citizenship application to be processed. Once the citizenship is approved and you can get your EU identity card and passport, you will no longer have to renew your French visa or carte de séjour. You can simply stay and forget that whole administrative nightmare was ever required of you, while using your new EU passport for official ID.

Having EU citizenship does not require you to apply for a visa in your home country, so you can simply show up in France and get a job or start your business. You will have nothing to prove to anyone. However, in order to reside legally in France as the citizen of another EU country, you should be exercising your EU treaty rights to live, study, and work. "Exercising your EU treaty rights" means that you can't show up in France and start mooching off of the French government. There are waiting periods to get benefits like health insurance and CAF, and you either have to have enough money to support yourself or be gainfully employed (or self-employed). There are no visa barriers to getting a job, but technically speaking, if you are just hanging around in France, aren't doing anything productive, you won't be eligible for training programs, unemployment, or any other type of financial support from France. You will also need to maintain private healthcare coverage until you can be covered in the French system, and if you have never been covered by the healthcare system in your EU country of citizenship, the process will take a long time.

Visa Summary

Who is it for?
EU citizen through family ancestry

VFS/TLS Appointment Fee: Not needed
Visa Application Processing Fee: None.
OFII fee: Not applicable.
Carte de séjour fee: None.

Where to apply: Directly through the country where you can get citizenship.

Length of visa: No visa required.

Renewal: None.

Path to residency and naturalization:
You can apply for French naturalization by decree after 5 years if you meet the financial stability criteria and speak French at a B1 level. Be sure to verify whether your country of nationality enables you to receive dual citizenship with another EU country, as not all countries allow this.

Health Insurance
The process for getting healthcare is slightly different for EU nationals who have never been on French healthcare or enrolled in another EU country's universal healthcare system. You will have to apply for PUMA (Protection Universelle Maladie) after establishing residence in France for more than 3 months, and you must prove your arrival dates and provide proof of your residence by providing multiple months worth of rent receipts, lease agreement, or utility bills to the CPAM office. Otherwise, you can get healthcare through your school if you are a student, through setting up a business or microentreprise, or through salaried employment.

You will need to maintain private healthcare until you are enrolled in the French healthcare system, which can take time if you are not working or registering a business. You will need to provide proof of healthcare coverage particularly if you are requesting a carte de séjour for your non-EU citizen spouse. If you are not working, the French healthcare system has to communicate with your EU country of citizenship about your status in their healthcare system, and these applications can take significant time to process.

Income & Savings Requirement
As an EU citizen, you will not need a minimum income or specific amount of financial resources in order to live and work in France. However, during the first 5 years of your residency will be greatly restricted from receiving French social benefits (CAF, RSA, etc.), unless you are contributing to the system through work and social contributions.

Work
You can do any type of work that you are legally authorized to do in France. You can work in a CDD or CDI contract, register a business, be a microentrepreneur, work part-time or full-time, or study.

If you work remotely, you still need to set up a French structure to pay French social charges and income taxes, whether that's through a portage salarial or French company you set up. Reread the section on Working Remotely in Part 1 to review your options, and schedule a consultation with Your Franceformation to discuss the best setup for your situation.

If you leave your job through being fired, filing a rupture conventionnelle, or being laid off for economic reasons, you can receive unemployment benefits and seek another job without worrying about visa issues. Even if you are fired "for cause" or resign from your job, you can remain in France, though you will not receive unemployment.

Taxation

Because you are living in France, you should declare your worldwide earnings and pay French taxes from your date of arrival in France. You will contribute to French healthcare and retirement funds through social charges on your earnings. If you are working remotely or self-employed, you still need to set up a French structure to enable you to pay social charges and taxes in France.

In the beginning, it will be important to keep records of your travel dates and time spent in France to determine whether or not you are a French tax resident, since you will not have a visa to attest to your residency and arrival date.

Establishing Residency

Unlike those who arrive in France with valid visas and who have an official arrival date recorded by OFII, you will not be tracked as a foreigner when you come and go from the EU. While this makes your life easier administratively in some ways, it means you will want to keep very good records of your time spent living in France to prove how long you have lived here. As EU entry points are no longer systematically stamping passports, you should keep records of your travels and ensure you establish a long-term address with bills and rent receipts in your name as soon as you can upon arriving in France. Determining your residency will be more reliant on bills in your name, such as utility bills showing consumption (of electricity, water, etc.).

This is especially important if you are an EU citizen who has never actually resided in another EU country. If you're an American or British citizen of Irish descent, but you've never had Irish healthcare, an Irish driver's license, or Irish insurance, you're still going to have to go through certain administrative procedures regarding exchanging your US state / UK driver's license (which you would not have to do with an Irish license unless you committed driving infractions.)

Finally, if you do plan to remain in France long-term and eventually want to consider applying for French naturalization (which still has its benefits even with another EU passport), you'll want extensive documentation on how long you've lived in France, how you've integrated, and the jobs you've done and taxes you've paid, for your citizenship application. French citizenship or extensive documentation of your residency would also be an insurance plan if France or your country of citizenship ever decides to leave the EU.

Part 3: Applying for a French Visa

Once you've figured out what type of visa you need and approximately when you would like to arrive in France, you can begin gathering the documents you'll need for your application.

For each visa type in this book, we have provided a suggested list of documents, which you should use along with the France-Visas "official" list to assemble your application. Be advised that both of these lists are guidelines and are the *minimum* that should be provided to have your visa or carte de séjour approved; having a complete application per these lists does not guarantee approval. Be sure to compare the list we've provided in this book to the official list you receive from France-Visas or from the préfecture, and to have everything on both lists for your appointment. Better to go to your appointment over-prepared than to be turned away for not having a surprise document you didn't know you needed!

We also want to stress the importance of ensuring that every document we instruct you to provide is included in your application when it is submitted to the visa processing center. We have had multiple occasions of VFS/TLS agents not taking all of the documents our clients have wanted to include with their applications, usually because they weren't familiar with that particular visa type. Since omitting essential information from your application can cause the consulate to email you for additional documents and otherwise delay your visa's approval, you want to be crystal-clear before the appointment of what they need to take, and insist they include it even if they don't think it's necessary. It is your job to advocate for your visa application and to know what to submit, even if the VFS/TLS agent's confusion (especially regarding rarer business visa types) is stressful.

You can understand the importance of ensuring your application is assembled correctly and you are confident before going into the appointment.

3.1 Accompanying Family Members

Generally speaking, visa applicants have the right to bring their minor children (except for programs like TAPIF, FACC, and Work Holiday, which specifically prohibit it) and their spouses to France with them as long as they meet the requirements for financial support. However, these accompanying family members will usually have the status of "visitor" unless they meet the criteria for other visa types and submit successful applications. Bringing other family members (elderly parents, siblings, adult children) will require the applicant to apply for a long stay "visitor" visa. The family members already residing in France can provide proof that they will provide financial support, lodging, and assistance with the application, but it will not help the applicant to get another status.

One of the advantages of the Passeport Talent visas is that the spouse of a Passeport Talent visa holder will get a "Passeport Talent - famille accompagnante" visa and subsequent carte de séjour, which enables the accompanying spouse to work. In some ways, this visa is even more advantageous than the initial Passeport Talent CDS, because it is similar to a Vie Privée et Familiale visa in that the family member is entitled to work, in any profession and with any status. This means that the Passeport Talent CDS holder is restricted in employment to the original CDS (tied to the salaried position, or business, or artistic proposal), but the spouse is not, and can choose to find a CDD or CDI, work part time or full time, or become an autoentrepreneur.

In most other cases, the spouse will get a visitor visa, which does not allow them to work. They will have to provide all of the same documents for the visitor visa and show proof of financial resources in order to get their own visa. Financial resources can include the spouse's projected salary or income upon arrival, based on a work contract or business plan.

Bringing Minor Children

If you would like to bring your minor children to France, the process is very easy. You will have to apply for visas for them individually at the

VFS/TLS office or local French consulate, which involves making appointments for them along with you, and paying the appointment fee.

Note that moving your minor children to France with a visa will make them French legal residents for purposes of family law, in accordance with the Convention of the Hague. This is the case even if both parents are not French and if only one parent has legal residence in France. Furthermore, being the parent of a minor foreign child living in France does not necessarily entitle you to a residence permit or work authorization in France. French courts are also unlikely to respect prenuptial agreements from abroad that cover child custody. Be aware of the potential issues for divorce and custody, and the potential restrictions on leaving French territory with your child, in case your relationship deteriorates after a move.

Minor children under 12 do not have to appear at the visa appointment in person; however, you are still required to make an appointment for each child and pay the appointment and application fee. Children 12-17 will have to be fingerprinted with parental authorization as part of the process.

Minor children require their own complete visa applications, including a long-stay visa form completed on the France-Visas website. There is a section on the long-stay visa application form where you can list family members who are accompanying you, as well as their relationship to you. Each form should list all family members in the group. They will also require their own passport, where a visa will be affixed, passport photos, and a birth certificate. If your children are young, you should ideally have these photos taken at a studio with an experienced photographer, so they are not rejected.

If you are not relocating with a partner, you will have to show some kind of document showing full legal custody and decision-making ability for the children. This could take the form of the other parent's death certificate, if deceased, notarized authorization from the non-custodial parent, documents showing the other parent has relinquished their rights, or court documents showing full custody.

Upon arrival in France, children do not participate in the OFII validation process or obtain a carte de séjour. Instead, minor children whose habitual residence is France can obtain a document called a DCEM, Document de Circulation pour Étranger Mineur, from the local préfecture. It serves as a residency permit for minors and can be presented to Schengen controls to demonstrate the child's ability to live in France. This process has been moved online and is covered in the *Fast Track to France* program.

Work
While it is extremely rare for minors to work in France due to strict labor laws, it is technically possible. If both parents are foreigners, the child's work authorization will depend on the parent's ability to work. For example, there are often casting calls for child models or for bilingual children to appear in films or television. The child would only be able to participate in such a project if at least one of the parents has the ability to work in France. If the parents have visitor visas, the child would not be eligible to work on the project.

Documents to Provide for Minor Child's Visa Application
- ✓ Long-stay visa application for each child, listing all family members traveling together
- ✓ Passport
- ✓ Passport photos
- ✓ Birth certificate
- ✓ Livret de famille, if applicable (French families)
- ✓ Proof of custody or notarized authorization from the second parent (if not relocating and applying together)
- ✓ Proof of parents' financial resources
- ✓ Copy of the proof of housing or an attestation that mentions the child(ren) by name
- ✓ Proof of pre-enrollment in school for children aged 3-16
- ✓ Visa insurance policy for children with "minor visitor" status

DCEM - Document de Circulation de l'Etranger Mineur
Minors residing in France do not need to go through the OFII procedure until they are 18; however, they do need a document called a DCEM to show that they live in France. You will need this document when you

travel with your children back and forth to the EU, to present along with your passports and cartes de séjour to prove that they reside with you.

The DCEM application is completed online after arriving in France through the Etrangers en France website and is valid for 5 years. You will have to apply individually for each child after completing the OFII procedure and provide documents such as your passport, visa or carte de séjour, proof of residence, proof the child is steadily living in France (such as proof of school enrollment), the child's birth certificate and ePhotos. The application is done through the parent's ANEF account and proof of parental authority will be required. This could be in the form of a marriage certificate or if you are a singe parent, they will require proof of sole custody such as a divorce agreement or death certificate. Certain documents are required to be officially translated into French. Once the application has been approved, the prefecture will send you a notification with an appointment to pick up the DCEM. The parent who applied and the child must both be present to pick up card and pay the 50€ fee with an excise stamp.

Documents to Provide for DCEM
- ✓ DCEM application through ANEF website
- ✓ Parent's passport, visa, & OFII validation
- ✓ Proof of residence
- ✓ Child's passport
- ✓ ePhotos
- ✓ Child's birth certificate with translation
- ✓ Livret de famille, if applicable (French families)
- ✓ Proof of custody or authorization from the second parent or marriage certificate, with translation
- ✓ Document such as school enrollment

When Children Turn 18
Children who are born in France to foreign parents are only French at birth if one of their parents was also born in France (double droit du sol), even if that parent does not have French nationality. Children who are born in France to foreign parents who were not born in France are not French at birth (there is no *jus solis* citizenship) but can obtain French nationality automatically before age 18 simply by requesting it. Minor

children whose parent(s) obtain French nationality are automatically naturalized along with their parent(s). Only one parent has to be a French citizen for the children to become French.

For minor children residing in France with foreign parents, but who were not born in France, they will have to complete the OFII process and obtain their own titres de séjour once they turn 18. If they have been living in France and completely educated in France since they were small children, they can have the opportunity to apply for naturalization as teenagers. It is VERY IMPORTANT that they complete immigration and naturalization procedures at the right time, and before leaving France to pursue education abroad. Otherwise, they risk having to start the immigration procedures from the beginning as adults, as if they had never resided in France.

In a particularly unfortunate situation, we were once contacted by a young man who had been living with his family in France since he was a young child. Upon reaching adulthood, his mother and sister had been naturalized, but he had not. During his studies, he became depressed, failed a year, and dropped out of his program, losing his "student" visa status and his legal status in France while he recovered.

As your children approach adulthood, it is important that they understand what they will need to do if they want to continue to live in France, to avoid a situation where they lose their status and have to leave a home they've known since childhood.

Procedures and requirements regarding children and their legal status differ depending on whether or not the child came to France before or after the age of 13 as well as how long the parents have been here when the child turns 18. In addition, things like whether or not the child would like to work are all variables to be taken into account when accessing your child's future situation.

Bringing Adult Children
If you have children over age 18 who would like to accompany you to France, they will have to apply for their own visa individually, and they

will be treated as adults. They will need to choose the visa type from this book that is most appropriate and meet all of the requirements on their own. Of course, if you are providing financial support, they could get a student or visitor visa relatively easily, especially if you attest that they will be living with you. Likewise, they will have to complete their own administrative procedures upon arrival, including the OFII visit and renewals at the préfecture.

Regroupement Familial

People who have been residing regularly in France for more than 18 months can bring immediate family members over to live with them through a process called Regroupement Familial. There are a few different ways in which this procedure might be appropriate, such as if a person living in France married someone back in their home country and wanted to bring over their spouse. Two foreign nationals from different countries who reside and marry in France can also go through a process called "regroupement familial sur place," which ensures that they maintain the right to remain in France together.

Note that only spouses and children are eligible for regroupement familial, and other adult family members (dependent parents, adult siblings) are not able to benefit from this procedure.

This process is started through the mairie (town hall) where the French resident lives, and requires a few administrative procedures, such as ensuring the resident's apartment is big enough for the arriving family members and that their financial resources are sufficient to support the whole family.

3.2 Tips for Using the France-Visas Website

In order to apply for your French visa, you will have to create a long-stay visa application on the France Visas website. After creating an account, you can create several visa applications for all members of your family, indicating the visa type you are applying for, the length of your stay, and all personal information about you and your family.

The form is relatively straightforward, but there are a few glitches and tricks you should be aware of. First, you should know that you have to select the visa application center where you will submit your application at the beginning of the process, and once you have selected a center, you cannot change it on the application. The application becomes coded for submission at that office (Los Angeles, London, Madrid...) and will only be electronically submitted to that center. If you ultimately decide to apply in a different center, you will have to re-do your visa forms in a new group.

Create a separate long-stay visa application for each member of your party, including children. The applications can however all belong to the same group.

Do not indicate a stay shorter than 12 months if you would like a renewable visa. In fact, explicitly state in your cover letter that you are planning on staying for 2 years or longer, so you receive a renewable visa. Some consulates will default to nonrenewable visas if you do not specify.

Indicate all accompanying members of your family on each form. For relatives in France, only list immediate family (parents, children, or siblings) who already live in France. You do not need to list everyone you know or random cousins. You are limited in the number of people you can add as family members, so indicate the people who are most closely related to you.

Do not list a partner as family if you are not engaged or planning to be married within the next few months. If they suspect you are going to

France to marry someone, they will want you to apply for a "vie privée" visa or for "regroupement familial."

It is perfectly acceptable to have accommodations in a rented apartment, AirBnb, or friend's home for a month or so while you look for permanent accommodation. List the name and address of where you will be staying, along with "rented apartment" or the name of the person who will be hosting you. You no longer have to provide proof of accommodation for any particular length of time unless you have very low financial resources. If you are a student, you'll need to provide accommodation for the first 90 days.

When identifying your arrival date in France, your arrival date, the start date of your temporary housing reservation, and your visa health insurance policy should all align and begin on the same date.

Your "financial resources" and "means of support" should be solely related to your reason for going to France. If you are going for a salaried position, it should be "income from this job and savings." If you are going for a self-employment visa, it should be "freelance income and personal savings." If you are going for a student visa, it should be "personal savings and support from parents/financial guarantor." You should not indicate a job as a source of income unless you are specifically seeking a visa for that job.

Reference one specific location as where you intend to stay. If you intend to travel within France or move around, you should still have a home base with a rented address that will remain constant throughout your time in France. Otherwise, you will be considered a tourist and will get a temporary stay visa.

Create your long-stay visa application here: https://france-visas.gouv.fr. We have a complete tutorial for the visa form and creating application groups and appointments in *Fast Track to France*, and we handle this for our clients.

3.3 Where to Apply for Your Visa

You must apply for a French visa in your country of residence or a country where you hold citizenship. If you live in a country where you hold a valid residence permit, you can apply at the local French consulate with proof of your local visa or carte de séjour equivalent (not a tourist visa). For example, an American citizen living in the UK can apply for a French visa at the French consulate in London, assuming she has a UK residency permit. An Indian citizen living in the US can apply for a visa in the US by showing a valid green card (but usually not a student visa). An American residing in Portugal with a Portugese residence permit can apply for a French visa at the consulate in Madrid, which processes visa applications for Spain and Portugal.

VFS Global is contracted to provide visa application services to the French government in Australia, Canada, the United States, and most of West Africa.

TLS Contact is contracted to provide visa application services in the UK and part of the Middle East.

In a couple of countries, like Algeria, both VFS and TLS are present, and your application city determines which company you use.

Unfortunately, you must use the third-party contractor company that accepts visa applications in your country, and there is no way to avoid them. You can only apply for a French visa directly at the French consulate in countries where the consulate continues to process long-stay visa applications, like New Zealand.

As of 2019, Americans can apply for a French visa at any VFS Global office in the US. Likewise, Canadians can apply for a French visa at any VFS Global office in Canada. Applicants are no longer restricted to submitting their applications at the consulate or VFS/TLS office for their region.

HOWEVER, the very first box you complete on your France-Visas website application is where your visa application will be submitted. Selecting a particular visa center will in turn generate a barcode for your visa application which links it to that visa center. When your application is submitted online, it will *only* be submitted to the visa application center you originally selected. Once you select a visa center for your application, you cannot change it.

This means that if you complete your visa application online for Boston, and then decide to make an appointment in New York, you will have to re-do your online visa application and select the correct visa center in order for the information to be received by the correct center prior to your appointment. We are repeating this information because we know of people who have made appointments at different centers and shown up to have to complete the forms again outside the office on their phones, because the forms were not properly coded for the visa center at which they were applying.

Normally, you will have to begin the France-Visas application process and generate those barcodes, then use the application barcode number to make your VFS/TLS appointment on their website.

Links for finding your local VFS/TLSGlobal / French visa application center and for creating your online French visa application are located in the Useful Links annex.

3.4 Making a Visa Appointment

Once you have completed the visa form on the France Visas website, you will need to make the visa appointment through the VFS Global, TLS Contact, or consulate website prior to finalizing the form. France Visas and VFS/TLS will not contact you to schedule an appointment; you will have to do that part yourself.

You can find the appointment page for your country by finding your local consulate or VFS/TLS office using the link in the appendix, and clicking on the "Prendre Rendez-Vous" button next to your local consulate's contact information. You will have to prepare the visa forms in advance and use the form's barcode on the VFS/TLS website when making the appointment. You can only make one appointment per visa application barcode and per passport number.

You can use this account to make multiple visa appointments together for people in your group, and paying the fee online. If you create a group with multiple people, you can schedule all of your appointments together. Each member of the group traveling must have their own appointment, pay the fee, and be physically present at the time of submission.

Children under 12 do not need to be physically present, but will have to have an appointment made on their behalf, and their parent has to submit a complete application with their passport and an ID photo, along with the other supporting documents.

The fee for an appointment is around €30, paid in your local currency. You will have to pay this fee online in order to schedule the appointment. This does not include the visa processing fee of €99, which is charged by the French consulate and is indicated separately for each visa type in its checklist. You will pay the visa processing fee at the visa appointment, for each applicant. Spouses of French citizens do not pay the visa appointment or application fee.

You can reschedule your visa appointment one time, up to 2 days prior to the appointment, and choose a new time at no additional charge, in the same visa center. If you try to reschedule less than 2 days in advance, or if you do not show up to your scheduled appointment, you will have to pay the fee again to schedule a new appointment. If you want to change visa centers, you will need to cancel the appointment and schedule a new appointment for a different center with a new application code. You can refer to VFS & TLS's respective refund policies regarding the changes.

While VFS & TLS used to release a full month's worth of appointments at a time mid-month, they now release appointments more regularly. During peak times (late spring and summer), it can be difficult to find an available appointment time, so start the reservation process early and check back regularly. Each visa center sets its own appointment times and releases new appointment slots on their own schedule.

Some centers also offer "prime time" appointments for an additional per-applicant fee, for appointments scheduled outside of normal business hours. While business hours are considered 9-4:30 or 5 PM, the prime time appointments are as early as 8 am and as late as 7 in some cases. A fee will be applied for each applicant.

Beginning in 2024, VFS has opened additional visa centers in other cities during the peak summer months when they process many student visas for the fall semester. These centers can process all types of visa applications, but charge an additional "convenience fee" per appointment. The extra fee, currently $100 per applicant, can seem high, it can still be less expensive than paying to travel to another city for a visa appointment, so do the math for your family.

VFS claims to offer a "visa at your doorstep" service, but when we have investigated this, it is primarily for universities with large groups of students who are in close proximity to a VFS center. It is not feasible to plan to use this service for submitting your visa application because the conditions were very restrictive.

3.5 Timeline for Applying

You can apply for your visa up to 90 days before you wish to arrive in France, or 90 days before the start of your program if you are enrolling in studies. If you have to travel to another city for your visa appointment, you should consider when it will be most convenient for you to travel.

Depending on the consulate or VFS/TLS office, new visa appointments become available 4-6 weeks in advance. At certain times of year (like winter), you will have no trouble finding an appointment for the next day or the next week. From April through September, however, it can be more difficult to secure an application, and you should plan to do so as soon as the appointments for that month open up. This can involve creating an account and logging in regularly to check appointment availability.

If you are scheduling your visa appointment in advance, remember to factor in things like waiting for Campus France approval (3 weeks for standard, 3 business days for rushed) or DREETS approval of work contracts (8 weeks) plus a bit of a buffer between when you submit all of your information and when you can expect to receive your approval for your visa appointment.

Once you apply, it typically takes 10-14 calendar days to receive your passport back with your visa stamped inside. However, we recommend that you apply for your visa at least 1 month before your scheduled departure to ensure you get your passports back on time. This is especially important if there are French holidays or holidays in the country where you are applying, or if you are applying during the spring and summer when more applications are processed.

Student visas: you will have to wait 3 weeks for Campus France validation, OR pay a rush fee for confirmation within 3 business days. If you are *already* accepted to a university or language program, you can complete the CF process and visa application documents in 7-10 days. If you are applying to a language program and are *not* accepted yet, expect it to take 14-21 days from choosing a language school and paying the deposit to submitting Campus France documents. If you are applying to university programs, the application process will take around 3 months. Note that not all countries' applicants have to pass through Campus France and Études en France first.

Visitor and family visas: Allow 7-10 days to gather documents and prepare the application, but these can be done relatively quickly.

Profession libérale visas: Allow 6-8 weeks to write the business plan and do the financial projections. A good rule of thumb is that the more easily you can get letters of support and collaboration, and the clearer your idea for your business, the faster you're going to be able to put everything together. If you are starting a brand-new business, you may want to take up to 12 weeks so you can hammer out all of the details of your business. Most Profession Libérale business plans do not require pre-approval as of the publishing of the 2024-2025 edition, but this seems to be in the works. You should leave 2-3 weeks for processing time after your visa appointment.

Passeport Talent Entrepreneur visa: These are approved by the Ministry of the Economy, require a €30.000 investment in starting a French business, and are subject to A LOT more scrutiny than the "profession libérale" visa in terms of viability and planning. Therefore, expect these applications to take about 12-16 weeks to prepare before submitting the business plan to the Ministry of the Economy for approval. After submission to the MOE, you can typically expect a response within 2 weeks, and you need to build in a buffer in case your initial submission is rejected and you need to improve it. We do not advise going to the visa appointment until you have received the business plan's approval from the Ministry of the Economy. Actual visa processing time once the application has been submitted can vary widely. In the US, you can expect it to take around 3 weeks, while in Canada, it can take 30-45 days.

3.6 The Visa Application Submission Process

Once you have made a visa appointment with your local French consulate or VFS Global / TLS Contact office, you will physically go to your appointment and bring the required documents. It is not an interview, and you will not be asked too many questions about your visa application aside from your travel dates and the purpose of your trip.

Prior to your visa appointment, you must finalize and submit all of your visa forms on the France-Visas website, which sends them electronically to the visa center you have selected. If you make an appointment at a different visa center than the one you initially selected on your forms, you will need to redo a new set of visa forms with the correct centers. Forms submitted electronically to the VFS center in Chicago, for example, cannot be retrieved by VFS in San Francisco.

Note that this is the only aspect of the visa application submitted electronically, and you must bring the printed, finalized forms with physical copies of all accompanying documents to your appointment in person. Bring originals (for agents to review if necessary) and photocopies for them to include with your file.

At the designated appointment time, the VFS/TLS official will take your official document checklist, provided with your visa application form from the France Visas website, and ask you to submit each document on the list, along with your photos and your passport.

The VFS/TLS offices typically have a photo booth as well as photocopying and printing services available for an additional fee. They may also have prepaid mailing envelopes available for returning your passport(s). Please fill out the mailing envelope with the address where you will be staying prior to your departure for France. The address where your passport is mailed does not have to match the address on your application.

The VFS/TLS official you interact with has no authority over your application and can't answer any questions about what the French embassy will approve. Their job is to verify that you submit what's on the list, that your insurance policy meets certain requirements, and to pass it on to the French embassy, which makes the decision and issues the visa. So, it is fairly useless to argue with the VFS/TLS official about the list or to try to get information from them about your submission.

The VFS/TLS office will not take any original documents, but will only take photocopies. They will, however, take your original passport, and take your fingerprints. Each day, VFS/TLS sends all of the visa applications overnight to the French Embassy in Washington, DC, where they are processed before being returned to you by tracked FedEx envelope, which you can pay for. Similarly, VFS/TLS offices in Canada send completed files to the French consulate in Ottawa, and TLS Contact in the UK sends all files to the French consulate in London for processing.

Assembling Your Documents

It is helpful to organize documents using paperclips or sticky flags so individual sets of documents can be easily handed over, but you should not use staples, and you shouldn't use a binder with tabs or anything fancy. The visa application center will take all of the papers out of whatever you bind it in, and it will just take extra time at your appointment.

You should ensure that you have a separate copy of the relevant paperwork for each visa applicant. For example, a set of 5 applications for a family should include 5 copies of the temporary housing reservation and the parents' bank statements, one set with each individual visa application. Each person's visa application form will have a document checklist, which needs to be accompanied by a copy all of the relevant documents. Yes, it kills extra trees, and no, there's nothing you can do differently.

Estimated Visa Processing Time

The French Embassy advises that visa processing can take 21 business days after your visa appointment. For this reason, we typically advise our clients to schedule their visa appointment at least 1 month before their intended departure date.

The vast majority of our clients get their passports returned to them, with visas inside, within 7-10 calendar days of their appointment. It may take a couple of extra days if the embassy emails you to request additional documents (see below). Longer processing times usually only happen if you are not a citizen of the country where you are applying (e.g. a Mexican citizen with a green card residing and applying in the US) or if you are from a list of countries that requires additional processing checks.

Requesting Additional Information
Check your email regularly, as the French embassy may contact you by email for additional information about your application. For example, if your visa insurance policy doesn't meet the requirements or the policy's proof of coverage letter doesn't provide all of the required information, they will contact you to ask for an updated policy. Similarly, if they feel that you don't have enough money in your bank account, they will ask for additional proof of funds.

You should send the documents they request as soon as possible, as failing to provide the information within 7 calendar days could lead to your visa application being returned, unprocessed. For business visa applications, they are a bit more lenient with waiting for documents if they request something unexpected. If you can't provide a document right away, we recommend replying to the consulate to let them know when they can expect to receive it.

We tell our clients that if the French embassy asks for additional information, it's a good sign. It means they are ready to issue the visa on the merits of your application, and the information you send back will enable them to check their last box and to proceed with finalizing your visa. After all, if they were going to reject you, they would have just sent back your passport with a rejection letter.

What if you don't have a document?
To make the process as painless and as smooth as possible, you should go to your appointment prepared with every document on your checklist, and inquire before the appointment if there are any

documents you're not sure about or aren't sure how to get. However, sometimes the information you get prior to the appointment is incomplete.

If the document list appears to be wrong, and you don't have something they say you need, write an attestation on a blank piece of paper explaining why you don't have the document, to include with your file. In one memorable situation, a client was held up at the VFS/TLS office in Los Angeles because the France-Visas document list was wrong. She was applying for a visa as a freelancer (profession libérale) and despite having checked off the correct boxes on the long-stay visa form, her document list included items for someone starting a business, like company formation documents.

She messaged us because the VFS/TLS official was going to mark her application "incomplete" since she hadn't provided these documents she didn't need! We quickly wrote an attestation in French identifying the documents she didn't have, explained why they weren't needed for her proposed business structure, and indicated that the list included them in error. We emailed it to her, and the VFS/TLS official included the document with the rest of her application. She successfully got her correct visa type, and the document checklist for that visa type has since been updated on the France-visas platform.

Getting Status Updates on Your Application
You can sign up for email updates on your visa's status to know when it has been received by the French embassy, when it is processing, and when it will be returned to you. However, we find that the status updates are not very reliable and are not always sent in the correct order. You will not know whether your visa has been issued until you receive your passport back and receive either a visa or a rejection slip.

3.7 Common Reasons for Visa Rejections

Around 3.8 million requests for French visas are processed by French embassies and consulates around the world during a single typical calendar year. Around 300,000 visas of all types were issued. The French consulates make determinations about who gets a visa and who does not based on several factors: your income, your credentials, what your stated purpose is in requesting the visa, and how likely they think you are to violate the terms of your visa by doing something you're not supposed to.

Your job, in assembling the visa application, is to paint a clear picture of exactly who you are, where your money is going to come from, and what you will contribute to France by being here. You want to show exactly what you will be doing with your time and ensure that all of your stated plans fit neatly into one of the "boxes" we've outlined in this book.

France is not a place where having lots of different simultaneous projects and stepping outside the box is appreciated. If they don't understand what it is you want to do when they are reviewing your visa, your chances of getting that visa are not good. Conversely, if you present a clear and compelling case for one visa type and the documents you provide give sufficient supporting evidence for your claims, you're very likely to be approved.

Put together a visa application like you are putting together a court case: with supporting evidence and documentation. You have no obligation to turn over exculpatory evidence that can torpedo your "case," so focus on the facts and build your case narrowly. Include only what needs to be included, nothing more. No unnecessary explaining.

Don't speculate about what you could do or what you might do. Don't equivocate. Don't give them ammunition to look for a reason to reject you. Don't lie by omission, but don't be overly forthcoming about your motivations. The more information you give them, the more information they have to process and analyze before issuing your visa.

Include in your visa application only that which can be proved with supporting documentation and that which shows a well-thought-out plan for what you will do upon arrival.

Here are some of the most common reasons I've seen for visa rejections.

1.   Being unclear in your intent.
If you apply for a visa and do not present a plan for what you are going to do while on that visa, and how it will impact your life, you may end up with a rejection or a visa you don't want, like the long séjour temporaire. Equivocating or being ambivalent about what you're going to do once you arrive in France, or being unsure of the future you are creating, or trying to tell the French consulate what you think they want to hear will not work.

Certain clients have expressed to us that when they applied for visas on their own, their initial visa applications were rejected or approved only for a temporary visa because they didn't want to seem too sure of themselves in planning to stay in France for multiple years. The resulting miscommunication meant they'd have to go through the additional expense and process of returning to their home country to get the new visa. If your plan is to stay for multiple years in France, it's okay – and encouraged – to say so. Project yourself into the future. What are the next few years going to look like for you? If you're a student or an au pair, what are the academic programs you might do *after* those initial programs end? If you're doing a work contract, how will the job help to build your career and insinuate you into your field and networking opportunities in France?

Be clear on how moving to France impacts your life plan and how this visa enhances that plan.

2.   Saying you're going to work (but you're not applying for a work visa).
Indicating on your visa application that you plan to work, seek employment, or be self-employed while you're not applying for a work visa is a sure way to get your visa application rejected. This seems to be

most common with students, who put that they plan to support themselves on cash savings and find a babysitting or part-time job upon arrival. While the student visa technically allows its bearers to work part-time, working should not be a motivation for requesting the visa.

Similarly, applying for a visitor visa and indicating that you plan to work remotely or run a business remotely can lead to rejection. Referencing any type of work on your visa application other than work specifically linked to your visa is a bad idea. If your visa application is rejected for this reason, it will be impossible for you to prove that you have decided *not* to plan to work in France or to seek employment upon arrival. You will have to wait even longer to reapply for a new visa.

3.   Saying you're going to be with a romantic partner.
If your relationship is serious enough for you to be moving to a new country to be with someone, it's serious enough to make things official, through marriage. At least, that's how the consulate will see it.

A common issue we see is people applying for student or visitor visas to move to France and "test out" the relationship with a previously long-distance significant other. They aren't ready to get married, and so look to other visa types that would enable them to live in France.

The problem arises when the partner is going to potentially be a source of income (financial guarantee) or of housing. If you have none of your own financial resources and plan on relying on someone to whom you are not legally attached, you are risking major problems should anything happen in your relationship. A romantic partner who is not legally bound to you has no obligation to provide you with anything. Abusive situations aside, you would be completely stranded without a job, without money, and without a place to live if things didn't work out for whatever reason. Don't put yourself in that situation. The consulate won't allow you to either.

4.   Saying you're looking for a job.
Applying for a visitor visa to work remotely or to look for jobs with the intention of switching visa statuses is also a no-no. You should expect

to maintain the same visa status for at least two years before switching, and any indication that you do not intend to maintain the status you are applying for will result in your application being rejected.

If you do come to France with a particular visa type with the intention of finding a job, keep that out of your initial visa application, as actually *getting* a job is merely speculative. When you actually find a job, you will have to return to your home country to apply for a new visa unless you have already been in France for more than a year and renewed your visa once.

5.   Not having your documents in order.

Since the VFS/TLS takeover of the French visa application procedures in 2018, there have been lots of problems with visas being misprocessed, the wrong visa types being awarded, or long delays. Part of the problem was that the VFS/TLS bureaucrats were not familiar with the different French visa types or the documents required for them, and in some cases, they weren't requesting everything they really needed for the French embassy to process the requests. And anyone who did their visa application more than a year ago and who does not have experience with the process in several locations is not a good source of information.

Moral of the story: bring ALL of your documents, and even the ones you don't think you need. We've provided complete checklists in this book for each visa type, and you should bring things that aren't on the official list and even documents you don't think you need. Having more documents that you can pull out of your binder if they ask is better than not having them and having to book a new appointment.

And, make sure they take all of the documents you've prepared, even if they don't ask for them or they aren't officially required. Cover letters, project plans, extra bank statements, the works.

6.   Applying for the wrong visa type for what you want to do.

It should go without saying, but applying for a visa you're not fully qualified for and don't have adequate proof for will very likely result in a rejection. This includes ensuring that for business and self-employment visa applications, your business model and description align with the type of business registration you have selected for your activity. We go into this in more depth in the *Complete French Business Incubator.*

There is not a lot of wiggle room in French visa applications, and the stated requirements are the *minimum* to get you a visa. You can certainly meet all of the requirements and still be rejected, so don't apply for a visa you're not eligible for. It will simply be a black mark on your file and can be held against you if you reapply for a different visa type within a short period of time.

Again, you should narrowly construe your visa application for the specific thing you're applying to do, and avoid referencing any personal projects or ideas that do *not* fit that plan.

7. **Not having enough money or a high enough salary.**
If you do not have enough personal cash resources to meet the minimum requirements for your visa or will not earn enough doing whatever job you plan to do in France, you will not get the visa. Ensure that you have at least the minimum cash requirement for your visa type and can show at least 3 bank statements with those amounts. Do not rely on someone outside of your family for income or support, and do not plan to provide a financial guarantor for visa types other than student or visitor.

8. **Not having economic ties for your project to France.**
The consulates have a lot of leeway in accepting projects or not for any of the business visa types, and it is no longer sufficient to simply be self-employed. The consulates are specifically looking for your project's economic ties and future projects or clients *in France,* to prove you will have work-related reasons to be living and working in France. This could be letters from future and potential clients in France or other documents demonstrating why you are pursuing this particular project in France rather than elsewhere.

3.8 Rejections, New Applications & Appeals

The French consulate does not have to give you a reason for rejecting your visa application unless you are applying as the family member of a French citizen. It can therefore be quite difficult to ascertain the reasons for the rejection and to submit a new application. If your application is rejected, you have the option of submitting a new application, or of submitting an appeal. Of course, the best way to ensure your visa application is accepted is to consult a professional *before* you submit it, to ensure no red flags are raised and that all conditions for the visa application are met. It is far easier to avoid rejection in the first place than it is to modify and resubmit a failed application.

Sometimes, there is no real reason for your rejection, other than the fact that they reject a certain number of applications and yours may not have made the cut that day.

A new application is the easiest and fastest solution, because you can submit a new application as soon as you can get a new appointment. There is no waiting period for when you can try again. However, in order to be successful the second time, you have to know what, if anything, was wrong with your application in the first place. Sometimes, it's a simple procedural error, or not providing enough supporting documents. Other times, it's a bell that is very hard to unring, like stating you are going to work or look for a job, when you shouldn't be. If you put on one application that you plan to find employment, how do you *disprove* that you're going to be job hunting on the next application?

If you are able to travel to France on just your passport and are going for studies or on a visitor visa (not to work), you may consider going for up to 90 days as a tourist, and then returning several months later to apply for a new visa. Obviously, you would not be able to work or start a planned job on the "tourist" status. Having a cool-down period before submitting a new application and taking the time to make the application more focused can help to ensure approval the second time around. It can also give you the opportunity to network and find potential clients and collaborators in France if you are submitting an self-employment or business visa application.

Another option is to file a "recours," or an appeal, with the Ministry of the Interior. This process involves sending your complete file, along with all supporting documents, to Nantes for processing. We do not recommend doing this without having a professional examine your file and helping you to prepare a new application and then the appeal, because 90% of rejections are upheld while only about 10% are overturned. In order to successfully appeal the decision, you would have to prove that the consulate initially made an incorrect decision based on the information provided, while typically it's more appropriate to simply file a new application with additional information and supporting documents to strengthen the original application. The appeals process can be lengthy, and then you will still have to submit a new application through the local French consulate or VFS/TLS office.

Part 4: Arriving in France after Receiving Your Visa

Your visa will be issued with the start date you've requested, and once your passport has your visa in it, it will be mailed back to you. You should receive a notification, but you will not know for sure whether your visa has been issued until your passport is returned. You have a little bit of leeway on the exact date you should arrive in France, so if you end up not leaving on the exact date you specified, it's okay.

Validating a VLS-TS

Most long-stay visa types require you to validate the visa online through OFII and be invited in for an OFII visit. This procedure is applicable to all visa types except for "Passeport Talent" visas and "EU family member" carte de séjour applicants.

Once you arrive in France with your VLS-TS, you will have to validate your visa through OFII, the Office Français d'Immigration et d'Intégration. This section describes the updated OFII procedure that was 'dématérialisé', or digitalized, as of February 2019. You will need to complete the OFII registration procedures in order to renew your visa at the end of the first year. Your visa will be validated online through the ANEF website, and you will create an account that you can use to change your address or request a renewal when the time comes.

You must complete the OFII validation procedure within 90 days of arriving in France, which should also be within 90 days of the start date of your visa. Ideally, you will submit your OFII registration very soon after arrival and have all of your OFII appointments before this 90 day period is over. If not, don't worry too much. As long as you submit the OFII registration within the 90 days, you should be fine. The great thing is that the new online procedure should prevent registrations from being lost and misplaced, which sometimes happened when everything was done on paper. Be aware that the earlier you validate the visa with OFII, the earlier you will be invited in for your required OFII procedures, which increases your likelihood of completing everything before you need to begin the renewal process.

Certain departments are extremely behind when it comes to inviting people in for OFII appointments. While some get their OFII convocations within days or weeks of submitting their online validation, and have their appointments 2-3 weeks later, other OFII offices have months-long wait times to even receive a convocation for a visit. It is impossible to predict, although we do know which departments tend to have longer wait times than others.

Passeport Talent & EU Family Carte de Séjour Requests
For all Passeport Talent visa categories, your visa will typically be issued for 90 days, during which time you are required to submit a request for a carte de séjour online. You will typically need to provide many of the same documents as for your initial application, along with registering your business and providing proof of domicile.

When you have submitted your application online, you will receive an attestation that it has been submitted, followed by an approval, followed by a notification that your card is ready to pick up at your local préfecture.

Note that if you have an accompanying spouse, the main Passeport Talent applicant's request has to be submitted an an account created before the spouse can submit their CDS application through the online portal. It is therefore extremely important to secure a long-term lease quickly and submit the main Passeport Talent holder's carte de séjour application quickly, so it is validated and an account is set up with enough time to request the spouse's card before their 90-day visa expires. Don't worry if you're a Franceformation client - we will let you know what documents you need and what the deadlines are, so as long as you provide what we need on time, you shouldn't have to worry about the short timeframe for the carte de séjour request.

4.1 Arriving in France with Your Visa

When you arrive in France with a valid renewable long-stay visa, you will either have a 12-month visa which needs to be validated online within 3 months, or you will have a 90-day visa for which you will have to request your carte de séjour online before the visa's expiration date. Both of these procedures are done online through the ANEF (Administration Numérique des Étrangers en France) platform.

If you have a 12 month renewable visa, you will need to secure a valid address where you can receive mail, along with a French phone number, before validating your visa online.

If you have a 3-month Passeport Talent visa that requires you to apply for a carte de séjour directly, you will need to find long-term housing and obtain a "justificatif de domicile" before submitting a CDS application online. You are exempt from the OFII procedures below.

1. Find Long-term Housing.
In order to complete the OFII process online, you will have to have an address where you can send and receive mail. This will ideally be your permanent address for your whole year in France. If you have reserved temporary housing upon arrival, you should spend your first few weeks seeking a permanent place to live, and only register with OFII once you have found a longer lease. You will have to enter your address on the form, and provide a "justificatif de domicile" in the form of rent receipts, an electricity bill, or an attestation d'hébergement from your landlord.

Alternatively, if you have friends who live in the same region where you are located, you may ask them to use their address for the initial OFII registration. This allows you to begin the process earlier while you are still looking for your housing. If you find permanent housing in the meantime, you can change your official address at your OFII appointment by providing a "justificatif de domicile" in your name; otherwise, you can continue to use their address by providing an attestation d'hébergement from your friends at your appointment, and then changing your address once you sign a longer lease or renew your carte de séjour. Normally, you will not receive any mail from OFII or from anyone; they will invite you to your appointments by email.

2. Purchase a timbre fiscal dématérialisé.
A timbre fiscal dématérialisé is a virtual excise stamp you purchase to pay taxes on certain services from the préfecture. You will most likely only use these for your OFII procedure and your titre de séjour renewals at the préfecture. For Passeport Talent holders, you will wait to purchase your timbre fiscal until you are invited to pick up your carte de séjour at your préfecture.

The timbre fiscal for the OFII procedure can be purchased online right on the website where you complete the OFII procedure. You will need to have a credit or debit card available.

Go to https://administration-etrangers-en-france.interieur.gouv.fr/particuliers/#/ and click on the tab for "Acheter un timbre fiscal." You will have to select the amount of the stamp you need to purchase.

If you do not know for sure what amount you should buy, you will need to begin filling out the OFII form first, as it will tell you once you've begun to input your information. You should verify the amount before purchasing the stamp, as you cannot buy multiple stamps for the same OFII form.

After clicking through to purchase the stamp in the correct amount, you will download a document to receive a 16-digit code, which you will input into the last page of the OFII form. Write down the code or save it as a PDF for the next step.

3. Complete the Online OFII Validation on ANEF.
You will need your passport with your long-stay visa, your date of arrival in France, and the address where you are staying for this step. You can open up a second tab to begin this procedure at the same time as you purchase the timbre fiscal, since beginning the OFII form will enable you to learn the exact amount you have to pay. The amount varies based on the visa type.

On this page (https://administration-etrangers-en-france.interieur.gouv.fr/particuliers/#/), you will have to put in your name, visa number (on the top right corner of your visa), its start date, issue date, arrival date, and various personal information. You will also have to identify the visa type that you received (visitor, profession libérale, student, etc.), at which point you will have to select a code from a drop down menu specifically identifying the visa type. These codes are called CESEDA numbers, and they refer to the article in the Code de l'Entrée et du Séjour des Étrangers et des Droit d'Asile which establishes each particular visa type. There are multiple sets of codes for each visa type depending on the CESEDA's publication year. The UK often issues visas with codes from the 2016 edition, which start with 311 or 313, while the most recent set of codes come from the 2021 edition, and begin with 421 or 431. The codes remain the same in 2024.

At the end of the process, you will learn the price of your timbre fiscal. Complete the purchase of the timbre in a separate window, and enter the 16-digit code from the timbre fiscal to pay and complete the procedure.

Once you have entered all of the information and submitted the page, save it to PDF to keep evidence of your submission. The PDF will indicate that you have officially been registered with OFII and will prove that you have validated your visa. Your visa along with this validation document will now be considered your titre de séjour. You will not receive a physical plastic card ("carte de séjour") until your renewal.

4. Receive Your Convocation(s).
It will take several weeks for OFII to get back to you, but you will receive a convocation by email inviting you to one or two visits at the OFII office (depending on your visa type), and you will receive a separate convocation for each. Along with the convocation, OFII will provide a list of documents that you will need to bring along with your visa in order to validate it. Normally you will just need to bring your passport with your visa and your convocation. You will also be asked to bring any important medical records and your vaccine records to the medical visit.

If you do not receive a response from OFII within 6 weeks, you can try calling or emailing your OFII office at (city where your OFII office is located)@ofii.fr. We have included an appendix with a list of the OFII offices by department. You can also try going in person if you are close. If you opt to go in-person, avoid peak times like 9:00, 10:30, 1:30, or 15:00 when most appointments are scheduled. Try to go halfway between those peak hours. Some OFII offices have scheduled walk-in hours for people to ask questions and get information without an appointment whereas some will only open the doors at appointment times.

5. Go to Your OFII Visits.
Show up to the appropriate OFII office on the date and time indicated. Arrive 15-20 minutes early if possible, as arriving earlier will mean you will get an earlier ticket and get out of there faster.

Everyone (except students, temporary stay visa holders, and passeport talent holders, who are exempt) will get a convocation for a medical visit, which is a very basic exam where they test your vision and hearing, X-ray your chest for tuberculosis, and ask about your vaccinations. If you have a record of your vaccines, bring it if possible along with any important medical history. For the X-ray, you will have to undress from the waist up, so ladies, bring a scarf to cover yourself on the brief walk from the changing stall to the x-ray machine, and wear pants and a t-shirt so you only have to take off your shirt and bra. Some centers are not equipped for the X-rays. If this is the case for your OFII office, they will send you a letter indicating where you should make an appointment prior to your OFII visit. If you get the X-rays done at the designated office, there will be no extra charge. You will need to bring the results with you to your OFII medical exam.

Starting in 2024, OFII is normally not requiring US citizens to get chest x-rays for the medical exam. If you do not receive a convocation specifically for an x-ray, you do not need to bring one to the exam. OFII is rolling out this new procedure across France and it's possible that this new exemption will extend to citizens of other countries where tuberculosis is rare.

Once you have completed your required visits, you will need to keep your attestation of attendance at each one, and provide those documents as part of the renewal process. Make a photocopy of the attestations as soon as you can, along with a photocopy of your visa and passport's ID page, and save them in multiple places - on your phone, in your email, in the cloud. If you ever lose your passport or if you are walking around without your passport and are asked to present ID, it could come in handy. And you will replace the passport and visa much more quickly if you have copies.

6. If You MUST Miss an OFII Visit.

First of all, don't. You should be there on the days they invite you in, no matter how inconvenient it will be. Rearrange your schedule.

Starting this year, some OFII offices are asking you to confirm receipt of the convocation and confirm your attendance, to limit no-shows, and some offices are sending convocations by both email and snail mail. If the email asks you to confirm your attendance, be sure to do so.

If you absolutely, positively, 100% cannot make one of the appointment times, go to what you can. (Sometimes the two appointments will be scheduled together; other times they will be a few days apart.) Once you have missed the appointment(s), email the OFII office or go in person to reschedule. Going in-person is preferable, as they may not respond or reschedule you over email. Bring your passport and old convocation so they can easily look you up in their system. Be aware that if you do not complete all of your OFII visits and obligations in your first year in France, it may impact your ability to get a multiyear card at your renewal (if you are on a visa type that can lead to a multiyear card), so it's important to prioritize these visits.

DO NOT MISS THE SECOND APPOINTMENT. If you miss the appointment once, they will reschedule you once without too much of an issue. Miss the second appointment, and they are very likely to tell you that you're out of luck, and that you will have to go back home for a new visa at the end of the year.

You will not be able to renew your visa without completing the OFII validation process.

7. Keep Your Documentation.

You will receive an attestation for having completed your OFII medical and integration visits. You should scan these documents and keep them in a safe place with photocopies of everything to ensure you have them for your renewal. You will have to provide a copy of these attestations the first time you renew your visa, but not any of the subsequent times.

Once you renew, the préfecture will keep a record of which visit(s) you've done. If you're a student, you will only be required to do the medical visit, but if you then change your visa type to salarié, for example, you will get another convocation to do the integration visit as well. If you haven't done one of the required visits for your new visa type, you may have to complete it before they will give you your new visa status.

8. Set a Reminder to Renew Your Visa.

You will need to renew your visa/titre de séjour no earlier than 4 months before it expires and no later than 2 months before it expires. If you do renew later than 2 months you will need to pay a late fee. Some renewals are done online now, such as visitor visas, but some still require and in person appointment such as the professional libérale. We suspect that this in person requirement may change in the future but have no indication of when. Set a reminder in your Google calendar or on your phone for 4 months before your visa's expiration date so you can begin looking into what procedure applies to you, see how to make an appointment to renew if necessary and what the delay time is for appointments and start gathering your documents.

We keep track of our clients' visa renewal dates and remind them to start gathering the required documents, make renewal appointments if necessary, assist with making appointments, and provide services to our clients who need assistance with the renewal.

4.2 Signing the Contrat d'Intégration Républicaine (CIR)

If you arrive in France with a visa authorizing you to work which does not fall into the "Passeport Talent" categories, you will be required to attend a series of "France Orientation" sessions totaling 24 hours through OFII to teach you about living in France and to put you on a path to naturalization and residence. This is called the Contrat d'Intégration Républicaine, and it is one way to know whether you are on a path to long-term residence in France.

The Contrat d'Intégration Républicaine (formerly known as the Contrat d'Accueil et d'Intégration, or CAI) was created in 2006 and implemented in 2007, and it outlines your contractual obligations for maintaining your carte de séjour and living in France. If you do not respect the CIR, your carte de séjour can be withdrawn. Around 110.000 new arrivals in France sign an integration contract and complete their integration days each year.

To fulfill the CIR, you must first have a visa category that identifies you as someone who may be relocating permanently and durably to France. If you have one of the following visa types, you are not considered to be sustainably establishing yourself in France, and will not complete this formality. Without signing the CIR, you do not truly have a path to long-term French residency unless you switch your visa status. This includes:
- ✓ Visitors - only required to do the OFII medical visit, not the CIR
- ✓ Students, Interns, & Au Pairs - only required to validate online, no visits or CIR required
- ✓ Detached workers (ICT, Work Holiday, FACC, Travailleur Temporaire) - only required to do the medical visit, not the CIR

Certain other immigrants to France are exempt from signing a CIR and taking the training days:
- ✓ EU citizens and their spouses
- ✓ Passeport Talent holders (who typically have to have a master's degree, with few exceptions)
- ✓ Students who have completed 3 years of secondary education

or 1 year of university education in France
- ✓ Minors 16-18 who receive a carte de séjour VPF through regroupement familial

This means that you will take the OFII classes and sign the CIR if you have one of the following visa types and have not done any higher education in France: vie privée, salarié, profession libérale, entrepreneur (commerçant, artisan, industriel). You will be invited to your first OFII appointments in the weeks or months following the validation of your VLS-TS.

You may also be registered by the préfecture if you switch from an "exempt" visa type, such as au pair, intern, or ICT, to a *CIR required* visa type, like salarié or vie privée, without completing any higher education in France. The préfecture will forward your information to OFII to request the appointments on your behalf.

In either case, you will receive an email with a formal (read: mandatory) invitation to the medical visit and your first integration day:

Personalized orientation interview: A day with an entretien personnalisé (individual interview) and French language evaluation for understanding your needs and orienting you towards public services that may assist you, like France Travail (Pôle Emploi) if you arrive on a family visa and would like to find work. During this interview, an interpreter in your language will be made available if you need one, and you will sign your CIR.

Language evaluation: You will be evaluated on your French level, and if you do not possess an A1 level, you can be assigned a mandatory number of French class hours (100, 200, 400, or 600) to take before renewing your titre de séjour. When you reach the A1 level or finish your assigned courses, you will be issued a certificate of completion with your name on it, which must be presented for renewal.

Civics Education: A series of 4 modules on French Republican values, administrations and public institutions and how they operate, rights and responsibilities of French citizens & residents, healthcare, work, school and childcare options, housing, and more.

A final interview: After your parcours is complete, you will be invited for a final interview and provide additional resources if you need further assistance with professional integration in France.

If you do not respect the contract by repeated unjustified absence from your French classes or from your integration days, you may be notified that the préfecture is "canceling" your contract, which will prevent you from receiving a multiyear card. Note that some regional OFIIs are significantly behind in inviting new arrivals in for their integration days. If you are not invited in for the OFII visits as your renewal approaches, you don't have to worry about your card not being renewed, but you may not receive a multiyear card at that appointment. Typically, the préfecture will contact OFII on your behalf to inquire about your status and remind OFII to invite you in. Once you do complete the required sessions, you will be able to receive a multiyear card at your next renewal.

Completing all of the required OFII classes and Stages d'intégration and testing out of any required language classes are prerequisites for receiving a multi-year carte de séjour. We strongly discourage you from missing any appointments to ensure you are able to complete all of the classes before renewal so you can be eligible for a multi-year card, even if it means paying a late fee and having your appointment after your final Integration Day.

4.3 Signing the Contrat d'Engagement Républicaine (CER)

The "Contract of Commitment to Respect the Principles of the Republic" is a new mandatory agreement for foreigners seeking residence permits in France, which went into effect on July 8, 2024. By signing it, applicants pledge to uphold French Republic principles such as personal freedom, freedom of expression, equality of the sexes, human dignity, and secularism. Adherence to these principles will theoretically be enforced throughout your stay, and violations may lead to the refusal or withdrawal of residence permits and potential expulsion from France.

Respect for Personal Freedom: Signatories must respect the privacy of individuals, the sanctity of their homes and correspondence, their freedom of movement, and their ability to communicate freely. They must also respect individuals' choice of spouse.

Respect for Freedom of Expression and Conscience: Signatories commit to avoiding acts of proselytism through coercion, threats, or pressure. They must not obstruct others from expressing their own values, principles, opinions, religious beliefs, or convictions.

Respect for Sex Equality: Signatories pledge to avoid sexist behavior and discrimination based on sex. They must treat public service employees equally.

Respect for Human Dignity: Signatories agree to uphold laws protecting health and physical and mental integrity. They must respect the equal dignity of all humans without discrimination based on origin, opinions, religion, or sexual orientation. They must not exploit or create vulnerabilities and must protect minors' physical, emotional, intellectual, and social development.

Respect for the Republic's Motto and Symbols: Signatories must respect the motto "Liberty, Equality, Fraternity" and the national symbols, including the national anthem "La Marseillaise" and the tricolor flag. Public insults to these symbols are prohibited.

Respect for France's Territorial Integrity: Signatories commit not to challenge France's national borders or sovereignty through actions that disturb public order, incite such actions, or involve foreign interference.

Respect for the Principle of Secularism: Signatories must not question the legitimacy of public officials or demand modifications to public services or facilities based on personal or religious beliefs.

Failure to adhere to these commitments can lead to the refusal, non-renewal, or withdrawal of the residence permit and potential expulsion from France. It is now available to download and sign during any renewal procedure on the ANEF platform, and will also be required at in-person appointments.

Currently, on the online platform, there is no upload field for the Contrat d'Engagement, but it needs to be uploaded alongside the justificatif de domicile.

4.4 Renewing Your Visa

If you receive a "VLS-TS", or a "Visa Long Séjour valant Titre de Séjour" and validate your visa via the OFII process upon arrival in France, you can renew the same visa status at the end of your first year directly in France provided that you continue to meet the conditions for maintaining your visa.

In this section, we will discuss how to renew your visa if you are keeping the SAME visa type. You will need to renew your initial visa status at least once before you can switch to another visa status, unless there are exceptional circumstances. (And even with exceptional circumstances, you better write a good cover letter explaining what they are on your change of status application.)

Note that if you receive a "Long Séjour Temporaire" visa and you are "dispensé" (exempt) from the OFII appointments, you will not be able to renew your visa or change your visa status. Even if you do the OFII procedure (which is required for all work visa types), you cannot renew a non-renewable visa type such as "work holiday" or "salarié en mission" for example.

The renewal process differs depending on what type of visa you have. It is managed at the préfecture level for each region, and can vary slightly between regions depending on the different systems they put in place to manage applicants. If you need an appointment, you can make an appointment online through your préfecture's web portal and receive a convocation by email or download. Getting an appointment can often be a challenge, especially if you don't have a valid AGDREF number. Normally you cannot make an appointment for a procedure that should be completed online.

Most Visa Renewals are Now Online
In 2024, more and more administrative procedures are fully online, including visa and carte de séjour renewals. In many cases and in many departments, you only have to physically go to the préfecture to pick up your physical card after receiving a notification by text message or

through the ANEF platform.

All visitor visa and student visa renewals are now submitted online, and renewal applications need to be submitted between 120 and 60 days before the visa or carte de séjour's expiration date in order to avoid paying a €180 late fee. You do not need to make an appointment in your local préfecture; you simply have to connect to your ANEF account to submit the required documents.

Passeport Talent carte de séjour submissions and renewals are also entirely online through the ANEF platform.

Other work visa types and business visa types are still processed outside of the ANEF platform, which means if you have a salarié, travailleur temporaire, profession libérale, entrepreneur (commerçant, artisan, industriel), or vie privée et familiale visa or carte de séjour, you'll have to check with your local préfecture to see how to submit your application. Certain préfectures have implemented online procedures through démarches-simplifiées.gouv, while others require you to submit through an in-person appointment or by mail.

Renew Online through ANEF	Check Your Préfecture's Procedure
All Passeport Talent types	Vie Privée et Familiale
Visitor	Profession Libérale
Student	Entrepreneur (commerçant, artisan, industriel)
Au Pair	
EU Family Member	RECE (Recherche d'emploi création d'entreprise)
10 year resident card	
Changes of status for any of the visa types in the "Check Your Préfecture's Procedure" TO the visa types listed here	Travailleur Temporaire / Salarié
	Working Holiday and Jeune Professionnel (if possible)
	Changes of status to any of the visa types in this column

If You Have to Make Your Renewal Appointment
You can make your appointment to renew your titre de séjour up to 120 days before your current titre de séjour is set to expire. Some préfectures advise that you make your appointment even farther in

advance because there is so much demand, to ensure you can submit your renewal before your current titre expires. However, some préfectures don't allow you to make an appointment until closer to your titre de séjour's expiration date.

If you're going to need to travel shortly after you renew your titre de séjour, you can make your appointment farther in advance to have your appointment earlier (before your titre de séjour expires). Alternatively, you can make your appointment *closer* to your titre de séjour's expiration date, such that your renewal appointment is several weeks AFTER your current titre de séjour expires.

As of right now, it is OKAY if your renewal appointment is AFTER your titre de séjour expires. It happens all the time and is totally normal, even if you make the appointment when you're supposed to. As long as the date you make the appointment is before your titre de séjour expires, you won't have any issues with your renewal. However, as online renewals become more common and in-person appointments are phased out, préfectures have begun to apply penalties for renewals filed fewer than 60 days in advance.

If you are waiting for an important document for your renewal, like the *attestation des droits à l'assurance maladie* to show your enrollment with the French healthcare system, or if you have a self-employment visa and need to show more earnings, it can be advantageous to make your appointment late and pay the late fee.

(In fact, it used to be much worse - people would have their renewal appointments months after their cards expired, and would not be issued the new 1-year carte de séjour until it was almost expired. They'd have to make appointments to renew immediately upon receiving the new near-expired card, and the cycle would begin again. Fortunately, France has mostly moved past those days due to a few changes in legislation and how the cards are processed and produced.)

There can be some advantages to having your renewal appointment several weeks later than you are supposed to make it. For example, a client who is a tour guide on a "profession libérale" status arrived in

May, but the bulk of her activity and income are during the summer months. Taking a day off for an appointment in May or early June would mean she'd miss out on income for the day of her appointment, and she'd have little time to prepare when she's working. It also means that her most recent months of income are relatively low compared to what she's capable of making during the height of tourist season in the summer. If she makes her appointment in February and has her appointment in May, her file won't look quite as good as if she makes an appointment in early May for August or September. By having her appointment a couple of months after she is "supposed" to, she'll have higher income to show in her most recent months, and has leverage for requesting a multi-year carte de séjour. This type of situation would potentially be worth risking the €180 fee for filing late.

Scheduling Your Appointment

If you need an appointment, and once you've decided approximately when you'd like to have your visa appointment, you have a few options for scheduling depending on your department. You will have to learn about your specific department's renewal procedures and how to make an appointment by googling the city where your préfecture is, + "prise de rendez-vous renouvellement titre de séjour." Most prefectures do not allow you to enter the premises without an appointment so the days of spontaneously showing up to ask questions are obsolete. As always, do not rely on outdated information from those who have not renewed recently, don't have your visa type, or are in a different region from you.

Online: Most préfectures now have the option of scheduling your appointment directly online. You will need to log into the appointment calendar with your AGDREF number (see the next section), your full name, and the expiration date, and will have access to an appointment calendar so you can choose your own date and time.

Pro tip: Many préfecture websites are now showing the previous date for which they released appointments, so you can try to predict when more appointments are going to be released. You'll have to check back regularly to ensure you don't miss the release time.

By Email: Some préfectures have a contact form on their website which you complete and submit to get an appointment, but this now only works in case of glitches or errors that prevent you from making an appointment via their website.

By Phone: It is useless to try to call the préfecture to make an appointment.

In Person: Also an obsolete method, unfortunately.

By Mail: Some préfectures have you submit your complete renewal application by mail, send your récépissé back by mail and you only have to be physically present to pick up your card, or directly or send you a convocation for an appointment. If this is the case for your préfecture, make sure you send your complete renewal packet no later than 60 days before your titre de séjour expires, and send it by lettre recommandée avec accusé de réception (certified mail with delivery receipt) to confirm they have received it and to provide proof in case it's ever needed. You should send copies of all of your documents, not originals, if you have to make an appointment in this way.

Information You'll Need to Schedule
Your AGDREF number: This is a 10-digit number, usually starting with 99, that is listed on the side of your carte de séjour or on your OFII vignette in your passport or on your validation receipt. AGDREF stands for "Application de Gestion des Dossiers des Ressortissants Etrangers en France" and it will be your ID number of sorts while you are living in France. You will keep the same AGDREF number even if you switch visa statuses, and it will follow you until you are naturalized. (Or until you return to your home country to get a new visa type and start over with a new AGDREF number.)

Your Full Name: You will need to input your complete name, including all middle names, into the online form. If the form doesn't work for whatever reason, ensure that you are typing all of your names exactly as they appear on the visa or your carte de séjour, including all middle names.

Your Visa's Expiration Date: This will be listed on your initial visa, or on your titre de séjour. Remember that the date is listed day-month-year.

After Scheduling

Once your appointment is scheduled, you should receive a Convocation. A Convocation is an official document showing the date and time of your appointment and where you should present yourself on that day. You will need it, along with your passport and titre de séjour and all supporting documents, to access the préfecture and the appointment windows.

If you are not traveling, your titre de séjour (even if it's expired) and your convocation are enough to prove that you can legally stay in France. If you do not plan to leave France between your titre de séjour's expiration date and the date of your appointment, you can use these two documents to stay in France and get to your renewal appointment.

However, if you work or receive benefits of any kind (CAF, unemployment from France Travail), or if you plan to travel before your appointment, you should get a récépissé. A récépissé is a receipt which extends the validity of your current titre de séjour, usually by 3 months, until your appointment or after your appointment and before your card is ready. Your employer may require a récépissé to prove that you still have the ability to work legally in France, and France Travail will stop your benefits at your titre de séjour's expiration date without this document. For most préfectures, you can only request a récépissé if your titre de séjour is expiring within 15 calendar days, and most préfectures have moved this procedure online.

If your renewal procedure is online, you may receive a "Prolongation" document, which is the equivalent of a récépissé.

Going to Your Appointment

On the day of your appointment, you should arrive before your appointment time to ensure you can get in and out as quickly as possible. If you arrive on time, you will usually wait in a long line of people who have the same appointment time as you; arriving 15-20 minutes early will ensure you receive one of the first tickets for your appointment slot.

You will have to go through a metal detector and scan your belongings before entering the préfecture, so don't bring anything dangerous or questionable with you. You can bring food and drink, and you should do so in case you have to wait a while. Most préfectures will have vending machines in the halls with coffee and snacks.

At the desk in the hall where you renew, SAY "BONJOUR", present your convocation, carte de séjour, récépissé (if you have one), and passport at the desk to receive a ticket with a number on it, and wait for your number to be called. Ensure that your documents are organized and in order, and bring change for the photocopier in case you need to make extra copies of anything. The préfecture should also have a Photomaton machine if you need to take extra photos. Get your ticket before making copies or taking photos so you have something productive you can do while you wait to be called.

They will give you a CERFA form to fill out while you are waiting with your basic information and details about your stay in France. Usually this is in A3 format so it can serve as a file folder for your documents. Fill this out in black ink and use capital letters to ensure your handwriting can be read easily. These forms for the most part are also available online in case you want to prepare ahead of time, even if you have to recopy the information onto the form they give you.

As soon as you get to the window, SAY "BONJOUR" and present your convocation, ticket, passport, and carte de séjour / récépissé immediately. Next, present the CERFA form and the justificatif de domicile of less than 3 months. Usually the agent de guichet will then begin asking for specific documents in order. The more organized you are and the more quickly you can identify and hand over the documents, the happier everyone will be. Hand over photocopies, not originals, but have the originals handy in case they want to look. Ask if they want documents they don't ask for (but you think they might need) and let them decide whether to take them or not.

Your job is to make their job as easy as possible and to get out of there as quickly as possible. Don't chat too much, fret, or over explain. Be polite, and answer their small talk, but recognize that they are extremely busy and have a lot of appointments to get through, so the more efficient you can be, the better. If you're potentially eligible for a multi-year card, don't be afraid to inquire about it. The agent might not offer it, but could approve you for more than one year if they're in a good mood, you're organized, and everything seems to be in order. When requesting a multi-year card, we like to include a cover letter explicitly asking for it.

Once they take your documents and ensure they have everything, they will fingerprint you and ask you for your set of official photos. In the best-case scenario, they will immediately print a récépissé and affix a picture. Review it to ensure that all of your information is accurate. Note its expiration date and the status (for your ability to work) and make sure everything is spelled correctly. If everything is accurate, sign, and you're done! The agent will tell you to expect a text message to go pick up your new carte de séjour when it's ready. Don't hesitate to ask for an estimate if they don't give one.

Sometimes, after taking your documents, they pass it on to a superior for review and approval before giving you your récépissé. Don't worry, this is also completely normal. It just depends on the préfecture and their procedures. In this case, they will have you go sit down, pass on the file, and call you again once it has been approved. In the meantime, you can wait in the waiting room, usually for 45 minutes to an hour. Once you are called back, you will receive your récépissé, which you can review and sign, and then you're done.

Using Your Récépissé
You can also continue to work, travel, and receive benefits on the *renewal* récépissé you receive during your renewal appointment. The récépissé will be valid for 3 months after the appointment date.

Once you have submitted all of your documents, the préfecture will process your renewal application and produce your carte de séjour. This process takes several at least 6-8 weeks, so you should expect to receive your carte de séjour about 2-3 months after your appointment. Sometimes, it takes longer, in which case you may want to return to the préfecture with your expiring récépissé, passport, titre de séjour, and more photos, so you can get another valid récépissé for work or benefit purposes.

Picking Up Your New Carte de Séjour

The préfecture should advise you during your appointment of how you will be notified that your carte de séjour is ready for pick-up. Usually, they will send a text message with a date and time to pick it up, although some préfectures are still sending letters by mail. You will need the text message or convocation letter to go and pick up your card. Note that you need to provide a French mobile phone number, not a foreign phone number, to receive text messages and notifications.

If you do not hear anything within 10 weeks of your appointment, you should write to the préfecture using their online contact form to check your card's status. During peak times, carte de séjour renewals can take 4-5 months to be completely processed, so it's not necessarily a bad sign if your card isn't ready. And sometimes, it's merely a glitch and the text message or letter wasn't sent out. When Allison used to provide a self-addressed stamped envelope to receive notification for pick-up, a letter was never mailed to her and she always had to call to see if her card was ready. Once, a client never got text messages from the préfecture - until one year when she got 3 text messages in a row to say that her current renewal, along with her two previous renewals, was ready for pickup! (She had fortunately picked up her card each year.) For certain clients, we have written to the préfecture because we had no news and they respond saying the card is ready with instructions on when and how to pick it up.

Once you receive notification that your card is ready, you can go to pick up your card. You will need your passport, expiring titre de séjour, récépissé (if you have one) and the amount you will have to pay in timbres fiscaux, which can be purchased online. The préfecture will tell you in your text message or letter how much you will have to pay. Be sure to ask whether they accept the timbres fiscaux purchased online (most do now), or whether you should purchase the physical stamps from a tabac. Purchasing stamps from a tabac is becoming less and less frequent, and not all tabacs carry the stamps. Make sure you have the correct amount in the proper format when you go.

When you arrive to pick up your carte de séjour, you will have to show your convocation if you have one (in the form of a text message or a letter) and get a ticket. Expect to wait in line a bit before you can actually receive your card. Most préfectures have a room dedicated to card pick-ups, so the process should go relatively quickly. And once you have it in hand, you can do a little dance and note the expiration date so you know when to make your next renewal appointment.

ANEF rarely indicates when the card is ready for pickup, and ANEF agents cannot see the status of your renewal or answer questions about your application's progress. Occasionally, your ANEF account will not reflect the fact that you have picked up your new card, which can cause issues when it's time to begin your next renewal procedure. If this happens, you need to write to your préfecture so they can update your card's status to "picked up."

4.5 Changing Your Visa Status in France

If you are already in France with a valid visa and want to switch to a different work status, you can sometimes change your visa status without leaving the country, thereby maintaining continuity of your residence in France and ensuring the time you've already spent in France will count towards your eventual residency or naturalization application.

Changing your visa status is a long and complex process, and it is NOT easier to change your status than it is to get a certain visa type in the first place. Being in France already does not mean your application will be approved more easily. In fact, the préfecture can sometimes become suspicious of your motives for the original visa application if they think you applied for a "visitor" visa with the intention of finding work and getting a "salarié" visa, for example.

You should not take the change of status process lightly, as in extreme cases the préfecture can actually revoke your current status if they find discrepancies in your application. If you get a student visa, get PACSed or married with your partner soon after arrival, and immediately attempt to change your status, you might raise more than a few red flags. And once those red flags are flying, it will be difficult to avoid extra scrutiny on your application.

You should not expect to begin the change of status process until you have been in France for at least a year, and the process will take at least several months from the time you make your initial appointment until the time your new carte de séjour with your new status arrives.

We have also experienced some challenges with certain change of status applications as certain procedures have moved online, so be aware that you should anticipate a change of status request well in advance and that the procedure may not be clear when you begin.

The most important thing to know is that changes of status can take a significant amount of time, and they need to be fully reviewed by the préfecture. In some cases, this can take months, and in one instance, our client's change of status from Visitor to Passeport Talent Entrepreneur in Bordeaux took a full year to be granted. This cannot be rushed. If you wait until you have a project starting to submit your application or make an appointment, your request will not even be looked at in time.

1. Ensure you can change from your current visa type to the status you want.

Not all visa types can be changed to all other visa types. We have outlined most restrictions in each visa type's individual section in this book, and you should verify that your change is possible before attempting to change your status. Trying to do a change of status that is not possible will only waste your time and frustrate the préfecture agents that are trying to help you, if you are even able to speak to an agent. In fact, many agents do not have enough knowledge or experience in most cases to know what is possible, why it is possible, and whether or not you can have an exception to the rule (spoiler alert: you can't), so don't bother going around asking in six different offices if what you want to do is okay. In theory, all the information you need to know will be online but in practice this is not always the case, especially now with so many procedures being moved online.

A few examples of what isn't possible: you can't switch from any type of work visa to a student visa. So, if you do TAPIF and then apply to a master's program, you'll have to go home to get a new visa. You can't switch to ANYTHING from salarié en mission, jeune professionnel (FACC) or work holiday (vacances travail) visas. You can't switch to anything from Long-Séjour Temporaire, or renew it. There really aren't any exceptions to these rules.

Switching from a family-type visa, like a "vie privée et familiale", to another status like profession libérale, salarié, or other work visa types, is typically allowed if you are getting un-PACSed or divorced. If this is your situation, you should write a cover letter explaining your situation, outlining your work situation and income, and specifying that you are seeking a change of status because of the impending end of your relationship. If you are salaried and do not have a 10-year card, your employer will likely have to pay the OFII tax to keep you in your position. It's better to inquire about what to do and how to do it BEFORE formally ending the relationship.

2. Renew your current visa at least once, unless you have very compelling reasons not to do so.

If you have been on your current visa type for less than one year and want to switch statuses, you are very likely to have problems, especially if your visa status is visitor or student. The préfecture can get very suspicious if it thinks that you got a visa in order to circumvent the application process for another, more difficult visa type. They will suspect that you never intended to fulfil your obligations associated with your initial visa.

Changing status from student or visitor without renewing once would be difficult, if not impossible, for example. But if you are doing the TAPIF program, which ends after 7-8 months, and want to switch to another status, it is feasible. In the latter situation, you would not be avoiding your obligations under your visa type, but instead you would simply be seeking a new status because the program that allowed you to move to France has ended.

Seek professional guidance and schedule a consultation with us on this topic before you attempt to change your status if you have any doubts about your ability to do so. Sometimes it is easier and more cost-effective to return to your home country and to apply for a new visa rather than to wait and change your status in France, even if it causes your time in France to restart.

3. Make your appointment.

For a change of visa status, you will have to specifically request a "changement de statut" and identify both your *current* visa type and your *future* carte de séjour status (the one you want to receive.)

You may be able to complete your change of status request online through ANEF or Démarches Simplifiées depending on the change you would like to make. If your change of status requires an appointment, you will not be able to make an appointment for a change of status on the automatic online system, so you will have to call or use the email form and explain in detail what you want to do in a comments box. Expect to wait a few weeks to receive a response, and if your change of status is uncommon, the agents might not know the answer or how to do it.

4. Submit your application.
Some préfectures will require you to submit a complete change-of-status application by mail that they will pre-screen before they will give you an appointment. Others just have you make an appointment by web, email, or phone, and evaluate it after you submit it in-person.

Show up to the préfecture at the appointed date and time and submit the complete application with all of the recommended documents from the list they gave you and the list I've provided here. You want to treat the change-of-status process as being just as serious, if not more serious, as applying for the visa in your home country.

5. Wait for approval and your new carte de séjour.
You will maintain your original carte de séjour status until your new status is officially approved and you receive your new card. For example, if you are switching your visa status from student to profession libérale, you will not be able to start your microentrepreneur activity until you have received a récépissé with your new "profession libérale" status. The new card will enable you to register as a microentrepreneur, whereas your student status would not. Similarly, if you switch from "visitor" to "vie privée et familiale" by marrying a French partner, you will not be able to begin working until you get a récépissé or carte de séjour that specifies your new status and your ability to work.

In most cases, the récépissé you receive at your renewal appointment will maintain your former status until you go to pick up your new card. This is to give the préfecture time to review your application properly before officially allowing you to begin work. You should refer to the récépissé you receive at your appointment, which will specify whether your status has changed and what, if any, work authorizations you have and whether you can register a business activity.

4.6 Requesting a 10-Year Resident Card

If you are in France on a visa type that requires a Contrat d'Intégration Républicaine or have a Passeport Talent Carte de Séjour, you are entitled to submit a request for a 10-year resident card after 5 years of living continuously in France, or after 3 years of being married to a French person.

The benefits of residency, aside from having to go to the préfecture far less frequently, are numerous. Instead of having your application scrutinized and evaluated every year or every couple of years, your renewal becomes a mere administrative formality. To renew a 10-year card, you provide documents like a justificatif de domicile and a copy of your tax declaration, and your card is renewed automatically. It would be extremely rare for a 10-year card to not be renewed.

As a resident, you also gain the broader right to work in France, and your work rights are no longer tied to a particular job or status. If you were previously on a profession libérale status because you are a registered autoentrepreneur, you can apply for a CDI in a completely different field. You can resign from a salaried position and go back to school or start a company. You can get downsized from your job, ride out your unemployment benefits, and start your own business. The possibilities are endless.

Being a French resident also enables you to live and work in other EU countries more easily. While each EU country has their own policies for transferring your residency status and work rights, you may be able to get a more favorable immigration status in another EU country if you decide to move. You may not have to start over with the new country's procedures. This benefit, of course, has to be confirmed with an immigration professional from the target EU country, as each country retains the right to manage its own immigration and internal affairs.

Finally, you can spend more time outside of France while retaining the right to return to the country as a resident. You can spend 3 years total out of the 10 years living outside of France without losing your rights. If you need to spend months at a time at home to take care of an ailing parent, or if you want to take a temporary opportunity working in another country, it's possible.

What titre de séjour status do you need to apply?

You can apply for a 10-year resident card if you have one of the following visa types: salarié, passeport talent salarié or carte bleue européenne, scientifique / chercheur, profession libérale, entrepreneur (commerçant, artisan, industriel), profession artistique, passeport talent entrepreneur, vie privée et familiale.

You cannot apply for a 10-year resident card if you have any of the following visa types: visitor*, temporary stay, student, recherche d'emploi, stagiaire familial (au pair), work holiday, jeune professionnel (FACC), travailleur temporaire, salarié en mission.

*In some cases, if you have renewed a visitor visa for at least 5 years (usually more), your local préfecture may issue a 10-year resident card with the status of visitor, which does not necessarily enable you to work. You should not rely on maintaining a visitor status for 5 years in order to ultimately receive work rights in France. There is anecdotal evidence of some préfectures granting this status to people with a visitor titre de séjour who have also provided proof of paying taxes and obtaining at least a B1 level of French with an official language exam.

What time counts towards residency?

The 5 years of residency required must be *uninterrupted,* meaning you must not have left France to apply for a new visa during that time. If you come to France as an au pair for 2 years, then apply to TAPIF and work two years as an English assistant after returning home each time for a new visa, and then return to France with a passeport talent salarié, the clock resets with each new visa. Only the time spent with the Passeport Talent Salarié would begin the countdown to applying for residency.

Conversely, if you switch your status within France and do NOT go to your home country to apply for a new visa, all of the years count towards your residency application, including statuses that do not make you eligible for residency on their own. For example, if you arrive in France as a student for 2 years, then switch to Recherche d'Emploi for one year, then start freelancing with a profession libérale - entrepreneur visa, you will be eligible for a 10 year card after your second year as a profession libérale (2+1+2=5).

It is important to note, however, you typically don't get the option to request a residency card unless your current carte de séjour is up for renewal, so if you have a multi-year card when your 5 years accumulates, you will request your 10 year card at the following renewal, and may apply for naturalization in the meantime.

Minimum Requirements for a 10-Year Residency Application
Establishing long-term residency in France and receiving a 10-year resident card requires the following:

- ✓ At least 5 years of continuous presence in France while maintaining the terms of the visa.
- ✓ Financial stability, defined as earning SMIC (French minimum wage, currently about €1.767 per month gross monthly salary as of July 2024), or about €21.204 per year.
- ✓ If you are in a salaried position, being in a CDI and outside of your période d'essai.
- ✓ B1 level of French, as demonstrated by the DELF B1, OFII course certificates, or TCF exam results less than 2 years old. Note that this language requirement increased from A2 to B1 in 2024, though there are exemptions for those with medical issues and people over 65.
- ✓ Filing French tax declarations for 5 consecutive years, even if some years show zero earnings or zero taxes owed.

How to Apply for Residency
Applying for a 10-year residency card is straightforward, and it is done at the same time as your regular renewal procedure. Because préfectures now issue some multi-year cartes de séjour, you may be in France longer than 5 years before your renewal appointment enables you to apply. You cannot make an appointment to apply for residency outside of your normal renewal.

To request a 10-year resident card, you should prepare your carte de séjour renewal application thoroughly, as normal, and write an additional cover letter in French specifically requesting the card. Along with your regular application, you should provide a document evidencing your B1 level of French, and you should provide a tax summary from your local tax office showing your annual income and taxes paid over the duration of your time in France.

You will not necessarily know whether your request for the 10-year card has been approved during your appointment, so it may be a happy surprise when you go to pick up your card. If you requested a 10-year card and do not receive one, make sure you meet the requirements and request it again at the following renewal.

4.7 Applying for French Naturalization

Applying for naturalization as a French citizen is a separate process from getting a 10 year residency card. You do not have to be a resident with a 10-year card in order to apply, as you may not have received the 10-year card yet if you have switched statuses several times or have a multiyear card valid beyond your 5th Franciversary.

As of July 2023, requests for naturalization by decree are filed online with the NATALI platform on the ANEF website, while requests for naturalization through marriage are still currently filed via an in-person appointment at your local préfecture. You should check your préfecture's procedures.

Naturalisation through Descent or "Double droit du sol"
Several EU countries like Ireland and Italy offer citizenship through descent from a citizen, and allow the grandchildren or even great-grandchildren of citizens to also obtain citizenship. Unfortunately, France does not offer citizenship through descent. Acquiring French citizenship through blood requires a parent to be French and recognize the child, and it must be requested before the child reaches the age of majority. Being born in France does not automatically grant citizenship to a child until the child has lived continuously in France, completed schooling in the country, and requested it as a teenager. French citizenship can also be granted through "double birthright": meaning a child born in France to a non-French person also born in France would be considered eligible to request citizenship. You can clarify all of these items with an immigration professional.

Naturalisation par mariage
If you are married to a French citizen, there is a relatively simple, if not bureaucratically long process called naturalization "par mariage," during which you submit proof of your marriage and common residence for at least 4 years. (5 years if you and your spouse have not lived in France for the whole 5 years.) This process does not require any particular level of financial stability, and is considered a right. If the administration rejects your request, it has to motivate its response,

such as suspecting that the marriage is fake or identifying you as a 'threat to public order.' However, if you obtain French nationality through marriage and then get divorced within 2 years of receiving your nationality, it can be revoked.

Naturalisation par décret
Naturalization "by decree" (par décret) is the main type of French naturalization, which is independent from your personal relationships. It requires submitting a thorough application demonstrating your integration into France, along with proof of your income and job history. Typically, to be naturalized, you must be financially stable, which means making at least minimum wage (currently €1.767 per month in 2024 or €21.204 gross annual income) as a freelancer or an employee, consistently, for 3 years. If you are an employee, you should be in a CDI and outside of your trial period.

You must also have a stable visa status, like a salarié or profession libérale visa, which is continuously renewed during your naturalization process. It is not possible, for example, to transition from a student visa directly to naturalization, even if you have been in France for more than 5 years.

Finally, if you're applying by decree you'll have to demonstrate that you have at least a B2 level of French, and have an interview on French culture and history to demonstrate how you've assimilated into life in France. The Ministre de l'Intérieur publishes a Guide du Citoyen that can be used to study for the questions you might be asked at this interview.

Timeline
The procedure for naturalization by decree can take up to 18 months, during which time any changes to your visa status, income, or financial situation can derail your application. Quitting or being fired from your job, seeing a dip in your income because you switch from a salaried position to a freelance position, or even taking parental leave to have children can affect the success of your application. If your application is adjourned, you have to wait 2 years before you can reapply.

Application Procedure

As of 2023, all naturalization applications are processed through a new online system, NATALI (NATuralisations en LIgne), where you can upload documents and track your application's processing online. You no longer have to make an appointment to submit your application at your local préfecture. When your application is processed, you'll be invited for your interview at the préfecture, and then when it has been approved, you will be invited for your naturalization ceremony if one is planned.

Getting Help with Your Franceformation

When you're planning your move to France, the key thing to remember is that you're not just applying for a visa or doing certain specific administrative tasks. You're creating a whole new life and getting set up in a whole new system. All of the admin things you've set up over the course of your whole life up to this point - from becoming part of your country's healthcare system to opening a bank account to learning the language - are things you will have to work on and set up during your first year in France. You'll have blind spots, and you won't understand exactly how all of the different administrations interact. And that's why it's important to have professional guidance: because you don't know what you don't know. Many people who try to go it alone or only get help on certain items end up missing essential steps in their relocation process, which can make it difficult to complete all of the required tasks during your first year.

Getting professional assistance to determine your visa type and to help you to create and submit a thorough application is one of the best ways to practically ensure your successful arrival, but it's not enough to ensure your successful Franceformation. Of course, even professional guidance is not a 100% guarantee of getting your visa, but it can eliminate or reduce most of the potential issues with your application. Having assistance throughout the visa application process can also keep you on track and reduce the stress of not knowing what you should be doing and when.

All professional services we provide include the stipulation that if your visa application is not successful the first time, we will reevaluate and rework the complete application for a resubmission at no additional charge, within one year.

If you have already submitted a visa application unsuccessfully, please consult a professional before making any subsequent submissions.

Reapplying after one application failure is not ideal but possible; multiple application rejections significantly lower your chances of ever getting a French visa.

What is a "Franceformation"?

The concept of Franceformation ties in a few different ideas. The transformation of our client's lives, in all of the most practical ways through the emotional transformation that accompanies major life changes such as an international move. In English, the word "formation" is the creation of something new, or it can represent an orderly or organized structure. In French, the word "formation" is a training or educational program, and a Franceformation encompasses a period of learning about yourself, your dreams, and your abilities, along with more broad topics like living in France, the French visa and renewal process, and various French bureaucracy and administration. It also includes learning new language skills and adapting to a new culture and way of life. Finally, a formation is also a deposit of solid rock, which represents the solid foundation we create for the projects and life goals my clients develop.

Franceformation, / fræns fɔrˈmeɪʃən /, n.f.:

1. The creation of one's new life in France;
2. The personal transformation one undergoes when moving to France and incubating a new life;
3. The intense period of learning about oneself, about French bureaucracy, and about French language and culture, which occurs as one prepares to move to France and adapts to a new culture;
4. A full-service and support program to nurture you from the moment you decide to move to France, through your visa application, arrival, and beyond.

Are you ready to commit to yours?

You can leverage expertise to enhance and accelerate your Franceformation journey.

Consider that your future dream life in France is a huge canvas, and right now, it is blank. Our job while working together is first to outline the image you want to paint, and then, to paint by number, filling in colors all over the canvas until the beautiful image emerges. At the moment, if you're not even sure what visa type you'll apply for, you may not be able to envision the future image at all. And yet, it's there. The life that you want to create for yourself is inside of you, and our most important task is to extract it, without damaging it or telling you that for some reason, you can't have it.

Once we have played midwives to your new life goals, our next step is to nurture and protect them as they mature, and as we begin to paint inside the lines and bring the colors to life. In this stage, during the process of determining how to bring your dream to life, it's important to continually nourish it with positive energy and excitement, and to avoid naysayers and "realists" who will be "concerned" that you are wasting your time on something that may not come to fruition. You may have your own doubts during this stage, and it's important to question your doubts and fears to prevent them from taking over. *Il faut cultiver son jardin* — and pull the weeds as we go.

The higher your enthusiasm, your energy, and your belief in yourself, your project, and your ability to make the move, the faster we will be able to fill in the grid and bring your dream to life. We can quickly build momentum and create the outlines of your new life, but at the same time, we have to avoid moving too fast and burning out. It's a delicate balance, to build energy and momentum on one hand, while pacing ourselves on the other. If we're not careful, moving too fast, or *danser plus vite que la musique*, the first obstacle or challenge will derail your project and your belief in your ability to make it happen.

Our unique Franceformation process is a holistic process to help you identify what you want to create in each area of your life, to guide you through the visa process for creating it, and to facilitate your passage through the administrative challenges that await you during the visa application procedure and upon arrival in France. We want to ensure that you have all of the tools you need and awareness of all of the challenges and issues you'll face as an immigrant to France.

You may want to begin planning your Franceformation early on, or you may be ready to start the visa process imminently. If you want to get some initial advice and ask questions about what visa type may be the best for your situation, you may want to attend one of our free monthly Q&A sessions for feedback on your plans, or schedule a paid one-hour consultation to understand all of your options and talk through all of your questions.

Once you have an idea of which type of immigration you'll pursue and what your goals are, you can request a proposal from us, and we can have a brief chat to understand your timeline and discuss which of our packages may be a good fit for you if we're working together. During our a consultation, we'll discuss what actual barriers there are to beginning your move process, and what barriers you've created in your mind to hold up the process.

We'll discuss your overall readiness to make your move happen. A sense of "readiness" to take a big step isn't something that comes from outside of you. It is something that you create inside of you, and you do it by taking action. While sometimes our clients have concrete time constraints, like waiting for a child to graduate, or selling their house, many times, the time constraints are in their minds.

As we begin our work together, you'll get access to our complete library of materials to prepare you for your move to France and the administrative work that awaits you upon arrival. From a moving checklist of documents to gather and things to do before you submit your visa application, to tutorials on post-arrival procedures like enrolling your kids in school, registering your business, or filing your first French tax return, you'll be accompanied along every step of your journey.

The 5 Foundations of the Franceformation system:
Throughout our years assisting people in moving to France, not only have we developed the expertise required to help them determine the right visa type for their goals and to achieve success, we've also developed a thorough understanding of the other tools and support you'll need as you move through the relocation process. Using our

previous experience with many clients, we've developed useful documentation in five key areas to help you to fill in the colors of your Franceformation canvas more quickly and more vividly than you could do it on your own.

Mindset – When preparing for such a huge life changing event like an international move, your mindset is key, and questioning or reflecting on any doubts or challenges about your ability to move to France or your ability to bring your new dream life to fruition is key to ensuring your success. Cultivating your success mindset so you continue to grow personally and professionally is a lifelong journey.

Money – Figuring out and preparing for financial security throughout the move is an important part of allowing you to feel secure during the process and confident in your ability to make the move work. It's also an important aspect of the visa application, in that a certain amount of money in cash is required for each type of visa. We have created a workbook and resources for you to calculate your expected expenses during the move, money coming in and out, and how to generate extra money to put towards your moving expenses and savings, to help you create a full-color picture of your finances as you develop your moving timeline.

Professional Development — Your career may look different in France, depending on your skills, professional experience, and ability to continue working in your same field, or not. Salaries in France are lower, benefits are higher, and overall, the ability to get a sponsored work visa can vary greatly based on your experience and salary expectations. While we will determine your likely visa path before even beginning the process, you'll have access to professional development workbooks and professional guidance on developing your career options or business ideas into full-fledged projects and plans. Once you have an idea of where your skills and experience could take you in France, we'll be able to put together a coherent and compelling strategy for your professional launch and future success in France.

Language – Speaking French, or being dedicated to learning, is essential to creating a successful and fulfilling life in France. While you'll need to find other tools and resources to improve your skills, we provide vocabulary lists for our most important bureaucratic endeavors and help you to identify the gaps in your language knowledge that you'll want to address quickly.

French Admin Preparation – There are lots of small admin tasks you can do to get ready for your move to France, from collecting copies of official documents like your birth certificate and driving record, to getting insurance documents necessary for the visa application. The admin and bureaucracy tasks you need to complete before your departure are broken down into bite-sized items you can do at your own pace, with an explanation of why you need to do each task and what you'll need each document for. Once you arrive, you'll receive a email sequences to walk you through each administrative step we need to take care of upon arrival to set up your life for success.

Of course, depending on your service package, some packages include all of the French administration done for you, with follow-up support available. Decluttering the life you have now and letting go of various aspects of it is key to finding peace and happiness as part of your move. It's all too easy to bring the clutter (physical and emotional) with us, then wonder why we are frustrated, stagnant, and stuck in the new place as well as the old. Usually, when clients come to us to begin their Franceformation, they have already begun the process of ungrounding and of laying the groundwork for their new life in France, and our service helps them to see the full picture and ensure they don't miss any essential steps in the process.

Franceformation Relocation Services Packages

At Your Franceformation, we are passionate about helping individuals, couples, and families turn their dream of living in France into a reality. Our team specializes in guiding clients through the entire relocation process, from preparing visa applications and handling French bureaucracy to ensuring that all the necessary paperwork is completed for a smooth transition to life in France.

We work closely with clients for 3-6 months before their move, offering personalized support to prepare for the visa application and initial administrative tasks. Once they've arrived in France, we continue to assist them for an additional 6 months, making sure everything is set up correctly, from healthcare and banking to housing and insurance. Many of our clients choose to stay with us even beyond the initial move, relying on our expertise for visa renewals and long-term support.

At the core of Your Franceformation are values of integrity, dedication, and a deep commitment to making the relocation process stress-free and enjoyable. We understand that our clients are moving to France because they love the country and envision a life here, and we are here to make that journey as seamless as possible. Our goal is to ensure our clients complete all of the essential paperwork during the first year - so they are set up right, and have a sustainable future in France.

Our done-for-you client packages:

Business Creation, Self-Employment, and Artistic Packages

VIP Concierge Package for Business & Self-Employed Clients: Our VIP Concierge Package is designed specifically for business owners, entrepreneurs, and self-employed professionals, including remote workers and those with clients around the world, who are looking to establish or expand their ventures and who are becoming tax residents in France. This premium service offers hands-on, personalized support, guiding you through the intricacies of French business administration, legal requirements, and financial management. From setting up your business structure and handling taxes, to securing the right permits and navigating the auto-entrepreneur or micro-entrepreneur systems, our dedicated team will ensure that every step of the process is handled with care and expertise. In addition, we work closely with legal and accounting partners to cover the legal bits we are not able to handle ourselves. With tailored advice, exclusive access to expert consultations, and ongoing support, our VIP Concierge Package provides you with the peace of mind that your business is fully compliant and positioned for success in France.

Artist & Entrepreneur clients begin working with us 4-6 months before they plan to apply for their French Visa.

https://www.yourfranceformation.com/artist-entrepreneur/

Retirement & Sabbatical Packages

VIP Concierge Package for Retirement Clients: Our VIP Concierge Package is tailored for individuals and couples planning their retirement in France, offering personalized support to ensure a smooth and stress-free transition for those who do not plan to work in France. From securing the appropriate visa and managing healthcare registration to organizing your finances and navigating French bureaucracy, our team will guide you every step of the way. With this VIP package, you'll receive dedicated assistance to ensure that your retirement in France is as relaxing and fulfilling as you've always dreamed.

Our retirement & sabbatical clients often begin working with us less than 3 months in advance, although they can begin the process earlier if they wish to start Client Orientation and have the time to follow Fast Track to France earlier on.

https://www.yourfranceformation.com/retirement-sabbatical/

French & EU Family Packages

VIP Concierge Package for Families: This VIP Concierge Package is designed for families with a French or EU citizen parent who are looking for some extra help with the required paperwork and also with getting each family member settled in to life in France. We provide comprehensive support to help you navigate the complexities of moving with children, from managing school enrollments and healthcare registration to securing the right visas for every family member. Our team ensures that every aspect of your transition is taken care of, from requesting the carte de séjour and DCEMs to handling insurance and banking setup. With expert guidance, personalized recommendations, and ongoing support, we're here to ensure your family's move to France is stress-free and successful, so you can focus on creating a fulfilling new life together.

https://www.yourfranceformation.com/family/

How to Get Started with Us

There are two main ways to get started working with us:

1) If You're Ready Now - Request a Proposal

Many of our clients get to know us over the course of weeks and months through social media, webinars, and the free monthly Q&As before deciding to work with us. If this is you, and you're fairly confident you'd like to work with us, you can request a proposal on the Your Franceformation site, or email us and request a proposal for the package you'd like to purchase. We'll send you the package proposal, and you can review it to ensure it meets your needs. Then, you can have a chat with a member of the Franceformation team to ensure we can meet your travel date requirements and verify that it's a good fit before you register.

You can submit an inquiry for a proposal on our website, on the page providing information about your package.

2) If You Have More Questions - Schedule a Paid Consultation

If you're a bit farther out in the process and still have a bunch of questions you'd like to have answered before you start the process, you can schedule a paid call with Allison or another member of the Franceformation team. You'll get a full hour to ask all of your questions and benefit from our guidance, with no strings attached. If you do want to request a proposal and then sign up for our services within 90 days, we'll apply the consultation fee as a credit to whichever package you select.

https://www.yourfranceformation.com/consultation/

Our Clients' Praise for Your Franceformation

Throughout the time we have been assisting people moving to France, we have had the pleasure of working with many wonderful clients who valued our expertise and enjoyed the process of developing their relocation plan.

Here is a sample of some testimonials and kind words from our clients:

* * * * *

We had always wanted to live in Europe, but it was just never the right time. Even with a French language background, I really had no idea how to start the moving process and I didn't want to waste time scrolling through social media sites to see what others were doing. After joining the Facebook group, Americans in France, I bought Foolproof French Visas, contacted Allison, and started the whirlwind application and moving process.

I found Allison to be extremely professional and knowledgeable about all the administrative tasks we needed to complete. Now that we have made it through the first year in France and have a better understanding of the administrative processes, thanks to Allison and her team, we are excited to be able to take the time to enjoy the French lifestyle.

Anyone looking to move to France should consult with Your Franceformation on the visa and relocation process! There's no need to waste time trying to figure it out yourself.

- *Penelope Lespinasse, VIP Concierge Entrepreneur Client for Profession Libérale*

* * * * *

We were back and forth for 2 years about moving to France. We knew it would be a huge change especially because we have three children. I also knew it would be challenging to get our business open and going there and was nervous about all the documents and regulations. So much of what we were afraid of was the paperwork. We really wanted our children to have a different experience growing up and I really wanted to expand my business to Europe, but we were just terrified of the paperwork and the difficulty in transition for all the details.

I chose to work with Your Franceformation because I had connected with Allison on a call before and really felt like she understood the ins and outs of the system. I connected with her personality and straightforward approach. Looking back on it, with our successful approval, one of the best decisions was hiring Allison and her team to help us. We couldn't have imagined embarking on this journey alone without her support. We have been so excited to be immersed in the culture, have our children learning a new language, taking advantage of the beautiful country of France, enjoying the incredible wine and food, and now finding new ways to expand our business here.

The best advice I can give someone who is embarking on the journey to move to France is to seek assistance. I truly believe it's not something you should do on your own. Having a guide walking alongside you, every step of the way, has taken so much stress out of the process. It doesn't always mean it will be easy or perfect, but it's so wonderful to know you have Allison and her team alongside you to listen, support you, and find the solutions you need.

I would highly recommend Your Franceformation to anyone who is relocating to France, whether for retirement or to start a business.

- Eliza, VIP Concierge Entrepreneur Client for Passeport Talent Création d'Entreprise

⭐ ⭐ ⭐ ⭐ ⭐

After reading Foolproof French Visas and booking a session with Allison, I knew I didn't need to look elsewhere. Your Franceformation are experts and we placed our trust in them, rightly so. They made it so easy for us to go through the process by basically doing it all for us. All we had to do was show up!

While we were preparing for the move, it took significant stress off our shoulders to have the Your Franceformation team handling our visa applications. We were retiring from our jobs and starting to downsize our home in anticipation of the move. Adding the visa application process on top of already stressful events was just too much. With Your Franceformation, we've never had to stress about what to do next. The team is always one step ahead of us and sends us the information we need to get things done.

I've already recommended Your Franceformation to a couple of friends who are looking to move to France - one for work and the other for retirement, like us. Anyone even considering the move should do at least a consultation with Allison to learn more.

- *Corinne, Visitor Visa VIP Concierge Client*

* * * * *

I started to do the process of applying for a visa myself and was extremely frustrated with the website and the application. I had followed Allison's Facebook group "Americans in France" and she always had the answers for so many people who would post. I thought that if I didn't work with her I would never be able to do it myself. I had already been trying it myself for a month.

So, I chose to work with Allison after following her online and especially after our first conversation. She is charming, knowledgeable and reliable. She was extremely helpful and answered any of my questions with clarity and patience. I followed her instructions and was able to get my long term visa within a month after speaking to her.

Allison is friendly, reliable, available and gets the job done. Working with others in France is not so easy. They take forever to respond or don't respond at all. I recommend Allison highly and would use her services again.

- *Sharon, Visitor Visa VIP Concierge Package*

* * * * *

As new immigrants to France with limited French language skills, we were overwhelmed with the paperwork (driver's license / CPAM / visa renewal) and sought out help.

We chose to work with Allison because we didn't want someone who did the boilerplate thing but to work with someone who would provide a personalized solution. Allison could give us the personalized help we needed and we didn't want to mess it up by doing it ourselves. We first thought we had it together and then COVID hit and everything sort of changed. We couldn't keep up with everything and couldn't even make an appointment at the préfecture in Tours. We're cautious people and wanted to do it right.

Thanks to the help we received from Allison we did do it right! We can stay in France another year, the driver's license exchange went through and all the things we set out to do are done or well underway. By working with Allison we were able to benefit from her experience. Because she knows the system, she was able to handle new complications and find creative solutions or tap other resources to help solve our problems. We've recommended Allison many times and would recommend working with her under any circumstances.

- Sue and Dave, Visitor Visa Renewal VIP Concierge Package

* * * * *

From Allison we learned that when it comes to French bureaucracy, 'No doesn't mean no. We just have to reach a compromise.'
Before working with Allison, it was a struggle understanding the process because it's a very different bureaucratic step by step. We wanted to make sure we didn't duplicate efforts or miss an important step and we wanted our hands held for the bureaucracy.

Even if we thought we knew what we were doing, we would have wasted our efforts if we didn't know where to go. Working with Allison was worth every bit of the fee we've paid. After reading her book [Foolproof French Visas] we decided to work with Allison. The book was very comprehensive and she sounded very knowledgeable. She knew what she was talking about and was fully able to lead us through the process. I liked the fact that in the book she didn't keep any secrets. After reading it, I believed I could do it myself, but I just didn't want to! A lot of the info we found on our own was more applicable to British citizens who were retiring but we wanted an American guide.

Thanks to Allison's help we could finally move to France...and eat delicious bread ! We have our visa so we could move on to France and the next step of what we want to do in our lives. It's been a bit scary, but it's good to know we did the process correctly so we won't get sent home for not doing things the way they should be done.

By working with Allison we saved time and effort. We learned to trust in the process and were confident that as long as we followed the steps we would get there. Any American considering moving to France should work with Allison.

- Julie & Russ, VIP Concierge Entrepreneur Package for Passeport Talent Profession Artistique

* * * * *

Before working with Allison we didn't know what to do...we wanted to go to France and had no direction. I read Allison's book and realized that we needed more help than the reading materials, so we contacted her. Allison made everything very clear and gave us step by step instructions and as a result, we got to fulfill our dream. I don't think either of us were capable of following the steps without guidance. There were a lot of moving parts and Allison eliminated a lot of stress for us so we were able to engage with the rest of the transition. It was a big thing to have confidence and be assured we were doing the right things while we were doing the other things we needed to do. She cleared the way on a weedy path we couldn't get through ourselves; she had the lawnmower we needed.

Is there anyone else I would have worked with? No ! She's the girl. We had our initial talk, felt a connection, and felt like we could rely on her to do what needed to be done to get us to France.

And thanks to Allison's help, we're here! She made it simpler for us to get here. We moved with confidence each step of the way, confidence in her guidance. So much chatter on the internet with everyone saying different things but we listened to her and were confident she had the right information.

We got to come to France! We got to live our dream and come to France and be with our family! We're here for cheap wine, grandchildren, and delicious bread. And we're going to start our plans for building our house. I would always recommend someone work with Allison.

- Chris J., Visitor Visa VIP Concierge Package

* * * * *

Thanks to Allison's guidance, I successfully got my profession liberale visa. All of the questions and training provided by Allison helped me to think through the visa application and business plan and determine how to make money and earn a living in Paris.

I knew I wanted to move to France. Last fall/winter, I had a timeline but no real info on how to make it happen. I had no real knowledge/info about the visas or process, so it was a complete lack of info. I knew I needed to hire someone to help me. After seeing Allison on a video event, I decided to work with her because of her success rate getting the visas.

The biggest value in working with her is the success of obtaining my visa. She helped me to determine the right type (profession liberale), lay out the things needed and have everything set up in order to be successful in Paris.

With Allison's help and expertise, I was able to understand the French visa process, understand how to integrate into French culture & bureaucracy once I had arrived and establish a good plan for actually having a decent income in Paris. Considering that she does the full range of visas, I'd recommend anyone who wants to move to France work with Allison!

- Brian B., VIP Concierge Entrepreneur Package for Profession Libérale

* * * * *

We're here in France...and with a valid visa!
We really appreciated Allison's expertise and how calm she is. We often would hear her say things like, « It's fine, don't worry, I see this all the time, this is what we're going to do », reassuring us that whatever it was, it was completely normal. We didn't know what to expect from the French side but we knew that it wasn't going to be like walking into an English civil service office and that the American attitude wouldn't work. With Allison guiding us, we felt like we were in very competent hands.

When we first went on the VFS website on our own, we felt like they were asking us to give lots of information without telling us what we should be doing. It felt like we were shooting in the dark. The explanations they gave on the France-Visas site were not helpful at all and were confusing. We weren't confident we were going to easily fit into a box until Allison clearly explained it all. It really gave us peace of mind knowing that Allison was there to help us. We knew that if we were thrown some oddball thing at the interview, Allison would just be a message away to help us deal with it.

We actually didn't speak to anyone else and chose to work with Allison from the start. Allison offered a whole package with admin support that made us very comfortable with our choice. She offers a lot of info on the website and lots of comprehensive stuff in the package like recommendations for lots of other professionals. The fact that she's American really appealed to us too, because if you're dealing with a French person, they're seeing it from the French perspective, not from an American perspective.
Working with Allison really took a lot of uncertainty out of the process.

We recommend working with Allison under any circumstances - if someone needs help with moving, visas, applied for the wrong visa, or just don't know what to do next,

-Carol & Kerry, Visitor Visa VIP Concierge Package

* * * * *

As a non French speaking person, I needed help trying to navigate the complex French red tape. With my daily routine of caring for my mom, I didn't have the time and patience to navigate it all. I needed help even though my wife is French speaking, because she's a busy doctor and I was on my own.

I'd been participating in Allison's Facebook group and found it really informational. Allison just seemed like the obvious person to work with. She seemed outgoing, accessible and had a lot of information.

Thanks to the fact that I worked with Allison, I got my visa! With her there was no language barrier. In addition, Allison is up on modern technology and it was an easy process to negotiate. The use of technology was very helpful, as was having access to the Americans in France facebook group. Allison was very reassuring, she has published a book about this and I felt comfortable knowing she had the knowledge and had done it before for Americans.

Anybody wanting to come to France should definitely work with Allison! I know a lot of people who are looking to move to France during retirement. I would recommend any of those folks to her.

-Hugh, Family & Visitor Visa VIP Concierge Package

* * * * *

Thanks to Allison, I get to realize a lifelong goal of living in France! I was unsuccessful at applying for a work-visa on my own. With Allison's help, I can now legally work as a freelancer to support myself as I experience the French lifestyle and culture.

Between visiting the visa facilitation center, application fees and other expenses, I wasted a lot of time and money unsuccessfully applying for a visa to France. I originally tried navigating the process with free guidance from well-intentioned friends-of-friends. Unbeknownst to me, while they may have already been granted their visas, their situation was too different from mine to be applicable. I can now see how Allison's personalized assistance made all the difference. Working with Allison was a smart investment that paid off.

With Allison's help, I created a business plan that I am confident will support me abroad. I was granted an auto-entrepreneur visa and she helped me to correctly organize my French taxes and banking for a long, happy stay in France. Working with Allison was time-saving, there was no guesswork, and gave me confidence.

If you're looking to properly move to France for a year or longer, I recommend you contact Allison to help you navigate the process. There are so many steps to take and factors unique to each person's move, that going it alone or following what "someone else did," may not get you the results you want. With Allison as my visa coach, I got guidance specific to me and was granted a visa. Thank you, Allison!

- Joanne, VIP Concierge Entrepreneur Package for Profession Libérale

Franceformation Courses & Digital Products

Fast Track to France

The Fast Track to France program is an 11-module online course that helps you to navigate the French relocation process with confidence and ease. Designed to help you cut through the complexity of moving to France, this comprehensive program provides you with the tools, resources, and expert guidance to ensure a smooth transition, while guiding you through the 9 Areas of Franceformation, from career and finances to housing and making friends. Recently revised and updated for 2024-2025, Fast Track to France is available as part of all our service packages or as a stand-alone option, and covers everything from visa applications and housing to healthcare, taxes, and banking. Whether you're preparing for your move or already settling in, this program offers the support you need to successfully build your new life in France.

Www.yourfranceformation.com/fast-track/

Our clients say:
* * * * *
Overall the application process was positive. In general it was a step by step process & hidden things in the application that were confusing were made straightforward through the program. It made everything less stressful and a lot easier.

In previous years with other countries, I've had trouble with visa applications and sought out someone who had experience and knowledge because if not it seemed like the luck of the draw for people who didn't really know the ins and outs.

I decided to work with Allison because I saw some reviews on her Facebook page of positive experiences. She has good knowledge of French bureaucracy & visas. She knows different kinds of situations for visas so you know what you qualify for and she knew the information needed for the visa I was applying for.

I would recommend Allison to anyone who wants more general information on the process and different types of visas.

- Nick, Fast Track to France student

* * * * *

I have been using Fast Track to France and the Complete French Business Incubator to plan my move to France and develop ideas for my business. The programs are very well-organized, and going through them in order helps me to get the answers I need, before I even know to ask the questions. I'm not even half-way through the program content yet, and I've gained so much clarity about my move to France and what I need to do to make it happen this year! I'm so glad I purchased Fast Track to France and that I have these resources for my move.

- Pat, Fast Track to France and Complete French Business Incubator student

The Complete French Business Incubator

The Complete French Business Incubator is an all-in-one course designed for aspiring entrepreneurs ready to launch and grow their business in France. This program walks you through every step of setting up and managing a business in France, from navigating French regulations and legal requirements to creating a solid business plan, mastering taxes, and handling accounting. With expert guidance, detailed resources, and ongoing support, the Complete French Business Incubator ensures you have everything you need to succeed as an entrepreneur in France. Whether you're just getting started or looking to expand, this course is your key to building a thriving business. Since 2017, this program has been helping individuals write their business and project plans for the four self-employment visa types: Profession Libérale Entrepreneur, Passeport Talent Entrepreneur, classic Entrepreneur, and Passeport Talent Profession Artistique. This program was revised, updated, and fully re-recorded for 2024-2025!

Foolproof French Visas: Complete 2024-2025 Edition
Www.yourfranceformation.com/business-incubator/

* * * * *

Before working with Allison on my move to France, I struggled with knowing what visa to apply for, if I had a good case and how to plan my time in the States. I therefore decided to work with Allison because she seemed knowledgeable and the price point was right where I wanted it to be. While working with her, I received a clear program and assistance understanding things I needed to do in order to obtain my visa successfully.

Allison has a knack for knowing what will and won't work for a business plan. Her Complete French Business Incubator program helps you get clear on your business before putting your plan together. Another added benefit is that taking the time to set this up really does put you in a great position to start a business in France.

Thanks to Allison, my husband and I were both successful in obtaining our profession libérale visas and were able to relocate to France with our three children. I highly recommend Allison's program and services.

- Lindsay, Complete French Business Incubator student

The French Admin Tracker

The French Admin Tracker is a 64-page digital planner designed to help you organize and track all the essential tasks involved in relocating to France. With sections dedicated to visa checklists, housing, utilities, banking, insurance, and more, it ensures nothing is overlooked during your move and your first year in France. The tracker also includes pages for scheduling daily tasks, keeping notes, and managing everything from the état des lieux of your new apartment to exchanging your driver's license. This planner is your step-by-step guide to making a smooth transition to your new life in France.

Www.yourfranceformation.com/books/

The Franceformation Relocation Admin Success Survey

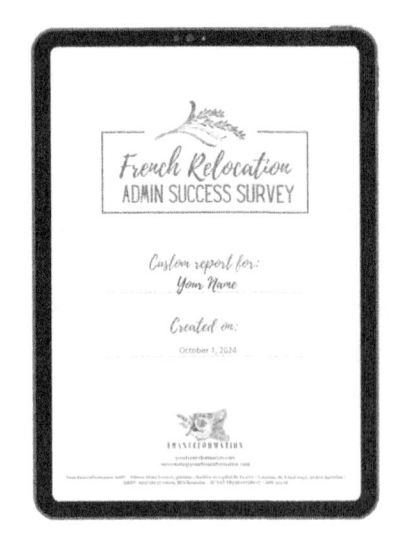

Franceformation Relocation Admin Success Survey: The Franceformation Relocation Admin Success Survey is a comprehensive 100+ question survey designed to help you ensure that all your French administrative tasks are complete during your first year in France. Covering everything from visa status, housing, banking, taxes, and healthcare, to children, pets, and business setup, this survey generates a personalized report highlighting any overlooked areas. Verified by the Franceformation team, the report provides tailored recommendations, partner referrals, and an optional fee quote for additional support to help you stay on top of French bureaucracy and ensure your long-term success in France.

Www.yourfranceformation.com/books/

Also by Allison Lounes

The 5 Decisions Big Dreamers Make Before Their Franceformation helps you determine whether you're ready to take the leap and move to France, and, if you're not yet ready, to show you how to get there. After working with dozens of clients who successfully and enthusiastically made the transition to living in France - and a handful of former clients who ultimately gave up pursuing their dream, Allison has identified the qualities most commonly embodied by the people who seem to effortlessly rise to the challenge of pursuing their international move. What makes them different, and how do they think differently about themselves and about their move? And are there beliefs or behaviors you can embrace in your own life to help you get ready to get ready to Franceform?

Link to purchase: https://www.yourfranceformation.com/books/

Allison Grant Lounes, Creator of Your Franceformation

I'm Allison.

I'm a visa specialist and consultant for people moving to France to help them imagine and align with their dream lives, get the right visa for creating the life they envision and navigate the French bureaucratic procedures that will enable them to achieve their goals. I created Your Franceformation, in order to work with highly motivated, creative, and heart-centered people who want to design a whole new life for themselves in France, who struggle with finding the right path for bringing their new life to life, and who would like to be fully supported as they blossom and *s'épanouir* into who they truly are.

What separates Your Franceformation from other relocation consultants is that we ONLY work with passionate people who are moving because they love France, the French language, and French culture, and they want support in creating a new life here. Because of this, clients receive personalized support and unbridled enthusiasm as they take their leap of faith into a new life, whether they're retiring or taking a sabbatical, seeking employment and visa sponsorship, or creating or moving a self-employment activity to France. Because our clients are fully supported from the very beginning - from figuring out the right work opportunity and visa for them, through the labyrinth of a full year of French administration, to understanding culture shock and the roller coaster of cultural adaptation, all the way to the finish line of their first visa renewal, they can truly flourish and thrive in their new home.

In this interview, I'll introduce myself and talk about how I became a

Franceformation relocation consultant and began helping people to achieve their goal of moving to France, and I will also identify the different ways we support our clients. I believe immigration is getting harder just as it's becoming more critical to creating a globalized, interconnected, and more empathetic world, and along with my wonderful team members, I'm on a mission to help make dreams bigger and the world smaller, one Franceformation at a time.

https://www.yourfranceformation.com/2021/11/22/bonus-episode-allison-grant-lounes/

Who are you, how long have you been in France, and how did you end up here?

After studying abroad for a year in college, I completely fell in love with Paris, and I moved back the fall after I graduated. I've been in France for over 10 years, and I started out as a student in a master's program in comparative literature in a French university. I was excited to study directly in a French university, not only because it improved my French so much, but also because I paid a grand total of €452 for a year of tuition AND a year of student health insurance. The same master's (not a lucrative one, I might add!) would have cost me $40,000 in tuition if I'd stayed at Columbia University.

As many Americans do, I spent the first two years teaching English with TAPIF to finance my studies. (You used to be able to do TAPIF while enrolled as a student, which is no longer the case.) Initially, I wasn't sure if I intended to stay in France, and I was applying to PhD programs back in the US. Ultimately, I began a second master's degree to be able to stay in France, and I found a job working in an American accounting firm, where I learned all about expat taxes and tax treaties.

I ended up getting married to my French boyfriend, enabling me to get French residency easily. But part of what pushed me to marriage, perhaps before I was ready (I was young!), was that fear of not being "good enough" to manage to stay in France on my own, of not finding the right job or the right kind of living to enable me to live my dream. While I don't regret being married, I do think that going the relationship route impacted my confidence in my ability to navigate the job and administrative challenges for myself, and it puts pressure on the relationship. And of course, if the relationship doesn't go well (I was lucky, but know people who weren't), it can create a whole set of problems for people who want to stay in France after ending a marriage.

What I want is to give people the freedom to create their dream lives in France, whatever that may look like, and to navigate the immigration process outside of the typical confines of employment sponsorship or marriage. The truth is that I believe those paths to relocation - while they seem easier - stifle creativity, limit freedom, and ultimately suffocate those who benefit from them. In choosing entrepreneurship, and in helping my clients to be fully informed about the different immigration possibilities and develop their own professional projects and career paths, I hope to empower them to embrace the true freedom that comes from creating their dream life outside of patriarchal and capitalist immigration structures and from becoming a citizen of the world.

What gave you the idea to move to France in the first place?
My aunt, a biology professor and a researcher, spent a year in Paris when I was 6. She taught me some French and told me about Paris, and I always wanted to come here. I always knew I'd study abroad in France.

In high school, after a friend died, I wanted to leave, to travel as far as possible, and I almost considered spending my senior year of high school doing an exchange program. I didn't, but moving to France, first to study abroad for a year and then to live permanently, ended up being an important part of my grieving process. It helped me to get away from everything and get back to myself: the pleasure of discovering new places, the peace from having beautiful surroundings, and the challenge of expressing my thoughts in a new language helped to heal my brain and my heart. I needed a complete change in my life to examine what I really wanted and how I could use my gifts to impact the world.

What were your biggest challenges when moving?
When I studied abroad, I had the full support of Columbia's study abroad program and its administrators, and they were available to answer lots of questions about French administration and completed a lot of the bureaucracy stuff on our behalf. When I moved independently, I was practically drowning in all of the stuff I had to do and figure out on my own. Even though I was completely fluent in French, I felt like I was constantly missing something or figuring out something important after-the-fact.

Plus, the isolation and lack of connection were very difficult. I suffered a lot from anxiety and panic attacks, and bouts of depression. But it took me a while to figure out what was going on, because I was mostly high-functioning. I was grateful for having social media and apps like Skype to stay in touch with family and friends back home for free, because I was very lonely for the first few years.

How did you start helping people move to France?
The fact that I could study independently for so little money made me wonder why other people, especially other students, weren't taking advantage of the opportunity to study abroad on their own instead of paying an American university program upwards of $40,000 for the same classes. Obviously, the American university programs provided a service helping with French administration and housing and all of that stuff that made things so much easier for their students, but there was no reason why highly motivated and intelligent individuals couldn't enroll directly in French universities instead, saving thousands. I thought I had made a really important discovery, and was excited to share it with people, so I started writing about how I did it and offering to guide other students through the process.

Initially, I wrote a book, which instead became a website, and then after a couple of years, I began offering services. When I started, it was hard to get information even from official French sites, and it was practically impossible to get information in English. Facebook groups didn't exist yet, and the internet forums that existed weren't super useful and didn't always have the right information. I really pioneered a lot of the accessible how-tos of French bureaucracy and a lot of people found my site that way.

As I added more information to my site, I began offering services, first to students who wanted to study independently as I had, and then to others who wanted to move independently and work as freelancers or remote workers. The appeal of helping clients to work on all kinds of different businesses and launch many different types of entrepreneurial projects was exciting, because I love coming up with new business ideas and brainstorming how to make them work. Ultimately, in 2021, after Covid, I created Your Franceformation and began hiring team members who share my vision for the resources and support we can offer to the community of Americans and other Anglophone immigrants in France and who want to move here. Now, we are a small team with a common mission of understanding the unique challenges of relocating to France and of supporting our clients as they arrive and thrive in France.

Have you helped anyone like me before?
In the 10 years I've been helping people move to France - and over 12 years since I began writing, I've made it my mission to make French bureaucracy as accessible and as easy to understand as possible. I've helped all kinds of clients, from EU citizens needing help with specific administrative problems like converting a driver's license or registering for unemployment benefits, to students applying for degree programs so they could seek employment in France, to aspiring self-employed people and entrepreneurs who wanted to make their own mark on the world by leaning into service as they moved.

Each person's path to France is unique, and yet, our Franceformation clients all share certain commonalities and dreams. They seek to radically shift their lives, and they need the tools not just to overcome the concrete barriers of bureaucracy, but to revolutionize their mindset so they can fully embrace their dream.

What do you look for in a client? How do I know if we'll be a good fit to work together?
At Your Franceformation, we love working with people who dream big and who have lots of ideas and plans. They're not just looking for one job

narrowly in one field where they've already worked for years, nor are they people who are "settling" for "just" taking French classes - they're people who are open-minded about all of the possibilities and willing to trust the process.

Sometimes, clients come to us with a very strong vision of what they want their future life in France to look like, and those people are fun to work with because the strength of their belief makes our work exciting and invigorating. Other times, the only clear desire is the desire to come to France, and we work together to fill in the grid and to imagine the possibilities for the move. In the second case, the challenge can be in refusing to get bogged down in worrying about whether a particular idea will work. In clients who don't have a specific vision yet, we have to work to establish trust, so I can pull desires out of the client to weave the application, without them feeling like we're imposing our vision for their future life, or choosing what is easiest for the work, and without triggering a belief that "it will never work." If the client develops reluctance or resistance while we're working together, it becomes very, very difficult to co-create anything.

Why should I work with you instead of someone else?
Many relocation professionals tend to work with large international companies and be very problem-oriented. Their client is the company moving its employee, and their objective is to anticipate and solve problems of bureaucracy as they arise. It can be a great approach, and it's one I've used occasionally, but it can set people up for failure.

Why? Because when you only address individual administrative and practical issues while ignoring the identity shift it takes to successfully transform your life through an international move, you risk being blindsided by your limiting beliefs or being held back by your fears. Instead, we can't promise that the journey to living in France will be without challenges and difficulties, but we do promise that you can trust us to be on your side and to confront any such challenges along with you whenever they may come up.

Other small businesses handling French admin tasks for newly-arrived English speakers often call themselves "hand holders" and they provide hourly service, often for a low rate, doing any personal admin task on an hourly basis. I don't love the term "hand holder" because of the term's connotations. We hold someone's hand when they're scared, or unsafe, or in pain, and we hold someone's hand when we're in love. None of those analogies are appropriate for the type of service we offer. Instead, we want to be your cheerleaders, and we want to make you aware of all of the different aspects of the new life you'll create.

What if I don't know exactly when I want to move to France?
A lot of times people resist setting a fixed departure date because they're waiting: waiting for the money to be there, waiting to find the right job, waiting to be 100% certain that things are going to work out. But the truth is, if you wait until the circumstances are perfect, you're probably never going to move. You have to begin taking action first.

Part of what we do is help our clients get ready to get ready, and reassure them that what they want to create is in fact possible with the correct visa and the right administrative setup. They take the first step by deciding to work with me on creating their dream, and we weave it into a vision at the same time as we're working on whatever leads their visa application. Being emotionally and psychologically ready for the challenges of an international move, combined with a career or job change, and speaking in a new language, and living in a new culture, all takes time. Committing to the move without committing to the work of getting ready to get ready is nonsensical. And some of the packages take several months to put together, anyway, meaning that you'll be doing the work of getting ready as we're working together on the professional vision. Our approach is holistic: we support you as a human working on a major life-altering project, just as much as we support and inform you about the administrative aspects of the move.

If you don't have a specific start date in mind, we can begin with a nonrefundable deposit to schedule in a tentative date and to get you access to the tools and materials I use to help clients acclimate to the reality of their move. We can reevaluate your plans as the date of our first meeting to work on your application approaches, and push back the start date a bit at no additional charge, while locking in the payment plan you chose, if you're truly not ready. You can also begin by enrolling in *Fast Track to France* and exploring the resources there

How do I know I'm ready to start the process and talk to you?
Each client has her own path to being ready to begin, and her own timeline for getting ready to be ready. Some clients have been working towards the idea of a move to France for months or years, and others have just begun the process. Aligning all of the elements of the move and of your energy so you can set yourself up to thrive and find a new level of personal fulfilment in your life can take time, but it can move more quickly when you have guidance from someone who is experienced with the particular blocks and challenges you're likely to face and who can help you navigate through them with ease.

The truth is that only you can know if you're ready to make the commitment and if you're willing to invest your time, energy, and money into making your move a reality. An international move isn't cheap, but the time and frustration you save by having help frees you up to focus on your dreams and imagining the life you want to create for yourself, instead of the nitty-gritty of the mundane administration that can trip you up and create resistance to what you want.

Removing the mental blocks and resistance to your dream is just as important as, if not more important than navigating the actual bureaucratic gatekeeping. When we work together, I can hold up a mirror to help you see what's holding you back. The personal transformation that will enable you to leave behind your current life and to create a new reality for yourself is well-worth it, but it will cost you the life you currently have and test what you are willing to give up.

What if I'm not able to invest in professional assistance for my move to France?
Having your finances in order and enough money for the visa Powers That Be is a very important part of a successful visa application - unless you're applying as the family member of a French citizen and therefore don't need to prove income and financial resources for your application. So we completely understand if investing in assistance is out of the realm of possibility at the moment.

Once you have a general idea of what kind of visa you'll go for and its requirements, you'll know approximately how much money you'll need to begin saving, and you can set a monthly savings goal to begin working towards your move. You can also research the amount of money you'll need for specific moving expenses, like a plane ticket from your location to France at the time of year you'll want to move, and the average cost of a small studio apartment in the area where you want to live.

You can begin saving for your move and working on envisioning exactly what you'd like to do in France. You may want to first invest in the *Fast Track to France* program, which has a complete module on the financial consequences of moving abroad, from helping you to figure out a budget for savings and a move, to understanding the French admin you'll need to navigate during the relocation process. Once the move is in the realm of financial possibility, it will be easier to align you with an employment opportunity and a visa type and to determine how you specifically may benefit from personalized assistance. When you move closer to your goal, the path will become clearer.

It's okay if you're not ready. And it's okay if you're getting ready to be ready. Financial constraints can be very real, but if you're going to commit to completely changing your life, you owe it to yourself. Let it take as long as it takes, but denying yourself the support you'll need to ensure your success is only going to prolong the struggle.

Kimberly Mousseron, International Mobility Consultant with Your Franceformation

Kim was born and raised in western Massachusetts. She started learning French in the 7th grade and continued to do so throughout her studies. Kim received her BA in French and International Relations from Mount Holyoke College and a MA in French from Middlebury College. She spent her junior year of college studying abroad in Paris and another year in Paris for her MA program. Then, after a year of teaching French and taking graduate courses at Boston College she moved back to France (for good this time…yes, she really had been bitten by the French bug!) and became a TEFL (Teaching English as a Foreign Language) certified instructor.

Kim met her future French husband while working at a law firm in Paris. After several years of living and working in the city of light, they relocated to Montpellier where she has lived for over 25 years. Over the years, Kim has worked for an investment bank, a law firm, taught English at all levels and translated. Immediately before joining the Your Franceformation team Kim spent seven years working in the field of study abroad helping American students who came to study in France. In addition to arranging their lodging, she accompanied them as they adjusted to their new "French" life, doing everything from organizing cultural adaptation sessions and developing re-entry workshops to making doctor appointments and helping them maneuver the grocery store or the pharmacy.

Kim has always enjoyed playing a role in supporting the American community in France. She is an active member of the American Women's Group of Languedoc Roussillon, previously serving as club

President, Vice President and Secretary. The club brings together American and international women for social gatherings, cultural activities and charitable events in addition to keeping close relations to the US Consulate in Marseille. She has also served in various roles for the Federation of American Women's Clubs Overseas (FAWCO is a UN accredited organization) working with women around the world to help Americans abroad with voting, tax and banking issues in addition to creating awareness on global issues and working together for charitable causes. While in study abroad, she served on the board of the APUAF (Association of American University Programs in France) organizing and attending workshops with professionals on a large range of topics concerning American students in France (health & safety, Campus France & visas, race & identity).

Kim and her French husband have two children who were both born and raised in Montpellier. Like her, they have dual nationality (American/French) and a French driver's license. Even after all of the years she has been in France, she is still amazed at how much there is to do and see. She enjoys visiting surrounding towns and villages, hiking in the mountains, spending time at the nearby beach, tasting new food and learning about wine. She loves sharing her knowledge and helping others discover France, its history, people, food, culture... in hopes that they will love it just as much as she does.

To learn more about Kim and hear the story of her life in France and how she joined the Franceformation team, you can listen to her interview with Allison here:https://www.yourfranceformation.com/2023/01/04/episode-53-introducing-kim-mousseron-international-mobility-consultant-with-your-franceformation/

Allison's Acknowledgements

Writing and publishing the first edition of *Foolproof French Visas* in 2019 was a solitary process, and I am grateful that since 2021, I have had the pleasure of hiring wonderful team members to support our Your Franceformation clients and who have also been instrumental in researching some of the changes and edits for this book.

The Franceformation team members who joined me are a pleasure to work with, and working with them has made supporting our clients easier and more fun than ever.

A wholehearted thank you and a ton of gratitude to my Franceformation team:

Michelle Wild, our Online Business Manager, who can make a mean Notion task board, who keeps me focused on our priorities, and who has designed and implemented so many of the systems and resources we have created to keep Your Franceformation running, growing sustainably, and fully supporting our clients and each other. She is the genius behind the French Visa Quiz.

Kim Mousseron, who brings her expertise from working in study abroad programs, who is a detail-oriented researcher, and who meticulously read and reread this book. She identified key parts to rewrite and research further for changes, found good resources outlining changes to certain administrative processes, made sure I finished all my sentences.

Lacey Bertrand-Reilly, the newest member of the Franceformation team who joined in November 2023 to fill our client support and admin position. She has provided wonderful feedback and assistance in the editing process, and has been a fantastic addition to our team.

Amy Gruber, a communications consultant and former client who has assisted with developing so many of our business plan materials and who helps support our Entrepreneur clients.

Lauren Clanet, whose fresh eyes and clarifying questions provide immensely valuable feedback on the information and support we provide in this book and develop for our clients for the 2022 Edition. Lauren was a part-time member of the Franceformation team from April 2021-December 2022.

Becky Hope-Ross of Busy Bee Organizers, our previous social media manager, who helped us grow and develop our social media strategy.

Our many wonderful partners who have helped us to provide even better service and more comprehensive information to our clients this year, through consultations, services, and informational webinars with us: Althémis Notaires, Axa Agence Internationale, Beaux Villages Immobilier, Cabinet Roussel-Olive, Chase Buchanan, Currencies Direct, Ellaw Avocats, Expand CPA, Fab French Insurance, France Media Inc., French Riviera House Hunting, GarantMe, Hoxton Capital, Let's Get Franced, Leggett Immobilier, Lumon, Monceau CPA, Mondassur, Qonto, and more.

Thank you to everyone in the Americans in France community who has written to me with questions or comments about the previous editions of *Foolproof French Visas*, to help improve it for later editions, and for teaching me or providing the opportunity to learn much of what I know about French visas and moving to France.

Thanks especially to our awesome clients who trust us to guide them on such an important journey, their relocation to France, and whose field experiences give us valuable data so we can explain how French administration works in the real world.

Appendix: List of Documents You May Need

Identification Documents

Your Passport: You will need a valid passport, issued less than 10 years ago, containing at least two available blank pages, and **you will need to submit your original passport to the VFS/TLS office for them to affix the visa**. This means you will be without your passport and unable to travel from the time you submit your visa application until the time it is returned to you, typically about 2-3 weeks maximum.

Please ensure that your passport is valid for at least 3 months beyond the end date of the visa you are applying for (although we recommend 6 months). If you are applying for a 1-year visa, your passport should be valid for at least 18 months beyond your visa's proposed start date. Please also ensure that the name on your passport is the same as your name on your other documents.

If you have lost your passport or had it stolen, you will need to reapply for a 10 year passport. Emergency passports are valid for only 1 year and so would not meet the requirement of having a passport which is valid for at least 3 months after your visa expiration date. In addition, emergency passports do not allow you to travel into France.

The UK sometimes issues passports valid for longer than 10 years because they add time remaining on the previous passport to the 10 years of the new passport. Unfortunately, the EU does not accept the validity of passports beyond 10 years, so France will consider that such a passport expires 10 years after its date of issue.

If you are in France, you will have to bring your original passport to each appointment with you(renewals, change of status, etc), but you will never have to leave your original passport at the préfecture.

ANTS-standard passport photos: The photo should be 35 mm wide and 45 mm high. The size of the face should be 32 to 36 mm (70 to 80% of the picture) from chin to forehead (excluding hair). You can have these pictures taken with the proper format at the VFS Global / TLS Contact office for around $13. In France, these pictures can be taken at any Photomaton machine. ePhotos are also taken at the Photomaton machine and include a code which can be entered into official websites.

ePhoto: This is a set of photos that meets the requirements above, which contains a 22-digit code and an electronic signature. It is NOT simply a scan of a passport-format photo. The code can only be used one time, within 6 months, to submit your photo electronically for one online procedure. A set of ePhotos can be obtained from an app like SmartphoneID, a photomaton machine, or a photographer advertising "official photos."

Basic Administrative Documents

Cover Letter: For most visas, we find it very useful to provide a one-page cover letter outlining the reasons for the application and move to France, your means of financial support, and the activities you intend to undertake while in France. If you are applying for your visa outside of France, you can write this in the language of the country you are applying from, or in English.

Bank Account Statements. You need to show adequate means of financial support during your stay in France. Different types of visas have different financial requirements, depending on whether you are able to work. If you have both French and foreign accounts, provide recent statements for both. The consulate and the préfecture want to see funds available in cash, rather than money in investment accounts.

For your visa application (Entrepreneur & Passeport Talent Entrepreneur): It is difficult to open a French bank account as a non-resident and without a French visa without an "economic tie to France," which is typically owning property or a business. With our Passeport Talent Entrepreneur and classic Entrepreneur clients, we advise beginning the process early to open a non-resident bank account with one of our banking partners, on the basis of investing money in a French business. It is highly recommended to have a French bank account open for these visa application types.

For your visa application (Everyone else): If you do not have an economic tie to France, you should wait to open your French bank account until you have arrived in France with your visa. A French bank account is not a requirement for your application and will be very difficult if not impossible to open before you arrive.

For your renewal: The préfecture has increasingly been requiring bank statements in French and in Euros, so you need to open a French brick and mortar bank account soon after arrival, and ensure you meet the financial resources requirement in your French account. This means having French bank statements that either show a year of net SMIC, or regular deposits from your foreign account of at least net SMIC per month. We recommend a monthly transfer of at least €1500. You should open an account with an actual French bank in addition to any currency service you may use. We can provide recommendations.

Foreign bank statements: Non-French bank statements in your country of origin are fine for visa applications. If you try to use these for renewal, you will likely be required to provide complete certified translations for all documents, at a cost of €40-50 per page.

Banking and investment issues: Most people are able to open and maintain a French bank account and bank accounts in their home country without issues. Americans sometimes have problems due to banking regulations like FATCA. If you experience difficulty opening or maintaining an account in France or the US, please contact us and we can refer you to non-profit organizations that may be able to assist you.

Expected departure date. Visa processing times are usually 10-15 business days. We typically recommend leaving at least one month between your visa appointment and your planned departure date. Your departure date should be no more than 90 days after your visa appointment date. You are not going to be required to provide your plane ticket, and we do not recommend providing a round-trip ticket in case the embassy decides to issue a temporary stay visa instead of the visa you apply for, based on a return date you provide.

Certificat de coutume: A document stating that you are not already in a legal partnership and are free to get married or PACSed. For a foreign person getting married or PACSed in France, or a French person getting married or PACSed abroad. https://fr.usembassy.gov/fr/mariage-en-france-attestation-tenant-lieu-de-certificat-de-coutume-et-de-celibat/

Transcription de l'acte de mariage / de l'acte de naissance: A document from the Service d'État-Civil in Nantes registering a foreign marriage or birth with the French authorities.

Livret de famille: An official family book registering marriage, divorce, and children's births. Some EU countries aside from France also require registration of foreign marriages by their citizens and issue a livret de famille. If this is the case for your EU country, you will have to show the EU registration for official purposes in France.

Financial Guarantee: If you are on a STUDENT or VISITOR visa and you do not have sufficient financial resources on your own, you will need a notarized financial guarantee from a family member. You CANNOT work or make reference to any earned income when applying for these visa types.

Préinscription scolaire / school pre-enrollment: A document showing children aged 3-16 have been pre-enrolled in school in France prior to receiving their visas. For elementary and maternelle (preschool) aged children, you will pre-enroll them by contacting the mairie in the town where you will live. For middle and high school students, you will need to contact the school where they will be enrolled directly. If you have reserved temporary housing for your arrival in France, you can typically pre-enroll the children in school based on that address, and finalize their enrollment in your neighborhood school once you have secured long-term housing. We have detailed explanations of these procedures in *Fast Track to France*.

Certificat de scolarité: A certificate issued for children enrolled in school, which shows their school location and their home address and proves that they are living in France on a regular basis. You should receive one for each child at the beginning of the school year.

Contrat d'intégration républicaine: A contract requiring you to agree to respect the values of France and complete certain trainings to help you integrate into French culture. Only available to people with certain visa types who are on a path to residency and naturalization. https://www.ofii.fr/wp-content/uploads/2020/12/CIR-CONTRAT.pdf

Contrat d'Engagement à Respecter les Principes de la République: a new contract foreigners in France must sign to receive a carte de séjour, which identifies the republican values you must agree to respect as a resident of France.

Housing

Proof of place to stay for at least the first month or so upon arrival. If you are heading to an area with a particularly difficult housing market, you may want to reserve 4-6 weeks of housing.

If you have a friend or family member who has a residence near where you'll be staying, you can put that person's address and indicate that you'll be staying there 'while looking for permanent housing.' You will need that person to provide an "attestation d'hébérgement."

You can do a long-term lease through a trusted agency that works with expats, although many will issue a secondary residence lease, which we do not recommend.

You can rent an Airbnb, hotel room, or hostel room for the first 3-4 weeks, so you have a place to stay upon arrival while you look for a permanent housing situation. Note that you will not be able to do many administrative formalities until you have a permanent place to live, and you will need to prioritize finding a long-term primary residence lease as soon as possible after arrival.

Students should provide proof of a place to stay for at least 90 days.

Justificatif de domicile: A bill with your name on it showing your residential address in France. Can typically be a utility bill, like gas, electricity, water, or property tax. Can also be a fixed phone or internet bill or in some cases, a cell phone bill. Rent receipts should be official and look like invoices, and are more likely to be accepted if they come from an agency rather than an individual. Required for proving where you live and should usually be less than 3 months old.

Attestation d'hébergement: An attestation from someone hosting you stating the dates you will be staying with them, along with a copy of their utility bill and their official ID.

Healthcare Documents

Proof of catastrophic health coverage: Visitor visa applicants and EU citizens and their spouses need catastrophic health coverage for 12 months; It must be a policy appropriate for 365 days of travel, cover all of the EU/Schengen space, and have €30,000 of coverage with no deductible. Not required if you are a student, on any salaried work visa, a business creator, or the spouse of a French citizen, although you can purchase such insurance if you feel safer doing so. These policies typically do not cover pre-existing conditions or routine healthcare. We provide referrals for our clients to multiple health insurance providers.

Attestation des droits à l'assurance maladie: A document issued by CPAM when your registration for the French healthcare system is finalized, proving that you are covered and indicating the dates of coverage. You will need this document or a private healthcare plan for a visitor visa renewal.

Certificate of Coverage: If you have been sent to France on an employment contract by an employer outside of France, you may qualify for an "expatriation" exception which allows your employer to keep you on payroll outside of France and pay social charges in your home country, which can be significantly cheaper for the employer. In the US, the company/employer can request this document from the Social Security office before sending you to France for your temporary contract. It precludes you from both paying into the French system and from being covered by CPAM. You will require a comprehensive private coverage policy for the duration of your certificate of coverage's duration. It can be valid for a maximum of 5 years, at which point you will have to shift onto the French system.

S1 / S1 Refusal: An S1 is a document issued by an EU country when you contribute to the healthcare system in a different country from where you live.

Carte vitale: The green card that enables you to receive reimbursement for healthcare expenses more quickly from the healthcare system. This card does not prove your coverage (as it can be inactive) and is issued shortly after the attestation des droits.

Business & Entrepreneur

Attestation de vigilance URSSAF: A document demonstrating that you have made all of your declarations to URSSAF and paid your social charges.

Avis de Situation or INSEE form: A document showing your microentreprise registration and activities, which also shows that your registration is still active and up to date.

Déclaration de chiffre d'affaires mensuelle / trimestrielle: Your monthly or quarterly declaration of your gross income to URSSAF for the purpose of paying social charges.

Lettre d'engagement: A letter from the accountant or attorney responsible for registering your business, or a contract with them for doing the business registration and/or bookkeeping.

Statuts: The articles of incorporation of your company (SARL, EURL, SAS(U)). "Projet de status" if the statutes are not finalized or signed and filed.

BPI Attestation: Usually a document showing if you have received credit or financing for your business project. We typically provide an attestation that the company is being financed through personal funds and does not require loans.

Domiciliation: A contract for the registered business address of your company. Note that this must be an address you own, have a long-term lease for, or have an official commercial lease for.

Attestation de l'origine des fonds: An attestation from a bank or a bank statement showing where the money you are investing in your business came from. It's an anti-money-laundering measure and also ensures you are investing your own funds in creating the company.

Attestation du caractère réel et sérieux du projet de création d'entreprise (from the Ministry of the Economy): A certificate attesting that the Ministry of the Economy has reviewed your business plan, financial projections, and company creation documents and believes that your project is viable.

Avis de la plateforme: Certificate from the DGEF, Direction Générale des Étrangers en France, on your project's viability, for Entrepreneur (commerçant, artisan, industriel) applicants. Requires the approval of the local DREETS and the Main d'Oeuvre Étranger or MOE.

Commercial, Industrial, Artisanal form: A form requesting information about your business project, location, and previous businesses you've run, for the Entrepreneur (Commerçant, Artisan, Industriel) visa.

Certificat de dépôt des fonds: Certificate from a French authority certifying that you have deposited the social capital in an escrow account for the purpose of creating your company. Identifies the investors and the amounts invested.

Kbis: Official company registration document (for an SARL/EURL, SAS(U) or other) issued by the Greffe du Tribunal de Commerce with your company's business registration details, including your tax numbers (SIREN, SIRET, APE code, and TVA number), official business address, and company director/president address. You may also have this if you have a commercial activity as a microentrepreneur, but not for other types of microentrepreneur activities.

Bilan: A company's complete accounting report produced by your accountant for a fiscal year.

Procès-verbal de nomination du gérant: A legal document naming the company's director or president, which is included with company creation documents.

Attestation de non condamnation: An attestation from the business owner stating they have not been convicted of any crimes that would preclude them from legally owning and operating a business in France.

Background check / extrait de casier judiciaire: Criminal background check demonstrating that you have not been convicted of any felonies or crimes that would preclude you from owning and operating a business in France. A foreign background check is also used for naturalization requests if you have lived in France for less than 10 years.

P237: Bordereau de situation fiscale, a document from the tax office demonstrating that all personal income taxes have been paid.

Salaried Work Visas

Autorisation de travail: Approval from DREETS stating that the company can hire an applicant for a particular position and approving the work contract. This is required when the applicant has a "situation de l'emploi opposable."

Fiche de paie: Your French salary slip. Needs to be produced by an accountant and show all pay, deductions, benefits, etc.

Contrat de travail: Your official work contract with complete job description and work conditions. See the introduction to the Salaried Work Visas section to see the legal requirements for work contract clauses.

Au pair contract: A document outlining the au pair's relationship with the host family, including job responsibilities and pay. The contract should include certain essential information, like where the family lives, how long the contract lasts, conditions for leaving or being let go, tasks and work hours (25h max per week with 1 day of rest), pocket money, housing, free time and days off, language classes, and insurance.

Déclaration préalable à l'embauche: A procedure for declaring a new employee to URSSAF and the relevant authorities in the 8 days preceding the employee's first day of work.

Déclaration préalable au détachement SIPSI: A procedure for employers to declare their detached workers who will be working in France, prior to requesting an ICT visa.

Attestation de la qualité innovante de l'entreprise: A certification from the Ministry of the Economy to recognize a company doing innovative work, which allows the company to access certain benefits, like being able to hire foreign employees through the Projet Economique Innovant or Jeune Entreprise Innovante schemes.

Proof of qualifications or professional experience: Certificates and transcripts from all trainings and degree programs, high school, college, and graduate diplomas. Can also include documents reflecting previous business registrations, previous work contracts and tax documents or pay stubs for previous related employment.

Convention d'accueil / CERFA 16079*03: A contract between a host institution and a researcher to outline the researcher's relationship and affiliation with the host institution, the nature of the research, and how the researcher is paid.

CERFA 15614*04: Éléments du contrat de travail justifiant une demande de carte de séjour "Entreprise innovante".
https://www.service-public.fr/particuliers/vosdroits/R46144

CERFA 15615*01: Éléments du contrat de travail justifiant une demande de carte de séjour "Carte bleue européenne".
https://www.service-public.fr/particuliers/vosdroits/R46145

CERFA 15616*01: Éléments du contrat de travail justifiant une demande de carte de séjour "Salarié en Mission". https://www.service-public.fr/particuliers/vosdroits/R46146

Certificate of Social Contributions: a document provided by the hiring company attesting that they have made all of their declarations and are up to date in their social contribution payments.

Glossary of Common Terms, Acronyms & Initialisms

AE / Autoentrepreneur / ME / Microentrepreneur: A simplified structure for tax reporting when one is self-employed in France. It is also referred to as microentrepreneur.

AGDREF number: Application de Gestion des Dossiers des Ressortissants Étrangers en France. This 10-digit code begins with 99 and is the foreigner identification number which will follow you throughout your time in France. It is generated automatically when you validate your visa through the OFII portal.

AGESSA: Association pour la GEstion de la Sécurité Sociale des Artistes, the government association which collects and manages social security contributions for artists based on the sale or licensing of their art, recordings, or other original works.

Alternance / Apprentissage: a type of internship or work study program where students work in a professional capacity to complement their studies. The length and organization of these programs varies widely depending on the program of study, but students usually split their time between work and class time during their academic year.

AMELI: Assurance Maladie En LIgne is the website for French healthcare. Each insured person has an individual account to access online and communicate with employees of CPAM, check records, etc.

ANEF: L'Administration Numérique pour les Étrangers en France is the website that aims to make all procedures concerning foreigners in France, including residence permits and access to nationality, available online.

ANTS: Agence Nationale des Titres Sécurisés. The government agency which produces secure documents, such as passports, cartes de séjour, and driver's licenses. Renamed **France Titres** in February 2024.

APE code: Activité Principale Exercée, identifies the primary industry in which a business or self-employed person operates.

Apostille: A legalization of an official document for its use by a foreign government. In some cases, birth certificates, marriage certificates, and other official documents from outside of France may require an apostille in certain situations. In the US, apostilles are affixed by the Secretary of State / Secretary of the Commonwealth of the state issuing the document.

APS: Autorisation Provisoire de Séjour. This is formerly the name of the visa type now called Recherche d'Emploi / Création d'Entreprise for graduates of French universities. You may see older documentation referring to this visa type as APS. An "autorisation provisoire de séjour" can now also refer to a temporary authorization issued to refugees and certain immigrant categories before their cartes de séjour are issued.

Arrêté de Nomination: A contract for the TAPIF program, indicating you have been hired and which school district and establishments you will be working in.

Avenant: An addendum or addition to modify a contract. An avenant could modify a work contract, for example.

CAF: Caisse des Allocations Familiales, a government agency that provides child benefits, housing aid, and other financial assistance to families that qualify based on their income.

Campus France: An online portal for higher education in France which has a directory of universities, their academic and degree programs and which provides application processing assistance to students from certain countries, including the US. Students can apply to certain university programs directly from the Études en France portal.

Carte vitale: A healthcare card scanned at your doctors' appointments, demonstrating your access to French healthcare and facilitating your reimbursements.

CCI: Chambre de Commerce et d'Industrie, registers certain types of commercial businesses.

CDD: Contrat à Durée Déterminée. A salaried work contract for a fixed amount of time. Typically for less than 12 months, these contracts must be issued for a specific reason and are strictly regulated by French labor law.

CDDU: Contrat à Durée Déterminée d'Usage, a salaried work contract specific to artists and performers, for rehearsals and performances eligible for the intermittent du spectacle status.

CDI: Contrat à Durée Indéterminée. A salaried work contract for an indefinite length of time. Usually these come with a trial period of up to 3 months, after which they become permanent.

CDM: Chambre de Métiers, registers artisanal businesses.

CDS: Carte de Séjour (common online). Fairly interchangeable with TDS/"titre de séjour".

CERFA: An official administrative form, developed and regulated by the government. The acronym CERFA refers to the now-defunct French administration which developed and standardized all government forms, called the Centre d'Enregistrement et de Révision des Formulaires Administratifs. Each official CERFA form has a number to identify it which also indicates the most recent version. An administration will request, for example, CERFA-12345*4 in which 12345 is the form number and 4 is the most recent edition. All CERFA forms can be downloaded online for free.

CESEDA: Code de l'Entrée et du Séjour des Etrangers et du Droit d'Asile is a legal code created in the mid-2000s which brings together all the rules relating to the rights of foreigners, from residence permits to the right to asylum.

CFE: Centre de Formalités des Entreprises

CFE: Cotisation Foncière des Entreprises, an annual local tax on business locations.

CGI: Code Général des Impôts

CIDFF: Centre d'Information et de Droits des Femmes et de la Famille, an association which provides legal assistance to women who are victims of domestic violence or want legal advice. A good resource for women who need assistance with divorce or immigration law issues in France. There are regional offices for each department. https://paris.cidff.info/

CIEP: Centre International d'Etudes Pédagogiques, now France Education International, for accrediting and assessing French language studies and administering language tests like the TCF and DILF/DELF/DALF.

CLEISS: Centre de Liaisons Européennes et Internationales de Sécurité Sociale

CNDA: Cour Nationale des Demandes d'Asile, located in Montreuil, Seine-Saint-Denis.

CNFE: Centre National des Firmes Étrangères, an administration which registers foreign companies operating with employees in France, but which do not have a formal subsidiary or branch office registered in France.

CNI: Carte nationale d'identité, a French ID card for citizens, which is sufficient for traveling throughout the Schengen space. Your CDS is not a CNI, and must always be accompanied by your passport when used for official ID purposes.

CPAM: Caisse Primaire d'Assurance Maladie, the French healthcare administration which oversees enrollment in the French healthcare system, issues your carte vitale (healthcare card) and processes reimbursements for medical care.

CRE: Centre de Réception des Etrangers, a division of the préfecture.

CRECI: Centre de Réception des Etudiants et des Chercheurs Internationaux, the préfecture's department which processes student and researcher visas and renewals.

CNOUS / CROUS: Centre (National / Régional) des Oeuvres Universitaires et Scolaires, an administration for student services and restaurants in universities

CVEC: Contribution de la Vie Etudiante et de Campus, a fee for campus life and activities if you are enrolled directly in a French university during the academic year. For the 2024-2025 academic year, this fee is €103.

DAP: Demande d'Admission Préalable, an application for admission to a French university in the first year of License (undergraduate degree)

DCEM: Document de Circulation pour Étranger Mineur, a residency permit for minor children living in France with their parents.

DGEF: Direction Générale des Étrangers en France, an online platform for assessing certain profession libérale projects, providing autorisation de travail, or a convention de stage.

DGFiP: Direction Générale des FInances Publiques, where the tax is paid on hiring foreign workers as of 2023 (formerly the OFII tax.)

DILF / DELF / DALF: A series of standardized French language tests which grant a diploma for each level of language study. DILF is Diplôme Initiale en Langue Française and is for beginner levels A1 or A2. DELF is Diplôme d'Etudes en Langue Française, for intermediate levels B1/B2. And DALF is Diplôme Approfondi en Langue Française, for advanced levels C1 and C2.

DIRECCTE: The DIrection Régionale des Entreprises, de la Concurrence, de la Consommation, du Travail, et de l'Emploi. In 2021, this administration was replaced by DREETS, but you may still see DIRECCTE written or referred to in some places, both in this book and by other French administration documents that have not yet been updated.

DREETS / DRIEETS: Direction Régionale (Interdépartementale) de l'Économie, de l'Emploi, du Travail et des Solidarités, which oversees the regional economy and approves immigration to the region based on its economic situation.

ECTS: European Credit Transfer and Accumulation System, the system for standardizing and assessing coursework and credit hours across European universities.

EEE / EEA: Espace Économique Européenne / European Economic Area. A group of 30 European countries with a free-trade agreement.

EEF: Études en France, the application process to apply for studies in France through the Campus France portal. We use Campus France and EEF / Études en France interchangeably.

EES: Entry/Exit System: the new passport scanning system going into effect throughout the Schengen area on November 10, 2024, to track the entry and exits of non-EU nationals into Schengen.

ENIC-NARIC: European Network of Information Centres – National Academic Recognition Information Centres, the European administration which validates foreign diplomas and credentials for use in Europe.

ETIAS: EU Travel Information & Authorization System, a pre-travel visa waiver application which will enter into effect in 2025. This will require all visitors to the EU who do not hold a visa, titre de séjour, or EU passport to complete a travel preauthorization form, which will cost €7 and be valid for 3 years.

FACC: Franco-American Chamber of Commerce, sponsors of a temporary work program for American college graduates who want to temporarily work in France.

FLE Qualité: Français Langue Etrangère Qualité, an accreditation label for French as a second language classes in France. FLE is pronounced "fleu".

France Services: a set of fonctionnaires who can provide access to online procedures and assist with admininstrative procedures for CAF, ANTS, retirement pensions, CPAM, energy, taxes, unemployment, renovation credits, the post office, and public legal services. Certain France Services offices are located in mairies, while others travel throughout rural areas.

France Titres: Formally simply known as **ANTS**, Agence Nationale des Titres Sécurisés, this is a French public administrative establishment under the supervision of the Ministry of the Interior. Its mission is to produce secure documents, such as passports, cartes de séjour, and driver's licenses.

France Travail: Formally, **Pôle Emploi**, this is the French unemployment administration. All salaried employees pay an unemployment tax, but only employees on a salaried visa type or a family visa type are eligible to receive paid benefits if their unemployment ends.

Gratification de stage: compensation for interns is called a "gratification" rather than a salary. The minimum wage for interns is 4,35€ per hour in 2024 and is mandatory starting in the 309th hour of the internship.

Greffe du Tribunal de Commerce: The commercial court, which registers companies in France and provides company registration documents such as the Kbis.

GUDA: Guichet Unique des Demandes d'Asile, for asylum seekers to file requests online.

Guichet Unique (Guichet électronique des formalités d'entreprises): This is a secure internet portal, through which all companies are required to declare their creation (since January 1, 2023). INPI had been designated by the government as the operator of this site.

ICT: Inter Corporate/Company Transfer, or "salarié en mission" for a temporary work assignment in France.

INPI: Institut National de la Propriété Industrielle is a public administrative institution placed under the supervision of the French Ministry of Economics, Finance and Industrial and Digital Sovereignty. All companies are registered through INPI as of 2023. It also governs trademark registration and other intellectual property in France.

INSEE: Institut National de la Statistique et des Études Économiques, the French governmental organization which keeps statistics on business registrations, salaries, and more.

Intermittent du Spectacle: a tax status for performers that provides a type of unemployment insurance for artists and performers which helps them stabilize their income. Artists' performance income includes an unemployment contribution. If they perform enough hours to register for Intermittent du spectacle status, they can receive a stipend from Pole Emploi to complement their income for months when they perform less.

JEI: Jeune Entreprise Innovante, a status awarded to certain tech startups that meet the criteria and request JEI status from the Ministry of the Economy.

Kbis: the registration document of a French company or corporation. It is like the company's birth certificate, and lists the company owners, the registered address, SIRET/SIREN and TVA numbers, along with the activity code for the company. It can be requested from the Greffe (business court) and must be less than 3 months old for most purposes.

Licenciement: the process of being fired or let go from a work contract, initiated by the company. *Licenciement économique* refers to a layoff from a company in financial difficulty, while a *licenciement pour faute grave* is being fired for serious and just cause. *Licenciement abusif* is being fired for bullshit.

MDA / La Maison des Artistes: The government association which manages social security contributions for visual artists and authors.

Mon Espace Sante: This is an individual digital space which allows you to store and share your health documents and data in complete confidentiality. This is a fairly new service and is not obligatory but useful.

Mon Master: the online platform where French students apply for admission to master's programs at French universities. Students who are applying to master's programs from abroad will not use this platform.

NATALI: NATuralisation en LIgne. As of February 2023, this online service allows users to complete the formalities necessary for applications for naturalization or reintegration into French nationality by decree. As the procedure is now completely dematerialized, an account allows users to follow the progress of the application and respond to requests for complementary documents without having to file in person.

NOEMIE: Norme Ouverte d'Échange entre la Maladie et les Intervenants Extérieurs is an IT standard which speeds up data exchange with the CPAM. Notably, it enables CPAM to send certain information about your healthcare expenses directly to your mutuelle so you are fully reimbursed more quickly.

OFII: Office Français de l'Immigration et de l'Intégration; where you register your visa.

OFPRA: Office Français de Protection des Réfugiés et des Apatrides.

OQTF: Obligation de Quitter le Territoire Français. A legal document informing you that you are being directed to leave France within 30 days. Typically this also prevents you from applying for a visa or returning to travel for a certain length of time.

PACS: Pacte Civil de Solidarité, a type of legal civil partnership between two adults, of the same or opposite sex. A sort of 'marriage lite' which does not have all of the same benefits as marriage, especially in immigration and estate and financial planning for inheritance purposes.

Parcoursup: the online platform where students in France apply for admission to undergraduate programs at French universities. Students who are applying to university programs for the first time from abroad will not use this platform.

PASS: Plafond annuel de la sécurité sociale. This is the maximum salary amount taken into consideration for calculating certain assistance such as sick leave payments, maternity and paternity leave stipends, and certain pension amounts. For employers, it is a reference to determine the appropriate rate of social charges to pay on salaries and the taxable amounts of severance packages. Some internship wages and various aides and stipends are expressed as a percentage of the PASS. In 2024, the PASS is set at €46.368, or €29 per hour.

PEP: Période d'Expérience Professionnelle, the mandatory professional experience, typically in the form of a 6-month internship at the end of a master's program.

Personne morale: An entity such as a company, government agency, NGO, or international organization, or other group considered a legal person in French law.

Personne physique: An actual human person.

Point d'Accès Numérique (PAN): Préfectures now offer a Point d'Accès Numérique to facilitate the completion of online procedures for those without a computer or internet access. The PAN is typically a set of computers staffed by a préfecture employee who cannot assist with appointments or take applications, but who can assist with computer use and scanning and uploading documents to various administrative websites. Find your nearest PAN... by looking online.

Pôle Emploi: see *France Travail*. Name of this administration changed in 2024.

Portage salarial: a company that will act as an intermediary for businesses that want to employ individual salaried workers in France. The portage company bills any client companies, establishes payslips, pays social charges, and pays the employee's salary. It can be used to establish certain salaried visa types.

PUMA: Protection Universelle MAladie, the universal healthcare scheme.

RCS: Registre des Commerces et des Sociétés, a business registration number for certain types of businesses registered with the CCI, which must be on official business documents.

RECE: Recherche d'Emploi / Création d'Entreprise visa

Registre des Étrangers Établis Hors de France: A registration through the French consulates for French citizens living outside of France, which enables them to receive consular services and vote in national elections

RM: Régistre des Métiers, a registration number for artisans registered with the Chambre de Métiers.

RSA: Revenu de solaridé active, a minimum income payment for people with no other financial resources or income. In 2024, RSA is set at €607,75 per month for a single person or €911.63 for a couple with no children.

Rupture conventionnelle: A process by which the employee and the employer mutually agree to end a work contract, preserving the employee's ability to receive unemployment allocations.

SAS / SASU: Société à Actions Simplifiées (Unipersonnelle). A second type of French corporation, which has one or more investors.

SARL / EURL: Société à Responsabilité Limitée, a type of French company. An EURL is an Entreprise Unipersonnelle à Responsabilité Limitée, which is a one-person SARL.

Schengen Area: A collective of 23 countries of the EU plus 4 others which have eliminated routine border controls between them. Austria, Belgium, Croatia, Czechia, Denmark, Estonia, Finland, France, Germany, Greece, Hungary, Iceland, Italy, Latvia, Liechtenstein, Lithuania, Luxembourg, Malta, Netherlands, Norway, Poland, Portugal, Slovakia, Slovenia, Spain, Sweden, and Switzerland

SIE: Service des Impôts des Entreprises, the tax office for businesses, including autoentrepreneurs.

SIP: Service des Impôts des Particuliers, the tax office for individuals.

SIPQ: Service de l'Immigration Professionnelle Qualifiée, the immigration office which processes professional and business visas and cartes de séjour.

SIPSI: Système d'Information sur les Prestations de Services Internationales, an online system for declaring foreign workers seconded to France.

SIREN: Système d'Identification du Répertoire des ENtreprises, a 9-digit code assigned by INSEE to your business upon registration. It will never change for the life of your business.

SIRET: Système d'Identification du Répertoire des ÉTablissements, a 14 digit code which includes the 9-digit SIREN and the 5-digit NIC (Numéro Interne de Classement) number. The SIRET can change for different business locations, and if a business's address changes, the SIRET will also change.

Situation de l'emploi non-opposable: DREETS cannot refuse to award a work authorization to the foreign employee, due to the job's specialized nature, the employee's qualifications, and/or the high salary.

Situation de l'emploi opposable: DREETS can refuse to award a work authorization, because the company has to prove they tried to hire someone with work papers for France before being able to sponsor a foreigner.

SMIC: Salaire MInimum de Croissance, French minimum wage for full-time, 35-hour/week contract. SMIC is calculated on an hourly and a monthly basis (151.67 hours per month) and rises each quarter with inflation. At the time of publication of the 2024 Edition, SMIC is €1.767 gross income per month, or €1.400 net income per month. This corresponds to annual gross income of €21.204, and annual net income of €16.800. Hourly SMIC is €11,65.

STEP: Smart Traveler Enrollment Program, a US Department of State enrollment program for Americans living or traveling overseas. You can register online to receive updates about travel to specific countries.

TAPIF: Teaching Assistant Program in France.

TCF / TCF-ANF / TCF-DAP: Test des Connaissances du Français, a standardized French language test valid for 2 years which can be used to demonstrate your language skills for university admissions or a job search. **TCF-ANF** is Test des Connaissances du Français - Accès à la Nationalité Française, which can be used to demonstrate a sufficient French level (B1) to be naturalized. The **TCF-DAP** is the Test des Connaissances du Français - Demande d'Admission Préalable, which is for candidates to license / undergraduate programs in French universities.

TDS: Titre de séjour. A long-stay visa validated by OFII becomes a titre de séjour. A TDS is the equivalent of a CDS.

Timbre Fiscal: An excise or tax stamp. This stamp is a method of payment for French administrative procedures and can be purchased online (for a virtual stamp) or at a tabac (for a physical stamp). Note that there are two different websites for purchasing a timbre fiscal depending on whether you are validating your visa through ANEF or picking up a carte de séjour at the préfecture.

TVA: Taxe sur la Valeur Ajoutée, known in English as VAT or Value-Added Tax.

URSSAF: Union de Recouvrement des cotisations de Sécurité Sociale et d'Allocations Familiales, the French tax agency which collects social charges on salaries and self-employment income.

VAE: Validation des Acquis et de l'Expérience. A procedure at the university level which assigns university credit for previous studies which did not lead to a degree, or to work experience in your field.

VLS: Visa Long Séjour

VLS-T: Visa Long Séjour Temporaire, a non renewable visa type

VLS-TS or VLS-VTS: Visa Long Séjour (Valant) Titre de Séjour

VPF: Vie Privée et Familiale, a visa type for people living in France for family reasons, such as being the immediate family member of a French citizen.

WARP card: Withdrawal Agreement Residence Permit, a carte de séjour for British citizens in France before December 31, 2020, who elect to remain French residents after Brexit.

Appendix: CESEDA Visa Codes

CESEDA is the Code de l'Entrée et du Séjour des Étrangers et du Droit d'Asile, and each visa type has a code that corresponds to the article and section in the CESEDA book which establishes that visa or carte de séjour. You may need to reference this chart when validating your visa online through the ANEF website.

Visa Type	New CESEDA Code (2021) Old CESEDA Code (2016)
Vie privée et familial	L312-2 R431-16 6 L211-2-1 R311-3-4
Visiteur	R431-16-16 R311-3 5
Etudiant	R431-16-16 "autorisé à travailler à 60%" R311-3 6 "autorisé à travailler à 60%"
Salarié	R431-16-7 "voir autor. de travail" R311-3 7 "voir autor. de travail"
Travailleur temporaire	R431-16-8 "voir autor. de travail" R311-3 8 "voir autor. de travail"
Passeport Talent Création d'Entreprise	R421-16 R313-20 5
Passeport Talent Famille Accompagnante	R421-22
Stagiaire	R431-16-17 R311-3 10
Salarié détaché ICT (+famille)	R431-16 11 R311-3 13
Entrepreneur Profession Libérale	R431-16-9 R311-3 14
Recherche d'emploi / création d'entreprise	R431-16-14 R311-3 15
Jeune au pair	R431-16-18 R311-3 16

Appendix: Useful Links

Ameli: healthcare registration for students, https://etudiant-etranger.ameli.fr/#/

Campus France / Etudes en France: https://www.CampusFrance.org/en

Centre National des Firmes Étrangères: https://www.cnfe-urssaf.eu/

CIDFF: https://paris.cidff.info/

CLEISS: Centre de Liaisons Européennes et Internationales de Sécurité Sociale: https://www.cleiss.fr/faq/accords_de_securite_sociale.html

CVEC fee payment for university students: https://www.etudiant.gouv.fr/fr/cvec-une-demarche-de-rentree-incontournable-955

Etudes en France 2024 guide: https://www.usa.CampusFrance.org/etudes-en-france-application-guide

Etudes en France fee payment: https://www.usa.CampusFrance.org/pay-the-etudes-en-france-application-fee

Find your visa application center: https://france-visas.gouv.fr/fr_FR/web/us/a-qui-sadresser

France Visa Application Site: https://france-visas.gouv.fr/

Link to online OFII procedure: https://administration-etrangers-en-france.interieur.gouv.fr/particuliers/#/vls-ts/demarches/etape/numero-visa

Link to purchase a timbre fiscal for the online OFII procedure: https://administration-etrangers-en-france.interieur.gouv.fr/particuliers/#/achattimbreselectroniques

Purchase a timbre fiscal for a carte de séjour: https://timbres.impots.gouv.fr/

Request a carte de séjour from a Passeport Talent visa type: https://administration-etrangers-en-france.interieur.gouv.fr/particuliers/#/espace-personnel/connexion-inscription

Request validation of a work contract, internship agreement, or business plan: https://administration-etrangers-en-france.interieur.gouv.fr/immiprousager/#/authentification

Schengen Trip Calculator: https://ec.europa.eu/assets/home/visa-calculator/calculator.htm?lang=en

Service d'Etat-Civil à Nantes: for ordering marriage certificates and birth certificates registered with the French government for marriages and births of French citizens abroad https://www.diplomatie.gouv.fr/fr/services-aux-francais/etat-civil-et-nationalite-francaise/

Service-Public page on cartes de séjour: https://www.service-public.fr/particuliers/vosdroits/N110#0

STEP: Smart Traveler Enrollment Program with the US Department of State: https://step.state.gov/

TAPIF application: https://tapif.org/

TLS Contact for making a visa appointment in the UK: https://fr.tlscontact.com/

VFS Global: Create an account or log in to make an appointment: https://visa.VFS/TLSglobal.com/usa/fr/fra/login

Vie Publique: a website that covers new laws and public debates in

Allison Grant Lounes & Kim Mousseron
France: **vie-publique.fr**

Women for Women France: womenforwomenfrance.org

Appendix: Préfecture and OFII Offices By Department

We have compiled a list of préfectures and OFII offices for each department, along with their contact information. These departments' websites will be your main resources for validating and renewing your visa, getting your carte de séjour, and various other administrative procedures during your time in France. The table of préfectures & OFII offices is not formatted for ebook editions, so please refer to the pdf or print editions for this information.

To learn how to make an appointment, renew your visa, understand the documents you need to provide, and where your OFII office is located, please go to the préfecture's website. Note that in some departments, certain applications or renewals can be done online, mailed in, or submitted at a sous-préfecture in a different city. That information is available on your préfecture's website.

As of 2024, all of the préfectures have updated their websites, making them more homogeneous in look, with the exception of Paris. Certain procedures however may vary from préfecture to préfecture so please be sure to check your préfecture specifically.

01 - Ain: Bourg-en-Bresse Ain préfecture 45 Av. Alsace Lorraine 01012 Bourg-en-Bresse www.ain.gouv.fr	OFII for l'Ain: Lyon 7, rue Quivogne 69286 Lyon Cedex 02 Tel. : 04 72 77 15 40 Email: lyon@ofii.fr
02 - Aisne - Laon Aisne préfecture 2 Rue Paul Doumer 02000 Laon www.aisne.gouv.fr	OFII for Aisne: Amiens Résidence Le Belvédère, bât. D 275, rue Jules Barni 80000 Amiens Tél. : 03 22 91 28 39 Email: amiens@ofii.fr

03 - Allier - Moulins Allier préfecture 2 Rue Michel de l'Hospital 03000 Moulins www.allier.gouv.fr	OFII for Allier: Clermont-Ferrand 1, rue d'Assas 63000 Clermont-Ferrand Tél. : 04 73 17 02 69 Email: clermont-ferrand@ofii.fr
04 - Alpes-de-Haute-Provence - Digne-les-Bains Alpes-de-Haute-Provence préfecture Rue de la préfecture 04000 Digne-les-Bains www.alpes-de-haute-provence.gouv.fr	OFII for Alpes-de-Haute-Provence: Marseille 61, boulevard Rabatau 13295 Marseille Cedex 08 Tél. : 04 91 32 53 60 Email: marseille@ofii.fr
05 - Hautes-alpes - Gap Hautes-Alpes préfecture 28 Rue Saint-Arey 05011 Gap www.hautes-alpes.gouv.fr	OFII for Hautes-Alpes: Marseille 61, boulevard Rabatau 13295 Marseille Cedex 08 Tél. : 04 91 32 53 60 Email: marseille@ofii.fr
06 - Alpes-Maritimes - Nice Alpes-Maritimes préfecture 147 Bd du Mercantour 06200 Nice www.alpes-maritimes.gouv.fr	OFII for Alpes-Maritimes: Nice Immeuble Space, bât. B 147 boulevard du Mercantour 06200 Nice Tél. : 04 89 15 81 70 Email: nice@ofii.fr
07 - Ardèche - Privas Ardèche préfecture 4 Bd de Vernon 07000 Privas www.ardeche.gouv.fr	OFII for Ardèche: Lyon 7, rue Quivogne 69286 Lyon Cedex 02 Tél. : 04 72 77 15 40 Email: lyon@ofii.fr
08 - Ardennes - Charleville-Mézières Ardennes préfecture 1 Pl. de la préfecture 08000 Charleville-Mézières www.ardennes.gouv.fr	OFII for Ardennes: Reims 2, rue du Grand Credo 51100 Reims Tél. : 03 26 36 97 29 Email: reims@ofii.fr
09 - Ariège - Foix Ariège préfecture 2 Rue de la préfecture Préfet Claude Erignac 09007 Foix www.ariege.gouv.fr	OFII for Ariège: Toulouse 7, rue Arthur Rimbaud CS 40310 31203 Toulouse Cedex 2 Tél. : 05 34 41 72 20 Email: toulouse@ofii.fr / integration.toulouse@ofii.fr

10 - Aube - Troyes Aube préfecture 2 Rue Pierre Labonde 10000 Troyes www.aube.gouv.fr	OFII for Aube: Reims 2, rue du Grand Credo 51100 Reims Tél. : 03 26 36 97 29 Email: reims@ofii.fr
11 - Aude - Carcassonne Aude préfecture 52 Rue Jean Bringer 11000 Carcassonne www.aude.gouv.fr	OFII for Aude: Montpellier 130 Rue de la Jasse de Maurin 34000 Montpellier Tél. : 04 99 77 25 50 Email: montpellier@ofii.fr
12 - Aveyron - Rodez Aveyron préfecture 7 Pl. Charles de Gaulle 12000 Rodez www.aveyron.gouv.fr	OFII for Aveyron: Toulouse 7, rue Arthur Rimbaud CS 40310 31203 Toulouse Cedex 2 Tél. : 05 34 41 72 20 Email: toulouse@ofii.fr / integration.toulouse@ofii.fr
13 - Bouches-du-Rhône - Marseille Bouches-du-Rhône préfecture 1 Pl. de la préfecture 13006 Marseille www.bouches-du-rhone.gouv.fr	OFII for Bouches-du-Rhône: Marseille 61, boulevard Rabatau 13295 Marseille Cedex 08 Tél. : 04 91 32 53 60 Email: marseille@ofii.fr
14 - Calvados - Caen Calvados préfecture 1 Rue Daniel Huet 14000 Caen www.calvados.gouv.fr	OFII for Calvados: Caen Rue Daniel Huet 14038 Caen Cedex 9 Tél. : 02 31 86 57 98 Email: caen@ofii.fr
15 - Cantal - Aurillac Cantal préfecture 2 Cr Monthyon 15000 Aurillac www.cantal.gouv.fr	OFII Cantal: Clermont-Ferrand 1, rue d'Assas 63000 Clermont-Ferrand Tél. : 04 73 17 02 69 Email: clermont-ferrand@ofii.fr
16 - Charente - Angoulême Charente préfecture 7-9 Rue de la préfecture 16000 Angoulême www.charente.gouv.fr	OFII for Charente: Poitiers 86, avenue du 8 mai 1945 86000 Poitiers Tél. : 05 49 62 65 70 Email: poitiers@ofii.fr

17 - Charente-Maritime - La Rochelle Charente-Maritime préfecture 38 Rue Réaumur 17000 La Rochelle www.charente-maritime.gouv.fr	OFII Charente-Maritime: Poitiers 86, avenue du 8 mai 1945 86000 Poitiers Tél. : 05 49 62 65 70 Email: poitiers@ofii.fr
18 - Cher - Bourges Cher préfecture Pl. Marcel Plaisant 18000 Bourges www.cher.gouv.fr	OFII for Cher: Orléans 4, rue de Patay 45000 Orléans Tél. : 02 38 52 00 34 Email: orleans@ofii.fr
19 - Corrèze - Tulle Correze préfecture 1 Rue Souham 19000 Tulle www.correze.gouv.fr	OFII for Correze: Limoges 19, rue Cruveilhier 87000 Limoges Tél. : 05 55 11 01 10 Email: limoges@ofii.fr
2A - Corse-du-sud - Ajaccio Corse-du-sud préfecture Cr Napoléon 20000 Ajaccio www.corse-du-sud.gouv.fr	OFII for Corse-du-sud: Marseille 61, boulevard Rabatau 13295 Marseille Cedex 08 Tél. : 04 91 32 53 60 Email: marseille@ofii.fr
2B - Haute-Corse - Bastia Haute-Corse préfecture Rond point Maréchal Leclerc de Hautecloque 20200 Bastia www.haute-corse.gouv.fr	OFII for Haute-Corse: Marseille 61, boulevard Rabatau 13295 Marseille Cedex 08 Tél. : 04 91 32 53 60 Email: marseille@ofii.fr
21 - Côte-d'Or - Dijon Côte-d'Or préfecture 53 Rue de la préfecture 21041 Dijon www.cote-dor.gouv.fr	OFII for Côte d'Or: Dijon Cité Dampierre 6, rue Chancelier de l'Hospital 21000 Dijon Tél. : 03 80 68 30 10 Email: dijon@ofii.fr
22 - Côtes-d'Armor - Saint-Brieuc Côtes-d'Armor préfecture 3 Pl. Général de Gaulle 22000 Saint-Brieuc www.cotes-darmor.gouv.fr	OFII for Côtes-d'Armor: Rennes 8, rue Jean-Julien Lemordant 35000 Rennes Tél. : 02 99 22 98 60 Email: rennes@ofii.fr

23 - Creuse - Guéret Creuse préfecture Bâtiment Martin Nadaud 4 Pl. Louis Lacrocq 23000 Guéret www.creuse.gouv.fr	OFII for Creuse: Limoges 19, rue Cruveilhier 87000 Limoges Tél. : 05 55 11 01 10 Email: limoges@ofii.fr
24 - Dordogne - Périgueux Dordogne préfecture 2 Rue Paul Louis Courier 24000 Périgueux www.dordogne.gouv.fr	OFII for Dordogne: Bordeaux 55, rue Saint-Sernin CS 90370 33000 Bordeaux Tél. : 05 57 14 23 00 Email: bordeaux@ofii.fr
25 - Doubs - Besançon Doubs préfecture 3 Av. de la Gare d'Eau 25000 Besançon www.doubs.gouv.fr	OFII for Doubs: Besançon 3, avenue de la Gare d'Eau 25000 Besançon Tél. : 03 81 65 22 00 Email: besancon@ofii.fr
26 - Drôme - Valence Drôme préfecture 3 Bd Vauban 26000 Valence www.drome.gouv.fr	OFII for Drôme: Grenoble Parc de l'Alliance 76, rue des Alliés 38100 Grenoble Tél. : 04 76 40 95 45 Email: grenoble@ofii.fr
27 - Eure - Évreux Eure préfecture Bd Georges Chauvin 27000 Évreux www.eure.gouv.fr	OFII for Eure: Rouen Immeuble Montmorency 1 15, place de la Verrerie 76100 Rouen Tél. : 02 32 18 09 94 Email: rouen@ofii.Fr
28 - Eure-et-Loir - Chartres Eure-et-Loir préfecture 1 Pl. de la République 28019 Chartres www.eure-et-loir.gouv.fr	OFII for Eure-et-Loir: Orléans 4, rue de Patay 45000 Orléans Tél. : 02 38 52 00 34 Email: orleans@ofii.fr
29 - Finistère - Quimper Finistère préfecture 42 Bd Dupleix CS 16033 29320 Quimper www.finistere.gouv.fr	OFII for Finistère: Rennes 8, rue Jean-Julien Lemordant 35000 Rennes Tél. : 02 99 22 98 60 Email: rennes@ofii.fr

30 - Gard - Nîmes Gard préfecture 2 Rue Guillemette 30000 Nîmes www.gard.gouv.fr	OFII for Gard: Montpellier 130 Rue de la Jasse de Maurin 34000 Montpellier Tél. : 04 99 77 25 50 Email: montpellier@ofii.fr
31 - Haute-Garonne - Toulouse Haute-Garonne préfecture 1 Rue Sainte-Anne 31000 Toulouse www.haute-garonne.gouv.fr	OFII Haute-Garonne: Toulouse 7, rue Arthur Rimbaud CS 40310 31203 Toulouse Cedex 2 Tél. : 05 34 41 72 20 Email: toulouse@ofii.fr / integration.toulouse@ofii.fr
32 - Gers - Auch Gers préfecture 3 Place du Préfet Erignac 32000 Auch www.gers.gouv.fr	OFII for Gers: Toulouse 7, rue Arthur Rimbaud CS 40310 31203 Toulouse Cedex 2 Tél. : 05 34 41 72 20 Email: toulouse@ofii.fr / integration.toulouse@ofii.fr
33 - Gironde - Bordeaux Gironde préfecture 2 Esp Charles de Gaulle 33000 Bordeaux www.gironde.gouv.fr	OFII for Gironde: Bordeaux 55, rue Saint-Sernin CS 90370 33000 Bordeaux Tél. : 05 57 14 23 00 Email: bordeaux@ofii.fr
34 - Hérault - Montpellier Hérault préfecture 34 Pl. Martyrs de la Résistance 34000 Montpellier www.herault.gouv.fr	OFII for Hérault: Montpellier 130 Rue de la Jasse de Maurin 34000 Montpellier Tél. : 04 99 77 25 50 Email: montpellier@ofii.fr
35 - Ille-et-vilaine - Rennes Ille-et-Vilaine préfecture 3 Av. de la préfecture 35000 Rennes www.ille-et-vilaine.gouv.fr	OFII for Ille-et-Vilaine: Rennes 8, rue Jean-Julien Lemordant 35000 Rennes Tél. : 02 99 22 98 60 Email: rennes@ofii.fr
36 - Indre - Châteauroux Indre préfecture Pl. de la Victoire et des Alliés 36000 Châteauroux www.indre.gouv.fr	OFII for Indre: Orleans 4, rue de Patay 45000 Orléans Tél. : 02 38 52 00 34 Email: orelans@ofii.fr

37 - Indre-et-Loire - Tours Indre-et-Loire préfecture 15 Rue Bernard Palissy 37000 Tours www.indre-et-loire.gouv.fr	OFII for Indre-et-Loire: Orléans 4, rue de Patay 45000 Orléans Tél. : 02 38 52 00 34 Email: orelans@ofii.fr
38 - Isère - Grenoble Isère préfecture 12 Pl. de Verdun 38000 Grenoble www.isere.gouv.fr	OFII for Isère: Grenoble Parc de l'Alliance 76, rue des Alliés 38100 Grenoble Tél. : 04 76 40 95 45 Email: grenoble@ofii.fr
39 - Jura - Lons-le-Saunier Jura préfecture 8 Rue de la préfecture 39000 Lons-le-Saunier www.jura.gouv.fr	OFII for Jura: Besançon 3, avenue de la Gare d'Eau 25000 Besançon Tél. : 03 81 65 22 00 Email: besancon@ofii.fr
40 - Landes - Mont-de-Marsan Landes préfecture 24 Rue Victor Hugo 40021 Mont-de-Marsan www.landes.gouv.fr	OFII for Landes: Bordeaux 55, rue Saint-Sernin CS 90370 33000 Bordeaux Tél. : 05 57 14 23 00 Email: bordeaux@ofii.fr
41 - Loir-et-cher - Blois Loir-et-cher préfecture Pl. de la République 41000 Blois www.loir-et-cher.gouv.fr	OFII for Loir-et-cher: Orléans 4, rue de Patay 45000 Orléans Tél. : 02 38 52 00 34 Email: orleans@ofii.fr
42 - Loire - Saint-Étienne Loire préfecture 2 Rue Charles de Gaulle 42000 Saint-Étienne www.loire.gouv.fr	OFII for Loire: Lyon 7, rue Quivogne 69286 Lyon Cedex 02 Tél. : 04 72 77 15 40 Email: lyon@ofii.fr
43 - Haute-loire - Le Puy-en-Velay Haute-loire préfecture 6 Av. du Général de Gaulle 43000 Le Puy-en-Velay www.haute-loire.gouv.fr	OFII for Haute-loire: Clermont-Ferrand 1, rue d'Assas 63000 Clermont-Ferrand Tél. : 04 73 17 02 69 Email: clermont-ferrand@ofii.fr

44 - Loire-Atlantique - Nantes Loire-Atlantique préfecture 6 Quai Ceineray 44000 Nantes www.loire-atlantique.gouv.fr	OFII for Loire-Atlantique: Nantes 93 bis, rue de la Commune de 1871 44400 Rezé Tél. : 02 51 72 79 39 Email: nantes@ofii.fr
45 - Loiret - Orléans Loiret préfecture 181 Rue de Bourgogne 45000 Orléans www.loiret.gouv.fr	OFII for Loiret: Orléans 4, rue de Patay 45000 Orléans Tél. : 02 38 52 00 34 Email: orleans@ofii.fr
46 - Lot - Cahors Lot préfecture Pl. Jean Jacques Chapou 46000 Cahors www.lot.gouv.fr	OFII for Lot: Toulouse 7, rue Arthur Rimbaud CS 40310 31203 Toulouse Cedex 2 Tél. : 05 34 41 72 20 Email: toulouse@ofii.fr / integration.toulouse@ofii.fr
47 - Lot-et-Garonne - Agen Lot-et-Garonne préfecture Place Verdun 47920 Agen www.lot-et-garonne.gouv.fr	OFII Lot-et-Garonne: Bordeaux 55, rue Saint-Sernin CS 90370 33000 Bordeaux Tél. : 05 57 14 23 00 Email: bordeaux@ofii.fr
48 - Lozère - Mende Lozère préfecture 2 Rue de la Rovère 48000 Mende www.lozere.gouv.fr	OFII for Lozère: Montpellier 130 Rue de la Jasse de Maurin 34000 Montpellier Tél. : 04 99 77 25 50 Email: montpellier@ofii.fr
49 - Maine-et-Loire - Angers Maine-et-Loire préfecture Pl. Michel Debré 49100 Angers www.maine-et-loire.gouv.fr	OFII for Maine-et-Loire: Nantes 93 bis, rue de la Commune de 1871 44400 Rezé Tél. : 02 51 72 79 39 Email: nantes@ofii.fr
50 - Manche - Saint-Lô Manche préfecture Pl. de la préfecture 50002 Saint-Lô www.manche.gouv.fr	OFII for Manche: Caen Rue Daniel Huet 14038 Caen Cedex 9 Tél. : 02 31 86 57 98 Email: caen@ofii.fr

51 - Marne - Châlons-en-Champagne Marne préfecture 1 Rue de Jessaint 51000 Châlons-en-Champagne www.marne.gouv.fr	OFII for Marne: Reims 2, rue du Grand Credo 51100 Reims Tél. : 03 26 36 97 29 Email: reims@ofii.fr
52 - Haute-Marne - Chaumont Haute-Marne préfecture 89 Rue Victoire de la Marne 52011 Chaumont www.haute-marne.gouv.fr	OFII for Haute-Marne: Reims 2, rue du Grand Credo 51100 Reims Tél. : 03 26 36 97 29 Email: reims@ofii.fr
53 - Mayenne - Laval Mayenne préfecture 46 Rue Mazagran 53000 Laval www.mayenne.gouv.fr	OFII for Mayenne: Nantes 93 bis, rue de la Commune de 1871 44400 Rezé Tél. : 02 51 72 79 39 Email: nantes@ofii.fr
54 - Meurthe-et-Moselle - Nancy Meurthe-et-Moselle préfecture 6 Rue Sainte-Catherine 54000 Nancy www.meurthe-et-moselle.gouv.fr	OFII for Meurthe-et-Moselle: Metz 2, rue Lafayette 57000 Metz Tél. : 03 87 66 64 98 Email: metz@ofii.fr
55 - Meuse - Bar-le-Duc Meuse préfecture 40 Rue du Bourg 55000 Bar-le-Duc www.meuse.gouv.fr	OFII for Meuse: Metz 2, rue Lafayette 57000 Metz Tél. : 03 87 66 64 98 Email: metz@ofii.fr
56 - Morbihan - Vannes Morbihan préfecture 10 Pl. du Général de Gaulle 56000 Vannes www.morbihan.gouv.fr	OFII for Morbihan: Rennes 8, rue Jean-Julien Lemordant 35000 Rennes Tél. : 02 99 22 98 60 Email: rennes@ofii.fr
57 - Moselle - Metz Moselle préfecture 9 Pl. de la préfecture 57034 Metz www.moselle.gouv.fr	OFII for Moselle: Metz 2, rue Lafayette 57000 Metz Tél. : 03 87 66 64 98 Email: metz@ofii.fr

58 - Nièvre - Nevers Nièvre préfecture 40 Rue de la préfecture 58000 Nevers www.nievre.gouv.fr	OFII for Nièvre: Dijon Cité Dampierre 6, rue Chancelier de l'Hospital 21000 Dijon Tél. : 03 80 68 30 10 Email: dijon@ofii.fr
59 - Nord - Lille Nord préfecture 12, rue Jean sans Peur 59039 Lille Cedex www.nord.gouv.fr	OFII for Nord: Lille 107, boulevard de la Liberté 59000 Lille Tél. : 03 20 99 98 60 Email: lille@ofii.fr
60 - Oise - Beauvais Oise préfccture 2 Av. de l'Europe 60000 Beauvais www.oise.gouv.fr	OFII for Oise: Amiens Résidence Le Belvédère, bât. D 275, rue Jules Barni 80000 Amiens Tél. : 03 22 91 28 39 Email: amiens@ofii.fr
61 - Orne - Alençon Orne préfecture 39 Rue Saint-Blaise 61000 Alençon www.orne.gouv.fr	OFII for Orne: Caen Rue Daniel Huet 14038 Caen Cedex 9 Tél. : 02 31 86 57 98 Email: caen@ofii.fr
62 - Pas-de-Calais - Arras Pas-de-Calais préfecture Rue Ferdinand Buisson 62000 Arras www.pas-de-calais.gouv.fr	OFII for Pas-de-Calais: Lille 107, boulevard de la Liberté 59000 Lille Tél. : 03 20 99 98 60 Email: lille@ofii.fr
63 - Puy-de-Dôme - Clermont-Ferrand Puy-de-Dôme préfecture 1 Rue d'Assas 63000 Clermont-Ferrand www.puy-de-dome.gouv.fr	OFII for Puy-de-Dôme: Clermont-Ferrand 1, rue d'Assas 63000 Clermont-Ferrand Tél. : 04 73 17 02 69 Email: clermont-ferrand@ofii.fr
64 - Pyrénées-Atlantiques - Pau Pyrénées-Atlantiques préfecture 2 Rue Maréchal Joffre 64021 Pau www.pyrenees-atlantiques.gouv.fr	OFII for Pyrénées-atlantiques: Bordeaux 55, rue Saint-Sernin CS 90370 33000 Bordeaux Tél. : 05 57 14 23 00 Email: bordeaux@ofii.fr

65 - Hautes-Pyrénées - Tarbes Hautes-Pyrénées préfecture Pl. du Général Ch de Gaulle 65000 Tarbes www.hautes-pyrenees.gouv.fr	OFII Hautes-Pyrénées: Toulouse 7, rue Arthur Rimbaud CS 40310 31203 Toulouse Cedex 2 Tél. : 05 34 41 72 20 Email: toulouse@ofii.fr / integration.toulouse@ofii.fr
66 - Pyrénées-Orientales - Perpignan Pyrénées-Orientales préfecture 24 quai Sadi Carnot 66951 Perpignan www.pyrenees-orientales.gouv.fr	OFII for Pyrénées-Orientales: Montpellier 130 Rue de la Jasse de Maurin 34000 Montpellier Tél. : 04 99 77 25 50 Email: montpellier@ofii.fr
67 - Bas-Rhin - Strasbourg Bas-Rhin préfecture 5 Pl. de la République 67073 Strasbourg www.bas-rhin.gouv.fr	OFII for Bas-Rhin: Strasbourg 4, rue Gustave Doré CS 80115 67069 Strasbourg Cedex Tél. : 03 88 23 30 20 Email: strasbourg@ofii.fr
68 - Haut-Rhin - Colmar Haut-Rhin préfecture 11 Av. de la République 68000 Colmar www.haut-rhin.gouv.fr	OFII for Haut-Rhin: Strasbourg 4, rue Gustave Doré CS 80115 67069 Strasbourg Cedex Tél. : 03 88 23 30 20 Email: strasbourg@ofii.fr
69 - Rhône - Lyon Rhône préfecture 18 Rue de Bonnel 69003 Lyon www.rhone.gouv.fr	OFII for Rhône: Lyon 7, rue Quivogne 69286 Lyon Cedex 02 Tél. : 04 72 77 15 40 Email: lyon@ofii.fr
70 - Haute-Saône - Vesoul Haute-Saône préfecture 1 Rue de la préfecture 70013 Vesoul www.haute-saone.gouv.fr	OFII for Haute-Saône: Besançon 3, avenue de la Gare d'Eau 25000 Besançon Tél. : 03 81 65 22 00 Email: besancon@ofii.fr
71 - Saône-et-Loire - Mâcon Saône-et-Loire préfecture 196 Rue de Strasbourg 71000 Mâcon www.saone-et-loire.gouv.fr	OFII for Saône-et-Loire: Dijon Cité Dampierre 6, rue Chancelier de l'Hospital 21000 Dijon Tél. : 03 80 68 30 10 Email: dijon@ofii.fr

72 - Sarthe - Le Mans Sarthe préfecture Pl. Aristide Briand 72100 Le Mans www.sarthe.gouv.fr	OFII for Sarthe: Nantes 93 bis, rue de la Commune de 1871 44400 Rezé Tél. : 02 51 72 79 39 Email: nantes@ofii.fr
73 - Savoie - Chambéry Savoie préfecture Château des ducs de Savoie 73000 Chambéry www.savoie.gouv.fr	OFII for Savoie: Grenoble Parc de l'Alliance 76, rue des Alliés 38100 Grenoble Tél. : 04 76 40 95 45 Email: grenoble@ofii.fr
74 - Haute-Savoie - Annccy Haute-Savoie préfecture Rue 30E Régiment d'Infanterie 74000 Annecy www.haute-savoie.gouv.fr	OFII for Haute-Savoie: Grenoble Parc de l'Alliance 76, rue des Alliés 38100 Grenoble Tél. : 04 76 40 95 45 Email: grenoble@ofii.fr
75 - Paris - Paris Paris préfecture 1 bis rue de Lutèce 75004 Paris www.préfecturedepolice.interieur.gouv.fr	OFII for Paris: Paris 83, rue de Patay 75013 Paris Tél. : 01 85 56 15 55 Email: paris@ofii.fr
76 - Seine-Maritime - Rouen Seine-Maritime préfecture 7 Pl. de la Madeleine 76000 Rouen www.seine-maritime.gouv.fr	OFII for Seine-Maritime: Rouen Immeuble Montmorency 1 15, place de la Verrerie 76100 Rouen Tél. : 02 32 18 09 94 Email: rouen@ofii.fr
77 - Seine-et-Marne - Melun Seine-et-Marne préfecture 12 Rue des Saints-Pères 77000 Melun www.seine-et-marne.gouv.fr	OFII for Seine-et-Marne: Melun 2 bis, avenue Jean Jaurès 77000 Melun Tél. : 01 78 49 20 00 Email: melun@ofii.fr
78 - Yvelines - Versailles Yvelines préfecture 1 Av. de l'Europe 78000 Versailles www.yvelines.gouv.fr	OFII for Yvelines: Montrouge 55 rue Etienne Dolet 92240 Malakoff Tél. : 01 41 17 73 00 Email: montrouge@ofii.fr

79 - Deux-Sèvres - Niort Deux-Sèvres préfecture BP 70000 79099 4 Rue du Guesclin 79000 Niort www.deux-sevres.gouv.fr	OFII for Deux-Sèvres: Poitiers 86, avenue du 8 mai 1945 86000 Poitiers Tél. : 05 49 62 65 70 Email: poitiers@ofii.fr
80 - Somme - Amiens Somme préfecture 51 Rue de la République 80000 Amiens www.somme.gouv.fr	OFII for Somme: Amiens Résidence Le Belvédère, bât. D 275, rue Jules Barni 80000 Amiens Tél. : 03 22 91 28 39 Email: amiens@ofii.fr
81 - Tarn - Albi Tarn préfecture Place de la préfecture 81013 Albi www.tarn.gouv.fr	OFII for Tarn: Toulouse 7, rue Arthur Rimbaud CS 40310 31203 Toulouse Cedex 2 Tél. : 05 34 41 72 20 Email: toulouse@ofii.fr / integration.toulouse@ofii.fr
82 - Tarn-et-Garonne - Montauban Tarn-et-Garonne préfecture 2 All. de l'Empereur 82000 Montauban www.tarn-et-garonne.gouv.fr	OFII Tarn-et-Garonne: Toulouse 7, rue Arthur Rimbaud CS 40310 31203 Toulouse Cedex 2 Tél. : 05 34 41 72 20 Email: toulouse@ofii.fr / integration.toulouse@ofii.fr
83 - Var - Toulon Var préfecture Boulevard du 112ème Régiment d'Infanterie 83070 Toulon www.var.gouv.fr	OFII for Var: Marseille 61, boulevard Rabatau 13295 Marseille Cedex 08 Tél. : 04 91 32 53 60 Email: marseille@ofii.fr
84 - Vaucluse - Avignon Vaucluse préfecture 2 Av. de la Folie 84000 Avignon www.vaucluse.gouv.fr	OFII for Vaucluse: Marseille 61, boulevard Rabatau 13295 Marseille Cedex 08 Tél. : 04 91 32 53 60 Email: marseille@ofii.fr

85 - Vendée - La Roche-sur-Yon Vendée préfecture 29 Rue Delille 85000 La Roche-sur-Yon www.vendee.gouv.fr	OFII for Vendée:Nantes 93 bis, rue de la Commune de 1871 44400 Rezé Tél. : 02 51 72 79 39 Email: nantes@ofii.fr
86 - Vienne - Poitiers Vienne préfecture 7 Pl. Aristide Briand 86000 Poitiers www.vienne.gouv.fr	OFII for Vienne: Poitiers 86, avenue du 8 mai 1945 86000 Poitiers Tél. : 05 49 62 65 70 Email: poitiers@ofii.fr
87 - Haute-Vienne - Limoges Haute-Vienne préfecture 1 Rue de la préfecture 87000 Limoges www.haute-vienne.gouv.fr	OFII for Haute-Vienne: Limoges 19, rue Cruveilhier 87000 Limoges Tél. : 05 55 11 01 10 Email: limoges@ofii.fr
88 - Vosges - Épinal Vosges préfecture Pl. Foch 88000 Épinal www.vosges.gouv.fr	OFII for Vosges: Metz 2, rue Lafayette 57000 Metz Tél. : 03 87 66 64 98 Email: metz@ofii.fr
89 - Yonne - Auxerre Yonne préfecture 1 Pl. de la préfecture 89000 Auxerre www.yonne.gouv.fr	OFII for Yonne: Dijon Cité Dampierre 6, rue Chancelier de l'Hospital 21000 Dijon Tél. : 03 80 30 32 30 Email: dijon@ofii.fr
90 - Territoire de Belfort - Belfort Territoire de Belfort préfecture 1 Rue Bartholdi 90000 Belfort www.territoire-de-belfort.gouv.fr	OFII for Territoire de Belfort: Besançon 3, avenue de la Gare d'Eau 25000 Besançon Tél. : 03 81 65 22 00 Email: besancon@ofii.fr
91 - Essonne - Évry Essonne préfecture Courcouronnes, Bd de France, 91000 www.essonne.gouv.fr	OFII for Essonne: Créteil 13-15, rue Claude-Nicolas Ledoux 94000 Créteil Tél. : 01 41 94 69 30 Email: creteil@ofii.fr

92 - Hauts-de-Seine - Nanterre Hauts-de-Seine préfecture 167-177 Av. Frederic et Irene Joliot Curie 92000 Nanterre www.hauts-de-seine.gouv.fr	OFII for Hauts-de-Seine: Montrouge 55 rue Etienne Dolet 92240 Malakoff Tél. : 01 41 17 73 00 Email: montrouge@ofii.fr
93 - Seine-Saint-Denis - Bobigny Seine-Saint-Denis préfecture 1 esplanade Jean Moulin 93007 Bobigny www.seine-saint-denis.gouv.fr	OFII Seine-Saint-Denis: Bobigny 13, rue Marguerite Yourcenar 93000 Bobigny Tél. : 01 49 72 54 00 Email: bobigny@ofii.fr
94 - Val-de-Marne - Créteil Val-de-Marne préfecture 21-29 Av. du Général de Gaulle 94000 Créteil www.val-de-marne.gouv.fr	OFII for Val-de-Marne: Créteil 13-15, rue Claude-Nicolas Ledoux 94000 Créteil Tél. : 01 41 94 69 30 Email: creteil@ofii.fr
95 - Val-d'Oise - Cergy Pontoise Val d'Oise préfecture 5 Av. Bernard Hirsch 95000 Cergy www.val-doise.gouv.fr	OFII for Val-d'Oise: Cergy Immeuble Ordinal Rue des Chauffours 95002 Cergy-Pontoise Cedex Tél. : 01 34 20 20 30 Email: cergy@ofii.fr

Printed in Great Britain
by Amazon